THE PRACTICE
OF PLANNING
Strategic, Administrative,
and Operational

THE PRACTICE OF PLANNING
Strategic, Administrative, and Operational

Leon Reinharth, Ph. D.
Professor of Management
School of Business Administration
Montclair State College

H. Jack Shapiro, Ph. D.
Professor and Chairman of the Management Department
Bernard M. Baruch College (City University of New York)

Ernest A. Kallman, Ph. D.
Professor of Management and Information Systems
School of Business Administration
Montclair State College

 VAN NOSTRAND REINHOLD COMPANY
NEW YORK   CINCINNATI   ATLANTA   DALLAS   SAN FRANCISCO
LONDON   TORONTO   MELBOURNE

Van Nostrand Reinhold Company Regional Offices:
New York Cincinnati Atlanta Dallas San Francisco

Van Nostrand Reinhold Company International Offices:
London Toronto Melbourne

Copyright © 1981 by Litton Educational Publishing, Inc.

Library of Congress Catalog Card Number: 80-16372
ISBN: 0-442-21917-2

Manufactured in the United States of America

Published by Van Nostrand Reinhold Company
135 West 50th Street, New York, N.Y. 10020

Published simultaneously in Canada by Van Nostrand Reinhold Ltd.

15 14 13 12 11 10 9 8 7 6 5 4 3 2 1

Library of Congress Cataloging in Publication Data

Reinharth, Leon.
    The practice of planning.

    Includes bibliographical references and index.
    1. Corporate planning. I. Shapiro,
Harris Jack, joint author. II. Kallman, Ernest A.,
joint author. III. Title.
HD30.28.R42   658.4'012   80-16372
ISBN 0-442-21917-2

To
Francoise Reinharth
and
Sandra Kallman
and
in loving memory of
Louis Shapiro

Foreword

There are two kinds of organizations in this competitive world of ours—the hunters and the hunted. The hunters are constantly aware of their environment and the changes taking place in it. They watch what other organizations are doing and assess what the organizations are likely to do. They consider their strategic options, adopt strategies, evaluate their success, and change strategies when necessary. They build plans to support their chosen strategies and develop systems to ensure that their plans are carried out. The hunters are the most successful organizations.

The hunted organizations graze peacefully in the fields of their endeavors, generally aware of what is going on around them, but rarely looking into the future. They do not worry about strategic options, and they do not plan. Instead, they react to the threats and opportunities that come to them. Some of these organizations are successful; most are not.

Let us consider an analogy using wolves and caribou. Caribou are good at what they do. They have been doing it a long time and feel confident about it. They migrate over well-established courses, find the food they need, reproduce, and don't think much about it. Caribou don't worry much about wolves since they are larger and faster. Moreover, a caribou can thrash one or two wolves in a fight any day.

Wolves know this, so they get organized into packs large enough to handle caribou. Then they plan. Their strategic goal is simple—bring down enough caribou to eat regularly. Their strategy is to first go after the easy targets— caribou weak from age or illness and the unattended calves. Since there are not enough elderly, sick, or careless caribou, the second strategy is to develop techniques to catch a healthy caribou—a faster animal—and to kill it without getting kicked to pieces.

The administrative and operational planning that follows is complex. It involves a system of scouts to keep careful watch on the caribou herd, assess the geography, and estimate the likely course of action of the caribou—i.e., which way they will run. When the wolves believe that only a few escape routes exist, they station individual wolves along the route they believe the caribou will use to escape. Then, the remaining pack members charge the caribou herd and start it running. If a caribou follows the route the wolves are guarding, they pursue it. The caribou easily outdistances the wolves; however, when the first wolf tires, another wolf is waiting. When the caribou finally tires, the wolf in pursuit can hold it until the rest of the pack shows up. Working together, the wolves can bring down the caribou and dine handsomely.

Of course, even the best plans do not always work. Sometimes no caribou follow the expected course. Sometimes several do, but they stick together so that no matter how tired they are, a small pack of wolves cannot attack them successfully. Sometimes a caribou outruns the wolves, or fights its way out. That is why wolves tend to be lean and why they constantly try to improve their planning.

But note that wolves kill a lot of caribou. And caribou seldom kill wolves. The moral of this story is that it is better to be the hunter than the hunted. In the organizational context, the hunters plan, and the hunted react. This is most obvious in the overtly competitive corporate world. In addition, government organizations compete for funds and personnel allocations, charities compete for donations, and artistic groups compete for audiences and grants. The organizations that plan—the hunters—tend to be the successful ones. And they make life miserable for the hunted, who can only respond to the initiatives of the hunters and are therefore always late.

The purpose of *The Practice of Planning* is to help you make your organization into a hunter—or a better hunter. The authors, who have had extensive experience in the business world, now teach at business schools. They have had time to reflect on their experiences and those of others and to organize this wealth of experience into this guide for successful planning. The book is valuable for (1) students of planning, (2) middle managers who must understand the structure of the strategic plan for an entire organization, play a role in developing the plan, and formulate congruent administrative plans for their part of the organization, and (3) operating managers who are particularly concerned with operational planning within their division, department, or section.

Each of the chapters survived passage through my less-than-gentle editorial hands. The chapters were then tested in courses for middle managers at the business schools where the authors teach. Two of the chapters have served as the basis for articles in *Planning Review,* the journal of the North American Society for Corporate Planning.* The readers of *Planning Review* expect the contents to be instructive and to be beneficial in improving their planning performance. The articles succeeded. The finished product is the book you now hold. For guidance in becoming a sleek and successful hunter, I suggest you read it.

MALCOLM W. PENNINGTON
Senior Editor, *Planning Review*
President, The Marketing & Planning Group, Inc.

*For more information on the North American Society for Corporate Planning or *Planning Review,* contact the society at 1406 Third National Building, Dayton, OH 45402, or telephone (213) 228-4849.

Preface

Planning is necessary at all managerial levels in an organization and yet it is different on each level. Nevertheless, most planning books concentrate on strategic planning, which is normally the domain of the few executives in top management. As a result, most middle-level and operational managers have no clear guidelines regarding the workings of the planning functions at their levels, nor are they given a framework for understanding the interaction among the various levels of planning.

In *The Practice of Planning: Strategic, Administrative, and Operational,* all levels of planning are covered. In addition, the usually neglected subjects of the implementation and control of a company's plans are treated in some detail. Thus, the reader is given a comprehensive picture of the planning process.

An overview of each type of planning process—strategic, administrative, and operational—is presented. From this, practicing managers will be able to determine how planning applies to their own functions as well as which aspects of planning apply to the rest of the organization. The student of planning will be able to learn about the scope of the planning function and to appreciate the interrelationships among the various levels of planning.

The planning approach is described for several types of firms and for various functions within the firm. Answers are provided for such questions as:

What is planning?
What kinds of plans are there?
Who is responsible for planning?
How much planning does an organization need?
Where do you start?
How do you know if it is working?
When do you stop?
Who should participate?
How does planning fit in with the rest of the business?
What does planning mean to a computer and management information system?

The chapters can be read in sequence or independently. The reader can pick and choose as little or as much information as is needed. The choosing process is aided by clearly delineated sections and subheadings. In many ways, the book is a combination textbook, handbook, refresher, and reference. It should be useful to business people, students, and scholars.

Each chapter is supplemented by related journal articles, which present the (sometimes conflicting) perspectives of academicians and practitioners and provide additional information. At the end of each chapter, annotated references describe related works of importance.

In addition to the numerous examples and anecdotes that amplify the points in each chapter, a major case study is included. The case is that of a real company with real decisionmaking situations: Alexander & Alexander Services, Inc., the second largest insurance brokerage, consulting, and actuarial firm in the world. Many of the actual experiences of this firm parallel the processes covered in the text. Through analyzing the case, the reader will get a further appreciation of the situational nature of planning.

There are nine chapters. Chapter 1 describes the systems approach to viewing organizations. It dwells on the managerial subsystem of the organization, that area where decisionmaking and planning take place. From this point, a definition of planning is developed, and comments are made on its success to date and on management's role in the process. The chapter concludes with some candid comments reflecting management's attitude toward planning.

An overview of the entire planning process is the basis for Chapter 2. It is a prescriptive explanation of what should take place. A model presents the key elements of the organization and their relationship to each other—i.e., objectives, policies, search mechanisms, data needs, strategies, implementation, and evaluation. This framework fosters sound current decisions.

Strategic planning is the focus of Chapter 3. It begins with the premise that strategic planning takes place in all organizations for better or for worse. The chapter then describes the various methods that are available to planners for use in the selection and ranking of the firm's limited resources for closing the "gap" between where it would like to be and where it will be if it does nothing. These methods include capital investment approaches (average rate of return, payback, various present value methods, etc.) and the adaptive search method. The situational nature of planning is also discussed.

Chapter 4 deals with administrative planning—i.e., creating a maximum performance potential through the structuring of the organization's resources. The emphasis is on organizational structure and the acquisition, allocation, and development of resources. This is medium-range planning. Its time frame is shorter than strategic but not as brief as operational planning.

The lowest level of planning—operational planning—is covered in Chapter 5. Its purpose is the efficient day-to-day utilization of resources in one area of operation. This type of planning has high certainty and short time periods. Included is a detailed description of the operating budget and its various types: appropriation, fixed, and variable. Break-even analysis, the sales budget, production and inventory budgets, materials budget, purchase budget, direct labor budget, manufacturing expense budget, selling and expense budget, administrative expense budget, and cash budget are also explained. In addition, there is a section on presenting the budget. Finally, the operations research tools for allocation, inventory, queuing, sequencing, routing, replacement, maintenance, and competition are presented.

Chapter 6 explains the other side of the budget picture—the functions of implementation and control. This chapter discusses how the planner's decisionmaking tools become the basis for making sure the plan gets carried out—or changed if that is what is needed. Through the invocation of the control function, the linkage among the levels of planning becomes quite clear. Operational plans are limited by the administrative-level resources, and both in turn are governed by the premises established at the strategic level. In addition, the importance of people to the planning process is emphasized through a discussion of the behavioral aspects of management: motivational approaches, management feedback, budget (and variance), accounting reports, ratios, internal reports, graphical techniques, work measurement and samplings, forms design, records management, etc.

Chapter 7 integrates the strategic, administrative, and operational plans in a unified organizational plan. The interrelation among the various levels is explained as a series of goals and constraints. Two major examples, one real and one fictitious, are drawn in detail to explain the integration concept and the goals-constraint interaction.

Since planning is a form of decisionmaking, Chapter 8 begins with a discussion of the decisionmaking process. Since an essential element of decisionmaking is information, the chapter describes what information is, where it comes from, how to get it, and how it flows through the organization. Distinction is made between the different kinds of information required for each kind of planning and for each level of management. This leads to a discussion of management information systems (MIS), the function of an MIS, how to build an MIS, and where computers come into MIS and the decisionmaking process.

Chapter 9 examines various articles that attempt to predict corporate environments between now and the year 2000. Corporations will change, and these changes will impose new planning requirements. The focus will continue its shift from goods to services. Quality of life will gain more popularity against monetary income as a prime personal goal. The entrepreneur will reemerge as a necessary style for the corporate leader. Computer-based models will aid the optimization of management action. Lastly, it is suggested that bringing all this planning about is the real challenge to management in the next 20 years.

It is appropriate to mention some of those connected with creating *The Practice of Planning.* First, Malcolm Pennington, whose sharp insights and gentle red pencil brought some order out of our rough-draft confusion. Next, Violet

Glod, who took scratches and arrows and snips of paper and shaped them into paragraphs and chapters on her typewriter. And finally, the many who gave advice, example, and encouragement, including Clif Buys, Tom DeLorenzo, Bill Doniger, Art Gravina, Jim Krok, Marijane McDonough Whiteman, Frank Mertz, Jim M. P. Moore, Jack Northrup, Nancy Ranft, Richard Shimpfky, and Lee Supper.

LEON REINHARTH, Ph.D.
H. JACK SHAPIRO, Ph.D.
ERNEST A. KALLMAN, Ph.D.

Contents

1
Nature and Scope of Planning

PLANNING: THE GREAT PR SUCCESS

Planning is management's attempt to anticipate future occurrences. In the past 10 years, planning has completely reversed its image. Once a specialized function, found only in the largest corporations and for the most part ignored by their members, planning is now a "socially accepted" business function. There is hardly a manager who would deny its virtues. Planning is taught in business schools, companies run planning seminars, journals devoted to planning are published, and professional planning societies exist. For the individual manager, however, this reversal of the planning image often represents only a public relations success. The only difference between planning now and planning in the 1960s is that today it is not fashionable to deny planning or its worth. Thus, it is common for managers to express the reservation that "Planning is not for this organization at this time," or perhaps "It's not for this department."

In other words, the public relations success has made planning an acceptable function to encourage others to do but not necessarily one that individual managers want to do themselves. Why are there so many advocates and so few practitioners of the planning process? Why do so many give lip service to something that so few want to do? Why is something that looks so easy so difficult to perform? Why is there so much talk and so little action?

THE ORGANIZATION AS A SYSTEM

An organization may be viewed as a system—a system that is greatly influenced by what takes place in the outside environment. Such an open system receives energy, material, and information as input from this environment. According to its own purposes, the system operates on or reacts to these outside influences and transmits output back to the environment. As a very simple example, a manufacturing plant receives raw material, creates a product, and sends it into the marketplace.

Kast and Rosenzweig (1974) define five major subsystems within an organization: (1) goals-and-values, (2) technical, (3) psychosocial, (4) structural, and (5) managerial. The *goals-and-values subsystem* describes the functions and purposes of the organization. This subsystem deals with why the organization exists and how it is going to approach reaching its objectives; e.g., a computer manufacturer decides it is in business to sell computer systems to small American firms through a network of distributors. If the goals-and-values subsystem is inconsistent with the external environment, feedback from the environment will force a change in the goals of the organization through the subsystem. In the previous example, if there is no market for computers among small American firms, then the computer company's purposes and goals have to change.

The *technical subsystem* provides for transformation activities. For instance, in a computer firm, this would include the manufacturing function, the preparation of software, and all the other activities necessary to bring the product to market. *Psychosocial subsystems* are concerned with group and individual behavior and are most directly related to the personnel function and the achievement of high motivation, satisfaction, and general human welfare. *Structural subsystems* are concerned with how the firm is organized. They determine what departments the firm has, what the reporting structure is, what degree of specialization each department has, and other aspects of the firm's formal relationships. All four subsystems overlap, and they all interact with the environment. Finally, they are permeated and influenced by, and in turn influence, the *managerial subsystem*. This subsystem "spans the entire organization by relating the organization to its environment, setting the goals, developing comprehensive, strategic and operational plans, designing the structure, and establishing control processes" (Kast and Rosenzweig 1974).

THE MANAGERIAL SUBSYSTEM

The managerial subsystem pervades the entire organization. According to Churchman (1968), "it is the subsystem that thinks about the overall plan and implements its thinking." The managerial subsystem operates on three levels within the organization: (1) operating, (2) coordinative, and (3) strategic (Johnson et al. 1973). On the operating level, it seeks efficiency and effectiveness in the accomplishment of objectives. Through coordinative activities, it seeks to integrate the internal activities of the system. And on the strategic level, the goal of the managerial subsystem is to relate the organization to the environment and prepare a comprehensive system of plans. Examined from the dimensions of environmental interaction, time, criterion of value, and decisionmaking, the strategic level appears to be open to environmental interaction, concerned with the long run, achieving a desired level of performance, and dependent upon judgmental rather than computational decision techniques (Kast and Rosenzweig 1974). This contrasts with the other levels of the managerial subsystem, which tend to be more closed to environmental influences, as well as short run, optimizing, and computational.

This systems view of the organization and the managerial process as a subsystem substantially changes the role of managers from that traditionally described for them. Now the situations they face are dynamic, uncertain, and often ambiguous. They are not in full control of all the factors of production, and they are restrained by many environmental and internal forces (Kast and Rosenzweig 1974). As Sayles (1964) expresses it: A systems concept emphasizes that managerial assignments do not have those neat, clearly defined boundaries; rather the modern manager is placed in a network of mutually dependent relationships.

The organization represents the system to be managed. According to Johnson et al. (1973), this management "is accomplished via managers planning and controlling organizational endeavor (toward objective accomplishment) by means of an information-decision system."

THE PLANNING DEFINITION

The previous section has shown that the open-systems view of an organization implies a planning function. And it is through the managerial subsystem that the planning function operates to adapt the organization to the external environment. In simple terms, the planning function can be defined as making decisions now about the future. This future-oriented decision process involves setting objectives, gathering and organizing information, determining feasible courses of action and choosing among them, implementing the actions, and monitoring the results to insure compliance with the objectives. If the objectives are not being met, modified or alternate plans are employed.

Can there be an operational definition of planning that applies to all organizations? We think not. Planning differs among different organizations and among the various levels in an organization. What planning means to one company is not the same for a company of similar size in a different industry. And what planning means for a young company may be different from what it means to a more mature company in the same industry.

Size alone, or number of employees, or marketplace are not common denominators of the planning function. A young company may be served adequately by a simple survival plan, whereas a more mature company in the same industry will need a formal planning function. A small firm in a high-technology area may have a desperate need for planning, whereas a large firm in a static industry may have less need. The planning needs of any organization are individual and situational. Thus, managers must understand the industry their firm operates in, the size and maturity of the firm relative to others in the industry, and the specific objective the firm has in the marketplace. Above all, they must know whether a particular functional area or the entire firm is the subject of the plan.

If the entire firm is the subject, planning takes place on the strategic level. If one of the functional areas, such as marketing, is being planned for, then planning will take place on the administrative and operational levels. To develop the appropriate plan, managers must have the proper perspective on the firm's situation.

The concept of the value of planning varying by industry was brought home dramatically to us as the result of our research on the motor-freight industry. Our purpose was to determine whether firms with a highly developed long-range planning function were more profitable than those with less developed planning functions or those that only planned in the short term. It was concluded that there was no difference in profitability between the two groups. Whether a carrier planned formally for the long term or did not plan at all except for day-to-day occurrences did not affect the level of profitability. There were highly profitable carriers in both groups and carriers with minimal profits or losses in both groups.

Why does long-range planning seem to be of little value to this particular industry? The answer seems to lie in the regulated nature of the industry. Those areas that are normally considered strategic—markets, prices, labor policies—are all stringently controlled for the motor carrier either through government regulations or strong union action. The only area where management has some control is in the day-to-day operation. Thus, except for *ad hoc* planning for acquisition or rate increases, continuous long-term planning does not seem to be the prime place for a motor carrier to expend resources. We concluded that each industry must be examined individually to determine the value of various kinds of planning. Then resources should flow to the kind of planning that is found to be most suitable.

THE VALUE OF PLANNING

As mentioned previously, planning means different things to different organizations. The value of planning to a given organization depends on its objectives, needs, and circumstances. Even so, planning has sufficient value so that, whatever the situation in an organization, it is always beneficial.

One of the benefits of the planning process is that it enables management to make rational decisions. When the planning process is followed, as shown in Chapter 2, managers are presented with alternatives to choose from which have undergone a thorough analysis reflecting all available facts. This minimizes the use of emotion, intuition, and guesswork. When they are used, it is because no better approach is available.

The capability of making rational decisions based on a thoughtful analysis puts management in the enviable position of being able to act when necessary rather than simply react. As a result, management maintains the initiative. When quick response is essential, management will be ready because alternatives have been decided and their priorities have been established. If something should go awry, the contingency plan is in place. Thus, the computer manufacturer that wishes to market to small firms in the United States might have as its second alternative to move into overseas markets and, as its third, to approach larger American firms. If forecasted demand for the first priority is not realized, the firm's management would be prepared to move immediately to the overseas alternative. Thus, the organization is able to capitalize on opportunities and ward off threats more effectively.

In order to have an effective planning process, management must define relationships within and without the organization. This definition alone constitutes one of the major benefits of the planning process. Defining who is responsible for each organizational function insures that each function lies in someone's area of responsibility. In addition, management can determine whether each function is properly placed and whether the responsible individual has the authority to execute the required actions. It also insures that only one area is responsible for a given function.

Defining an organization and its relationships is usually more valuable if the managers themselves—not just top management—participate. In this way, the definitions are not imposed on those who must operate within them, but rather they reflect the understanding and willingness of the managers themselves. Such an approach fosters communication and cooperation. Managers will be more willing to be responsive to the needs of another department when they are sure that the responsibility is theirs, and they will be more willing to seek assistance from other areas if they are confident that such help is properly due them. In summary, defining relationships as part of the planning process opens up the lines of communication in an organization.

Organizations are dynamic. They change—in fact, they must change. When organizational change is random, however, it is difficult to determine where the firm changed from or whether it is better off for the move. Planning elminates that dilemma. When the planning process is in place—when management is committed to planning and is operating according to the model in Chapter 2—an organization can change rapidly—and from a known position. The new position is rationally chosen, and it can be defined and evaluated relative to the original base. Thus, planning provides for the constant change in an organization, but the change is controlled and directional.

A good planning process, which allows all levels of management to participate, builds confidence in an organization for it gives everyone a long-term perspective. It shows that management has a direction, that decisionmaking is under control, and that the total organization is working to achieve the same objectives.

Finally, planning provides a standard of performance. The plan states what will be done. At any time, the level of achievement can be compared to this standard. On the operational level, the standards are set through a budget; this is the goal against which expense performance is measured. On the strategic level, corporate objectives, such as a certain level of annual gross revenue, become the standard by which management can be evaluated. This facet of planning provides an element of control at all levels of management. Management monitors performance and perceives whether changes should be made in order to maintain the standard, or it may indicate that the standard needs to be changed. In either case, the planning process provides the guidelines for rational, controlled action.

Planning can be undertaken from many perspectives, depending on the needs of an organization. The challenge to management is to discover the kind(s) of planning the organization needs and to invoke the part of the process that will achieve the greatest overall return.

FEAR OF PLANNING

Many people would prefer to avoid planning if they could find a substitute means of achieving the same ends. Among the planning-related fears that business people reveal are:

- It is hard to plan (and I might not do a good job).
- It puts constraints on my actions (if it's not in the plan, I can't do it).
- It forces me to make decisions (and that makes me vulnerable).
- Making a plan provides a yardstick for critique and evaluation (and I might not measure up).
- Planning brings direction and organization out of chaos (and removes a very good excuse).
- Planning brings its own chaos and disruption (when managers resist or choose not to follow the plan).

Are the consequences of these fears necessarily the ones suspected? Can more positive consequences be achieved? If managers could somehow be induced to embark upon a planning project, they would soon learn that their fears were unfounded. Here is one example. A small but fast-growing electronics company was grossing about $10 million per year when it was persuaded by its auditors to institute an elementary budgeting system. This basic planning function would highlight which funds would be spent by each functional area. There were separate budgets for administration, finance, production, and marketing. The company had no other formal planning system nor any inclination to plan. The proposal to budget and the required thought process were both severely resisted by all but the financial officer. Fears were rampant among managers. (Suppose I overspend? Suppose I forget to include something? Should I put in for more than I need to protect myself? What expenses can I dump on another area?) But the auditors prevailed. Historical data were prepared, showing expenses in each area over the prior 3 years. Each officer was asked to project expenses for the next 2 years. This historical information had an astounding effect. For the first time, the managers had some idea of the costs for the functions in their operation. Moreover, they could see immediately where their greatest expenses were and where they had the most cost control. Thus, they could concentrate their efforts on those areas with the greatest payoff. The managers recognized that the budget allowed them to see just how well they were performing. Such specific evaluation was much more desirable than a nebulous feeling of "doing a good job." Finally, under-budget performance became a source of pride.

One of the authors served as a consultant to this company, and the institution of the budget was important for him as well. By forcing management to assign his fee to a specific functional area, the budget clarified that he was primarily on board to assist in the production area. However, it was agreed that, from time to time, he could be made available to the marketing department as well. This made it clear to the consultant where to spend his time and provided a framework within which the managers could more efficiently use his services. The planning process also forced the company's management to evaluate the worth of the consulting services. Moreover, the decision to budget a specific amount for the services removed the production manager's constant fear that he would be criticized for the amount he spent.

PLANS VS. PLANNING

Although plans are valuable, the planning process itself is more important. An organization gains significant benefits just by moving through the organized, logical, and systematic process of developing a plan. Some of the benefits are immediate; for example, weaknesses, strengths, threats, and opportunities are discovered during the analysis phase. Even the initial step of defining the purposes and goals of the organization often provides top management with a much needed clarification of where the organization is headed, through which it can evaluate its decisions.

Planning is a continuing management function; it is never finished. The planning process includes many stages—from goal-setting to analysis, to strategy formulation and evaluation, to implementation. Implementation is always followed by feedback and control: that is, the original premises developed are continually tested against reality, and, as reality changes, the planning process must be reinstituted and the premises (and analyses) reworked. In other words, the plan—the result of the planning process—is dynamic, constantly adapting to changes in the internal and external environment. That is the way it should be, because a static plan would be of no value to a dynamic organization.

As mentioned previously, planning is a management function, and it cannot be effective in an organization without the active participation of all levels of management. However, although each level of manager has responsibility for some aspect of planning, the initial support must come from the top (the chief executive), and the commitment must be evident to everyone in the organization. Top management will focus on the strategic long-range aspects of the plan, leaving administrative planning to middle management and the day-to-day operational aspects of the planning cycle to lower levels in the organization. At whatever level planning is being done, it is part of an integrated, companywide effort. And the chief executive is the chief planner.

This involvement by top management formalizes the planning process. As Chakraborty and David (1979) point out in the article starting on p. 12, ". . . if top executives do not put their influence behind the planning process and create the environment to bring about order out of disorder at their own level, the tasks of lower level managers become more difficult and the planning activity inefficient."

Additionally, Cleland and King (1974), in the article beginning on p. 19, point out that planning must be done by those individuals in those organization units that will ultimately be responsible for implementation. This conclusion diminishes the idea of the "professional" planner and strengthens the case for the key people at all levels becoming adept at, and knowledgeable about, planning. The professional planner, one schooled in planning techniques, whether consultant or employee, guides the process but does no actual planning.

Several variables affect the process, and thus the planning system is dynamic. These variables and their interaction provide a framework through which plans are made and executed. Chapter 2 details that framework.

CANDID COMMENTS

Through interviews and questionnaires, evaluations of their planning functions were solicited from more than 500 chief executive officers (CEOs). The firms ranged in volume from $3 million to over $100 million, with the majority ranging from $10 million to $30 million. Some were local operations, while others were national or covered major segments of the country. None were international firms.

A number of the CEO's responses are excerpted here. They reveal a wide range of corporate attitudes toward planning, ranging from the nonbeliever, to the unsophisticated planner, to the more formal planner.

1. *Just lucky, I guess* . . . We operate day by day, week by week, and month by month in a very informal manner. We are a small company with about 175 employees and a very good profit margin. Sometimes I wonder how we do it.

2. *Have it your way* . . . We are very informal—apparently quite unsophisticated. Long-range, even intermediate-range, planning is not formally done. We are fairly successful though, doing it "our way."

3. *Have sons (and stock), will plan* . . . We are a relatively small company. The firm is managed by the president, the sole owner of all the stock. Planning assistance is obtained from certain long-term supervisory employees. More

specific planning methods probably should be employed now that two young sons have entered the business.

4. *What about the second time around?* . . . We are a closely held corporation, with stockholders and directors involved in our day-to-day activities. All planning is done by the supervisor of each function meeting with the owner-president of the company. We are able to plan and replan virtually every day.

5. *Decisions on a full stomach* . . . Policies are suggested to the company president. Upon approval, they are put into effect by the vice president and general manager. Breakfast meetings are held every two weeks and are attended by the president, vice president and general manager, controller, operations manager, and personnel supervisor.

6. *I'd rather do it myself* . . . Most plans regarding growth and changes are made and carried out by myself (president). I have consulted different employees—traffic manager, sales manager, and the like—but have never really had a good idea from them on anything but immediate problems. They have never done any long-range thinking.

7. *Youth takes over* . . . We are in a transitional period, going from very informal to formal planning. The executive committee functions as the board of directors, with the younger members pushing for more formalized long-range planning.

8. *A family affair* . . . The president, his three brothers, and a nephew—all employees of the company—plus a close personal friend, make up the six-man board of directors. The president formulates short-term and intermediate-range plans for specific projects by informal conferences with the members of the board. Day-to-day operation of the company is controlled by a three-man executive committee consisting of the president, one brother, and the nephew. The president personally implements the results of the informal planning policy. Nothing is committed to writing, and he monitors his own progress.

9. *The staff approach* . . . Planning is done principally by an executive staff. It meets for 3 to 4 hours on the first and third Monday of each month. Membership consists of corporate officers, each of whom is responsible for one or more activities of the company.

10. *Management by objectives* . . . We're starting a management-by-objectives program for our company. We have developed companywide objectives and then objectives for each geographic location and then each department. We are just getting the program to work smoothly and are starting to stretch out the length of our advance planning.

11. *Committee decisions* . . . Our company is managed by an executive committee consisting of the president, executive vice-president, treasurer, operations vice-president, sales vice-president, and maintenance vice-president. The planning function is the responsibility of the president and executive vice-president, who are also directors. Most of the planning is informal. Courses of action are determined based on the recommendations of the executive committee, but

the responsibility for all major decisions rests with the two directors on the committee. Implementation of plans adopted rests with the officers in whose area of responsibility the action is to take place.

12. *The budgeting approach* ... Our planning is almost entirely devoted to budgeting. Every quarter we make sales projections for the next 12 months, revising previous projections as appropriate. At the same time, expense levels are budgeted for each of nearly 200 expense items at each of 16 locations plus the home office.

For several years, we tried 5-year projections of the same nature, but gave these up as a "pie in the sky." Our overall corporate goals are profitability and growth, but aside from the budget, no formal goals are established for growth. Rather, it is approached *ad hoc* as new sales opportunities develop or acquisitions become attractive.

13. *Projections* ... Projections are made for 1 year or 13 four-week periods. Comparisons are then made to actual performance. No capital purchases or major decisions are made without approval of two of the three officers.

14. *Automation creeps in* ... We operate under a complete budget system with all data on electronic data processing. This provides at least 5 years' historical information. The budget is upgraded quarterly with actual performance.

15. *Unreliable, but* ... I have found that long-range planning is unreliable. However, beginning this year, taking into account economic and political indicators, we have gone to a very fundamental and companywide goals-planning system. Everything is committed to paper, and each department supervisor and higher-level manager participates in the process. It is too early to tell whether we will be successful.

16. *All inclusive* ... Planning, both long-range and short, is done by the president, vice-president, operations manager, sales manager, and traffic manager during informal meetings every Friday. Long-range plans and forecasts are discussed monthly, whereas, day-to-day and shorter-term projects are discussed each week. Occasionally, the long-term goals are set by the president-owner and formalized in a brief letter to the others mentioned above. Progress toward the long-range goals is monitored formally each March, and steps toward the goals are noticed and commented on at the weekly meetings.

17. *Y'all join in* ... Planning is developed through the "staff" by any person with an idea. Staff meetings are held weekly at a planned luncheon with no interruptions! Most long-range plans are forecasted judgment decisions. They are approved by the board of directors and are implemented by the officers and staff. This is particularly true in the case of capital investments.

18. *Once a year with adjustments* ... The primary thrust of planning is an annual plan. Strategizing or long-range planning is done periodically. Strategic issues are discussed, however, in each year's plan and monitored for progress. In a constantly changing economic scenario, these plans are adjusted, and contingency plans are set up each year.

19. *What can I say?* ... Formal annual planning is based on objectives, strategies, and tactics. The resources, time frames, and results are formally described for each strategy and tactic. The financial results of these programs are combined into an operating budget for the year, which in turn is compared, location by location, with the actual results each period.

20. *Or else* ... Annual profit plan also includes a 5-year forecast of sales, earnings, and capital requirements. This must be submitted to the executive committee of our parent corporation to be incorporated into the parent's profit plan.

21. *Amen* ... All this talk of planning seems unnecessary to me. How any company could expect to survive and not undertake long-range planning is unthinkable.

REFERENCES

Chakraborty, S. and G. S. David. 1979. Why managers avoid planning. *Planning Review* 7(3): 17–19, 34–35.

The authors endorse the concept that top management must create a positive planning environment, or otherwise subordinates will give in to their fear and avoid planning. *Reprinted herein on pp. 12–19.*

Churchman, C. W. 1968. *The Systems Approach.* New York: Dell Publishing Co.

A classic explanation of the elements of a system and the method of thinking about an organization with a systems perspective. Links are made to management information systems and the planning function.

Cleland, D. I. and W. R. King. 1974. Developing a planning culture for more effective strategic planning. *Long Range Planning* 7(3): 70–74.

Reports the authors' empirically based conclusion that the success of long-range planning in an organization is less sensitive to the parameters of the planning techniques than it is to the overall culture within which the planning is accomplished. *Reprinted herein on pp. 19–29.*

Johnson, R. A., F. E. Kast, and J. E. Rosenzweig. 1973. *The Theory and Management of Systems.* 3rd ed. New York: McGraw-Hill.

Three focuses of the systems approach are presented: (1) systems philosophy, (2) systems design and analysis, and (3) systems management.

Kast, F. E. and J. E. Rosenzweig. 1974. *Organization and Management: A Systems Approach.* 2nd ed. New York: McGraw-Hill.

Explains the managerial role in a complex and dynamic organizational society through a systems perspective.

Sayles, L. R. 1964. *Managerial Behavior.* New York: McGraw-Hill.

A basic text in the field of management.

Why Managers Avoid Planning And What Top Management Can Do About It

Samir Chakraborty
and
Gabriel S. David

In many cases, there is no firm commitment to planning by the senior officers of an organization, because planning is regarded as an exercise that has little relevance to present reality—results are not seen for a considerable period of time. This attitude is often reflected by subordinates, for if top executives do not put their influence behind the planning process and create the environment to bring about order out of disorder at their own level, the tasks of lower level managers become more difficult and the planning activity ineffective. The climate usually ends up accentuating the painful aspects of planning and the average manager's chances of planning success are significantly diminished.

Disorganized operations affecting a manager's area are another major barrier. Managers can be prevented from effectively organizing their own operations, even when planning is carried out within their area of responsibility. If operations above the level of an individual manager are disorganized, the incentive to plan and organize will be reduced. Not only will attempts at planning for future improvements fail, but operations will gradually deteriorate through lack of systematic attention and action.

Planning is perceived as a complex task and is therefore often avoided. In order to choose realistic objectives and effective methods for implementation, the manager must be able to relate causes with effects based on the best available information concerning the future environment and current operations. This requires an articulation of assumptions with a high degree of clarity, which is often unsettling. The longer the time span of the plan, the greater the inter-relationships and dependencies and, hence, the more difficult the task. In a rapidly changing environment such as ours, complexity is a fact of life and the manager must accept this if he is to prepare for the future. Our inability to cope effectively with complexity is not necessarily inherent. Although planning is not limited to the chief executive officer and senior executives in most organizations, they have more power to reduce this complexity by actively participating

Reprinted from *Planning Review,* a journal of the North American Society for Corporate Planning, 1406 Third National Building, Dayton, Ohio 45402.

in the planning process, and also by acting as major catalysts in changing attitudes towards the planning activity.

The discipline for effective planning is often lacking. In addition to forcing the manager to face present reality and the complexity of the future, planning imposes discipline in the conception, development and implementation stages of the plan. To develop a plan, the manager must structure his thoughts, build an abstract representation of the future environment and quantify the consequences of the relationships that he is postulating. The manager must then derive standards of performance for the monitoring and control of his operations. The plan, therefore, provides a mechanism for continuous review and accountability—both aspects of control—which people resent and even fear because they are often misused. Again, the officers of the company have the power and responsibility to change the internal environment and the application of the planning and control system. It is one thing to use a planning and control system as a means for encouraging managers to learn from their experience and improve their operations. It is another thing to provide data to superiors to police and control their subordinates. There is great potential in management science techniques, quantitative models, computerized systems, etc., but they are useless if the proper management attitude toward planning does not exist in the organization.

Many managers fear "The Plan" and staff planners. They fear that planners exists to curb their independence and encroach on their territory. Planning thrusts them into complex situations with a great degree of uncertainty, situations with which they often cannot cope. The plan provides information to others within the organization, thus decreasing privacy and exposing errors in forecasting and judgment. It enforces cohesiveness and integration and appears to pose a threat to the independence of the manager. In organizations where the motives and operating principles of superiors are suspect, it would be risky for a manager to expose himself. Secrecy and minimal involvement are the safest approach, for if there is no documentation, there is no easy way of assessing performance.

Managers, therefore, have good reasons for avoiding planning. They will not naturally seek complexity, discipline and exposure unless properly rewarded. The environment for effective planning must be instilled, cultivated and implemented within the organization by senior executives. It is very unlikely that planning will be accepted voluntarily by lower management without this impetus.

The basic responsibilities of a manager require him to organize the activities of his area of responsibility and contribute to the total profitability and effectiveness of the organization. He must, therefore, plan effectively. The planning process imposes a mental discipline which exposes intuitive inconsistencies. Furthermore, the plan provides a frame of reference which is essential to the learning process. The value of this critical management activity far exceeds the psychic and other costs the planning process may impose. The question, there-fore, is not one of " planning versus no planning," but rather questions of how to plan, how much, in what form and at what level.

CHARACTERISTICS OF INEFFECTIVE PLANNING

It is well known that a major part of an executive's time on the job is spent coping with crises and that a very small part of his or her time is spent on plan-ning. Of the time spent on planning, at least half of the "planning" is crisis initiated. The worst time for planning, however, is when one is fighting fires. Views on the environment are distorted, tension is high, impatience sets in and the "ostrich mentality" prevails. Procedures designed to get the organization out of a crisis are often elevated to the level of general policies and strategic plans, only to lead the organization into the next crisis. Crises are often the result of pat actions or inaction. Crises invite fast action, but planning needs adequate research, objectivity and thoughtful deliberation. Planning, in short, requires time.

Actions necessary to get an organization out of a crisis are usually not those which will prevent it from falling into the next crisis. Policies and operating pro-cedures on how to fight fires prepared after the fact are by their nature dif-ferent from policies and strategic plans designed to eradicate the causes of the fires. Confusion about this difference leads managers to respond to symptoms rather than causes. Constant crises are degenerative, and the more crises managers must face, the less time they can afford to devote to their prevention through planning. Crises have some value in that they may transmit to the organiza-tion a sense of urgency and dissatisfaction with the results of non-planning. Top management should not waste the opportunity of attempting to change organi-zational attitudes toward planning after a crisis. The major drawback of this approach is that managers overreact to a crisis situation, making the problem worse.

A consequence of a lack of formal planning is that managers learn very little from either their own experience or that of others within the organization be-cause there are no common, consistent reference points for assumptions, im-plications and standards of performance. Major attributes of a good manager are that he learns from experience, enriches the knowledge of others within his organization by formalizing information dissemination and thereby enhances the learning process for others—his subordinates, colleagues and superiors.

Managers also tend to confuse "planning efficiently" with effective planning. Their major concern seems to be form rather than function. But, no matter how efficient the form in which planning is carried out, if it is done for the wrong reasons, it will not be done effectively and the complexity of managing the area of responsibility will increase exponentially. Since managers attempt to cope with problems by attacking them sequentially rather than in parallel—and they frequently have no alternative if they are inundated with problems—any management control system which may exist cannot provide them with the necessary support for effective decision making unless key aspects of operations are linked to the relevant plans. Moreover, the problems which force managers to attack problems sequentially also force them into taking a short-term view. Planning, under these circumstances, is likely to be a scheduling of day-to-day activities, since the span of attention of the harassed manager is inversely proportional to the intensity and number of crises with which he has to deal at any point in time. The greater the number of crises, the quicker the performance of managers and their subordinates declines. And the higher up in the organization one goes, the greater the necessity for planning in parallel rather than sequentially, and the greater the value of effective long-range and strategic planning.

Confusion within the organization tempts managers to jump to simplistic, naive solutions. Managers do not use their creativity but, rather, resort to taking the path of least resistance in order to cover themselves. Determinism prevails when this occurs and decision making processes are neglected. Executives within the organization may claim, especially in private, that "problems are simple and the solutions obvious," but no one is willing to do anything about them because "he was not asked" and after all "it is not his problem." Actions are limited to the necessary minimum, which usually means only when crises occur; and even then it is more of the same. Confusing activity with results and efficiency with effectiveness, managers gradually lose sight of the real goals of planning. They begin increasingly to concentrate on staying busy.

The "Staff Meeting" syndrome is very often present when the organization is faced with a crisis. In the absence of formal effective plans, it is extremely difficult to identify the causes of a crisis, so discussion rarely goes beyond the stage of identification of the symptoms before it reverts into a "witch hunting" session. The discussions become biased, the people defensive and the mechanism which can make the organization fast on its feet and, in addition, prevent similar problems from occurring in the future are ignored. Meetings, under a crisis situation, are not conducive to learning. There is a serious lack of relevant information and most meetings are adjourned without having identified the real problem, let alone the solution to it.

As previously mentioned, effective planning requires a management environment which emphasizes openness, interdependence and visibility. Accurate and relevant information is required to develop and effectively implement a plan. In organizations where the planning discipline has been instilled, the absence of necessary information is obvious and procedures are established to obtain it. In an organization which does not have an effective planning environment, on the other hand, information is more often used as a power base. It is, therefore, often withheld no matter how critical it is to the success of the total organization. In fact, there may be a positive incentive to withhold it, since the worse the people without the key information are made to appear within the organization, the better the one who withholds the information looks.

Without effective, integrated plans, chances are the organization will not have developed well integrated and complete operational goals, standards of performance, milestone markers and formal information systems for monitoring total task performance. It becomes, therefore, difficult to evaluate performance and give reward appropriately. Distrust and blaming of others is not the only negative consequence of such situations, for the environment can become so unhealthy that it not only discourages co-operation but, to the contrary, encourages suspicion and backstabbing.

Closely related to the previous symptoms is the gradual creation of an operational leadership vacuum. When things get out of hand, there is a great probability that the top executives of the organization, feeling insecure, will isolate themselves mentally, if not physically. They will be inclined to suspect the motives of their subordinates, ascribing to the latter their own failures. This stance, in the absence of any formal standard of expectations and performance, will most likely leave lower level managers unsure as to where they stand. Since the organization has no integrated plans or well articulated goals, these managers will simply not know where to turn. While some will try "to keep the ship afloat," others, capitalizing on the opportunity, will become more political and increasingly cater to the vanity of their superiors. The latter in return will give these "trusted" subordinates more power. When two classes of people—the "ins" and the "outs"—exist in the organization, a lot of energy will be expended by the "ins" to neutralize, if not remove, the "outs." A business organization transformed by inept leadership from an economic entity to a political circus can be doomed to failure, especially when people are pushed aside and an exodus of competent managers and personnel begins. To save the organization when it reaches this point, one needs to initiate a thorough "house cleaning," starting from the top.

The advantages of planning, budgeting and establishing standards of performance are that they help keep managers honest, protecting themselves and their organization against their own weaknesses. Plans, budgets and standards can make the difference between success and failure.

EFFECTIVE PLANNING ENVIRONMENT CHARACTERISTICS

Let us now turn to what enables effective corporate planning. Some characteristics of effective corporate planning were indicated in previous parts of this paper. We will now bring these into focus and elaborate.

Planning activity must be initiated by, encouraged by and have an ongoing commitment from the very top levels of management. Senior executives can change the corporate climate from one of conflict to one of cooperation and openness. When top management defines overall objectives from which one starts structuring a management environment, the assumptions, judgments, choices and decisions for implementation made at the top level define constraints and limits that guide the judgment of lower management. That is why, unless the chief executive and other senior executives of the organization contribute to the process of creating order, the chances for success by lower management are marginal.

Those who constitute top management should be people who recognize patterns in the relationships between the external environment and the corporate organization. This pattern recognition capability is critical for successful planning because planning activity and the resulting plans must be created along integrated, consistent, formal and well documented lines. They must include specific definitions of:

- The major business assumptions regarding the external environment and how the environment affects the goals of the organization.
- The goals to be pursued—both qualitative and quantitative—and the translation of these goals into operational objectives.
- The resources and operations necessary for the accomplishment of objectives and the specific cause and effect relationships linking them together.
- The key indicators that show whether the choice of decisions and operations will enable achievement of the objectives of the organization. As part of this activity, there should also be a specification of the meaning of deviations.
- The measurements and feedback mechanisms that will best generate the "current status information" and to what depth they will reach.
- A management information and control system that will apply the measurements, generate the control data, analyze the information generated and transmit it to appropriate levels of action.

Operationally, effective planning processes are:

Model-Based: That is, plans are based on abstracted representations of the "environment" in which the manager is working. The greater the perceptiveness of the manager and the greater his ability to handle complexity, the more encompassing, long-range and elaborate these models tend to be. As the manager learns from experience, he should consolidate and formalize the knowledge he has gained by restructuring and upgrading his models.

Process/System Oriented: This implies specification of the significant "means to ends" and cause and effect relationships. Furthermore, all these relationships must be connected together as a system through cross impact analysis. The latter, for our purposes, may be viewed as an assembly of interconnected subsystems and elements, such that the value of any part of the system is judged not independently but only in terms of its contribution to the overall objectives of the system.

Iteratively Implemented: Management is not an exact science. Many things are done in a semi-scientific way and by "trial and error." In strategic planning, models are developed, goals and strategies for implementation derived, and an assessment of the logical consequences of the assumptions and expected results is made. If the results are unrealistic, unfeasible or unsatisfactory, the process is repeated. Thus, through successive iterations, a plan which is acceptable is formulated. Later, during the process of implementation, the managers may discover that there were many things they did not consider because they did not know how to handle them or predict their behavior. It must be remembered, however, that if it were not for the existence of a plan, there would be no way to recognize what was left out. Thus, a well articulated plan serves as a basis for learning and improvement.

Sustained by the Ongoing Information Systems: Many organizations develop plans, but stop short of specifying the signals, measurements and feedback mechanisms which will provide indicators for performance evaluation. In this way, the necessary linkage between planning and control is missing. Operations, therefore, do not provide the necessary information for sustaining the planning activities of the organization. As a result, line and staff managers live in two different worlds, the planning efforts of the organization go to waste and the "information" generated internally is considered useless by top managers. Operations keep plodding along as usual and performance review sessions become fencing matches and tension-generating exercises.

It is not an insurmountable task to link the elements of the planning and control processes. The major requirements are that managers: a) discipline themselves to define the feedback they want and how often they wish to have it, and to specify the possible implications of variations in the feedback; and b) aid the designers of control systems to provide them with information which refers not only to the results from their operations but also to the validity of the various environmental assumptions (both external and internal) which link plans to operations.

Top management should insure that the role and status of the corporate planner are clearly understood. The effective planner is a "power-broker" between different sections of the organization and, while the planner is usually not personally involved in the generation of substantive plans for any division, he or she is responsible for helping create an environment in which plans can be developed, integrated and executed. The planner is also a problem solver, the major problems being human problems.

SUMMARY

In this paper, we have shown some of the things that top management can do to change the planning environment of an organization. These are changes that will conserve the time of both managers and executives. They will help the organization get out of firefighting and into preventive planning. But above all, they will help upgrade the managerial capabilities of an organization and change the climate from one of suspicion, backbiting and mutual conflict to one of creative co-operation.

Elaborate systems and computers are not needed for a planning process such as the one described. More important than hardware are the conceptual framework and the intellectual discipline that framework imposes. And most important is the intellectual discipline that must be encouraged by top management to permit the development of effective planning procedures throughout the organization.

Developing a Planning Culture for More Effective Strategic Planning

David I. Cleland
and
William R. King

The literature of long-range planning is replete with justifications of the need for strategic planning and admonitions concerning its critical importance. However, both the literature of planning and its practice, as manifested in a variety of organizations as diverse as industrial firms, educational systems and law enforcement agencies, are deficient in specifying proven techniques and methodologies for marshalling organizational resources to effectively implement strategic planning.

Over a period of years, the authors have consulted with a variety of business organizations and public agencies in the development and implementation of long-range planning processes. From this work has come an empirically-tested conclusion that the success of long-range planning in an organization is less

Reprinted from *Long Range Planning,* June 1974, Vol. 7, No. 7.

sensitive to the parameters of the planning techniques than it is to the overall *culture* within which the planning is accomplished. Since most of the non-pontifical literature of planning focuses on planning techniques and specifications for planning processes, these conclusions suggest a critical void in planning methodology.

A PLANNING CULTURE

The basic premise of the approach to long-range planning described here is that meaningful, long-range planning must be done by those individuals and organizational units who will ultimately be responsible for executing the plan. If this was not true, the question of organizing for planning would have a deceptively simple answer . . . organize a "planning department." However, although professional planners clearly have an important role in planning, there are few illustrations of "delegated planning" which are truly successful. Those few instances where success with such an approach is claimed tend to measure success in terms of planning-related performance measures rather than overall organizational performance measures. For instance, one company found that the installation of a formal planning department significantly enhanced planning performance—deadlines were met more frequently, and the amount of documentation was increased. However, after several years, it was ascertained that only the trappings of planning had been improved: the substance was unaffected. When an analysis was made of the quality of planning in terms of its impact in the organization and on such things as the range of alternatives considered in the planning process, it was discovered that no significant influence could be determined. Thus, while the forecasts were more sophisticated and the plans more voluminous, the allocation of significant resources to a planning department had not led to greater creativity, to new concepts of the business or to higher profits. Since all of these are reasonable expectations for planning, the company determined that the planning department was not the whole solution to their planning problems.

An alternative to the simplest "one-dimensional" approaches to planning, which are exemplified by the vesting of planning responsibility in a planning department, is the conscious creation of a *planning culture*. This multi-dimensional concept of a "culture" is interpreted here to mean *an accepted and demonstrated belief* on the part of organizational participants as to what is important and valued within the organization. This culture reflects the accepted knowledge, attitudes, and philosophies of both those who guide the organization and those who operate it.

In the planning context, a culture is a clearly established bias concerning the importance and effectiveness of long-range planning which is accepted and demonstrated in daily actions and attitudes by both planning participants and organizational operatives. This means that long-range planning is an accepted and

continuing way of life in the organization—not just a necessary evil which is carried on cyclically.

THE NEED FOR A PLANNING CULTURE

The development of a planning culture is obviously not a simple task, since it requires that planning be made endemic to the value system of managers. In our experience, fully five to eight years may be required under optimum conditions. Yet, to ignore planning is to make oneself the victim of the planning of others, and to "go through the motions" of planning without inducing a planning culture is to simply make the same error in a more resource-consuming way.

The need for a long-range planning culture can be deduced from a number of symptoms—each tending to inhibit prospective planning—which we have frequently found in organizational planning activities. Among these are:

- A tendency for the organizational member to view his current domain from the standpoint of the discipline in which he first acquires credentials, regardless of its broader scope and requirements for more diverse considerations.
- A "tunnel vision" in which an individual fails to recognize the multiple objectives of the organization even though he has moved to a general management position and can no longer afford the luxury of the simplistic efficiency-oriented objectives which are the forte of the middle manager.
- A bureaucratic organizational structure designed more for maintaining efficiency and control in current operations than in fostering long-range innovation.
- The lack of an "organization" designed specifically for bringing out the innovation necessary to develop new products and services.
- An assumption that the chief executive or, alternately, a professional planning staff should *do* the long-range planning.
- An incentive system wherein performance oriented toward an ability to produce short-range results is rewarded more highly than that oriented toward long-range opportunities.
- The introduction of radically new planning systems into organizations without proper concern for their effect on the motivations and behavior of those who will implement them.

In the ensuing sections of this paper, we shall discuss these symptoms as they are found in various organizations together with proven organizational approaches for alleviating them. Taken collectively, these organizational responses constitute the basis for an organizational planning culture.

DISCIPLINARY AND ORGANIZATIONAL
PAROCHIALISM

An understandable tendency on the part of educated human beings to view the world from the standpoint of their particular experiential and educational background is one of the facts of organizational life which must be overcome if planning is to be effectively performed and implemented. Two varieties of such parochialism which abound in organizations as diverse as engineering-dominated technical firms and public school systems need be considered—disciplinary parochialism and organizational parochialism.

In *disciplinary* parochialism, the executive still thinks (even unknowingly) in a narrow, specialized function in which he was educated and in which he won his first kudos. Having won his credentials and a degree of success in a specialty such as engineering, he never totally recognizes the narrowness of his education and views that discipline as the most important one in the organization. Such an individual is inclined to spend excess time supervising the engineering aspects of a strategy, since it is familiar and "comfortable" and to minimize his personal involvement in areas such as marketing, even though they may be of critical importance to success.

Perhaps the best illustration of this sort of phenomenon is the aerospace firm whose top executive ranks were dominated by engineers. The firm considered itself to be the quality-leader in its field; yet, its record of obtaining contracts was poor. As the aerospace "crunch" of the early 1970s occurred, a formal study was conducted. The study revealed that the firm had seldom obtained a contract that was handled on a truly competitive basis. Moreover, when contrasted with its more successful competitors, it was apparent that its lack of success could be attributed to naive marketing. Such simple elements of modern aerospace marketing as frequent contact by high-level executives with customers, the allocation of "salesmen" (with a euphemistic title to embellish their image) to major customers, and the close control of these salesmen through briefings and debriefings were not even recognized as deficiencies by the organization's executives. They had never recognized that they could not sit back and rely on the obvious quality of their products to sell themselves, because their concern was with the product and its technical performance rather than with the broader range of considerations which their job necessitated. Truly, they were the victims of the disease of disciplinary parochialism.

Of course, one way of avoiding this natural tendency toward parochialism is to surround the general manager with advisors chosen from various backgrounds. Since his success is reinforced by other specialists who have assisted him in moving up the ladder, the disciplinary parochialist often surrounds himself with those who are known and have been trusted within his field of specialty. Thus, even as he moves up the ladder into positions requiring a broader perspective, his view is not broadened by his access to advisors.

Organizational parochialism is similar; it is the tendency of a manager to view his organization as the center of affairs and to focus attention on a coveted product line which has already been successful—another form of myopia.

The pervasive tendency of some managers to spend product development funds in areas which are known and familiar—thus extending existing product lines—even in the face of overwhelming evidence of a changing market, is indicative of this sort of narrowness and reliance on the choice of "comfortable" alternatives.

The resolution of the problems of parochialism is not simple. The development of a planning culture is itself a partial answer, since a recognition and acceptance of the importance and pervasiveness of planning places pressures on the planning participants to produce plans which involve the consideration of wide ranges of alternatives. Thus, the desire for "good" planning in the planning culture sense is, in part, self-fulfilling.

Moreover, the basic premise of this approach as previously stated—that planning must be done by those who will ultimately be involved in executing the plans—serves to reduce the impact of parochialism. This is so since most organizations will find that their opportunity array does not match either their formal organizational or disciplinary structure. Therefore, managers will necessarily be involved in multi-disciplinary and inter-organizational planning activities which will serve to reduce their parochialism, or at least to reduce its effect on the organization.

ORGANIZATION FOR PLANNING

The structure of most complex organizations is built around some form of vertical structure—often drawn from military or church models—which is characterized by a form of bureaucracy. The visible elements of such bureaucracies are a division of labor, specialization, "chain of command," an objective system of policies and procedures—all having as their purpose the assignment of subtasks to units of people who are "expert," and the creation of "departments" where people of similar skill, training and values are brought together. Under such an organizational arrangement, problems of *efficiency* and *control* in the *current* operations can be dealt with decisively.

Unfortunately, such a vertical organization may not deal effectively with the problems and opportunities of planning long-range organizational strategy. Such organizations characteristically display poor strategic responsiveness and the preemption of strategic decision-making by current operating problems. A conflict of *innovation versus efficiency* is inherent in these organizations, and the basic premise of the organization invariably allows efficiency to dominate the conflict.

The development and implementation of long-range strategy require an extensive assessment of the environmental and competitive forces outside of a given organization. If done properly, long-range planning can very well point out the obsolescence or the threat of obsolescence of a given product line, a market strategy, or similar strategic activity. To ask a given line executive to do this is indeed proper but to provide him with an organizational milieu which will be facilitative, rather than hindering, is also essential.

The particular structure which can best provide such a facilitative environment is inherent in the nature of strategic planning. The result of the planning process should be new products, services, markets, etc.; a whole complex of new opportunities and relationships, both within the organization and in the marketplace. Such innovative opportunities begin as an idea—perhaps held by a research scientist, a field salesman, or a general manager. These ideas are the basic building blocks of future organizational strategy; the point from which the future central purpose of an organization evolves. As these ideas emerge and grow in maturity, they eventually become (assuming they survive) new products, services, reorganizations, etc.

Ideas are, therefore, the harbingers of future strategies. An emerging idea can make a current product obsolete, and point the direction for a change in organizational strategy. Not only must the emergence of ideas be facilitated, but the idea must be "managed" to determine if there is anything worth pursuing. In its early life stages, the idea will face a high mortality potential as the victim of high market risk, technical or economic infeasibility, etc.

The bureaucratic, control-oriented, efficiency-seeking organization will often serve to stifle any ideas not flowing directly from the executive suite. Therefore, some organizational structure must be created to encourage ideas, to nurture them and to ensure that they are allowed to develop to their fullest.

Such an organizational form—*the matrix organization**—has been used in a variety of contexts for precisely this purpose. As applied to strategic planning, the matrix organization simply means that *projects* or *project teams,* headed by project managers, are set up to be "in charge" of an emerging idea. The project manager becomes an entrepreneur who "sells" the project across the organization. As well, he pulls together a team to further evaluate the idea from the standpoint of need, marketability, investment requirements, etc. In effect, the idea is "managed" via the project manager as it moves from the inception to fruition.

For example, one company (a large decentralized conglomerate) set up a project team to study the technology and marketability of an airport security system. Members of the project team were recruited from the various divisions

---

*The matrix organization consists of integral teams superimposed on the vertical structure of the organization. The matrix form of organization is found extensively in the defense industry. See for example: Mee, John F., "Matrix Organization," *Business Horizons,* (Summer 1964).

of the company to form an integral team of experts to evaluate and make strategic recommendations to top management concerning the emerging idea.

Project teams can also be used in strategic planning in the "search" phase which precedes the generation of specific ideas. Illustrative of this is the large firm which set up interdisciplinary project teams made up of upper middle managers to investigate broad opportunity areas for new products and services. The teams "divided up the world" on the basis of the federal government executive department's spheres of concern. This was done not so much because the government represents a large potential customer, as it was to take advantage of the large influence of government programs on expenditures to be made in the future by the private sector and other governmental levels.

The teams proceeded by analyzing agency plans and by assessing the impact of these plans on other elements of the economy. Then, they "matched" these projections with their own plans to develop a number of specific opportunities worthy of detailed analysis.

The result of this process was about seven major new product opportunities which were approved by top management for immediate expenditures. Of these, about four are likely to reach full fruition and provide the firm with significant future profits.

Of course, the advantage of such a structure is not solely in their project element. The matrix form makes projects and functions complementary. Line managers have an extra-functional resource to use in developing strategies and exploring opportunities. The greater adaptability and responsiveness thereby achieved provide direct benefits to planning and—through the interdisciplinary and interfunctional nature of the team—an additional system of "checks and balances" against the pitfalls of parochialism.

Thus, the utilization of project teams and matrix organizational forms constitutes a basic part of the planning culture. In instituting such a system, an organization is saying: "Innovation is so important to this organization that a one-dimensional organizational structure is inadequate. To foster innovation, ideas will not only be encouraged, but formally managed until they reach fruition or are shown to be infeasible."

ROLES OF THE CHIEF EXECUTIVE AND PLANNING STAFF

Just as an "organization" which can facilitate strategic planning is an essential element of a planning culture, so, too, is an understanding of the role to be played by various other elements of the organization.

For instance, since the chief executive is ultimately responsible for the strategic and long-range development of the organization, his role can be exaggerated. While he must, in fact, *do* planning, he cannot do it alone. The chief executive must develop goals and strategies and approve plans developed by lower-level managers, but he cannot himself devote time to developing plans. He must effectively use his staff and lower-level managers in a project team environment to ensure that the best of organizational thought and creativity are brought to bear in planning.

Thus, in the final analysis, a primary contribution of the chief executive to strategic planning is in the acceleration of the acceptance of a planning culture. The example set in word, but more importantly in deed, by the chief executive will, in large measure, determine the aggressiveness and creativity which will be applied to planning by others and the meaningfulness of the plans which they produce. One chief executive who believed in the adequacy of a memo announcing a new planning process and stressing its importance eventually found that many of his line managers were "going through the motions" of participation in planning without really making it an important part of their activities. His personal involvement in planning meetings and a series of phone calls placed to key individuals over the duration of the most intensive segment of planning activities served to have the process be immediately taken more seriously.

In providing motivation and facilitation, the chief executive must be skillful in his use of his planning staff. While they are professional planners, they must not be allowed to do the planning or to dominate the planning process. Their role, like that of the chief executive, is facilitative. However, the chief executive facilitates both substantively, by contributing to planning, and culturally, by "selling" planning to his organization.

The planning staff must play only a substantive facilitative role in providing forecasts, assumptions, alternative strategies, etc., to be considered by the manager-planners. If they try to play the planning cultural role of the chief executive, they may well be viewed as "technocrats with a cause." Then they, like the efficiency experts, operations researchers, and a host of others before them, will be relegated to the "back room" of the organization, and their "cause" will not play a significant role in determining the organization's destiny.

ACCOUNTABILITY AND PLANNING-RELATED INCENTIVES

In organizations which do not have a planning culture, the attitude that . . . "long-range planning is not really important because we'll all be dead in the long run anyway" . . . usually means that accountability for long-range results is poor. If the system of awards and punishments favors current performance at the expense of the long-run, a powerful, anti-planning culture emerges to deter the executive from giving his attention to the long-range future of the organization.

If the manager has profit center responsibility, this short-run, tunnel vision is reinforced. This is illustrated by the division manager who, when asked to develop long-range strategy for his organization, came up with a strategy which essentially extended existing product lines. This manager had been successful and the prevailing incentive system provided for short-term profit performance. Indeed, there was little recognition, either in merit increases or promotion opportunity, for innovation in the development of long-range strategies. Thus, the success of a given product line reinforced a propensity to develop strategy along proven lines. The manager was doing just what could reasonably have been expected of him; yet the firm somehow naively believed that it could expect otherwise. Although planning should be participative and nonthreatening, once plans have been approved and accepted by the managers, they should be accountable for them. In this, as in perhaps no other way, can managers be forced to explicitly consider the short-term versus long-run trade-offs which are essential to good planning.

Of course, this principle has been accepted by many who have found it difficult to implement. The only effective way of doing so—within the context of an organizational environment in which personnel are constantly changing responsibilities—is to have the plans follow the individual, i.e., to trace the individual's planning performance back to previous jobs. The authors know of several firms who have tried to do this—none of them with a degree of success which could be taken to indicate its feasibility. However, if such a system can be developed, a reward structure which is, in part, based on planning performance can be implemented. When the organization does this, it reaps benefits which can go far beyond the reward-punishment syndrome, since the knowledge that "good planning pays" is itself a powerful element of a planning culture.

A PLAN FOR IMPLEMENTING PLANNING

One of the most common reasons for the failure of planning to "catch on" in an organization is the commonly-voiced assertion that the "process is often more important than the product." While it is true that the planning process can pay benefits for the organization in terms of the broader horizons, greater creativity, and better understanding of objectives on the part of planning participants, it is also true that a radically new planning process can disrupt an organization, threaten managers, and lead to ineffective planning.

The process of introducing a planning procedure into an organization is a subtle one of taking advantage of a preliminarily-established planning culture and, in turn, of reinforcing that culture. Planning cannot be introduced into an organization not yet ready to accept it; and, conversely, successful planning reinforces itself.

Thus, the effective implementation of planning in an organization which has not previously done formalized planning requires that an *implementation strategy* be developed. An implementation strategy is a step-by-step procedure for taking advantage of the existing characteristics of the planning culture in such a way as to enhance the likelihood of planning being accepted and meaningfully used.

The basic nature of such a strategy is its sequential nature. An "all at once" introduction of a comprehensive planning process is almost inevitably doomed. A sequential process which has been successfully implemented by a technical products firm begins with a series of internal "workshops" which deal with the theory and state-of-the-art of long-range planning. These workshops focus on both the positive and negative aspects of planning in going into the advantages which can be gained as well as the practical failures with planning both within the firm itself and by other firms with which the consultant-seminar leaders are familiar.

The output of these seminars is a better appreciation of planning as well as some specific ideas as to the most fertile areas within the company for the initial implementation of planning. When the "best" area is selected, a planning activity can begin.

In one organization, the budgeting area was selected for major initial effort since it was well understood and because the seminars had revealed that the current system would be detrimental to innovative planning. In another organization, the new product area was selected for initial formalized planning because of its potential payoff.

In this way, the value of planning—so much talked about in the literature and by those executives who wish to make greater use of it in their organizations—can be demonstrated in concrete terms. As with the introduction of any major change in an organization, "nothing succeeds like success," so that those who would oppose the *concept* of formalized planning, or ineffectively perform themselves in such a process are placed in the position of objecting to a "proven" approach. Usually, this approach attracts those who wish to join the coming thing—thus ensuring the success of planning.

SUMMARY

A planning culture—an accepted and demonstrated belief in the efficacy of strategic planning—is a critical element for the success of organizational long-range planning. Such a culture is defined here in terms of appropriate organizational response to commonly-found symptoms which serve to inhibit effective planning.

Parochialism—both organizational and disciplinary—is one such symptom. Traditional organizational forms which focus on control and efficiency in the short-run, rather than the innovation and creativity which are so critical to long-run survival, are both symptomatic of basic organizational planning bottlenecks as well as reinforcers of parochialism.

Other inhibitions of planning are reward structures, which in turn reinforce both parochialism and the bureaucratic organization, and the narrow views of the roles to be played by chief executives and professional planners in planning which are implicitly held in some organizations.

Thus, the elements of a modern planning culture, as developed here, are a philosophy which emphasizes the participation of the manager in planning, a matrix organizational structure for planning, an expansive view of the role of the chief executive as a planning facilitator, a technocratic view of the role of a planning staff in planning, a system of accountability and reward for planning, and a plan for the implementation of planning.

With such a culture, the benefits of planning are not left to vague assurances that . . . "the value is in the process rather than in the plans themselves" . . . since such a structure lends itself well to the assessment of planning effectiveness in terms of both long-run impact and the short-run organizational change which can be induced through effective strategic planning.

2
The Futurity
of Current Decisions:
A Framework for Planning

The framework for planning is built upon the concept of the *futurity of current decisions*. This framework is a tool used to identify and respond to future opportunities and threats as moderated by other relevant factors. An integration of known data, projected occurrences, and subjective needs and requirements within the planning framework, provides the mechanism for an organization to arrive at current decisions. These decisions are then used to guide the company through the uncertainties of the future, and to help it arrive at its goals and move toward its objectives.

For example, let us consider how this planning framework might apply to the homebuilding industry. Companies in the industry must make current decisions in order to survive in the future. At times, homebuilding is drastically cut back primarily due to high interest rates on mortgages, the difficulty in obtaining mortgage money, and the unusually high down payments demanded by lending institutions. The slowdown in construction should result in strong future demands if potential purchasers can meet the demands set forth in the financial environment.

According to Ehbar (1980), economic growth will substantially increase living standards, and two out of every five families may qualify as upper income by 1990. If this is so, then this information would be a very important input in the framework for planning. In addition to other factors, such as Americans' desire to own single-occupancy private homes, a company in the homebuilding industry might very well make current decisions to develop plans and allocate implementing resources in order to increase its share of the homebuilding market in the next decade.

The foundation for the framework is the formulation by the company of its objectives and goals. There can be little doubt that, unless an organization's missions, functions, and intentions are translated into objectives and goals, they will remain dreams and well-meant intentions without ever becoming reality.

An *objective* is a highly desirable ambition toward which a firm works; it is usually unattainable within a planning period. A *goal,* however, is a milestone along the path toward an objective; its attainment is planned within the planning period. For example, a firm's stated objective is to be the most profitable in the industry. The many steps that must be taken in order to achieve this objective, such as developing new and more economical sources of raw materials and improved sources of distribution, are goals. The Alexander & Alexander case study presented herein clearly indicates that A&A, which is a large insurance brokerage, actuarial, and consulting firm, uses objectives and goals as the heart of its planning process (see p. 351).

After formulating a company's goals and objectives, the planners must analyze its strengths and weaknesses in reference to its internal makeup and external activities. (For an example, see pp. 358–367 in the A&A case study.) These comparative strengths and weaknesses help point the way and develop the criteria for goal attainment for the firm.

The planning framework must also include a search mechanism to help the planners seek out feasible alternatives. After the alternatives are identified, they can be rank-ordered for possible implementation. Rank should be assigned by using corporate policies and comparative profiles as evaluation guidelines. Next, each alternative must be analyzed in depth in order to define the administrative and operational strategies required to implement and fund it. The analyst must consider, among other factors, staffing, financing, administering the gathering of resources, a timetable, and the operational programs required for each. After the analysis is complete, and the comparisons have been made, the moment of truth arrives—the responsible officers of the company must select and implement a decision. (A&A seems to have faced up to these difficult decisions and arrived at satisfactory answers; see p. 345.) Until implementation occurs, goal achievement simply remains a gleam in the eye of the planner. The job of completing the framework is almost over—the addition of control devices and the development of a set of contingent strategic, administrative, and operational plans will make it an integral planning structure.

Obviously, the desired end product of the preceding information process is not an aggregation of plans; rather, it is a systems approach for planning that includes the entire planning space, i.e., strategic, administrative, and operational. Figure 2-1 gives a clear picture of the systems-approach concept by showing the relationships among the various components of a planning system.

To further clarify the planning framework, some of the more abstract ideas are explained in the next section.

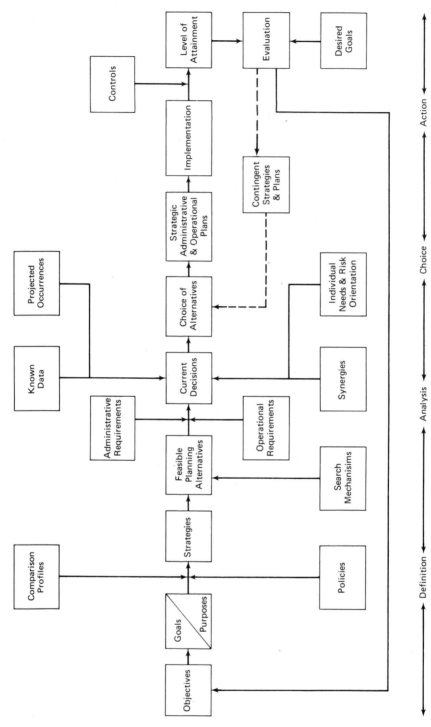

Figure 2-1. Framework for planning.

OBJECTIVES AND GOALS

To supplement the previous discussion, the concept of objectives and goals can best be illustrated by use of examples:

- The National Aeronautics and Space Administration's objective is to reach the stars. One of its goals is to have reusable space vehicles circling the earth in the 1980s.
- The objective of every professional football team is to win the Super Bowl. Its immediate goal, for example, might be to acquire a proven head coach or a new first-string quarterback.
- The United States' objective is not to be dependent upon foreign oil in the future. One of its goals is to achieve the more efficient use of that oil by requiring automobile manufacturers to increase substantially the average miles per gallon performance of the vehicles they produce.

If a company is to logically determine and develop its goals, it must first decide what its corporate objective is. It must determine what business it is in and what business it would like to be in. The answers to these questions are more difficult than might be imagined. For example, is Holland America in marine transportation or in the resort hotel business? Neither? Both? Is one of its objectives to carry more freight and passengers than any of its marine-line competitors or to entertain more guests than Las Vegas hotels? Should it plan to increase its gambling revenue or its freight revenue? Obviously, the ability of planners to set goals and objectives and to determine strategies depends upon their knowing what the firm's objectives are. According to Barnard (1938), a classic writer in the field of management, it is the top executive's function "to formulate and define the purposes of the organization." Goal-setting is of little value to a firm that has not determined what its objectives, purposes, or both really are.

STRATEGIES AND POLICIES

The ways and means used to direct a firm toward its goals, within a definitive time frame, are its strategies and policies. Both are used to help management achieve its stated goals. *Strategies* are plans of action that lead to major company commitments. *Policies* are guidelines to action, usually based upon past experience. The strategic planner takes a comprehensive company view of goal accomplishment, whereas the policymaker operates in a more limited vein. Policy is basically an ongoing procedure to help management solve specific problems, such as preventing errors from recurring, implementing and testing strategy, making use of specialists, and coordinating the control and decisionmaking processes.

There is obviously a means-end relationship between objectives, goals, strategies, and policies. For example, if a firm's objective is to be self-capitalized, then one of its goals might be to reduce its outstanding bank loans. In turn, to accomplish this goal, it could develop a strategy to increase its cash accumulation. The firm could adopt a new credit policy whereby, instead of billing on "1-percent/10-day, net/30-day" terms, it would use terms of "1-percent/10-day, net/30-day, and 1-percent interest per month on all unpaid balances over 30 days." Concurrently, the company could switch from paying its own bills on a net 30-day basis to a net 45-to-60-day basis. Putting aside their possible ramifications, these policies would lead the company to greater cash accumulation and, in turn, to lowered outstanding bank loans—as well as closer to self-capitalization.

COMPARISON PROFILE

The *comparison profile* is an organization's basic tool in determining its planning alternatives. It matches the organization's competencies, capabilities, and competitiveness against firms, in its own field and in other fields, that have the same or similar characteristics. The comparison profile considers internal business areas such as research and development, total operations, overall management, marketing, and financial services, as well as areas external to the firm such as the political system, laws and government regulation, culture, and society. It determines the relative strength of each of these areas by using a series of operational measures such as (1) personnel abilities, (2) facilities and equipment, (3) group climate, (4) productivity, and (5) group structure. The comparison profile also takes into account investment costs, state of technology, competition, perceived market trends, and organization support.

Take the case of a wheelchair and crutch manufacturing concern that has stopped growing in terms of sales and profits. After performing a comparison profile, it finds that it is in excellent financial shape, has extremely good manufacturing facilities with excess capacity, and a good marketing and distribution organization. However, it has a very limited research-and-development (R&D) capability. Its objective is to resume growing in order to improve its return on investment and increase the price of its common stock. The company's comparison profile, when compared to others in the industry, indicates that it should acquire an emerging medical-equipment manufacturing firm that has developed several innovative products but that has been unable to produce them in quantity due to financial problems.

A company's comparison profile, when matched against another, usually successful, company, indicates its strengths and weaknesses. When compared to the profile of a company in the same industry, it indicates whether its alternatives, such as expansion, development, or remaining static, are feasible. Matched against a company in an industry that it is considering entering, the profile would indicate whether such a plan is feasible. For example, a professional football team may have a choice of increasing the seating capacity of its stadium, doming the stadium, or investing in a new major-league soccer team. Obviously, it could match its comparison profile against those of other football teams or against those of soccer teams. The results of such matches would be of tremendous help to the planners who must choose among the feasible alternatives.

PLANNING ALTERNATIVES AND
SEARCH MECHANISMS

It is impossible for an organization to have knowledge of all planning alternatives. However, the adequacy of new and different possibilities uncovered by the search for alternatives will depend upon the time, effort, and money an organization is willing to spend. The search mechanism uncovers inventions, new products, acquisitions, divestments, and joint opportunities for the evaluation of the strategic planners.

Let us assume that the wheelchair and crutch manufacturer has found several planning alternatives. In addition to the possible acquisition of the medical-equipment manufacturer, the company is considering: (1) acquiring a group of nursing homes, (2) acquiring a manufacturer of electromechanical valves, (3) increasing its own in-house R&D capability, or (4) selling the entire business to a conglomerate listed on the New York Stock Exchange. The firm's comparison profile is compared to profiles of other firms. This analysis, in conjunction with the stated company policies, enables the firm to rank-order the four alternatives. If policy dictates that the company should not engage in businesses outside its field, including service businesses, the first two alternatives will have low rankings. The ranking of the third alternative, to increase the company's in-house R&D capability, will depend upon how long it will take for the fruits of such an undertaking to be realized and how much it will cost. Finally, the fourth alternative, selling the company, could rank very high if it met the needs of the individual stockholders and top management, or very low if management opposed the idea. Thus, many factors are considered in evaluating planning alternatives, with corporate policies and comparative profiles being very important analytical tools.

The planning structure must be designed so that it can test the feasibility of new opportunities and rank them against each other. In order to determine the effect of each alternative on the entire system, administrative requirements for staffing, financing, and other resources must be a part of this analysis. Likewise, operational alternatives and problems must also be part of the input. Once completed, the feasibility test paves the way for the planning decision.

CURRENT DECISIONS

As previously stated, the concept of the futurity of current decisions is the keystone of the planning framework. Current decisions are based upon (1) who makes the decisions and (2) how the decisions are made. It is commonly accepted that effective managers are those who make decisions that are timely, logical, and acceptable to those who are responsible for executing them. If a manager is unwilling to make decisions, he or she will inevitably lose authority, respect, and allegiance of subordinates, as well as legitimization of the role itself. How decisions are made is a well-studied process. For example, Simon (1960) classifies the decisionmaking process into four steps:

1. the intelligence activity: the perception of decision need or opportunity
2. the design activity: the formulation of alternative courses of action
3. the analysis activity: the evaluation of the alternatives for their respective contributions
4. the choice activity: the selection of one or more alternatives for implementation

Thompson (1967) dimensionalizes the process into (1) beliefs concerning cause-effect relationships, and (2) preferences among possible outcomes.

Some practitioners and academics believe that decisionmaking is the most important function a manager has to perform. When a manager's field of expertise is in corporate planning, then his or her decisionmaking function can be crucial to the company's existence. Obviously, the decisions to manufacture the Edsel, develop the SST, develop and produce artificial leather, and process fish flour are examples of crucial decisions that were extremely costly. On the other hand, the decisions to manufacture Mustangs, build 747s, develop and produce nylon, and process quick frozen foods were extremely profitable. All of the decisions must have taken into consideration such concepts as the individual needs and risk orientation of the decisionmaker, synergies, all the known data, data on projected future occurrences, and administrative and operational requirements. Decisions made today involving solar energy, the strip-mining of coal, gasohol, and nuclear energy will greatly affect energy-producing companies for years to come. Overall, the concept of the futurity of current decisions is the primary cornerstone of corporate success and failure.

SYNERGIES

When two actions are joined and their outcome is greater than that which would have resulted if the two actions had remained independent, then positive synergy exists. If the joint outcome is less than the sum of the outcomes of the two independent actions, then negative synergy exists. For example, assume that the

Little Company, with a debt of $3 million payable at an interest rate of prime plus 1½ percent, is acquired by the Giant Company. Giant, which borrows its money at the prime rate, refinances the debt of the acquired company through its own banks. As a result, it generates a savings of $45,000 without materially changing anything in the combined debt structure. This is positive synergy.

The Little Company had been classified as a "small business" when bidding for government contracts. However, it can no longer claim that advantage. In fact, without changing its operation, it has been closed out of the small-business market. This is negative synergy.

Synergy, like an organization, can be broken down into different categories. The most common types of synergy that are investigated in the developing and choosing of planning alternatives are:

1. *Management.* Will the combination increase competent top-level management?

2. *Facilities and personnel.* Will the combination result in greater and more efficient use of facilities and personnel?

3. *Financial.* Will the combination result in decreased financial costs and easier and cheaper access to capital markets?

4. *Research and development.* Will the results of R&D be used by the entire combination?

5. *Labor.* Will the combination result in increased or decreased labor problems?

6. *Markets.* Will the combination enhance the competitive position of the firm? Will it open up new channels of supply? Will it open up new markets?

There can be little doubt that synergistic effect plays a major role in an organization's formulating and selecting plans and alternatives. For example, in 1977, General Electric Company acquired Utah International. Before deciding to do so, however, General Electric carefully evaluated the financial synergy (the conversion of General Electric common stock into unmined uranium ore) and the marketing synergy (opening of new Japanese markets).

INDIVIDUAL NEEDS AND RISK ORIENTATION

The choice of a planning alternative depends not only on the risk orientation of the decisionmakers, but also upon their individual needs and motivations. The psychological makeup of these people plays an important part in the selection of alternatives, as do the planning group's and organization's needs. For example, a decisionmaker with a low-risk orientation and antiwar sentiments would probably not consider acquiring a defense-oriented R&D company regardless of its potential return on investment. On the other hand, a decisionmaker with a high-risk orientation and strong need for achievement would probably dismiss immediately any suggestion to acquire a manufacturer of plumbing fittings because it is in a static industry. Thus, an organization should consider the subjective needs of planners when forming its planning group.

The methods used to choose alternatives are too complex to discuss here. However, once alternatives are chosen, a series of strategic, administrative, and operational plans are made, and then the detailed methods, guidelines, and approaches required to achieve the goals are specified.

IMPLEMENTATION AND CONTROL

"The best-laid plans o' mice an' men gang aft agley"—especially those that are neither implemented nor controlled. All over the country, file cabinets are overflowing with companies' best-laid plans—plans that were carefully conceived and developed, but neither funded nor manned.

Obviously, there is a world of difference between conception and implementation. Fully implementing its plans does not insure a firm that its goals will be achieved. Many brilliant strategies, backed with excellent policies and full managerial support, have failed due to a lack of control. The control function of the planning framework must be as well thought out and put into action as every other function in the framework. If not, the company is bound to fail to achieve its goals. This end phase (i.e., control) involves the careful monitoring of ongoing results in order to reach the firm's desired goals. Thus, the primary mission of a control group within an organization is to constantly monitor the data being generated by the implemented plans and to bring to management's attention any and all deviations.

EVALUATION AND CONTINGENT PLANS

The data supplied to the decisionmakers by the control group must be carefully analyzed to determine progress toward goal achievement. When the control criteria point toward time delays, money overruns, shortages of materials, lack of personnel, capital shortage, and so forth, managerial action must be taken. The magnitude of such action depends upon how large a gap exists between the desired goals and the current level of attainment. If the gap is minor, the current strategy is maintained until the goal is achieved, and then the process is reinitiated. On the other hand, if the gap is serious enough to cause lasting damage to the company, then previously designed *contingent plans* are called into play. Every well-conceived strategic plan must include a contingent plan to prevent the catastrophes that can result from planning failure. The contingent plan should be designed, not to slow the bleeding of the firm so that it will die more slowly, but rather to stop the bleeding so that the firm will become healthy again.

The two articles at the end of this chapter present other ideas and approaches to the concept of planning frameworks (see pp. 12-29). In "Making Strategic Planning Work," Koontz (1976) provides a framework for planning by developing his premise that

> ... the basic cause of disillusionment with strategic planning is the lack of knowledge in four areas: (1) what strategies are and why they are important; (2) how strategies fit into the entire planning process; (3) how to develop strategies; and (4) how to implement strategies by bringing them to bear on current decision.

In "The Two Purposes of Business Planning," Roney (1976) approaches the concept of a planning framework a bit differently.

> The *protective* purpose is to minimize risk by reducing uncertainty surrounding implications of potential business conditions and by clarifying near and long-term consequences of selecting alternative goals and strategies. The *affirmative* purpose is to realize greater financial and competitive success than would be possible without a sound planning program . . ..

REFERENCES

Barnard, C. I. 1938. *The Functions of the Executive.* Cambridge, Mass.: Harvard University Press.

Addresses the topics of informal organization, limitations of financial rewards, motivation, decisionmaking, and inducements and contributions. It is a classic in the field of management.

Ehbar, A. F. 1980. The upbeat outlook for family incomes. *Fortune* (February 25, 1980), 122-134.

A discussion of how modest economic growth in the 1980s will lift millions of Americans into the upper income brackets.

Koontz, H. 1976. Making strategic planning work. *Business Horizons* **19**(2): 37-47.

What does strategy really mean? The author's guidelines for the effective implementation of strategic planning help to clarify this very important, but widely misunderstood, concept. *Reprinted herein on pp. 51-65.*

Roney, C. W. 1976. The two purposes of business planning. *Managerial Planning* **25**(3): 1-6, 40.

Why should your company have a planning function? Since generally accepted principles do not exist, chief executives have trouble answering this question. Roney claims that the need for accepted principles has become acute. *Reprinted herein on pp. 40-50.*

Simon, H. A. 1960. *The New Science of Management Decision.* New York: Harper & Row.

Deals with formal organizations. The author believes that organizations are obviously very important but have been ignored in the literature. More importantly, he develops and presents the concept of limited or bounded rationality.

Thompson, J. 1967. *Organizations in Action.* New York: McGraw–Hill.

The central concept of this reference book is that the organization seeks to seal off its core technologies from environmental influences and therefore technology dictates organization structure.

The Two Purposes of Business Planning

C. W. Roney

Formalized business planning programs have spread rapidly to the majority of major U.S. corporations. Why? Whenever I ask chief executives and planning officers *why* a formal planning program is needed, I get a different answer. Their answers suggest that there are no generally accepted purposes of business planning. This is confirmed by business literature: much has been written on *how* to plan—but not *why*. Without a generally accepted purpose of planning, it is not surprising that generally accepted standards for accomplishing that purpose, in practice, also do not exist. In this article, I state a point of view on *why* companies must plan—that is, on the *purposes* of business planning. These purposes have certain implications for practice which will be discussed in the conclusion.

SCOPE AND CONTENT OF
BUSINESS PLANNING

Since business planning principles are almost as numerous as the number of practitioners, it would be surprising if all would agree on the terms they use.

Roney, C. W., "The Two Purposes of Business Planning," *Managerial Planning,* November/ December 1976.

But, for the sake of convenience, let it be assumed, here, that business planning at least consists of defining a business' goals (for the planning period) and activities which will be instrumental in those goals' achievement. Very often, instrumental activities are so numerous that *completion* of each activity, and/or a combination of activities, itself may be a significant measure of accomplishment. I call such intended accomplishments, "objectives." Business plans usually contain a few goals; several objectives (for each managed unit of the business); and many instrumental activities. I refer to instrumental activities and objectives, collectively, as "strategy" for goals' achievement.

WHY IS PLANNING SO POPULAR?

Without generally accepted principles of business planning, it is amazing that the growth of formal planning programs has been so explosive; but there is no doubt that it has been. By 1974, the proportion of major U.S. corporations with formal long-range planning programs probably had grown to more than 80%. A recent survey by Fulmer and Rue (1973) revealed that 314 of 386 companies responding to a questionnaire (81%) had long-range plans. But about half had begun long-range planning only during the most recent five years. Service industries were the least practiced: 45% of service companies with long-range plans had begun to prepare them during the most recent two years.

The precise reasons for these programs' recently rapid emergence probably are as numerous as the companies which have undertaken them. But, I think that many chief executives too often have undertaken formal planning simply because so many successful companies are doing it. I doubt that many have a clear understanding of the *specific benefits* which should be expected from a planning program. In other words, a lot of planning is being done by executives who don't know why—except that they were told to do it.

When the chief executive's suggestibility does not explain his planning program's genesis, I believe that desperation often does. Many planning programs apparently have been undertaken as one way of dealing with the explosion of complexity and uncertainty in business conditions. During the last half-decade, changes in important decision-making considerations have occurred more rapidly than ever—violent shifts in U.S. and international economics; volatility in monetary markets; changing federal fiscal and legislative behavior; uncertainties surrounding availability and costliness of basic commodities; changes in spending patterns of both consumers and businesses; and intensified scrutiny of accountable executives' past (and forecasted) performance by stockholders and regulators. All of these recent complexities, and many others, have compounded the risk chief executives take when making major commitments of corporate resources. It is not surprising, therefore, that many have welcomed planning's promise of better methods for formulating corporate goals and selecting strategies to achieve those goals.

Neither of these motives—emulation of "fashionable" practices, or desperate flight from uncertainty—is a very good reason for the Chief Executive to undertake a planning program. As, it has turned out, however, there is growing evidence that the results have not been as questionable as the motives. Sound planning *has* become closely associated with successful management. In part, this is because planning produces a reduction in uncertainty about business conditions' potentials and their implications for effective strategy.

THE TWO PURPOSES OF BUSINESS PLANNING

The dilemma of increasing complexity in business circumstances naturally has been paralleled by growing uncertainty surrounding decisions involving major corporate commitments. Consequently, it is becoming both more difficult—and more important—to assess the full scope of alternative present-day commitments in light of their likely future consequences. If the planning process can reduce uncertainty surrounding alternative commitments, a business' risk is greatly reduced. Moreover, research is beginning to reveal that, in the process of clarifying alternatives, businesses become more effective competitors. Thus, the purposes of planning are both *protective* and *affirmative*.

The Protective Purpose of Business Planning

As just noted, the success of modern top management decision-making often depends upon the executive's ability to deal with *increased commercial risk* engendered by a rising level of uncertainty in business conditions.

- The dilemma of uncertainty
  As uncertainty surrounding business conditions increases, the probability also increases that a business' present goals and/or strategy are inappropriate for its future circumstances, and consequently, that levels of competitive and financial risk will rise, over time.
- The protective purpose of business planning
  One purpose of business planning thus is to reduce uncertainty surrounding future implications of potential changes in business conditions and thus the risk which that uncertainty imposes on making selections from alternative goals and strategies to achieve goals.
- The fundamental mechanism of business planning
  Planning accomplishes a reduction of uncertainty and risk through the fundamental mechanism of clarifying alternative goals, and activities which are instrumental in goal-achievement (strategy).

Few problems which companies face can be solved by only one course of action: there often are several apparently viable solutions. But some are more expensive than others; some may be dangerous competitively; others may be limited by regulation, etc. Management's challenge in planning thus is to discern the fullest possible range of viable alternatives and their likely consequences. Then, the most beneficial alternative may be selected. This process of clarifying and selecting from alternative goals, and then strategies, is the essence of effective business planning.

Simply dictating the goals and/or strategy of a business arbitrarily thus is counter-productive to the purpose of planning. Certainly, that approach often is taken; but as long as it is, competitive risk will mount disproportionately, versus other companies which have prepared their plans in the context of more thoroughly clarified alternatives. As simple and obvious as this commonsense principle may seem it has been frightening, for me, to witness the profusion of planning programs which violate it.

Let us then re-acknowledge that companies which design their planning programs in such a way that alternative goals and strategies are defined and assessed thoroughly, before selections are made, should enjoy a much lower level of risk that . . .

- even if accomplished, goals and strategies will lead to unfortunate consequences; and
- even if goals are reasonable, strategies will not be appropriate, thus making plans infeasible.

The Affirmative Purpose of Business Planning

While one purpose of sound business planning is to reduce the probability of errors in decision-making (protective benefits), a second purpose is to increase the probability of commercial success. The *affirmative* purpose of business planning is to realize greater financial and competitive success than would be possible, otherwise. Statistical research has shown that the chief executive reasonably can expect this benefit.

Intuitively, one would expect the well-planned company to perform better than poorly planned companies. But the task of justifying that expectation with statistical evidence is not an easy one, because the factors which determine a company's performance of course are not limited to its planning. In addition, the quality of a plan is difficult to measure and thus to correlate with performance. Notwithstanding these difficulties, students of management have begun to direct their research toward the returns which businessmen can realize on an investment in sound business planning. While such inquiries have not been sufficiently extensive to provide definitive answers, some encouraging evidence has emerged.

Stanford Research Institute (1957). The Stanford Research Institute (1957) studied differences between 210 companies with exceptional growth in sales and earnings, versus 169 companies with growth rates significantly below the average, during 1939–1949, and again during 1949–1956. The studies' findings pointed clearly to planning as a distinguishing characteristic of fast-growth companies.

- Fast-growth companies tended to have "organized programs to seek and promote new business opportunities," and "an affinity for growth products or fields."*
- "Only 12 of the 210 growth companies studied were staying in the fields that are characterized by low rates of growth."

After 1949, some slow-growth companies grew faster; some previously fast growth companies' growth decelerated; and others' growth rates were maintained. Here, again, the companies with faster growth rates in 1949–1956 "report a greater activity in planning than do the groups whose growth has slackened."

Thune & House (1970). Thune and House (1970) contrasted the financial results of seventeen manufacturing companies which practiced formal planning, covering a period of at least three years, with nineteen others which did not. The thirty-six contrasted companies were selected from ninety-three survey respondents for purposes of industry similarity and statistical balancing. Three statistical comparisons of planners and non-planners were made, covering a span of at least seven, and up to fifteen, years:

- Planners versus non-planners *before* "planners started planning;
- Planners versus non-planners *after* "planners" started planning; and
- Both groups' performance before versus *after* planners began planning.

Planners' performance improved after they started planning. More importantly, planners outperformed non-planners *after, but not before,* planning had begun—in the following measures:

- Earnings per share.
- Earnings on common equity, and
- Earnings on employed capital.

*Other characteristics of fast-growth companies were "proven competitive abilities in present lines of business;" "courageous and energetic management, willing to take carefully studied risks;" and "luck."

The probabilities that these differences in performance were due to chance was [*sic*] calculated and found to be quite low. Planners also outperformed non-planners, on the average, in growth of sales and stock price, but differences were not as reliable.

Because of the statistical design employed by Thune and House, it is a fair conclusion that the planning process can be accompanied by a significant improvement in financial performance, if not a competitive advantage, at least for manufacturing companies.

Another finding by Thune and House, of great interest, is the following. Correlations between company-size and performance measures were negative for formal planners and positive for "informal" planners. This evidence strongly supports the risk-reduction hypotheses proposed, earlier: to quote Thune and House . . .

"... among the informal planners the rich got richer; among the formal planners, the poor got richer."

This research thus may have provided a strong planning incentive to managements of smaller and medium-sized companies, and it may suggest the advisability of decentralizing planning activities in larger, diversified corporations.

Ansoff et al. (1970). While Thune and House were conducting their study, Ansoff et al. (1970) were pursuing similar research addressing success of acquisitions and mergers over a twenty year period (1947–1966). They contrasted manufacturing companies which had ongoing planning programs and/or specific acquisition plans to those which did not. The categorization method entailed assigning eight criteria to each company. Four criteria described the broad, systematic processes of planning corporate operations; four others described the systematic process of selecting acquisition candidates and effecting combinations. "Planners" were defined as those with six or more of the eight planning criteria. "Non-planners" were defined as those with three or less. 27.7% of the 93 companies finally selected for study were planners and 57.5% were non-planners. Each company had made at least one acquisition during the twenty year period of this study. Together, they had acquired 299 other companies. A majority of the "planners" had *both* corporate plans and acquisition plans.

Twenty-one variations of thirteen financial measurements were contrasted:

- Median rates of change before and after acquisitions were compared as follows—
  —Corporate planners versus non-corporate planners,
  —Acquisition planners versus non-acquisition planners, and
  —Corporate and acquisition planners, combined, versus non-planners;

—Comparisons of variability (or, predictability) in planners' and non-planners' financial performance also were performed. Presumably, this measure reflected the effectiveness of management controls.

In all cases, planners outperformed their unplanned counterparts. The most significant differences occurred in these measures:

- Sales growth;
- Earnings growth;
- Earnings-per-share growth;
- Growth in earnings/common equity; and
- Predictability.

Fulmer & Rue (1973). More recently, research conducted by Fulmer and Rue (1973) differed from the prior two studies, but virtue of (1) a broader scope of industries—including service, as well as manufacturing; (2) a larger statistical sample—386 companies; and (3) a shorter time span—3 years (1969-1971) versus 7-20 years in the others.

Like the studies of Thune and House and of Ansoff, et al., Fulmer and Rue discovered superior financial performance of durables manufacturers with plans encompassing a period of three years or more. However, Fulmer and Rue found that differences were much more pronounced in larger companies (over $75 million sales) than smaller, thus differing with Thune and House. Moreover, there was another difference of importance: No benefit of planning was discernable in the performance statistics of financial and other service industries, not even for non-durables manufacturers.

Unfortunately, there is very little explanation for the conflict between results of this and the earlier studies. Fulmer and Rue reported no before-and-after comparisons, as the other studies did. However, it may be significant that only durables manufacturers had, in the majority, been practicing formal planning for more than five years. Therefore, it is possible that the benefits of planning had not yet emerged, through learning, in the other groups. In this regard, we should remember that the prior studies examined much longer periods of performance.

Karger and Malik (1975). Karger and Malik (1975) also studied the effects of formal planning on financial success. Their research concentrated on three industries: chemicals and drugs, electronics and machinery. This, most recent study of its kind, is of particular interest because its investigatory definition of formal planning is more rigorous than definitions in the other studies mentioned previously.

The authors qualified formal integrated long range planning as follows:

Establishing a written plan for the overall organization and for each division and each plant in each division for at least the next five years—and a more expanded one to two year plan for each. The plans must be distributed to the involved executives after creation of the plan by a group effort—and the CEO operates the firm in accordance with the plan unless new data requires a revision. The study's ten-year time span (1964–1973) is the most current to date and includes the latest decade preceding the recent recession.

Research methods also reflected great care. A questionnaire mailed to chief executive officers first was tested by mailing it to a group of known planners and a group of known non-planners. Answers to the questionnaire did successfully distinguish planners from non-planners. Statistical analyses recognized the possibility that collected data might not conform to normal statistical assumptions: statistical tests were selected accordingly. Thus, in view of the care with which this research was conducted, Karger's and Malik's findings are highly credible. Happily, their results replicated the earlier studies. Statistical significance was most pronounced (and the possibility of chance results was the least) in machinery and chemical industries.

In the machinery industry, differences between planners and non-planners were dramatic. Planners' sales grew at an average annual rate of 19.6% versus 8.6% for non-planners. Planners' earnings per share grew at an average annual rate of 10.1% versus 2.4% for non-planners. Planners' net income had almost tripled (on the average) in ten years; but non-planners' had remained flat. Planners' average annual return on equity was 13.2% versus 7.1% for non-planners. Planners' average operating margins were 12.1% versus 7.8% for non-planners. Planners' P/E ratios averaged 16.0% versus 14.0% for non-planners. Similar differences were observed in the chemical industry and for the sample as a whole.

Summary of Benefits Discovered by Research

Empirical investigations of planning's effectiveness are immature both in their methodology and findings. Without a doubt, the above studies should be replicated to determine whether significant benefits yet can be demonstrated in financial and service industries—as well as to reveal the relative resiliencies of planners versus non-planners during the recent recession.

But the research conducted so far is mainly encouraging; and methods obviously are being developed to the point where we soon will be able to measure both the magnitude and limits of commercial benefits which chief executives may expect from their planning programs. So far, the following tentative conclusions appear to have been supported by evidence:

- As a result of initiating formal business planning, with a scope of time extending beyond the present year, the financial performance of manufacturing companies generally is improved significantly and ultimately may exceed competitors' (last four studies);

- The financial performance of manufacturers which begin to practice formal planning tends to improve when others' do not (Stanford Research Institute, 1957; Thune and House, 1970; Ansoff et al., 1970);
- Among the performance measures most sensitive to planning are those which generally are viewed as reflections of financial success—earnings per share, return on sales and return on investment (last four studies);
- Smaller and medium-sized manufacturers may benefit more from planning than their larger competitors (Thune and House) which nevertheless also can benefit significantly from planning (Fulmer and Rue, 1970); and
- Companies which implement acquisitions and which (a) previously have prepared corporate plans and/or (b) proceed according to specific acquisition plans, tend to experience significantly greater financial success than those which simply indulge in more "opportunistic" approaches (Ansoff, et al., 1970).

It is interesting to conjecture that there may be a limit to the effective organizational scope of planning, on the basis of Thune's and House's findings. If this is true, the advisability of decentralizing the planning function in multibusiness corporations may be worthy of serious consideration. On the other hand, Fulmer's and Rue's results may have suggested that a dominant corporate plan also may be financially beneficial in larger corporations. Reconciliation of differences between top management's plan and profit centers' plans thus would be of primary importance for success of multibusiness corporate planning endeavors. In any event, the two studies' inferences are not necessarily at odds.

Conclusion

Logical deduction, on the one hand, and empirical inference on the other, have led me to conclude that there are two complementary benefits of formal planning programs:

Protective benefits which, like insurance, help to reduce the likelihood of catastrophe caused by unforseen adversities in business conditions and/or erroneous top management commitments to goals and strategies; and

Affirmative benefits which promote the well-planned business' long-term financial and competitive success.

In my opinion, securing these two types of benefits constitutes accomplishing the two purposes of business planning.

METHODOLOGICAL CONSIDERATIONS

The two purposes of business planning which have been identified and discussed here imply some definite methodological conclusions. . . .

General

The most important methodological conclusion which I have drawn from the foregoing deliberations is this: *Successful planning approaches must place a premium on revealing the full scope of alternative goals and strategies at each level in the management organization.*

Modern Methods for Clarifying Alternatives

Powerful mathematical and computing techniques now exist to aid in clarifying a far broader scope of alternatives than would be possible without them. Because risk is lessened and the probability of success is increased, relative to the degree of thoroughness attained in clarifying alternatives, there is a competitive incentive to make maximum use of these new techniques.

Multiple "scenarios," reflecting alternative potential changes in economic, industry and market conditions can be constructed. Then, plans may be formulated to deal effectively with each contingency. By being prepared for changes in business conditions before they occur, contingency planners have an advantage over competitors who do not plan for contingencies. While their competitors assess a significant change, contingency planners can be taking immediate action by implementing thoroughly developed strategies.

Of course, contingency planning calls for a great deal of effort, not only in formulating the contingency plans, themselves, but in monitoring business conditions and developing "trigger points" which signal the imminent occurrence of contingencies and/or the need to initiate action.

POST-SCRIPT TO THE CHIEF EXECUTIVE

It is important for top management to realize that overnight miracles are rare: even the best of planning programs and management organizations require considerable persistence and encouragement from above to produce *affirmative* benefits. *Protective* benefits should be enjoyed much more immediately, however.

SUMMARY

To date, there has been no generally accepted purpose for business planning. Therefore, there are no generally accepted principles by which planning's purposes can be accomplished, although many useful methods have evolved in response to the growing interest in planning which has been evidenced by top management. The need for generally accepted planning principles has become acute because Business recently has encountered rapidly growing problems of uncertainty in commercial conditions and complexity of alternatives from which to select goals and strategies for goals' achievement. Little definite progress toward meeting this need has been made.

I believe that there are two purposes of business planning. The *protective* purpose is to minimize risk by reducing uncertainty surrounding implications of potential business conditions and by clarifying near and long-term consequences of selecting alternative goals and strategies. The *affirmative* purpose is to realize greater financial and competitive success than would be possible without a sound planning program: statistical research has shown that Management reasonably can demand this as an ultimate benefit. Affirmative benefits, like protective benefits, are the results of *clarifying alternatives.* Being prepared to adjust their strategies as and when business conditions shift, by implementing contingency plans, may be a characteristic of companies which have succeeded in thoroughly clarifying both potential business conditions and alternative strategies. As the complexity in business conditions increases, these companies should have a competitive advantage over others in which plans are not as well developed.

REFERENCES

Ansoff, H. I., et al., "Does Planning Pay? The effect of planning and successive acquisitions in American firms." *Long Range Planning:* December, 1970. Pp. 2–7.

Fulmer, R. M. and L. W. Rue. *The Practice and Profitability of Long Range Planning.* 1973. The Planning Executives Institute; Oxford, Ohio.

Karger, D. W. and C. A. Malik. "Long Range Planning and Organizational Performance, 1975." *Long Range Planning,* December.

Stanford Research Institute, as reported in *Why Companies Grow.* Nations Business; November, 1957. Pp. 80–86.

Thune, S. S. and R. J. House. "Where long-range planning pays off." *Business Horizons:* August, 1970. Pp. 81–87.

Making Strategic Planning Work

Harold Koontz

It is widely agreed that the development and communication of strategy is the most important single activity of top managers. Joel Ross and Michael Kami, in their insightful book on the lack of success of many large U.S. companies, said, "Without a strategy the organization is like a ship without a rudder, going around in circles. It's like a tramp; it has no place to go."[1] They conclude from their study that without an appropriate strategy effectively implemented, failure is only a matter of time.

Although strategies are important, their development and implementation have posed many problems. The term strategy is often valueless and meaningless, even though it may be mouthed constantly by academics and executive. As one prominent consultant declared with respect to strategic planning, "In the large majority of companies, corporate planning tends to be an academic, ill-defined activity with little or no bottom-line impact."[2]

Many corporate chief executive officers have brushed strategic planning aside with such statements as: "Strategic planning is basically just a plaything of staff men," or "Strategic planning? A staggering waste of time."[3] A number of companies and even some government agencies that have tried strategic planning have been observed wallowing around in generalities, unproductive studies and programs that do not get into practical operation. In one large company, a far too patient president watched a succession of top planning officers and their staffs flounder for twelve years, until his patience was finally exhausted and he insisted on practical action.

The basic cause of disillusionment with strategic planning is the lack of knowledge in four areas: (1) what strategies are and why they are important; (2) how strategies fit into the entire planning process; (3) how to develop strategies; and (4) how to implement strategies by bringing them to bear on current decisions.

NOTE: This article is adapted from a speech presented at the November 1975 meeting of the International Academy of Management.

1. Joel E. Ross and Michael J. Kami, *Corporations in Crisis: Why the Mighty Fall* (Englewood Cliffs, N.J.: Prentice-Hall, Inc., 1973), p. 132.

2. Louis V. Gerstner, "Can Strategic Planning Pay Off?" *Business Horizons* (December 1972), pp. 5–16.

3. *Ibid.,* p. 5.

WHAT STRATEGIES ARE

Strategies are general programs of action with an implied commitment of emphasis and resources to achieve a basic mission. They are patterns of major objectives, and major policies for achieving these objectives, conceived and stated in such a way as to give the organization a unified direction.

For years, strategies were used by the military to mean grand plans made in view of what it was believed an adversary might or might not do. Tactics were regarded as action plans necessary to implement strategies. While the term strategy still has a competitive implication, it is increasingly used to denote a general program that indicates a direction to be taken and where emphasis is to be placed. Strategies do not attempt to outline exactly how the enterprise is to accomplish its major objectives; this is the task of a multitude of major and minor supporting programs.

Failure of strategic planning is really one aspect of the difficulties encountered in making all kinds of planning effective. Although the sophistication with which planning is done has risen remarkably in the past three decades, and despite the fact that planning is considered the foundation of management, it is still too often the poorest performed task of the managerial job. As every executive knows, it is easy to fail in all aspects of effective planning without really trying.

WHY PLANNING FAILS

What are some of the major reasons why effective planning is so difficult to accomplish? By summarizing some of the principal reasons in practice in both business and nonbusiness enterprises, some light may be cast on the reasons for disillusionment and ineffectiveness in many strategic planning programs.

One of the major reasons for failure is managers' lack of commitment to planning. Most people allow today's problems and crises to push aside planning for tomorrow. Instead of planning, most would rather "fight fires" and meet crises, for the simple reason that doing so is more interesting, more fun, and gives a greater feeling of accomplishment. This means, of course, that an environment must be created that forces people to plan.

Another cause of failure is confusing planning studies with plans. Many are the companies and government agencies that have stacks of planning studies. But for a planning study to become a plan, a decision must be made that will commit resources or direction; until then it is only a study.

Problems also arise when major decisions on various matters are made without having a clear strategy, or without making sure that decisions, such as one to develop and market a new product, fit a company's strategy.

Another reason for failure is the lack of clear, actionable, attainable and verifiable objectives or goals. It is impossible to do any effective planning without knowing precisely what end results are sought. Objectives must be verifiable in the sense that, at some target date in the future, a person can know whether they have been accomplished. This can, of course, be done best in quantitative terms, such as dollars of sales or profits. But since many worthwhile objectives cannot be put in numbers, goals can also be verified in qualitative terms, such as a marketing program with specified characteristics to be launched by a certain date.

Perhaps the most important cause of failure in planning is neglecting or underestimating the importance of planning premises or assumptions. These are the expected environment of a decision, the stage on which a certain program will be played. They not only include economic and market forecasts, but also the expectation of important changes in the technological, political, social or ethical environment. They may also include decisions or commitments made, basic policies and major limitations. One thing is sure; unless people know and follow consistent planning premises, their planning decisions will not be coordinated.

Another problem area is the failure to place strategies within the total scope of plans. Anything that involves selecting a course of action for the future may be thought of as a plan. These include missions or purposes, objectives, strategies, policies, rules, procedures, programs and budgets. Unless strategies are seen as one of the major types of plans, it is easy to regard them as isolated directional decisions unrelated to other kinds of plans.

Ineffective planning may also be the result of failure to develop clear policies. Policies are guides to thinking in decision making. Their essence is defined discretion. They give structure and direction to decisions, mark out an area where discretion can be used, and thereby give guidelines for plans. Without clear policies, plans tend to be random and inconsistent.

Planning often suffers, too, from not keeping in mind the time span which should be involved. Long-range planning is not planning for future decisions, but planning the future impact of present decisions. In other words, planning is planning. Some plans involve commitments that can be fulfilled in short periods, such as a production plan, and others can only be discharged over longer periods, as in the case of a new product development or capital facilities program. Obviously, unless a decision maker does not try to foresee, as best as can be done, the fulfillment of commitments involved in today's decisions, he is not doing the job that good planning requires.

Another danger of planning lies in the tendency of people, especially those with considerable experience, to base their decisions on that experience—on what did or did not work in the past. Since decisions must operate for the future, they should be based on *expectations* for the future, not on experience and facts of the past.

Finally, a major cause of deficient planning is the inability of some people to diagnose a situation in the light of critical or limiting factors. In every problem (opportunity) situation, there are many variables that may affect the outcome of a course of action. But in every problem area there are certain variables that make the most difference. Thus, in a new product development program, the critical factors may be whether a proposed product will fit a company's marketing channels and competence, or whether its efficient production might require capital facilities beyond a company's financial ability. Clearly, the adept decision maker will search for, identify and solve critical factors.

MAJOR TYPES OF STRATEGIES

For a business enterprise at least, the major strategies which give it an overall direction are likely to be in the following seven areas.

New or changed products and services. A business exists to furnish products or services of an economic nature. In a very real sense, profits are merely a measure—albeit an important one—of how well a company serves its customers.

Marketing. Marketing strategies are designed to guide planning in getting products or services to reach customers, and getting customers to buy.

Growth. Growth strategies give direction to such questions as: How much growth and how fast? Where?

Financial. Every business, and for that matter every nonbusiness, enterprise must have a clear strategy for financing its operations. There are various ways of doing this and usually many serious limitations.

Organizational. This kind of strategy has to do with the type of organizational pattern an enterprise will follow. It answers such practical questions as how centralized or decentralized decision-making authority should be, what kind of departmental patterns are most suitable, whether to develop integrated profit-responsible divisions, what kind of matrix organization structures are used, and how to design and utilize staffs effectively. Naturally, organization structures furnish the system of roles and role relationships to help people perform in the accomplishment of objectives.

Personnel. Major strategies in the area of human resources and relationships may be of a wide variety. They deal with union relations, compensation, selection, recruitment, training and appraisal, as well as strategy in such matters as job enrichment.

Public relations. Strategies in this area can hardly be independent but must support other major strategies and efforts. They must also be designed in the light of the company's type of business, its closeness to the public, its susceptibility to regulation by government agencies and similar factors.

STRATEGY REQUISITES

For developing major strategies of any kind, there are a number of key requirements. If a company fails to meet them, its strategic planning program is likely to be meaningless or even incorrect.

Corporate Self-Appraisal

This requirement involves asking the questions: What is our business? What kind of business are we in? These simple questions, as many businesses have discovered, are not always easy to answer. The classic case is the railroad industry that too long overlooked the fact that its companies were in the transportation business, and not just the railroad business. Glass bottle manufacturers in the United States almost missed their opportunities by seeing themselves for too long as glass bottle makers rather than liquid container manufacturers, as plastic and metal containers came to be used in many applications in place of glass. Likewise, many believe that the steel companies over the world have stayed too long with the belief that they are steel makers, rather than in the structural materials business, which includes many materials not made of steel.

On answering this question, a company should be regarded as a total entity, its strengths and weaknesses analyzed in each functional area: marketing, product development, production and other operations areas, finance and public relations. It must focus attention on its customers and what they want and can buy, its technological capabilities and financial resources. In addition, note must be made of the values, aspirations and prejudices of top executives.

In assessing strengths, weaknesses and limitations, an enterprise must, of course, be realistic. In doing so, however, there is a danger in overstressing weaknesses and underestimating strengths. History is replete with examples of companies that have spent so much effort in shoring up weaknesses that they did not capitalize on their strengths. To be sure, weaknesses should be corrected to the extent possible. But taking advantage of identified strengths in formulating strategies offers the most promise.

Assessing the Future Environment

Strategies, like any other type of plan, are intended to operate in the future; thus, the best possible estimate of the future environment in which a company is to operate is necessary. If a company can match its strengths with the environment in which it plans to operate, opportunities can be detected and taken advantage of.

A prerequisite of the assessment of the future environment is forecasting. In general, modern businesses do a fairly good job of forecasting economic developments and markets, although, of course, there can be many errors and uncertainties. Few would have forecast the price impact of the oil-producing nation's cartel and the extent of inflation in recent years. A few companies have found rewarding results in forecasting technological changes and predicting technological developments. Some companies in highly regulated industries have even forecast political environments, particularly governmental actions that would affect their company. But only recently have companies, research institutes and government agencies even started the task of attempting to forecast social attitudes and pressures.

Clearly, the better an enterprise can see its total environment, the better it can establish strategies and support plans to take advantage of its capabilities in preparation for the future. However, experience to date indicates that, except for economic and market forecasts, it is difficult to get the forecast and assessment of other environmental factors into practical use. This can be done through an active and effective program that would use planning premises as the background for decision making, but this is one of the areas of planning that has especially not been performed well.

An important element of the future environment, of course, is the probable actions of competition. Too often, planning is based on what competition has been doing and not on what competitors may be expected to do. No one can plan on the assumption that his competitors are asleep.

Organization Structure Assuring Planning

If strategies are to be developed and implemented, an organizational structure which assures effective planning is needed. Staff assistance is important for forecasting, establishing premises and making analyses. But there is the danger of establishing a planning staff and thinking planning exists when all that really exists is planning studies, rather than decisions based on them.

To avoid ivory-towered and useless staff efforts, several things are needed. A planning staff should be given the tasks of developing major objectives, strategies and planning premises, and submitting them to top management for review and approval. They should also be responsible for disseminating approved premises and strategies, and they should help operating people to understand them. Before major decisions of a long-range or strategic impact are made, the staff group should be given the task of reviewing them and making recommendations. These few tasks can be advantageous in that they force decision makers to consider environmental factors, and also prevent the staff from becoming a detached and impractical group.

Another major organizational device is the regular, formal and rigorous review of planning programs and performance, preferably by an appropriate committee. This has long been done in well-managed divisionalized companies where division general managers are called in before a top executive committee. Perhaps it should be done at lower levels too. Doing so has the advantage of forcing people to plan, of making sure that strategies are being followed by programs, and where strategies do not exist or are unclear, making this deficiency apparent.

Assuring Consistent Strategies

One of the important requirements of effective strategic planning is to make sure that strategies are consistent, that they "fit" each other. For example, one medium-sized company had a successful sales record as the result of a strategy of putting out quality products at lower prices than its larger competitors, who did their selling through heavy and expensive advertising. Pleased with this success, and after adding to its product line through acquisitions, the company then embarked on an additional strategy of trying to sell through heavy advering, with disastrous effects on profits.

The Need for Contingency Strategies

Because every strategy must operate in the future, and because the future is always subject to uncertainty, the need for contingency strategies cannot be overlooked. If a regulated telephone company, for example, has had some of its services opened to competition (as has happened recently in the United States when other companies were allowed to furnish facilities that were once the monopoly of the telephone companies), and adopts a strategy of aggressive competition on the assumption that regulatory commissions will allow competitive pricing, the strategy would become inoperative if the commissions do not actually allow such pricing. Or if a company develops a strategy based on a certain state of technology, and a new discovery changes materially the technological environment, it is faced with a major need for a contingency strategy.

Where events occur which make a strategy obsolete (and they often can without warning), it is wise to have developed a contingent strategy based on a different set of premises. These "what if" kinds of strategies can be put into effect quickly to avoid much of the "crisis management" that is seen so often.

PRODUCTS OR SERVICES STRATEGIES

To develop strategies in any area, certain questions must be asked in each major strategy area. Given the right questions, the answers should help any company to formulate its strategies. Some key questions in two strategic areas will be examined; new products and services, and marketing. A little thought can result in devising key questions for other major strategic areas.

One of the most important areas is strategy involving new products or services, since these, more than any other single factor, will determine what a company is or will be. The key questions in this area may be summarized as follows.

What is our business? This classic question might also be phrased in terms of what is *not* our business. It is also necessary to raise the question: What is our industry? Are we a single product or product-line industry, such as shoes or furniture? Or are we a process industry, such as chemicals or electronic components? Or are we an end-use industry, such as transportation or retailing?

Who are our customers? Peter Drucker has long said that the purpose of a business is to "create a customer," although he could hardly have meant to create customers without regard to profits. In answering this question, it is important to avoid too great an attachment to *present* customers and products. The motion picture industry failed to avoid this when home television first appeared on the market and was considered a threat to movie theaters. They fought television for years until they realized that their business was entertainment and their customers wanted both motion pictures in theaters and on television. They then found one of their most lucrative markets in renting old movies to television and in using their studios and other facilities for producing television shows.

What do our customers want? Do they want price, value, quality, availability, service? The success of the Hughes Tool Company, for example, has been based largely on a shrewd analysis of what oil and gas well drillers wanted, and furnishing them with the exact drill bit, of a high quality, in the place the bit was needed, and with adequate service to support the product. Likewise, IBM's leadership in business computers has been due in large part to its knowledge of what customers wanted and needed; maintaining advancement of product design; having a family of computers; and developing a strong service organization.

How much will our customers buy and at what price? This is a matter that involves what customers think they are buying. What they consider value and what they will pay for it will determine what a business is, what it should produce, and whether it will prosper. The answer to this question will be a key to product or service strategy.

Do we wish to be a product leader? It may seem that the answer to this question would be obvious, but it is not. Some companies owe their success to being a close second in product leadership. The product leader will often have an advantage in reaching a market first, but such a company may incur heavy costs of developing and attempting to market products which do not become commercial successes, as well as those which do. One of the major airlines, for example, prided itself on being the leader in acquiring and putting into service new aircraft. But after suffering financial losses as a result of their extensive debugging of several new planes, they adopted the strategy of letting someone else be the leader, and becoming a close second.

Do we wish to develop our own new products? Here again, a company must decide whether it should develop its own new products, whether it should rely on innovations by competitors to lead the way, or whether it should lean heavily on product development by materials suppliers. In the chemicals field, such innovative raw materials producers as Du Pont and Dow Chemical discover new chemical compositions and then cast about to ascertain where they can be used in new products. Companies without adequate resources to mount a strong product research program can often find a gold mine of product ideas in the development of such suppliers.

What advantages do we have in serving customer needs? Most companies like to have a unique product or service that is difficult for a competitor to duplicate. Some larger companies look only for products that require a high capital investment in tooling and machinery, heavy advertising, strong engineering, expensive service organizations, and similar characteristics that tend to discourage the entry of smaller competitors into a market. Many larger companies also purposefully keep out of products with small volume markets—products that can be manufactured and marketed by small companies—feeling that the small operator can offer a personalized service and incur lower overhead costs than the larger company.

What of existing and potential competition? In deciding on a product strategy, it is important to assess realistically the nature and strength of existing competition. If a competitor in a field has tremendous strength in new products, marketing and service, as IBM has had in the computer field, a company should consider carefully its chances to enter the field. Even the large RCA Corporation found it had to swallow a loss of some $450 million after attempting unsuccessfully to compete with IBM with a head-on strategy.

How far can we go in serving customer needs? There are often important limitations. One is, of course, financial: a company must consider whether it has the financial resources to support necessary product research, manufacturing facilities, inventory and receivables, advertising and marketing, and a requisite service competence.

Legal limitations may also be important, as Procter and Gamble found when it was forced by the antitrust laws to divest itself of the Clorox Company (household bleach), or as certain pharmaceutical companies have found when their introduction of new products is held up by the Pure Food and Drug Administration.

Other important limitations may be found in the availability of suitably competent managers and other personnel. Thus, Ford, a well-managed automobile company, had difficulties in managing Philco. Litton Industries apparently found that running its shipbuilding subsidiary was beyond its managerial abilities.

What profit margins can we expect? A company naturally wants to be in a business where it can make an attractive profit. One of the keys is the gross profit margin, that profit above operating expenses which will carry overhead and administrative expenses and yield a desired profit before taxes.

What basic form should our strategy take? In formulating a product or service strategy, a company should determine the direction it wishes to go in terms of intensive or extensive product diversification. If it follows an intensive strategy, it might move in the direction of market penetration—going further in present product markets. Or it might decide on one of market development—going into markets it has not been in before. Thus, Reynolds Aluminum years ago expanded into such consumer products as aluminum kitchen wrappings. Or a company might concentrate on developing, improving, or changing products it already has.

If a company follows an extensive product strategy, it can go in three basic directions. First, it might concentrate on vertical integration. If it is a retailing company it might, as Sears Roebuck and Company has done so often, go into making products it sells. Or if it is a manufacturing company, it might go into retailing, as Sinclair Paints has done. Second, a company might diversify extensively by link diversification, going into products utilizing existing skills, capacities and strengths. Lever Brothers has done this for many years by expanding their operations to a large number of products marketed through grocery stores. A third kind of extensive strategy is conglomerate diversification, going into not necessarily related products with the hope of getting synergistic advantages from combining such skills and strengths as marketing, new product development, management and financial resources. The difficulty with this strategy, as many conglomerates have found, is that too rapid and too varied a program of acquisition can lead to situations that cannot be managed effectively and profitably.

MARKETING STRATEGIES

Marketing strategies are closely connected to product strategies, and must be supportive and interrelated. As a matter of fact, Drucker regards the two basic business functions as innovation and marketing. It is true that a business can hardly survive without these. But while a company can succeed by copying products, it can hardly succeed without effective marketing.

In this area, as in products and services, there are certain questions which can be used as guides for establishing a marketing strategy.

Where are our customers and why do they buy? This question is really asking whether customers are large or small buyers, whether they are end users or manufacturers, where they are geographically, where they are in the production-ultimate user spectrum, and why they buy. Xerox answered some of these questions cleverly and effectively when it saw customers not as copy machine buyers but rather as purchasers of low cost copies. As a result of their leasing program and charging on a per copy basis, this company has had phenomenal success. Likewise, the Farr Company, one of the nation's most innovative and successful air filter companies, has effectively marketed its engine air filters for locomotives and trucks by the strategy of considering its real customers to be the buyers and users of such transport vehicles rather than the equipment manufacturers. Thus, by getting large railroads and trucking companies to specify Farr filters on new equipment, they in effect forced the use of their filters on equipment manufacturers.

How do customers buy? Some customers buy largely through specialized distributing organizations, as is the case with medical and hospital supplies. Some buy through dealer organizations, as with automobiles. Others are accustomed to buying directly from manufacturers, as in the case of major defense procurement, large equipment buyers and most raw material users in such fields as chemicals, electronic components and steel products; but even in these cases, specialized distributors and processors may be important for certain buyers and at certain times.

How is it best for us to sell? There are a number of approaches to selling. Some companies rely heavily on preselling through advertising and sales promotion. Procter and Gamble owes much of its success to a strategy of preselling customers through heavy advertising and sales promotion expenditures (said to average 20% of every sales dollar). At the same time, a much smaller company in the soap and detergents field, the Purex Corporation, had great success in selling its liquid and dry detergents through the appeal of lower consumer prices and higher margins for retailers. Other companies may find their best strategy is to sell on the basis of technical superiority and direct engineering contacts with customers.

Do we have something to offer that competitors do not? The purpose of product differentiation is, of course, to make buyers believe a company's products are different and better than similar products offered by competitors, whether in fact they are or not. It is often possible to build a marketing strategy on some feature in a product or service that is different, regardless of the significance of the difference. This may be an attractive innovation in product design or quality, as in the case of Sylvania's push-button television sets. Or it might be an innovation in service, such as American Motors' all-inclusive automobile warranty. Obviously, what every marketer wants is a claim of product or service uniqueness in order to obtain a proprietary position.

Do we wish to take steps, legally, to discourage competition? There are many things a company can do to discourage competition, other than to run afoul of the antitrust or fair trade laws. Mere size and the ability to finance expensive specialized machinery and tools, or a geographically spread sales and service organization are among these. The success of the Hughes Tool Company in oil drilling bits and that of IBM in the computer field fall into this category. But even medium-sized companies can discourage the very small would-be competitors in the same way. Or a company's marketing strategy might be helped by innovative advertising and product image, which will entrench the company in a market and discourage competition.

Do we need, and can we supply, supporting services? A company's effectiveness in marketing can be greatly influenced by the degree of need for supporting services such as maintenance, and the ability to supply them. Often, certain foreign-made automobiles were slow in getting a position in the American market because of the lack of availability of dealer repair services. Mercedes Benz, for example, had difficulty in making much of a dent in the automobile market until it was able to establish service capabilities in at least the larger cities of the United States. Packard Bell enjoyed a strong position in television in the western states some years ago because of its strong service organization in this area; and for years because of this, limited sales to that area. The major telephone companies, the Bell System and General Telephone, have recently developed a marketing strategy for their industrial and commercial switchboard systems against the rising competition of special equipment manufacturers by emphasizing their prompt and competent maintenance service capabilities.

What is the best pricing strategy and policy for our operation? There are many strategies that can be used. Suggested list prices, quantity and other discounts, delivered or F.O.B. sellers' place of business prices, firm prices or prices with escalation, and the extent of down payments with orders or prices that vary with labor and material costs are among the wide number of variations. How goods or services are priced may be a matter of custom in a market, a marketing tool of a supplier, a matter of achieving price stability versus price cutting; or may reflect the understandable desire of a producer to guard against losses from uncertainty, as in the case of "time and material" contracts.

IMPLEMENTING STRATEGIES

Thus far, much of the emphasis has been on the development of clear and meaningful strategies. If strategic planning is to be operational, certain steps must be taken to implement it.

Strategies should be communicated to all key decision-making managers. It naturally does little good to formulate meaningful strategies unless they are communicated to all managers in the position to make decisions on plans designed to implement them. Strategies may be clear to the executive committee and the chief executive who participate in making them, but nothing is communicated unless they are also clear to the receiver. Strategies should be in writing, and meetings of top executives and their subordinates should be held to make sure that strategies are understood by everyone involved.

Planning premises must be developed and communicated. The importance of planning premises has been emphasized earlier. Steps must be taken so that those premises critical to plans and decisions are developed and disseminated to all managers in the decision-making chain, with instructions to generate programs and make decisions in line with them. Too few companies and other organizations do this. But if it is not done and if premises do not include key assumptions for the entire spectrum of the environment in which plans will operate, decisions are likely to be based on personal assumptions and predilections. The result is almost certain to be a collection of uncoordinated plans.

Action plans must contribute to and reflect major objectives and strategies. Action plans are tactical or operational programs and decisions, whether major or minor, that take place in various parts of an organization. If they do not reflect desired objectives and strategies, vacuous hopes or useless statements of strategic intent result. If care is not taken in this area, then certainly strategic planning is not likely to have a bottom-line impact.

There are various ways of ensuring that action plans do contribute to strategies. If every manager understands strategies, he can certainly review the program recommendations of his staff advisers and his line subordinates to see that they contribute and are consistent. It might even be advisable, at least in major decisions, to have them reviewed by an appropriate small committee, such as one including a subordinate's superior, the superior's superior and a staff specialist. This would lend an aura of formality to the program decisions, and important influences on implementation of strategies might become clear. Budgets likewise should be reviewed with objectives and strategies in mind.

Strategies should be reviewed regularly. Even carefully developed strategies might cease to be suitable if events change, knowledge becomes more clear, or it appears that the program environment will not be as originally thought. Strategies should be reviewed from time to time, certainly not less than once a year, and perhaps more often.

Consider developing contingency strategies and programs. Where considerable change in competitive factors or other elements in the environment might occur and it is impractical to develop strategies that would cover the changes, contingency strategies should be formulated. No one, of course, can wait until the future is certain to make plans. Even where there is considerable uncertainty, there is no choice but to proceed on the most credible set of premises. But this does not mean that a company need find itself totally unprepared if certain possible contingencies do occur.

Make organization structure fit planning needs. The organization structure should be designed to support the accomplishment of goals and the making of decisions to implement strategies. If possible, it is best to have one position (or person) responsible for the accomplishment of each goal and for implementing strategies in achieving this goal. In other words, end result areas and key tasks should be identified and assigned to a single position as far down the organization structure as is feasible. Since this sometimes cannot be done, there may be no alternative but to utilize a form of grid organization. Where this is done, the responsibilities of the various positions in the grid should be clearly spelled out.

In an organizational structure, the roles of staff analysts and advisers should be defined and used so that staff studies and recommendations enter the decision system at the various points where decisions are actually made. Unless this is done, independent staff work of no value to planning is the result.

Continue to teach planning and strategy implementation. Even where a workable system of objectives and strategies and their implementation exists, it is easy for it to fail unless responsible managers continue to teach the nature and importance of planning. This may seem like a tedious process and unnecessary repetition, but learning can be assured in no other way. Teaching does not have to be done at formal meetings or seminars. Rather, much of the instruction can take place in the day-to-day consideration and review of planning proposals and in the review of performance as superiors undertake their normal control functions.

Create a company climate that forces planning. As mentioned earlier, people tend to allow today's problems and crises to postpone effective planning for tomorrow. Therefore, the only way to assure that planning of all kinds will be done, and that strategies will be implemented, is to utilize devices and techniques that force planning.

There are many ways that an environment compulsive of planning can be created. *Managing by objectives* is one way; verifiable and actionable objectives cannot be set without some thought on how they are to be achieved. The rigorous and formal review of objectives, programs and performance will help create a planning environment. Similarly, *review of budgets* will force people to plan, especially if managers are required to explain their total budget needs and are not permitted to concentrate only on changes from a previous period. As pointed out earlier, a clear results-oriented organization structure and staff assistance in the actual decision process will help force planning. *Goals, strategies, policies and premises, if communicated effectively,* can also aid the planning process, especially since most people prefer to make decisions that are consistent with them.

Also, since strategies normally involve a fairly long-term commitment, care must be taken to insure that *long-range and short-range plans are integrated.* There are few day-to-day decisions that do not have an impact on longer-range commitments. In reviewing program proposals, even those that appear to be minor, superiors should make sure that they fit long-range strategies and programs. This is easy to do if managers know what they are and are required to think in these terms.

Strategic planning can be made to have a bottom-line impact. Effective top managers can assure this if they have carefully developed strategies and taken pains for their implementation. In fact, if a company or any other kind of organization is to be successful over a period of time, it really has no other alternative.

3
Strategic Planning

In the construction of a country it is not the practical workers but the idealists and the planners that are difficult to find.

Sun Yat-Sen

Strategic planning is applicable to not-for-profit, governmental entities as well as profitmaking organizations. Certainly, medical facilities, religious organizations, and the like are confronted with such decisions as whether to expand, contract, move, or discontinue some existing services. Under close study, one finds that all organizations engage in strategic planning.

Unlike mid-range tactical planning or short-range operational planning, strategic planning is primarily concerned with solving problems associated with external, environmental influences with long-range time horizons. Specifically, it attempts to master the future by answering the questions: What business are we in? What business would we like to be in? What business should we be in? Where will we be in x years if we do nothing? Where would we like to be in x years?

Companies have four possible alternatives to help them answer these questions:

1. Expansion within their own industry
2. Diversification into a new industry
3. Divestment of existing questionable assets
4. A strategy of wait-and-see

To choose one or more of these alternatives, companies must engage in strategic planning.

In turn, strategic planning requires the accumulation of huge amounts of information, the active participation of key officers, the ability to evaluate and analyze data under conditions of uncertainty about the future, and the psychological maturity of key officers to cope with risk-taking and decisionmaking. It imposes stringent conditions and arduous tasks upon the planners. This has its rewards, however, because the planning process may be far more important than the plan itself.

The length of time a firm projects into the future depends upon the industry it is in and its expected business environment (e.g., the anticipated availability of raw materials, market conditions, labor supply, and governmental controls). For instance, it is not unreasonable for companies engaged in manufacturing of aerospace hardware to plan 20 years into the future. On the other hand, 5 years ahead is just about as far as companies in the garment industry can plan. After a company has developed a scenario for its future, it compares where it would like to be to where it is now and to where it will be if it does nothing. The difference between where a company would like to be and where it will be in the future if it does not change is termed the *planning gap*. Strategic planning is primarily concerned with closing that gap.

The remainder of this chapter presents various methods that are available for selecting and ranking alternative projects in order to most effectively use a firm's limited resources for gap closing. (Also see the Alexander & Alexander case study, p. 367. Note that A&A's prime strategy for gap closing is internal expansion. A&A believes that more opportunity for growth exists in its own business than in any non-insurance-related businesses it could consider.)

The term *project* is not intended to convey a series of possible actions by a firm that would limit it to the modification or creation of new versions of existing company products and or services only. Instead, *project,* as used here, is meant to be more universal, to indicate possible shifting by a firm into new product lines and properties for divestment purposes, expansion of its position in its present product market, and proposed projects to improve intraorganizational unit efficiencies to promote overall company effectiveness.

For example, a firm engaged in the manufacture and sale of cigarettes might consider the evaluation and ranking of projects such as:

1. the purchase of radically new computer-controlled cigarette-making machinery
2. the design, development, and manufacture of such machinery for sale to the industry
3. the introduction of a new product that is a substitute for cigarette smoking
4. the sale of its pipe division
5. the purchase or start-up of a plant to manufacture cigarette lighters
6. the purchase of a plant to manufacture birth-control pills
7. the purchase of a professional soccer team
8. the investment of company funds in high-interest debt instruments

and so on. The list of possibilities is probably inexhaustible.

To help planners choose preferable alternative projects, various selection methods are examined, evaluated, and discussed in the following sections. The presentation begins with the simplest methods and proceeds to the most complex.

AVERAGE RATE-OF-RETURN METHOD

The average rate-of-return method is usually based upon straight-line depreciation.

ROR_{av} = Average book earnings/Average net investment

The higher the ROR of the project under investigation, the higher the criterion of evaluation ranks when compared to other projects being considered. This method has many shortcomings because it is based upon financial information only. Its major weakness is that it fails to take into account cash inflows and outflows and only considers accounting income.

PAYBACK METHOD

In the payback method, the time (usually in years) required to recover a firm's initial investment from its annual cash inflow is used to rank-order the alternative projects being considered. The shorter the payback period of a project, the higher its rank compared to other alternative projects.

The payback method fails to consider cash flow after the payback period, and therefore it cannot be considered as a measure of profitability over the long term. When this method is used, it is more logical to consider it as a constraint that must be met than as a time objective to be minimized or a profitability objective to be maximized. In the same context, it could be considered as one of the basic evaluating criteria when the firm employs a "satisficing" philosophy toward the strategic planning function. (Satisficing can be defined as doing well but not as well as would be possible if increased resources of time and material were expended. It is in fact the choosing of the first alternative that satisfies a predetermined set of criteria.)

PRESENT VALUE METHOD

There are two distinct present value methods based upon discounted cash flow. They provide for an objective basis of selecting and evaluating alternative projects. These methods consider the timing and magnitude of expected cash flow in each period of a project's life.

To help clarify the use and the differences between the two present value methods, let us assume that the following holds true for an alternative project under consideration:

1. The initial investment required is $15,000.
2. The cash-flow stream is an even series of $5000 per year for 5 years.
3. The required rate-of-return is 10 percent.

The *internal rate-of-return method** is based upon the discount rate that equates the present value of the expected cash outflow with the present values of the cash inflow. Projects are ranked by comparing the internal rate of return against a previously agreed upon rate of return known as the *handle* or the *cutoff.*

For the preceding example, the calculation would be:

$$\$15,000 = \$5000/(1+r) + \$5000/(1+r)^2 + \$5000/(1+r)^3 + \$5000/(1+r)^4 + \$5000/(1+r)^5$$

where r is the internal rate of return. Solving for r, we find the internal rate of return is equal to 19.85 percent. According to this method, the proposal would be acceptable because r is greater than the required rate of return of 10 percent.

In the *net present value method,*† all the cash flow is discounted to present value using a previously agreed-upon required rate of return. For our example, the calculation would be:

$$NPV = -15,000 + 5000/(1.10) + 5000/(1.10)^2 + 5000/(1.10)^3 + 5000/(1.10)^4 + 5000/(1.10)^5$$

Solving for NPV, we find that the net present value is equal to + $4153. According to this method, the proposal would be acceptable because the net present value is greater than 0 at the 10 percent required rate of return.

*Mathematically, the internal rate-of-return method can be represented by the following model:

$$\sum_{t=0}^{n} A_t / (1+r)^t = 0$$

where

A_t = the cash flow for the period t, whether it be negative or positive cash flow.
n = the last period in which cash is expected if the initial cash investment occurs at $t = 0$, the above model can be modified as follows:

$$A_0 = A_1 / (1+r) + A_2 / (1+r)^2 + A_n / (1+r)^n$$

Then r becomes the rate that discounts all future cash flows from A_1 to A_n, so that the sum of all the discounted flows equals A_0 at time 0.

†Mathematically, the net present value method can be represented by the following model:

$$NPV = \sum_{t=0}^{n} A_t / (1+k)^t$$

where

k = the required rate of return.

Projects are ranked by comparing all net present values above zero. The greater the net present value of a project, the higher its respective ranking. If any net present value falls below zero, it is automatically rejected. It indicates a rate of return less than the agreed-upon requirement.

In general, the net present value method and internal rate-of-return method lead to the same ranking decisions. However, if a choice is to be made between them, the net present value method is considered to have a stronger theoretical base, and therefore, to be the better choice (Hirshleifer 1958).

These two present value methods are forms of capital investment theory. They are used to evaluate each alternative project for its respective contribution to the firm; afterward, one or more of the alternatives are chosen for implementation. For each proposal, both negative (costs) and positive (revenues) cash flows are calculated over the life of the project. To compare projects, the cash flows being considered must be marginal to all other cash flows within the firm, since only additional revenues and costs generated can be considered. In capital budgeting, only cash can be used for reinvestments or paid to stockholders as dividends; therefore, cash, not accounting income, is important. If the firm has the cash, it can invest it in the hope of receiving even greater cash returns in the future. The greater the amount of return expected, the higher the project ranks compared to others being considered. In other words, after the projects have been enumerated and the cash flows determined, the worth of each proposal is evaluated with respect to its payoff.

Capital investment theory ignores the fact that investment decisions are not arrived at in a psychological or an environmental vacuum. The objective financial approach ignores the needs and motivations of the decisionmakers themselves. It also does not consider the concept of *satisficing* or *limited rationality* (Simon 1965), but is based upon the concept of *optimizing*—which is not possible because human beings are involved in the decision process.

Synergy is also completely ignored in present value methodology. Yet, the synergistic effects in the managerial, monetary, time, facilities, and public relations areas must be considered when selecting competing alternatives that require organization resources. In fact, the very structure of a firm may be dependent upon management's desire to maximize the effects of synergy. Since synergy does play a large role in dictating strategy, Steiner (1969), among others, believes that it helps to determine organization structure; to ignore synergy in the selection process is a mistake and can result in serious errors in decisionmaking.

ADAPTIVE SEARCH METHOD

The adaptive search method proposed by Ansoff (1965) attempts to bridge the apparent flaws in capital investment theories. It takes into account, to a limited degree, the perceptions and needs of the decisionmakers and the effects of synergy, as well as suggests a thorough search of the external environment.

Ansoff assumes that decisionmakers operate under conditions of partial ignorance, i.e., they are not capable of knowing all possible alternatives at any particular time. The idea of partial ignorance, when used in decisionmaking, is similar to the concept of limited rationality or satisficing. There is, of course, a marked philosophical difference when making decisions under partial ignorance as compared to making decisions under perfect knowledge, as is assumed in the previously presented methods.

The method presented by Ansoff is a four-step process:

1. *Perception of decision need or opportunity.* This step is based upon the premise that no firm is immune from the dangers of competition, product obsolescence, changes in demand, and new product innovations. Therefore, intelligence activity that continually reviews the environment for strategic threats and opportunities must be available.

The more dynamic the industry that a firm is involved in—such as aerospace, electronics, nuclear power generation, optics, and pharmaceuticals—the greater its need for an organization structure to provide a continuing monitoring system. Firms in more static industries, such as steel, automotive, packaging, and construction, may only require a structure capable of periodic review. Simon (1976) calls this step the "intelligence phase." Ansoff elaborates on this idea by separating the "perceivers" into three groups:

1. Reactors: companies that wait for problems to occur before taking action.
2. Planners: companies that anticipate problems.
3. Entrepreneurs: companies that anticipate both problems and opportunities, i.e., that are engaged in a continual search for opportunities.

2. *Formulation of alternative courses of action.* Traditionally, capital investment theory has required that decisionmakers know all of the possible alternatives at the time that the projects are ranked. In any strategic situation, this is not possible. Ansoff points out that during the strategic planning process, new alternatives will present themselves for consideration. The greater the scope of the search, the greater will be this flow of alternatives. Inventions, new products, acquisitions, divestments, and joint venture opportunities will present themselves for the evaluation of the strategic planners. The company must thus have a planning structure that will allow it to conduct an active search for these attractive opportunities. This structure must be designed not only to accommodate new opportunities, but also to evaluate and rank them in order to allocate the firm's limited resources among those chosen. Management should create an organizational climate of "sensitivity" to encourage the planners to "sense" attractive opportunities that are close by but still uncovered.

3. *Evaluation of the alternatives for their respective contributions.* The adaptive search method dichotimizes its criteria for judging the relative contributions of alternative projects by time. The first is the proximate-period (3 to 10 years) criterion which is return on investment (ROI); it is a measure of profitability

(return on investment) rather than operating profit (excess of revenues over cost) as used in capital investment theory. The ROI of each alternative project is measured against a threshold-goal criterion. The threshold is the minimum ROI that a firm is willing to consider for investment purposes, whereas the goal is a highly desirable ROI. Obviously, as one moves from the threshold to the goal, the element of risk increases. The choice of an alternative that falls within the threshold-goal range depends upon the risk orientation of the decisionmakers. As mentioned, the psychological makeup plays an important part in the selection of alternative projects. In a sense, the threshold-goal range becomes the proximate yardstick for the evaluation of opportunities. (Note: The general approach to strategic planning and evaluaton followed by A&A closely approximates the adaptive search method outlined here.)

The firm's long-term objective is to remain healthy and profitable after the proximate period. To do so, the firm must continually renew itself by entering new markets, developing new products, and bringing in new resources of people, capital, and equipment. According to Ansoff, planners should measure characteristics of the firm that continually contribute to its health and profitability. He offers the following list of long-term criteria, which deal with the continued improvement of the company's external competitive position, for consideration:

- Continuing growth of sales at least at the pace of the industry to enable the firm to maintain its share of the market.
- Increase in relative market share to increase relative efficiency of the firm.
- Growth in earnings to provide resources for reinvestment.
- Growth in earnings per share to attract new capital to the firm.
- Continuing addition of new products and product lines.
- Continuing expansion of the firm's customer population.
- Absence of excessive seasonal or cyclical fluctuations in sales and earnings and the consequent loss of competitive position through externally forced inefficiency in the use of the firm's resources.

These measures, when taken individually, are partial indicators of a company's strong competitive position. When taken together, they assure that a firm will have a long-term profitability potential in its competitive environment.

How does one evaluate and rank-order the possible alternative projects using the proximate and long-term criteria? The proximate criteria of ROI can be used to rank projects if the risk orientation of the planners is considered as part of the evaluation process. In addition, the needs of the board of directors, management, stockholders, and the public also play a vital part in the rank ordering. For example, could a publisher of children's books start a division to produce pornographic films? Regardless of the ROI or risk orientation, the firm would consider the diversification to be unfeasible. Yet the publishing company may very well consider entering the children's clothing industry—even if the ROI is lower and the risk higher. Alternative projects can be ranked using the ROI yardstick, but only after the constraints imposed by nonfinancial factors are taken into consideration.

After a ranking has been developed using the proximate criteria, modified by the organization's internal and external environments, the long-term criteria for each of the ranked proposals must be considered. Again, the subjective judgments of the planners and others are introduced, and the rankings based upon the proximate criteria are modified to satisfy the long-term objectives of the firm. This evaluation and reevaluation, based upon both objective data and subjective input of the planners gained through experience and knowledge, result in the final ranking of alternative projects.

4. *Choice of one or more alternatives for implementation.* Once they have been rank-ordered, projects must still pass fiscal feasibility studies and synergistic analysis. After these steps, the firm must be structured so that it can implement the chosen projects. In addition, it must set up a control mechanism to measure goal achievements and deviations. The firm must also be able to change its plans whenever necessary.

How can a firm determine whether it needs long-range planning including project evaluation and ranking? First, it must answer the questions posed in the introduction to this chapter on p. 66. If the answers can be summed up, "We are in the business we want to be in, and we will be where we want to be in x years if we do nothing," then obviously there is no need for planning. However, for most companies, the answer would be, "Even though we are in the business we would like to be in, we are not going to be where we want to be in x years if we do nothing. Therefore, we had better start planning to close the gap between where we are and where we would like to be in x years by either expanding our present product or service line, diversifying into new product markets, divesting ourselves of some of our present holdings, and/or attempting to institute new efficiencies in our present operations." At this point, the need arises for a mechanism with which to evaluate and rank gap-closing projects. Planners should not use the adaptive search method as a series of hard and fast guidelines, but rather as a tool to help themselves break free from the tunnel vision imposed by other methods. It is a mechanism subject to individual adaptation by each firm's needs. When used in this context, it becomes a valuable planning tool.

Although the **adaptive** search method is preferable to the other methods discussed, it does not consider in depth the behavior of the decisionmakers. The goal-directed behaviors as expressed in acognitive explanations, the needs, drives, and desires of hedonism, the ahistorical concepts of expectancy theory, and the linkage of performance and satisfaction for both individuals and groups responsible for planning are either ignored completely or treated superficially. Finally, the idea that strategic planning is essentially a manifestation of general systems theory has not received the attention it deserves. From an overall point of view, however, the adaptive search approach to strategic planning is a giant step toward realization that planning is a complex process that requires perceptual as well as objective input.

In "How to Design a Strategic Planning System," which begins on p. 76, Lorange and Vancil (1976) approach the problem of strategic planning in a chronological fashion. They enhance the concept that strategic planning, to be of value, must of necessity be considered an open system in a dynamic framework. Each company, due to the diversity of input into the strategic planning system, must develop its own individual plan.

"Long-Range Planning Is Not for Everyone" (Shapiro and Kallman 1978) is presented as a counterpoint to the concept that strategic planning is a panacea for all companies (see p. 86). Circumstances do exist where strategic planning may be an unnecessary and costly exercise. Obviously, "the less uncertain the future the less the need for a strategic planning function because there are fewer strategic alternatives with which to deal." The very fact that the government agencies set freight rates and routes in the trucking industry eliminates many strategic possibilities. Thus, the reader might ask, If we find our company in a similar set of conditions, should we manage it by the seat of our pants on a day-to-day basis? No! The other modes of planning—administrative and operational—are still of the utmost importance to insure the proper use of scarce resources. These important components of the planning process are fully discussed in the following chapters.

REFERENCES

Ansoff, H. I. 1965. *Corporate Strategy: An Analytic Approach to Business Policy for Growth and Expansion.* New York: McGraw-Hill.

The position a company would like to be in several years hence, relative to the position it will be in at that time if it does nothing, is defined as the "planning gap." The author presents the adaptive search method using a cascading effect as a logical way to close the gap.

Hirshleifer, J. 1958. On the theory of optimal investment decisions. *Journal of Political Economy* **66**: 95–103.

The two popular approaches to evaluating investment opportunities using discounted cash flows, net present value (NPV), and internal rate of return (IRR) are analyzed. The IRR method is shown to be based upon a misunderstanding of Fisher's original work on interest rates and investment evaluation. The conclusion is that, in general, the NPV method is superior to the IRR method.

Lorange, Peter and R. F. Vancil. 1976. How to design a strategic planning system. *Harvard Business Review* **54**(5): 75–81.

Presents in chronological fashion the process of setting up a strategic planning system in both a small and a large company. The authors believe that to remain effective, the planning process must be continually monitored and changed when necessary. *Reprinted herein on pp. 76–85.*

Shapiro, H. J. and E. A. Kallman. 1978. Long-range planning is not for everyone. *Planning Review* **6**(5): 27–29, 34.

In an empirical study of the trucking industry, it was found that companies in a regulated industry may not need long-range planning at all. Since the government controls routes and pricing and the union controls compensation, tactical planning may be far more important than strategic planning. *Reprinted herein on pp. 86–90.*

Simon, H. A. 1960. *The New Science of Management Decision.* New York: Harper & Row.

The organization of the future will depend largely upon new decisionmaking techniques. It will include automated programmed decision processes for governing daily routine operations. Automation and rationalization of decisionmaking are bound to alter the climate of organizations as we know them today.

——. 1976. *Administrative Behavior.* 3rd ed. New York: Free Press.

This study of decisionmaking processes in administrative organizations is addressed to both the student of organization theory and behavior and to the practitioner. Its objective is to construct a set of tools with which to describe how administrative organization works.

Steiner, G. A. 1969. *Top Management Planning.* Toronto: Macmillan.

A major all-inclusive work in the field of top-level planning, the book is written—from top management's point of view—for both the practitioner and the student of planning. The author believes that the major requisites for successful management are a first-rate planning system, charisma, and a sense of competitive urgency.

How to Design a Strategic Planning System

Peter Lorange
and
Richard F. Vancil

Every business carries on strategic planning, although the formality of that process varies greatly from one company to the next. Conceptually, the process is simple: managers at every level of a hierarchy must ultimately agree on a detailed, integrated plan of action for the coming year; they arrive at agreement through a series of steps starting with the delineation of corporate objectives and concluding with the preparation of a one- or two-year profit plan. However, the *design* of that process—deciding who does what, when—can be complex, and it is vital to the success of the planning effort.

A strategic planning system is nothing more than a structured (that is, designed) process that organizes and coordinates the activities of the managers who do the planning. No universal, off-the-shelf planning system exists for the simple and obvious reason that companies differ in size, diversity of operations, the way they are organized, and managers' style and philosophy. An effective planning system requires "situational design"; it must take into account the particular company's situation, especially along the dimensions of size and diversity.

While providing in this article some guidelines for designing strategic planning systems, we caution the reader to recognize that, for the reasons just stated, such generalizations can be treacherous. We do not aspire to prescribe a planning system for your organization, you must do the tailoring.

But some useful generalizations are possible, particularly in distinguishing between large companies and small ones and between highly diversified companies and less diversified ones. Size and diversity of operations generally go hand-in-hand, although exceptions to that rule are common. Several of the large airlines, for example, are in one business, and a number of mini-conglomerates with sales of less than $100 million have divisions in disparate industries. For convenience here, we shall talk about companies as "small" or "large," defining those labels in terms of the typical characterisitcs shown in *Exhibit I.*

Exhibit I. Characteristics of "small" and "large" companies

	"SMALL" COMPANIES	"LARGE" COMPANIES
Annual Sales	Less than $100 million	More than $100 million
Diversity of operations	In a single industry	In two or more different industries
Organization structure	Functional departments	Product divisions
Top executives' expertise in industries in which company operates	Greater than that of functional subordinates	Less than that of divisional subordinates

While your company may not neatly match either set of characteristics, an understanding of why an effective strategic planning system is different in these two types of companies may enable you to design a system that fits your situation. We should note that the characteristics of small companies also describe a "typical" division in a large, diversified business. Therefore, division managers in such companies can follow our discussion at two levels simultaneously: (1) in their role as a part of the corporate planning process, and (2) in their strategic planning role for their own "small" businesses.

There are six issues on which a choice must be made while designing a strategic planning system. With each issue the proper choice for large companies will be different in most cases from the one for small companies. The issues are: communication of corporate performance goals, the goal-setting process, environmental scanning, subordinate managers' focus, the corporate planner's role, and the linkage of planning and budgeting. We shall describe each of these issues in turn and briefly discuss why the design choice differs in the two corporate settings.

COMMUNICATION OF CORPORATE GOALS

A common roadblock in designing a formal planning system occurs when second-level managers ask headquarters for guidelines to focus the preparation of their strategic plans. These managers, uncertain how to tackle the assignment, may ask, implicitly or explicitly, "Tell us where you want us to go and the performance you expect from us, and we'll give you a plan of how to achieve it." These questions are not unreasonable, but acceding to them may violate the very purpose for undertaking strategic planning. To determine how goals should be communicated and how specific they should be is an important matter in planning system design.

When the president of *a small company* (or the general manager of a division of a diversified company) initiates the strategic planning process, he shares with his funtional subordinates his thoughts about the objectives and strategy of the business. In most situations, however, he does not make explicit his performance goals. Instead, he asks his functional managers to devise a set of action programs that will implement the strategy of the business in a manner consistent with its objectives. In a pharmaceutical company that we observed, the R&D, manufacturing, and marketing functions jointly proposed a series of possible programs for developing various new drugs and modifying existing ones. But often, of course, this "programming" process involves only a single department.

Usually, the managers concerned realize that there is no need to anticipate the results of their planning efforts by trying to establish goals before establishment and evaluation of the programs. This would be time-consuming and burdensome and might also create false expectations among the functional managers.

The programing process is oriented much more toward analysis of alternative actions than toward establishment of corporate goals, primarily because the functional managers involved in programming tend (properly) to have a parochial point of view. They have a somewhat shorter time horizon than the president and focus their attention on their own areas of the business. The president is the one who selects the action programs for achieving the goals he has set for the business. Functional managers do not need to know the president's performance goals, only that he wants the managers to recommend the best set of programs.

Because of its action orientation, the programming process usually lacks continuity from one year to the next. The objectives and strategy of the business may remain the same, but each year it is necessary to reexamine all existing programs and try to devise new ones. As a consequence, even though the programming activity commonly uses a three- to five-year time horizon, management pays little attention to the tentative goals established in the preceding year. Instead, the focus is on the current situation, the best set of action programs now, and the development of an achievable goal for the forthcoming year.

The diversity of the portfolio of business in *large companies* is often so great that it limits top management's capacity for in-depth perception and familiarity with each business. Consequently, management has to rely on the relatively unconstrained inputs from the divisions.

Division managers do heed corporate guidance in the form of broad objectives, but as a rule top management should delay development of a statement of performance goals for the corporation. Usually, a division manager is in a better position to assess the potential of his own business if he is unbiased by corporate expectations. Delay also permits the top executives to change their approach to the task. In the absence of a formal strategic planning process, top management may have developed explicit goals for itself; but it cannot be sure of the appropriateness of the goals when viewed in the context of a set of independently arrived-at divisional goals. Divisional recommendations stimulate a better job of corporate goal setting.

GOAL-SETTING PROCESS

From the division manager's viewpoint, should he or corporate management set the division's goals? This issue is sometimes cast as a choice between "top-down" and "bottom-up" goal setting. Actually, of course, management at both levels must agree on divisional goals. An important issue, however, remains: Which level in the hierarchy should initiate the process? In a homogeneous company, the same issue arises concerning the general manager and functional managers. The design of the planning system can strongly influence how this issue is resolved.

The goals that emerge from the programming process in *a small company* are tied to an approved set of action programs. Until the president has decided on the programs, no functional manager can set goals for his sphere of activity. Selection of a set of action programs, therefore, more or less automatically determines the performance goals for each functional unit. In many small companies—such as the pharmaceutical concern we spoke of—a "package" of action programs spells out the functional goals for every department, because of the interdependence of all the departments.

In a sense then, functional goal setting is a top-down process. The functional managers propose action programs, but the president with his business-wide perspective determines the programs and goals for his functional subordinates.

In *a large company* with a relatively diversified group of businesses, "capacity limitations" at the corporate level dictate a more or less bottom-up approach. The divisions initiate much of the goal setting, since it requires intimate knowledge of the industry-specific set of business conditions.

Establishing an effective croporate-divisional goal-setting climate in a large company is not easy. For the first year or two of a formal planning effort, the best approach in most situations is to allow the initiative for recommending divisional goals to rest with the division manager. This approach gives him support in running his business and encourages strategic thinking at the divisional level.

Later, after the corporate and divisional managers have gained experience in hammering out a mutually agreeable set of divisional goals, the division manager's annual proposal for divisional goals will become more constrained than in the early years. In a divisionalized, consumer goods manufacturer we know of, the first years of carrying on the planning process were viewed frankly as a learning experience for division managers in making plans operational as well as for top management in learning to appreciate the strategic problems of each business of the company.

The cumulative experience of negotiating the goal setting over the years improves the effectiveness of the process. Corporate management can help nurture this development by creating a system that maintains a proper top-down/bottom-up balance. One way to achieve this balance is by withholding an explicit statement of corporate goals for the first year or two, while requiring the division manager to recommend goals for his division.

ENVIRONMENTAL SCANNING

A strategic planning system has two major functions: to develop an integrated, coordinated, and consistent long-term plan of action, and to facilitate adaptation of the corporation to environmental change. When introducing and developing such a system, companies commonly concentrate on its integrative aspects. The design of the system, however, must also include the function of environmental scanning to make sure that the planning effort also fulfills its adaptive mission.

Corporate management, of course, provides subordinates with a set of forecasts and assumptions about the future business environment. Since each manager, initially at least, draws the strategic plans for his sphere of responsibility more or less independently of his counterparts, all managers must have access to the same set of economic and other environmental forecasts.

Environmental scanning in *small companies* is a strategically oriented task that can go far beyond the mere collection of data about markets, competitors, and technological changes. A company that, for example, enjoys a large share of the market for a product used by middle- and upper-income teenagers and young adults may devote considerable effort in analyzing demographic trends and changes in per capita income. A fairly accurate forecast of market size five years hence is possible to make and would be useful in appraising the potential for the company's growth.

The task of monitoring detailed environmental changes in *large companies* is too difficult to be performed by top management alone. Division management, therefore, is expected to study the external environment that may be relevant to their particular businesses. In these circumstances, headquarters typically provides only a few environmental assumptions—mainly economic forecasts.

Environmental scanning may play another important role in large companies that are interested in diversification through acquisitions. In one diversified electronics and high-technology company that set out to decrease its dependence on defense contracts, the vice president in charge of planning spent most of his time searching for acquisition opportunities. After establishing close ties with the investment community and certain consultants, he spread word of his company's intentions.

SUBORDINATE MANAGERS' FOCUS

In a strategic planning effort, where should the second-level managers direct their attention? What roles do the division manager, functional manager, and top management play? We shall consider these questions in terms of whether plans should be more quantitative or more qualitative, more concerned with financial detail or with strategic analysis.

Preparation of a functionally coordinated set of action programs for *a small company* may require a great deal of cross-functional communication. Much of this interchange is most efficiently expressed in dollar or other quantitative terms, such as numbers of employees, units of product, and square feet of plant space. Use of financial or quantitative data is appropriate for two reasons: (1) it helps each functional manager understand the dimensions of a proposed program and forces him to think through the implications of executing it; (2) it permits the president to select more confidently the set of programs to be implemented. The pharmaceutical company previously referred to, for instance, focuses on the funds flows that might be expected from the various strategic programs suggested by the functional departments.

In practice, the financial and quantitative aspects of functional planning become progressively detailed as the programming process continues, culminating in very specific plans that constitute the operating budget.

In a diversified *larger company,* top management wants each division to adopt a timely strategic outlook and division management to focus primarily on achieving that outlook. Particularly during the early years of the planning program, division managers should be permitted to develop as much financial detail in support of their proposals as they think desirable. As a result, they may generate more financial detail than necessary for strategic business planning. After a year or two, therefore, the corporate requirements for financial detail to support division proposals should be made explicit—and should be explicitly minimal.

Division managers should be asked to shift the focus of their efforts to identification and analysis of strategic alternatives, using their expertise to estimate quickly the financial implications. This focus has been a goal from the beginning, of course, but it is difficult to achieve at the outset. Failing to shift the focus is an even greater danger; the planning activity becomes a "numbers game" and never achieves its purpose.

Considering that the division manager may never have seen, much less prepared, long-range financial projections for his business, drawing them up should be a useful activity. Such projections help him lengthen the time horizon of his thinking; they oblige him to make his intuitive economic model of the business more explicit, which in turn enables him to forecast changes in financial performance. As a result, a division manager's initial planning efforts tend to be financially oriented and, in many respects, analogous to long-range budgeting. Corporate management should design the requirements of the system to mitigate the pressures that initiation of formal planning poses for a division manager.

One important caveat for the chief executive of a large company: he should never allow himself to get so involved in the development of business plans that he assumes the division managers' planning job. A situation that we investigated concerned the newly appointed president of a multinational company in the consumer products business, whose experience was mainly in marketing. He could not resist "helping" one of his divisions develop a detailed, more aggressive marketing plan. Such interference often inhibits the division from coming up with a realistic plan to which it can commit itself. In this case, quiet resistance effectively shelved the president's ideas.

CORPORATE PLANNER'S ROLE

A major issue in the design of the planning system is where the corporate planner fits. Strategic planning is a line management function; a sure route to disaster is to have plans produced by staff planners and then issued to line managers. Strategic planning is essentially a people-interactive process, and the planner is only one in the cast of characters involved. If the process is to function effectively, he must clearly understand his proper role. The corporate planner's function in small and large companies is quite different.

In *a small company* (or a product division of a large company), the planner performs the function of staff planning assistant to the president (or the general manager). While coordinating the planning activities of the functional managers, he concerns himself with the president's problem of selecting the best set of action programs. Only the president—and his planning assistant—has a business-wide perspective of the choices, and the assistant must do the bulk of the analysis.

Cast in this role, the planner may become a very influential member of the president's (or the general manager's) executive team. If he uses his power sensitively, he need not lose effectiveness with his peers running the functional departments. They can appreciate the necessity for cross-functional analysis of program alternatives. Managing the planning process is an almost incidental role for the assistant, since he merely formalizes the analysis that leads to a coordinated set of action programs.

In *a large company,* the corporate planner's organizational status can have significant symbolic value in conveying to division managers the importance of formal strategic planning and the difference between it and conventional budgeting. The planner's role initially is that of a catalyst, encouraging line managers to adopt a strategic orientation. He helps corporate management do a better job of resource allocation among the divisions, partly by assisting the division managers in strategic planning for their businesses. But he must not succumb to the temptation to become more involved in formulating the plans, or he may lose his effectiveness.

System maintenance and coordination is the planner's primary function as the planning effort matures; he monitors its evolution and maintains consistency. His tasks differ greatly from the mainly analytical role of the planner in the small company.

LINKAGE OF PLANNING AND BUDGETING

The steps in a typical planning system represent an orderly, gradual process of commitment to certain strategic alternatives. Each step is, theoretically at least, linked to those preceding. In financial terms, this linkage may be quite explicit; for instance, a division's profit forecast prepared in the first planning cycle may become the profit commitment for next year's operating budget. Although few companies expect to achieve this financial linkage in narrowing the choices, all the parties involved in the process should understand the intended relationship between the cycles.

How fast this narrowing should be is a situational design question that depends on the particular corporate setting. A tight linkage between planning and budgeting indicates that more strategic commitments have been made at an earlier stage. A loose linkage, on the other hand, implies that the narrowing process is slower and will occur mainly late, in the budgeting stage of the process.

Exhibit II. Slow versus rapid narrowing profiles in the planning process.

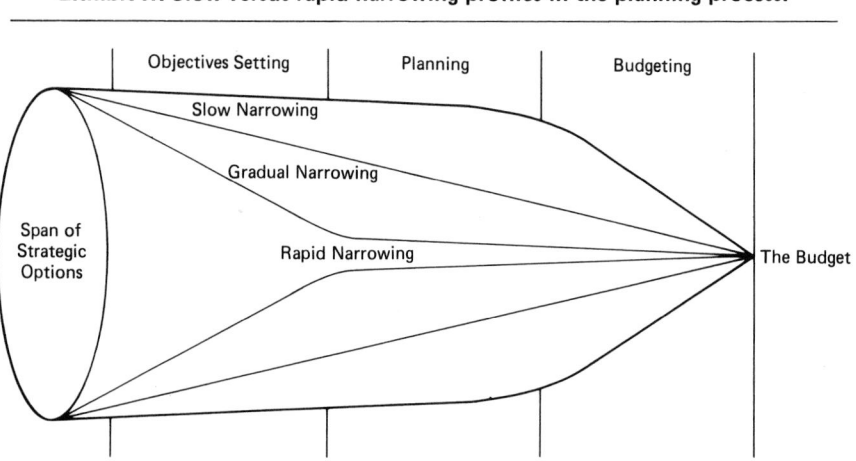

Exhibit II shows examples of slow versus rapid narrowing profiles. Notice that a company that does little narrowing in the early stages faces the task of considering a large number of strategic issues in the budgeting stage. This implies that either the company is equipped with an adequate organization to process an immense and "peaky" budgeting workload, or it will neglect some choices altogether, with the likely result that the quality of its allocation decisions suffers.

A small company with little diversity in its operations may wish to adopt an early or rapid narrowing process, since the functional and corporate executives involved are thoroughly familiar with the strategy of the few businesses in question. Then functional managers can proceed directly to the development of action programs to continue implementation of that strategy. Quantitative financial linkage between the selected programs and the resulting budgets is feasible, and "tight" linkage of this type is common practice.

In *a large company,* linkage is usually looser and the narrowing process more gradual. During the start-up phase top management should give division managers plenty of time to devote to strategic thinking about their businesses—but the lower-level executives must remember to differentiate that activity from long-range budgeting, with its related requirement of divisional performance fulfillment.

As the system matures, however, management can gradually accelerate the narrowing process without jeopardizing the creative aspect of planning. A natural result of this progress is a more precise definition of the linkage between the planning cycle and the budgeting cycle. A large producer of heavy equipment we know of, for instance, has "tightened up" the linkage between planning and budgeting. The top executives believe that this development is a natural consequence of their increasingly cohesive strategic points of view.

EVOLVING SYSTEMS

In sum, significant differences exist between the planning procedures used in the two types of companies we have examined. The issues that management must address, and our attempt to delineate what is good practice in small and large companies, are summarized in *Exhibit III.*

In companies that are not very diversified and are functionally organized—as well as product units of diversified corporations—top management carries on the strategic thinking about the future of the business. In such companies, a formal process to help organize that reflective activity is frequently unnecessary, in view of the few managers involved. Instead, formal strategic planning focuses on the development and review of innovative action programs to implement the strategy. The planning system reflects that focus: goal setting is top-down, linkage to

Exhibit III. Approaches to planning system design issues.

ISSUES	"SMALL" COMPANIES	"LARGE" COMPANIES	
		NEW PLANNING SYSTEM	MATURE PLANNING SYSTEM
Communication of corporate goals	Not explicit	Not explicit	Explicit
Goal-setting process	Top-down	Bottom-up	"Negotiated"
Corporate-level environmental scanning	Strategic	Statistical	Statistical
Subordinate managers' focus	Financial	Financial	Strategic
Corporate planner's role	Analyst	Catalyst	Coordinator
Linkage of planning and budgeting	Tight	Loose	Tight

SITUATIONAL SETTINGS

the budget is tight, and the staff planning officer plays a major role as cross-functional program analyst and environmental scanner.

In companies that operate in several industrial sectors and are organized into product divisions, initiating a formal strategic planning process is a major task. The first year or two of such an effort must be viewed as an investment in fostering a planning competence among division managers; the payoff in better decisions at the corporate level must wait until the system matures.

If the planning system is to survive as more than an exercise in pushing numbers into the blank spaces on neatly designed forms, it must evolve rapidly along several dimensions. A mature system, however, can be invaluable, helping both corporate and divisional executives make better and better-coordinated strategic decisions.

Any company—indeed, any organization—is a dynamically evolving entity whose situational setting is subject to change. Accordingly, to remain effective, the design of the planning process is a continuous task requiring vigilance and insight on the part of management.

Long·Range Planning Is Not for Everyone

H. Jack Shapiro
and
Ernest A. Kallman

Since the turn of the century management researchers, among others, have exhorted business firms to plan for their future. To us it seems obvious that the greater a firm's commitment to long-range planning, the greater are its chances for survival and success. Most managers and executives "know" that this is so—they do not have to perform lengthy and costly research on planning to support so obvious a truism. Nonetheless, we did a research study of long-range planning in the motor freight industry to find out whether long-range planning is a necessity for every company in the industry. It also asks if there is a boundary condition that differentiates between those companies that must plan continually, plan occasionally, or not engage in long-range planning at all. If there is such a boundary, what variables go into making it up? Are the variables controllable or uncontrollable? Can a model be devised that incorporates these variables? The answers to these questions can point the industry toward more efficient and effective use of its scarce resources.

We examined the planning practices and economic performance of nearly 500 Class I motor common carriers who participated in the study by completing questionnaires which were mailed to them. We also interviewed some carriers about their planning function. Most questionnaires were completed by corporate presidents or top level executives. In addition to the planning information gathered through the questionnaires, economic performance data and other general information about the respondents were obtained from the *Trines Blue Book of the Trucking Industry,* including carrier size, commodities handled, and geographic area. Data from *Trines* were used to calculate for each carrier the growth rate of five economic performance indicators over a ten-year period (1965-1974). The measures of business success used were: 1) gross operating revenue, 2) net earnings before taxes, 3) earnings to revenue ratio, 4) return on shareholder's investment (net income divided by average shareholder's equity) and 5) return on total investment (operating profit divided by the sum of average equity capital and average fixed liabilities).

The questionnaire which was sent to each carrier was designed to determine

Reprinted from *Planning Review,* a journal of the North American Society for Corporate Planning, 1406 Third National Building, Dayton, Ohio 45402.

the carrier's commitment to long-range planning based upon a time horizon of over one year. Part I of the questionnaire consisted of five definitions of planning. The respondent was asked to choose the definition of planning which most closely fits the kind of long-range planning performed by his company. If none of the definitions applied, there was a space provided for the respondent to describe what does take place.

Part II asked what year the planning described in Part I was first used by the carrier. Part III had fifteen questions, each of which reflected some aspect of the long-range planning process. There were five possible responses for each of these questions, each representing a decreasing frequency of occurrence, i.e., A = always or very high occurrence. O = often or something less than always, P = periodically or some middle range of occurrence, S = seldom or not very frequent occurrence and N = never or hardly any occurrence at all.

The completed questionnaire allowed us to categorize carriers according to their commitment to long-range planning. A composite score was developed from the responses and based on that score each carrier was placed in a group. Group one contained all the non-planners, or those whose planning was for one year or less. Groups two through five represented increasing commitments to planning with group five representing a carrier with a highly sophisticated planning function.

Replies from the 498 companies represented a response of 56.2 percent of the 886 firms polled. Of the 498, twenty were completely unusable. Complete economic data for the full ten-year period (1965 through 1974) could not be obtained for 93 respondents. This left 385 fully completed questionnaires with full ten-year economic data. Of these, 298 started planning in 1965 or before and the others started in the years 1966 through 1975. The 298 that started planning in 1965 or before constituted a rather large homogeneous group and were the basis for this study. The others, though providing some interesting information, were too small a sample from any one year to be usable in the major analysis.

The data gathered in the study were deemed sufficient to answer the previously posed questions by supplying answers to four basic questions. The first is whether there is a relationship between the size of the firm, its commitment to long-range planning and its economic performance. This is really two questions in one. Do firms which plan perform better economically, and does the smaller firm have to plan as much as the larger firm in order to do as well? The second major question is whether geographic area of operation has any bearing on the economic performance of a carrier relative to its commitment to planning. Does a carrier in one geographic area benefit more from planning than a carrier in another part of the country? A third question is concerned with whether a carrier handles general commodities or is a specialized carrier. The question is, does the amount of planning depend on the kind of freight handled? Do the different types of carriers plan the same way, and do they perform the same economically? The fourth question has to do with the length of time a carrier has actually been using a planning function. It was supposed that the longer a carrier had been planning, the better he would be at it and the better would be the economic results.

The results of the study indicate that there is no relationship between a carrier's size, planning commitment and economic performance. The degree of planning does not seem to have any material effect on a motor carrier's profitability. The sophisticated planner and the non-planner appear to perform equally well. If we examine just the largest carriers, there is still no difference in the profitability between the planners and non-planners. Similar results are found from analyzing the medium and small carriers separately. The presence or absence of a planning function does not appear to have a bearing on carrier profitability.

Since motor carriers operate in different geographic areas, perhaps the circumstances in some geograpahic areas require more long-range planning than do other geographic areas. However, the results show otherwise. The kind of long-range planning applied to operations in various geographic areas does not seem to affect economic performance. Nor does the kind of commodity handled seem to make a difference in the planning result. Non-planners who handle general commodities do no better or no worse than other general commodity carriers. The same is true for special commodity carriers. Planners and non-planners perform similarly. Likewise, the length of time a carrier planned does not have an effect on how productive a firm is. Those carriers which planned for ten or more years do no better economically than those which planned for only five or more years.

These findings are a surprise since scholars and businessmen constantly endorse the planning function as vital to the organization. Just why the practice of long-range planning does not aid the motor carrier in his quest for greater profitability calls for explanation.

One of the major reasons for the establishment of a long-range planning function is to provide for the future uncertainties that the firm may face. The greater the future uncertainties, the more sophisticated the long-range planning efforts. The less uncertain the future the less the need for a strategic planning function because there are fewer strategic alternatives with which to deal.

If the external environment for the motor carrier has fewer uncertainties than those of other firms in other industries, then the motor carrier has fewer strategic alternatives from which to choose. If the motor carrier company is limited in its strategic alternatives, then it does not need a sophisticated planning function to guide decision making. Furthermore, if the company has a sophisticated planning system, such a system might not be necessary. The fact is that, although there are many forces that influence a motor carrier, the organizational and environmental realities are such that it is extremely difficult to effectively plan for these forces on a long-term basis.

One major force in long-range decision making in the motor carrier industry is regulation by the Interstate Commerce Commission (ICC). The specific effects of the Motor Carrier Act of 1935 which brought truck transportation under the regulation and jurisdiction of the ICC are reflected in three major areas: rights to serve specific territories for specified commodities, rates charged for services rendered, and the financing of the regulated carriers. The importance and impact of this type of regulation can be seen from the fact that even such important decisions as expansion of the territory served and routes traveled are not under the direct control of motor carriers. Even the acquisition of another carrier must be justified to the ICC. The implication of these realities is that most of the major areas of strategic planning are not sufficiently under the carrier's control to make planning effective.

A second constraint on long-range planning is the labor intensity of the industry. According to *Trucking Trends,* 61.5 percent of carrier revenue went for wages and fringes in 1973. The wages and fringes are, to a large extent, controlled by the Teamsters Union. This means that the management of motor carrier organizations has little control over a large portion of its total cash flow, especially over the long run.

The third constraint is transportation costs. These include trucks and other equipment, fuel costs and road taxes. Motor carriers have no control over fuel price rises or road tax increases. Inflationary trends tend to constrain management's ability to control equipment and other costs.

All this helps to explain why the motor carrier industry has a limited capability for strategic response. There are some lesser reasons that may help explain why long-range planning does not seem to have an effect on carrier economic performance. The first is that the profit of the industry is generally low. The profit range runs from a few percent below zero to a few percent above that point. The losers do not lose too much, and the profit makers do not earn very much.

This low profit profile may be explained by the fact that rates are regulated and in times of inflation there is a lag before higher rates can be instituted. Carriers have to bear the brunt of cost increases until they can satisfy the requirements for being granted a rate increase. Thus, the major strategic area of price setting is not fully available to the motor carrier as a strategic alternative in his planning, and this seems to account to some degree for the low profit profile of the industry.

Second, the industry is composed of many family-owned firms and many that are quite closely held. It is possible that the objectives of such firms do not include the maximizing of the economic performance variables we have chosen for this study. Though economic performance may be important to a degree, there may be other advantages accruing to the owners which are not dependent on, or which negatively affect, these variables. For instance, large personal salaries, company automobiles, and the like are often part of the owner's remuneration.

Third, research and development are less fertile for the motor carrier than for other forms of business. The R&D function, in the sense that it is found in other industries, does not exist in the motor freight industry. There is little that can be done in the area of product development since in effect there is no product except service. There are, of course, attempts at developing materials handling equipment and more functional terminal facilities. Innovative use of computers and communications devices represents an area of current effort. However, such actions are not likely to make dramatic impacts on a firm's long-term position in the way a new wonder drug would for a pharmaceutical house. Instead of R&D, the industry has been more concerned with lobbying-type efforts such as those to increase payloads through influencing individual states to increase their maximum gross weight allowance.

The conclusion is that the motor carrier industry is a rather static one. It does not change much from year to year, either in its financial performance or in its managerial approaches. It is highly dependent on the state of the economy, the economic health of its major customers, the cooperation of the regulatory agencies (both state and federal), and the Teamsters Union (both local and national). Under circumstances such as these, planning opportunities are limited.

If a boundary condition does exist that differentiates between those companies that must plan continually, plan occasionally, and not plan at all, it would be extremely difficult to describe or define. The reason for this is that the industry is really quite closed to environmental influences, and consequently management has a very small degree of freedom in the area of strategic decision making. In such a situation the best of plans will not be able to alter or perhaps even predict future outcomes. Those carriers which are economically successful are perhaps performing well because of management attributes which go beyond just the planning function. In addition, there seems to be strong intuitive feeling that short-range planning wields a greater influence on motor carrier performance due to the high direct costs of a carrier's day to day operations.

A final thought for the motor carrier who does not use long-range planning is that perhaps he should examine very closely whether he should institute such a program. For the carrier who is planning and doing well, perhaps similar results can be achieved with less cost and effort in the planning area. For the successful non-planner, we urge no move toward formalized planning.

4
Administrative Planning

In contrast to strategic planning, which sets up the mission, objectives, and goals of an organization, administrative planning may be defined as the process that structures a firm's resources in order to create a maximum performance potential. This is accomplished through both the design of the organization structure and the acquisition, allocation, and development of resources.

It is useful to view the total planning process of an organization in terms of time frames. Administrative management deals with plans of medium range, an undefined period that is usually shorter than the scope of strategic plans and longer than the typical 1-year boundary of operational plans. The advantage of adopting time frames is that they avoid the confusion that can be caused by using the same managerial techniques for the various levels of planning. Thus, although budgeting is generally considered a tool of operational planning, a financial budget that controls the acquisition of capital assets is, in fact, an aspect of administrative planning.

POLICY FORMULATION

A crucial determinant of organizational effectiveness is the accurate transmission of top management's mission, objectives, and goals and the means it has selected to achieve them, to middle and lower levels of management. This communication is commonly achieved through the formulation of policies. Without such policies, operating management has no framework for effective decisionmaking.

Policies are guidelines for carrying out an action. They establish the limits, ranging from very broad to very narrow, within which certain types of action may be taken. For example, a company may proclaim broadly, "It is our policy to fulfill our social responsibilities," or, more definitively, "It is our policy to provide 10 days of paid vacation time per year to all employees with more than 1 year and less than 5 years of employment." A complete policy manual explains how companywide and departmental goals are to be achieved by providing guidelines to the actions of managers in the myriad situations that crop up in the daily operation of an organizaton.

Policies are thus one element of the planning process. Since administrative planners deal with the structuring of a firm's resources, they should not become involved in minor policies regarding plant layout, merchandise display, the handling of incoming orders, the servicing of customer complaints, coffee breaks, smoking, use of company automobiles, or distribution of paychecks. The administrative planner should be interested in the major policies dealing with product-market aims, selection of geographic areas, and policies dealing with the major functions of the organization.

Steiner (1969) provides the following classification of business policy areas:

1. General Management
2. Marketing
3. Production
4. Procurement
5. Research
6. Finance
7. Facilities
8. Personnel
9. Public Relations
10. Legal

Within each area, he lists subcategories for which policies are traditionally formulated. For example, in the personnel area, Steiner lists collective bargaining and union relations, communications systems, employment and recruiting, equal opportunities, hours of work, incentives and bonuses, pensions, selection, personnel services, training and education, wages and salaries, and working conditions. Under marketing he lists products and services sold, customers, pricing, and sales promotion, and each of these categories is then further broken down.

The actual formulation of these corporatewide policies may be done by the strategic planners who then pass them on to the administrative planners for implementation; or, they may be formulated by the administrative planners themselves. The strategic planners may limit their policy formulation to product-market targets, growth goals, and control structure and delegate the task of drawing up functional policies to the administrative planners. Whatever the technique used, policies are prerequisites to the implementation of an organization's strategic plans. (The formulation of policies to implement organizational goals is illustrated on p. 351 of the Alexander & Alexander case study.)

ORGANIZATIONAL STRUCTURE

The communication of strategic management's goals and objectives via the formulation of policy guidelines provides the framework within which administrative planners may carry out their task. Ideally, the past experience of other organizations as well as theoretical research should have produced a set of prescriptions or rules for current administrative managers to follow in designing the structure of their organizations. Unfortunately, despite the voluminous research and publications that exist in this area, there is no blueprint that indicates which organizational structures are most appropriate to the successful implementation of specific strategies. The theories that have emerged from the research, however, are helpful to our understanding of organizational variables and the interrelationships between strategy and structure.

Each of the major schools of management thought has dealt with the subject of organizational design in a manner consistent with its theoretical approach. Proponents of classical management theory were convinced that the "universal" principles of management, which they had identified, would serve as the foundation for the most appropriate structure for each firm. However, critics of the classical school, such as Simon (1976) and Lowell (1956), pointed out the contradictions that existed among the various principles. They demonstrated that these principles are valid only under certain conditions. Similarly, the early behavioral scientists believed that organizational structure should be determined mainly by its impact upon human behavior and motivation. Of course, they interpreted this impact in the light of the assumptions they held about human behavior. Since they assumed that the nature of humans was to be social and cooperative, they believed that the appropriate structure was one that permitted employees to express this social and cooperative nature.

There is a general consensus today that neither of these two approaches is adequate for determining the "right" structure for a specific organization. Nevertheless, they have made administrative planners aware that principles of management as well as human behavior and motivation must be taken into account in the design of an organization.

Over the last two decades, research has shown that there is no best way to structure an organization. Rather, theorists have discovered that "organizational variables are in a complex interrelationship with one another and with conditions in the environment" (Lawrence and Lorsch 1969). Thus, they have been leaning toward a "contingency approach" to organization design. Since the situation of each organization is unique, the design of each organization must be considered separately, according to the specific tasks it is trying to perform. Nevertheless, the contingency theorists have proposed different kinds of structures based upon underlying patterns discovered either in the operation of the organization or in its relationship with the environment.

The British sociologist Joan Woodward (1965) studied 100 firms in Great Britain to verify whether a classical structure was a prerequisite for organizational success, as has been claimed by adherents of classical theory. Her findings were not consistent with the theory. In reviewing her data, she discovered that firms that operated as job shops and those that used a process technology seemed to function more successfully within an organic structure. This structure is characterized by a more permissive management, greater delegation of authority, less tightly organized work forces, and less emphasis on clear-cut, written definition of duties. On the other hand, the mechanistic structure favored by classical theorists and typified by elaborate control procedures, close supervision of production workers, rigorous application of sanctions, and voluminous written communications and procedures was found to be more appropriate for mass production firms. Woodward therefore proposed that the proper determinant for an organization's design should be the technology it uses.

In a study of 10 organizations in three industries, Lawrence and Lorsch (1969) found that the degree of stability of the environment in which an organization functions plays a major role in determining the structure of the organization. For an organization to be effective, its internal processes must be consistent with the external demands of the environment. (If the external demands are predictable and stable, the internal structure may be engineered to provide maximum efficiency. In a staple food plant, the same can of soup may be produced in a standard manner day after day. If the external demands are not known with certainty in advance, the structure must be made flexible to cope with the unexpected. In a hospital, provision must be made for emergency surgery needs.)

Lawrence and Lorsch considered the major aspects of structure to be (1) differentiation based upon the specialized tasks of the various departments and (2) integration of the activities of the organization. Their findings revealed that in a diverse and dynamic environment, effective organizations have to be both highly differentiated and highly integrated, whereas, in a more stable environment, successful organizations have to be less differentiated, but must still achieve a high degree of integration.

Administrative planners thus have several options to consider as they prepare to design an appropriate structure for their organization. They can research other successful firms or peruse the literature for a model to be imitated. However, they must realize that no single organizational model fits all organizations, and their choice of a model may not be the best. On the other hand, they may evaluate the various theories of organizational design—those from the classical, behavioral, and contingency schools of thought—and select the framework that seems to provide the best approach to their particular situation. (Consideration of an appropriate structure for the achievement of the objectives of Alexander & Alexander is discussed on p. 373-374.)

Although an organization will benefit from the inherent strengths of the chosen framework, it will also have to cope with its weaknesses. The inescapable problem facing organization planners is that their organization's philosophy and strategic goals differ in some ways from those of other organizations and so require a unique structure. Recognizing this state of affairs, the British behavioral scientist Albert B. Cherns (1977) identified the following 10 basic principles of organization design to serve as guidelines and to be applied effectively by the administrative planner in conjunction with any model or conceptual framework the designer may prefer:

Principle	*Explanation*
1. Compatibility	The means to design must be consistent with the end to be achieved.
2. Minimal critical specification	At each stage of the design, what is critical should be identified and only that should be specified.
3. Variance control	If variances cannot be eliminated, they should be dealt with as near to their point of origin as possible.
4. Multifunctional principle, organism vs. mechanism	Design the organization so that it can achieve its objectives in more than one way. Allow each unit a repertoire of performance.
5. Boundary location	Roles that require shared access to knowledge or experience should be within the same departmental boundaries.
6. Information flow	Information systems should be designed to provide information to the organizational unit that will take action on the basis of the information.
7. Support congruence	The system of social support should be designed to reinforce the behaviors that the organization structure is designed to elicit.
8. Design and human values	A prime objective of organizational design should be to provide a high quality of working life to its members.
9. Transitional organization	There is a changeover period from old to new that requires a transitional organization.
10. Completion	The closure of options opens new ones, and at the end, we are back at the beginning.

Based on the work of Chandler (1962) and subsequent researchers, it is generally accepted that strategy formulation and implementation are interrelated phases of a total process, with strategy preceding structure. This is analogous to the architectural concept, "form follows function." Chandler concluded:

> The comparison emphasizes that a company's strategy in time determined its structure and that the common denominator of structure and strategy has been the application of the enterprise's resources to market demand. Structure has been the design for integrating the enterprise's existing resources to current demand; strategy has been the plan for the allocation of resources to anticipated demand.

Chandler's work compared the history of organizational change in 50 large companies (including Du Pont, General Motors, Standard Oil, and Sears, Roebuck) during the century following the Civil War. Chandler found that "American industrial enterprises have followed a recognizable pattern in the acquisition and use of resources." He discerned four distinct phases:

> . . . the initial expansion and accumulation of resources; the rationalization of the use of resources; the expansion into new markets and lines to help assure the continuing full use of resources; and finally, the development of a new structure to make possible continuing effective mobilization of resources to meet both changing short-term market demands and long-term market trends.

Three types of organizational structure evolved from Chandler's four phases of organizational development. The first type is the entrepreneurial business organization, where the firm is an extension of the interests, abilities, and limitations of the chief executive–founder. Its structure is characterized by the dominance of one function (e.g., sales or production) and concentration upon one major product line. Growing volume led the entrepreneurial firm to develop into the second type, the vertically integrated, functionally coordinated organization. At this stage, many firms added a few related product lines, but the decisionmaking structure remained centralized in the hands of a few home-office executives whose skills were generally restricted to the function in which they had specialized as they climbed up the managerial hierarchy. The chief executive devoted much time to coordinating these functional activities. This specialization by function resulted in a high level of functional efficiency.

As its markets became saturated, the functionally oriented firms turned to the introduction of new product lines in order to maintain its growth rate. However, product diversification places severe strains upon the functional structure. Allocation of resources and coordination among the product lines developed into an extremely complex, logistical operation, and conflicts increased, especially at the lower levels of the organization.

The third type of structure evolved in response to this situation. In the multidivisional product structure, responsibility for the profitability of specific product lines was delegated to divisional general managers who also assumed the functional responsibilities for their product areas. Top management at the home office found that it could coordinate and control the overall performance of the firm by retaining responsibility for the corporate finance function as well as for some general staff functions such as planning and research. In *My Years with General Motors* (1972), Sloan describes how General Motors evolved into this third type of organizational structure under his leadership. The success of the product-line divisional structure was enhanced by some significant by-products. The position of divisional manager proved to be an excellent training ground for developing general management executives for the central office. The product managers discovered that they could not succeed in their profit responsibility by merely concentrating on their areas of functional expertise. Rather, they had to accommodate the demands of all of the functional executives in their division. This development of general management skills enabled the product-structure organization to enter unrelated product areas. Furthermore, product diversification lessened the organization's dependence upon any single product line. It also enabled administrative executives to plan rationally for the replacement of products reaching the end of their life cycle with new products that had been developed in advance for this purpose. Thus, the R&D function became an important tool for the administrative planner, providing the firm with an ongoing innovative capacity to cope with domestic and, in recent years, foreign competition.

In addition, another type of structure has come to the attention of administrative planners. Shortly before the start of World War II, Albert Einstein wrote a letter to President Franklin D. Roosevelt pointing out that the German government was investing significant resources to develop an atomic bomb. Einstein warned that it could have a decisive effect on the outcome of a war. The United States government took this warning seriously and determined to embark, in complete secrecy, upon a crash program to develop this new weapon before the Germans. The scientists appointed to direct this program soon discovered that the methodology required to split the atom required a completely new and complex technology. No industrial firm, government agency, or university research center had the knowledge or facilities to take on the responsibility for this undertaking. The government, therefore, put together a temporary organization—the Manhattan Project—which had the single objective of building an atomic bomb. Scientists, engineers, and other specialists were recruited from private firms, university laboratories, and various government agencies. Of course, history shows that the project was successful. After the war, the project was disbanded, and most of the participants returned to their previous jobs.

A similar challenge arose in the late 1950s when the U.S.S.R. sent a satellite into earth orbit. Congress authorized the creation of the National Aeronautics and Space Administration to coordinate the American space effort. As each space project was authorized, a team of thousands of specialists was brought together from scores of governmental, educational, and private institutions to work toward accomplishing the mission. Upon its completion, most of the team members returned to their original organizations. Some remained to serve on subsequent NASA projects.

This mission or project-type organization is applied by private industry in high-technology capital-intensive projects that are beyond the scope of any one firm. In an attempt to compete with American aircraft manufacturers, who have long dominated the market, the major aircraft companies in several European countries formed a consortium to jointly design, produce, and market a new generation of aircraft. Pooling resources and operating under a project-type organization, this consortium has already produced the airbus, which is being aggressively marketed throughout the world.

The mission-type of organizational structure has also been used within individual firms. Many large corporations have found their bureaucratic structure to be increasingly hostile to product innovations. In an attempt to avoid such bureaucratic obstacles, small interdisciplinary groups, known as *venture teams,* are brought together with the objective of developing profitable new business ventures or products and marketing them successfully. These teams report directly to top management and operate autonomously throughout the R&D phase. Once a new product has reached the full-production and market stage, the team is reintegrated into the normal organizational structure.

The case history of the Litton Microwave Cooking Division (George 1977) illustrates yet another application of the mission-type organizational structure. In 1971, this operation had a sales volume of $13 million and was preparing for the national introduction of its microwave oven. Based on a market forecast, management's long-range plan called for building the sales volume to $100 million in 5 to 7 years, an ambitious compound growth rate of 40 percent per year. Therefore, management had to create both a structure and a climate that fit the strategy of rapid growth. It considered replacing the existing functional structure with a product-line organization, but decided it was inappropriate for the then-small firm. In addition, the functional organization seemed to fit best with the managerial personnel. Therefore, management decided to maintain the existing structure and to supplement it by using informal teams to carry out the key activities of the company.

Each task team was made up of a designated leader (who was generally a member of middle management) and representatives from several functional departments; members of top management participated on an "as required" basis. Separate task teams were assigned responsibilities in such diverse areas as new-product development, new marketing programs, cost-reduction activities, facility planning, private-brand business, and new business ventures. The team members learned to be innovative and responsive to change; they were encouraged to be receptive to outside ideas and to newcomers. In brief, the task-team structure provided the flexibility required for rapid growth, while the underlying functional organization supplied the stability needed to assimilate the organizational changes called for by this growth. Based on this combined organization design, the division achieved a 60-percent compound annual growth, and sales volume grew to $130 million in 5 years. More significantly, the division's profit increases have averaged 75 percent per year, indicating that management was able to maintain effective control throughout the growth period.

One may conclude from the examples just given that, although the mission- or project-type organization will not replace the three basic structures described by Chandler, it may complement them in certain situations. Large projects requiring input from several organizations are prime candidates for the mission structure, as are corporate-level projects that do not fit comfortably into the functional organization.

FUNCTIONAL PLANNING

The close relationship of the organizational structure to the effectiveness of a firm justifies the structure's importance to management executives. The administrative planners must continually review the structure to insure that it remains appropriate and relevant to the evolving strategy of the organization. In addition, they must be prepared to make major structural changes whenever new units are added to the operation due to merger, acquisition, or introduction of an unrelated product. Likewise, they must be ready to change the structure in the event of a radical shift in strategy. Nevertheless, administrative planners devote most of their time and energy to the allocation and use of resources; it is to this subject that we now turn our attention.

The strategic planners enunciate the mission of the organization and formulate the long-range objectives designed to accomplish it. It is the task of the administrative planners to translate these objectives into medium-range plans that will serve as guidelines for the achievement of the short-range goals of the operating executives. Since organizational life in industrialized societies is characterized by task specialization, allocation of resources is almost always implemented through the functional organization, whose structure is based upon the grouping of similar tasks. (The major exception is in the mission-type organization, which is discussed on p. 107.) Planning for international operations may also cross functional lines.

In an industrial firm, the product-market function is the key element—it determines the scope of all other functions in the organization. The same principle holds true for service, nonprofit, or governmental organizations, except that a unique service replaces the product concept and a term such as *client* or *public* is used instead of *market.* The importance of this function is evident, for the organization exists primarily to supply a product or a service to its clients or market. The administrative executive will thus initiate his or her planning task through the product-market function. (The analysis of four alternative areas of action to expand the product-market scope is demonstrated in the Alexander & Alexander case study, pp. 352–355.)

Which is more important—the product or the market? This question is somewhat like the chicken-or-the-egg dilemma. Basic marketing courses teach that in a free society, consumers demand products that will satisfy their needs, and entrepreneurs produce these products in response to the demand. This is undoubtedly true for the basic needs of food, shelter, and clothing. However, it does not take into account the myriad of products introduced due to technological breakthroughs, for which markets had to be developed. For example, both television and the hand calculator are considered necessities by many, yet originally they were luxuries that a hesitant public had to be sold on. For our purposes, product and market will be considered interdependent.

Suppose that the strategic planners of an organization formulate as an objective the doubling of the sales volume. They then turn over to the administrative planners the responsibility for achieving this objective, generally advising them of the resources available to implement the plan. The administrative planners may consider many alternative courses of action. Forecasts of national economic trends indicate that the gross national product may rise by 50 percent over the next 7 years. If the firm's sales volume generally follows the GNP, the planners may calculate that, by simply retaining their share of the market, the growth of the economy will enable them to accomplish half of the desired increase. However, plans are still required in order to maintain market share, and goals must be established for each of the major elements of marketing—product, promotion, channels of distribution, and pricing.

In evaluating the existing product line, an administrative planner must consider where each product is in the typical life cycle. Every competitive product passes through an introductory phase characterized by a generally low volume and relatively significant start-up costs. For the successful product, a period of rapid growth then occurs, reaching a peak during the mature phase. As market saturation is reached, sales gradually decline, to a point where obsolescence occurs and the product is ultimately taken off the market. Although this process is inexorable, the planner can alter the shape of the life-cycle curve for the benefit of the firm by adjusting the marketing mix at various stages of the cycle. For example, repackaging of a product during the maturity phase often gives it a new competitive status. Alternatively, if sales are about to decline, the price may be reduced, or advertising may be increased, or both. The planners may also consider entering new channels of distribution in order to open up new markets. The specific strategy they choose will depend upon how the project stacks up against competitive products; whether the strategy will contribute to the planned profit level of the product or firm; and the importance of the product's sales to the firm's total marketing effort.

During the administrative planning cycle, a certain portion of the total product line will inevitably reach the end of the life cycle and will have to be replaced by other products if market share is to be maintained or enhanced. New-product development and introduction are major components of the marketing function, and they present a significant challenge to the ingenuity of the administrative planner. Each new product must fit into the concept of the strategic marketing plan. As an example of how the product-fit problem may be handled, the article by Wind and Claycamp (1976) that begins on p. 111 proposes an integrative approach for planning product-line strategy.

Many product strategy alternatives are available to planners, as shown in the following examples.

1. *Product mix.* Colt Industries Inc. is a manufacturer of specialty steels, machine tools, and a wide range of other industrial products. The capital-goods industry, of which Colt Industries is a part, is subject to violent cyclical fluctuations. Colt Industries has attempted to cope with this instability by developing a mix of products for which demand does not peak and ebb at the same time. Thus, in recent years, it has phased out such products as generators, electric motors, and piston engines and entered the industrial gasket and aircraft landing-gear markets. As a result, Colt Industries doubled its volume and more than quadrupled its profits between 1972 and 1977, a period noted for the low level of capital-goods spending in the American economy as a whole.

2. *Single product line.* The stable, mature firm that wants to embark upon a new phase of growth is usually counseled to diversify its product line. However, when the new president of Interpace Corporation found the company saddled with a string of marginally profitable operations in nongrowth industries, he decided to weed out these unprofitable products and to focus the firm's resources on the one business it knew best—building and other construction materials. To avoid the construction industry's notorious cyclical disadvantages, Interpace is expanding its building product lines into residential, commercial, and industrial construction. By exploiting the different cycles of each of these markets, the firm expects to achieve both stability and growth.

3. *Change in product line.* The difficulties many manufacturing companies encountered during the 1974–75 recession led their managements to completely analyze and reassess their business operations. As a result, Borg-Warner Corp. decided to drop hundreds of marginally profitable products and to replace them with entirely new product lines. Within a 3-year period starting in 1976, Borg-Warner supplemented its basic automotive component line with product areas such as armored trucks and courier services, fire-detection systems, submersible pumps, and heat pumps. It also moved heavily into service industries, led by its

inventory financing arm, Borg-Warner Acceptance Corp. During this period, its profit margin doubled over 1975, and its long-term debt was reduced by almost 50 percent.

4. *New product lines.* Within 2 years of taking over the reins at Standard Brands Incorporated in mid-1976, the chairman and president implemented a strategy to change the firm's image from that of a food-ingredients business to that of a consumer food company. His next step was to broaden the image to that of a consumer product company. The 70 percent of earnings that had been contributed by the company's branded foods and beverages increased to 90 percent. Plans call for expanded effort in the areas of convenience foods and nutritional snacks. The effort is being led by a greatly expanded research staff, which is responsible for corporate growth with the major emphasis upon new-product development.

If administrative planners are to achieve the goals of the product-market function, product planning must go hand in hand with market analysis. This analysis should include:

1. A demographic profile of current and potential users of the product, as well as of users of competitive products.
2. A definition of the total market for the product.
3. The major characteristics of the relevant market.
4. Current and projected share of the market for the product.
5. Strengths and weaknesses of competitors' marketing.
6. Quantity and value of market by various channels of distribution.

Depending on their evaluation of these market statistics, administrative planners may then develop various strategies. For example, in a market study of San Diego County, the Times Mirror Company, publisher of the *Los Angeles Times,* found that the population of the county was projected to rise from 1.2 million in 1978 to 2 million by 1985. In addition, the educational level of the current and anticipated population was higher than the national average, thus promising a favorable potential for a cosmopolitan daily newspaper in the area. The publisher therefore decided to expand the distribution of the *Los Angeles Times* into San Diego County.

The marketing strategy of Iroquois Brands Ltd. is to search out unexploited niches in the food and beverage markets. Its planners seek opportunities for unique products that can fill specialty needs of the marketplace. Management's philosophy is to select a $5- to $8-million specialty item for which the firm will be the sole supplier to the market rather than a $50-million line that can be readily copied by a company such as General Mills, Inc. or General Foods Corp. In pursuing this strategy, Iroquois Brands has built up a $150-million business including Champale, Black Horse ale, Angostura bitters, Major Grey's chutney, Raffeto condiments and delicacies, and Yoo-Hoo chocolate-flavored drink.

In the development of a strategy for the product-market function, pricing and promotion must also be considered. A pricing decision takes into account such factors as profitability, competition, the characteristics of the product, market or sales expectations, and consistency with product-line price structure. The options available for the promotion of the product include advertising, public relations, point of sale material, contests, sweepstakes, and special offers. The final decision on marketing strategy should thus incorporate product, market, price, and promotion factors. A classic example of comprehensive marketing strategy is the campaign conducted each year by the four automobile manufacturers to introduce their new models.

Once the decisionmakers at all the affected levels have agreed upon the administrative marketing strategy, the functional planners attached to the operating divisions prepare detailed specifications of which resources and facilities will be needed to insure that these functions coordinate with and help to implement the marketing strategy. Thus, production plans are drawn up to indicate how and at what cost the manufacturing function will contribute to the fulfillment of the marketing strategy. The production planner must take into account plant facilities and locations, technological developments affecting tooling and other manufacturing equipment, and production engineering for more efficient methods, planning, scheduling and control systems, and personnel and organization factors.

Research-and-Development Planning

Planning for R&D should be integrated into overall corporate planning in the same way that all other major functional areas are. In past years, many top management groups were reluctant to become directly involved with R&D planning. This was partly due to the erroneous notion that R&D activities were primarily related to basic research, which was accepted as a necessary obligation to prevent competitors from exploiting a major scientific breakthrough, but were too uncertain to incorporate into the planning process. However, with the development of applied research, it was recognized that the R&D function could be, and indeed had to be, coordinated with the manufacturing and marketing plans if a firm was to achieve its objectives. Given the ever increasing number of new products that are introduced annually, the R&D emphasis has been shifting more and more to product development and testing, product evaluation, and product application. The experience of Weyerhaeuser Co. illustrates how important the effective management of the R&D function is. Since Weyerhaeuser owns an estimated $7 billion of untouched timber resources, investors have been aware that even a small increase in the use of wood fiber by Weyerhaeuser could cause a significant upward swing in profits. Yet the Weyerhaeuser management was frustrated that the R&D operations were not finding enough new products to make out of wood fiber. It was discovered that since R&D activities were financed out of general corporate funds, line managers had little incentive to apply the findings that emerged from the R&D effort. Furthermore, the uncontrolled and semiautonomous structure of the R&D function resulted in the specialists developing expensive projects, which the line managers did not want or did not know how to put into practical use. In a major overhaul, Weyerhaeuser built a $40-million research center at its corporate headquarters in Tacoma, Washington, and revamped its organizational structure so that each major operating group has to pay its share of R&D expenses out of its own budget. Line managers now have a major responsibility for deciding which projects to undertake. The new coordinated approach is expected to result in a much greater involvement of the business managers in the forward planning and direction of research.

Manpower Planning

Another major operational function, whose importance to successful corporate planning has been recognized belatedly, is personnel management. Even though chief executives realize that their most important, most frequent problems are with people, they have often been reluctant to use their personnel departments for solutions. They seem to lack faith in the ability of their personnel managers to supply information and assistance in the area of solving personnel problems. In part, this is because personnel specialists have not been trained to think in terms of the entire organization. Thus, many executive-development and organizational-development programs have been placed with separate organization planning units. Furthermore, many functional executives have been reluctant to avail themselves of the technical expertise of their colleagues in the personnel department because they regarded the staffing of their functions as their own responsibility. However, it has become obvious that effective organizational plans must deal with human resource requirements; failure to employ the specialized knowledge of the personnel executive may be detrimental to the planning process and costly to the organization.

At the same time that the personnel administration function has broadened into human resources management, it has become clear that manpower planning lies at the heart of all rational personnel activities. The prime objective of manpower planning is to incorporate the planning and control of personnel resources into overall company planning. Another objective is to coordinate all company personnel policies. Since functional managers in an organization are continually making decisions that affect personnel, the human resource specialists must be responsible for keeping personnel policies consistent throughout the company. Manpower planning is based upon a systematic analysis of personnel resources currently available within the firm, which are then matched to the company's objectives as set forth in the corporate plan. This comparison will reveal whether the personnel required by the plan is available from the present internal personnel supply.

If it is necessary to recruit from outside the firm, a forecast of external personnel supply is required. Implementation of the personnel plan should include the use of personnel and programs for improving the efficient use of personnel; the supply of personnel covering recruitment, promotion, internal mobility, and training of employees to prepare them for the jobs planned; and the personnel policies necessary to recruit and retain staff, including working conditions, remuneration, and industrial relations.

Financial Planning

Both the value of the resources and of the facilities authorized by the functional planners can be expressed in monetary terms. Thus, the financial aspects of each of the functional areas discussed previously were an integral component of the planning process and were alluded to in our comments about profitability, cost, and budgets. In "Integration of Financial and Marketing Plans" starting on p. 123, Hawkins (1978) shows how the financial plan coordinates the plans of the various functional areas of a firm. There is a very close relationship between the financial plan and the other plans of the organization; nevertheless, the financial manager has a unique role to play in corporate planning.

All corporate strategic plans enunciate a profit objective, to be achieved in terms of a percentage of sales or a return on investment. They also outline the capital budget needed to support the strategy. The administrative planners then allocate the authorized capital investment to the major divisions of the organization and establish profit goals for each. The operational planners are responsible for the day-to-day operations of the subunits of the firm and must be provided with the necessary materials, labor, and overhead components. The financial planners have to develop a system that translates these three planning levels into financial terms. This system includes balance sheets, income statements, and other accounting forms expressing the formulated plans in monetary units. Financial management then uses this system to fulfill its two major responsibilities—keeping the business solvent and providing the funds required for planned growth. To maintain financial liquidity, the financial executives must insure the proper balance between working capital and current liabilities, between long-term debt and income to pay principal and interest, and between dividend payments and retained earnings.

On the administrative planning level, the financial planner is primarily concerned with capital expenditure budgeting. In accounting practice, an expenditure that is expected to produce benefits over a period of time, usually longer than a year, is classified as a *capital item*. Since administrative plans cover a multiyear time period, authorizations for expenditures for physical plant, equipment, and the like fall into this category. The most important techniques for financial evaluation of capital expenditures, which were described in Chapter 3, are the payback method, the return on investment, and the time-adjusted rate of return. These techniques are used both by strategic and administrative planners. The strategic planner is likely to apply them to major corporate projects, while the administrative planner will usually be concerned with smaller divisional projects or to components of larger projects. The capital expenditures authorized by administrative planners are formally summarized in the *capital budget.* This budget enables management to evaluate the extent to which proposed capital expenditures tie in with strategic plans, cost and profit objectives, and available funds and personnel. The capital budget also permits management to compare a group of programs simultaneously and to observe the effects of the capital expenditure program upon the total corporate cash flow.

OTHER ADMINISTRATIVE PLANNING

The growing complexity of large corporations and the evolution of new forms of organizational structure have expanded the range of administrative planners beyond the major functional areas, as discussed in the following pages.

International Planning

Over the last quarter of a century, international trade has become a major factor in the world economy. Large corporations that had been conducting international operations from headquarters in their home countries have developed into multinational goliaths whose strategic plans encompass a global framework without reference to a specific national base. Other companies, which still identify with their countries of origin, exploit the structure of regional trading blocs, such as the European Economic Community. For example, a company might operate one or more manufacturing facilities in one country within a trading group and export the finished product to other countries in that group. Smaller companies may simply export their products to foreign countries or license a foreign producer to manufacture and sell their products and collect royalties.

History records many horror stories of economic loss in which firms tried to duplicate the success of a domestic product in a foreign market without recognizing that social conditions, moral values, attitudes of people, legal requirements, politics, tradition, and education all have an important bearing upon business success. As international operations have grown apace, it has become clear that the best approach for successful management is to centralize responsibility for strategic planning and to decentralize responsibility for local planning and operations. Under this approach, top management can maintain control over its corporatewide operations while taking advantage of the superior knowledge of local management regarding environmental conditions that often determine the success or failure of a product or service.

For example, it is highly unlikely that an American-based manager would know that, in certain Asian cultures, white—our color for purity—is associated with death, or that green—a color we identify with freshness—is associated with sickness. How many native Americans know that the Dutch consider blue to be feminine and warm, whereas Swedes perceive it as masculine and cold?

Perhaps the most publicized incident concerning ignorance of local conditions began during the mid-1970s when international opprobrium was heaped upon the management of the Swiss-based Nestlé Company. The firm was accused of causing the malnutrition and death of numerous infants in Africa after it introduced a powdered infant formula into that market. Operational planners had ignored that fact that many mothers were not sufficiently educated to read the label on the can of formula, which instructed them to boil the water before adding it to the powder. The water supply in many of the countries was contaminated. A decentralized structure in which operational planning is the responsibility of local management is more apt to avoid such failure. (As indicated on p. 347 of the case history, the management of Alexander & Alexander recognizes that the environments of its various international markets differ from those in the United States.)

However, this formula for success leaves unanswered the questions of how and where to position the administrative planning function. In practice, the size and nature of the international operation determines the role of the administrative planner. In large multinational firms, the regional divisions are almost autonomous; administrative planning is left to the regional management, while contact with top management is limited to the strategic level. In these circumstances, the administrative planners will generally follow the functional planning pattern described previously. When the international phase of a business is on a small scale and under close control of top management, the administrative planner is more likely to operate out of corporate headquarters and to apply strategic planning techniques, modified as to time frame, to the foreign operation. The planner will also coordinate functional planning with local management. For these situations, the administrative planner must add an international dimension to the planning process.

Project Planning

The mission- or project-type organizational structure was first developed for projects that required the participation of several organizations and later adapted to intraorganizational activities that did not fit comfortably into the functional structure. For the larger project involving many organizations, a temporary structure resembling a permanent organization is established, and the planning function is implemented at each level as has been described. However, when a team structure is created within an individual firm, the administrative planners must add a coordinating component to their continuing functional activities. Since the project is a one-time activity with a clearly defined goal, the planners must insure that each step in the project-planning process is undertaken at the right time and meshes with the other steps in the plan. In effect, they must create a subsystem or a microcosm of the corporate planning process to deal with the individual project.

For example, a project team may be established to develop and introduce a new product. The planning manager will elicit from the marketing manager a preliminary product-marketing concept, possible level of sales, and proposal of an ideal target launch date. These preliminary data are submitted to R&D, which assesses the project feasibility and estimates the time to complete the task and the cost of research. When R&D has come up with its proposed version of the product, it joins forces with the marketing and development engineering departments to conduct a full feasibility study. Such a study comprises certain elements of market research such as concept testing, process development, packaging development, costing, and investment needs. The planner then works with marketing to develop a detailed marketing-plan proposal that includes cost estimates, test-market plans, a comprehensive financial appraisal, and an examination of the project in relation to total corporate strategy. Prior to submission of the plan to top management for the final decision (whether to launch or reject), approval is requested from the financial executive. Obviously, project planning calls for coordination by the planning manager at every step of the process.

Cost-Reduction Programs

As corporate profits improve during the "up phase" of an economic cycle, internal controls tend to be relaxed. Rising profits absorb increasing costs, and management is likely to approve more risky and less profitable capital projects. When the inevitable downturn occurs, an unprepared firm is likely to launch a crash cost-reduction program, which may do more harm than good. It is far more desirable to approach cost reduction as a continuing program usually coordinated through the financial planning and control function. Such programs are often inaugurated by a chief executive who joins a firm during a period of flat or falling profitability.

For instance, in 1977, International Harvester Co. hired Archie R. McCardell as its president and chief executive officer. Two years earlier, while he was president of Xerox, Mr. McCardell instituted that firm's first cost-cutting program, which resulted, during its first year, in the discharge of some 8000 employees. Similarly, during his first 6 months at International Harvester, the payroll was trimmed by 3000 employees. Mr. McCardell has declared that his goal is to reduce operating costs by $500 million or almost 10 percent within a few years. The plan includes cutting the corporate staff of 1300 by 16 percent and granting early retirement to 2200 middle managers who are at least 55 years of age. Moreover, structural reorganization has accompanied the staff reductions. Engineering, purchasing, and inventory control functions have been centralized. A corporate planning group was established to help coordinate the strategies of the company's major operating divisions, and the firm almost doubled its capital-budget program in an effort to reduce production costs. The program thus crosses functional lines and compels coordination of the strategic, administrative, and operating levels of planning.

In 1976, when Samuel Addoms stepped into the presidency of Monfort of Colorado, Inc.—the largest feedlot operator in the country and the twelfth-largest meatpacker—he made cutting costs the company's foremost objective. In his first 2 years in office, Mr. Addoms cut expenses by $10 million by restructuring production tasks, trimming the labor force, and revamping the truck fleet. By reorganizing work schedules, about 15 percent of the jobs at Monfort's Greeley, Colorado, packing plant were eliminated, resulting in an estimated annual savings of $6.5 million. Mr. Addoms hired an experienced trucking executive to run the transportation unit; this executive replaced Monfort's older trucks with new, more fuel-efficient models, and revised the routing schedules to enable the drivers to obey the 55-mile-per-hour speed limit (previously, drivers had to exceed the speed limit to complete their run in the time allotted). In addition he increased the backhaul business (i.e., hauling goods for outside shippers on return trips to the plant) from 40 to 80 percent of returning trucks within 1 year. Finally, Mr. Addoms placed tighter controls upon capital spending by requiring that all projects have a 4-year payback or better.

CONCLUSION

In this chapter, we have explained how the administrative planning function is implemented through the design of the organization structure and the allocation of resources. Although the resource-allocation process is normally carried out through functional planning, the administrative planner has become involved in multifunctional planning in areas such as international operations, project planning, and cost-reduction programs. The next chapter will deal with the lowest level in the planning process, operational planning.

REFERENCES

Chandler, A. D., Jr. 1962. *Strategy and Structure: Chapters in the History of the American Industrial Enterprise.* Cambridge, Mass: MIT Press.

The pattern of development of the American corporation since the Civil War as revealed by a study of 50 companies; includes four detailed case studies.

Cherns, A. B. 1977. Can behavioral science help design organizations? *Organizational Dynamics* 5(4): 44–64.

Cherns proposes 10 basic principles of organization design, which he claims are valid for any enterprise and all strategies.

George, W. W. 1977. Task teams for rapid growth. *Harvard Business Review* 55(1): 71–80.

A vivid description by the president of Litton Microwave Cooking Division of how the addition of task teams to his functional organization facilitated its rapid growth.

Hawkins, C. L. 1978. Integration of financial and marketing plans. *Managerial Planning* 27(2): 17–24, 37.

This presentation to the 1978 International Conference of the Planning Executives Institute develops a step-by-step marketing plan and demonstrates how the financial plan coordinates the completed marketing plan with the other functional departments. *Reprinted herein on pp. 123-134.*

Lawrence, P. R. and J. W. Lorsch. 1969. *Organization and Environment: Managing Differentiation and Organization.* Homewood, Ill.: Richard D. Irwin, Inc.

Lawrence and Lorsch demonstrate that the most successful structure for an organization is one that is responsive to the demands of its environment.

Lowell, A. L. 1956. *Conflicts of Principle.* Cambridge, Mass.: Harvard University Press.

An analysis of the contradictions inherent in the principles of classical management.

Simon, H. A. 1976. *Administrative Behavior.* 3rd ed. New York: Free Press.

Traces the behavior of people in organizations back to the limited rationality and biological limitations of human beings and enunciates a set of principles for organizations that recognizes these human limitations.

Sloan, A. P., Jr. 1972. *My Years with General Motors.* Garden City, N.Y.: Doubleday and Company.

The former president of General Motors provides a fascinating first-hand description of the organizational steps he took to develop General Motors into the largest and most successful industrial organization in the world.

Steiner, G. A. 1969. *Top Management Planning.* New York: Macmillan.

A comprehensive survey of corporate strategic planning.

Wind, Yoram and H. J. Claycamp. 1976. Planning product line strategy: **40**(1): 2–9.

An integrative approach is proposed for planning product-line strategy. *Reprinted herein on p. 111–122.*

Woodward, J. 1965. *Industrial Organization: Theory and Practice.* London: Oxford University Press.

As head of a research team, Woodward surveyed 100 firms in Great Britain to test the proposition that classical structure was a prerequisite for organizational success. Her findings indicated that technology was a major determinant for the design of an organization.

Planning Product Line Strategy: A Matrix Approach

Yoram Wind
and
Henry J. Claycamp

Development of a strategic plan for the existing product line is the most critical element of a company's marketing planning acitivity. In designing such plans, management needs accurate information on the current and anticipated performance of its products. This information should encompass both (1) consumer evaluation of the company's products, particularly their strengths and weaknesses vis à vis competition (i.e., product positioning by market segment information); and (2) "objective" information on actual and anticipated product performance on relevant criteria such as sales, profits, and market share.

Whereas much has been written in recent years about the use of product positioning in strategic marketing planning,[1] little new information has been published about formal methods of using the product's actual and anticipated performance characteristics in terms of sales, profits, and market share as inputs

Reprinted from *Journal of Marketing,* Vol. 40 (January 1976), published by the American Marketing Association.
1. Yoram Wind, "The Perception of a Firm's Competitive Position," in *Behavioral Models of Market Analysis: Foundations of Marketing Action,* Francesco M. Nicosia and Yoram Wind, eds. (Hinsdale, Ill.: Dryden Press).

to the design of a strategic marketing plan for the firm's existing product line. Several attempts have been made to use product sales (or, more explicitly, stage in the product life cycle) as a guideline for marketing strategy, including specific recommendations on items such as the type and level of advertising, pricing, and distribution.[2] Yet these recommendations have usually been vague, nonoperational, not empirically supported, and conceptually questionable, since they imply that strategies can be developed with little concern for the product's profitability and market share position.[3]

In the 1970s, some attention has been given to various aspects of sales, market share, and profitability as guidelines for marketing planning. Most notable of these efforts are the Marketing Science Institute's PIMS (Profit Impact of Market Strategy) project, which examines the determinants of profitability in the modern corporation,[4] and the Boston Consulting Group's product portfolio analysis.[5] These approaches do not, however, provide a comprehensive approach for product line planning based on all three measures—sales, market share, and profitability—which are integrally tied to positioning the product by market segment. The objective of this article is to outline such an approach, based on the development of a product evaluation matrix.

THE PROPOSED APPROACH

The proposed approach to strategic product line planning has two definitional phases followed by five analytical stages. The definitional phases relate to the determination of the strategic product/market area under consideration and the relevant measurement instruments. The analytical phases include: (1) determination of current and past trends for the product line in terms of industry sales, company sales, market share, and profit; (2) integration of these four scales into a single analytical framework, the *product evaluation matrix;* (3) projection of future performance given (a) *no* changes in marketing strategy or competitive or

2. See, for example: Gosta Mickwitz, *Marketing and Competition* (Helsingfors, Finland: Centraltrykeriet, 1959); Jay W. Forrester, "Advertising: A Problem in Industural Dynamics," *Harvard Business Review,* Vol. 37 (March-April 1959), p. 100; Eberhard E. Schewing, *New Product Management* (Hinsdale, Ill.: Dryden Press, 1974); and Robert D. Buzzell et al., *Marketing: A Contemporary Analysis,* 2nd. ed. (New York: McGraw-Hill Book Co., 1972).
3. For an evaluation of the product life cycle literature, see: Rolando Polli and Victor J. Cook, "Product Life Cycle Models: A Review Paper" (Working paper, Marketing Science Institute, Cambridge, Mass., 1967); Rolando Polli and Victor J. Cook, "Validity of the Product Life Cycle," *The Journal of Business,* Vol. 42 (October 1969), pp. 385–400; and William E. Cox, "Product Life Cycles as Marketing Models," *The Journal of Business,* Vol. 40 (October 1967), pp. 375–384.
4. Sidney Schoeffler, Robert Buzzell, and Donald Heany, "PIMS: A Breakthrough in Strategic Planning" (Working paper, Marketing Science Institute, Cambridge, Mass., 1974); and Bernard Catry and Michel Chevalier, "Market Share Strategy and the Product Life Cycle," *Journal of Marketing,* Vol. 38 (October 1974), pp. 29–34.
5. The Boston Consulting Group, *Product Portfolio,* undated brochure.

environmental conditions, and (b) a variety of alternative marketing strategies; (4) performance of additional diagnostic analyses to provide further guidelines for the firm's marketing strategies; and (5) incorporation of possible competitive actions and changes in environmental conditions into projection analysis.

The Definitional Phases

Phase A. Define the relevant universe in terms of the relevant strategic product/ market area. This requires determination of:

1. *The product* of concern. The product definitions should be clear and unambiguous, and in all cases they should include the relevant sub-categories of the product class at both the company and industry levels.

2. *The strategic market* for the given product and the key segments within it. Again, the more specific the definition is, the more operational the resulting analysis will be. For example, separating the domestic from the international market for automobiles (excluding trucks) can be the first step toward establishing the strategic market for automobiles. Within this broad strategic area, further segmentation can be undertaken, for example, by separating the commercial market from the private market. This can provide sharper focus and meaning to the analysis of the product life cycle of subcompact, compact, intermediate, standard, sport, and luxury automobiles.

Phase B. Establish the relevant measurement instruments in terms of units (e.g., dollar sales or unit sales), necessary adjustments (e.g., sales per capita), and time (e.g., quarterly or annually).

The Analytical Phases

Phase A. Determine and examine the current and past trends in product sales, market share, and profit position in each relevant strategic product/market area. Specifically, it is necessary to establish the following:

1. *Sales position* for the given product in the strategic market area. Two simple plots of industry and company sales against time are required, followed by the identification of the stage of the product in the classical product life cycle. Each product can be assigned to one of at least three product trend stages: decline, stable (which can in turn be separated into decaying and sustained maturity), and growth. The assignment of a product to one of these three or four categories can be based on the rule established by Polli and Cook[6] or on

6. The Polli and Cook approach is based on the percentage change in a product's real sales from one year to the next. Plotting these changes as a normal distribution with mean zero, they determined that if a product has a percentage change less than $.5\sigma$, it is to be classified as in the decline stage. Products with a percentage change greater than $.5\sigma$ were classified as being in the growth stage, and products in the range $\pm .5\sigma$ were considered to be stable. For the application of this approach, see Rolando Polli and Victor J. Cook, "Validity of the Product Life Cycle." The *Journal of Business,* Vol. 42 (October 1969).

any other explicit criterion. A sample alternative criterion is:

If the annual sales trend over the past N years is:

- Negative, assign to the *Decline* category
- 0%–10% increase, assign to the *Stable* category
- Over 10% increase, assign to the *Growth* category

The determination of the specific criterion and number of categories is, of course, the responsibility of management, and it is likely to differ across industries and companies.

2. *Market share position.* The market share of the company's given product in the strategic product/market area should also be determined. As with the number of sales trend categories and the criterion for category assignment, it is also the responsibility of management to determine the number of market share categories and the assignment criterion. For illustrative purposes, three categories and their corresponding assignment rules are as follows:

- If market share is less than 10%, assign to the *Marginal* category
- If market share is 10%–24%, assign to the *Average* category
- If market share is over 25%, assign to the *Leading* category

The market share figures that establish the three categories may, of course, vary from one strategic product/market area to another.

This stage assumes the availability of market share data. In many product areas, such data are available through services such as Nielsen or the Market Research Corporation of America (MRCA). In other areas, a firm may have to rely on expert estimates or relevant secondary sources.[7]

3. *Profit position.* The firm's profit position in the given strategic product/ market area must be specified. Again, it is management's responsibility to establish explicit profit categories. These categories—whether based on return on sales, investment, or equity—should be stated explicitly, and at least three levels should be established to distinguish between *below target, target,* and *above target* profit performance.

The three separate analyses of sales, market share, and profitability result in the assignment of each product, in each of the market segments of any given strategic product/market area, into one category in each of the three areas. This is illustrated in Figure 1, which also includes the plotting of the past trends in company and industry sales, market share, and profitability.

Phase B. Once the unidimensional analysis suggested in Phase A is completed, it is necessary to combine the four unidimensional scales—for industry sales,

7. Louis W. Stern, "Market Share Determination: A Low Cost Approach," *Journal of Marketing Research,* Vol. 1 (August 1964), pp. 40–45.

PLOT THE PAST TREND

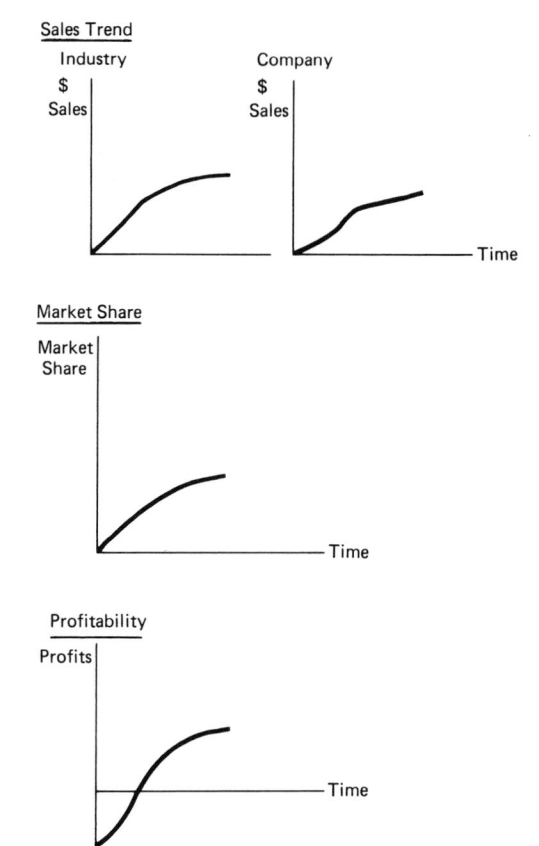

Figure 1. Establishing a product's sales, market share, and profit position (current and past trends).

company sales, market share, and profit—into a comprehensive scheme. The integration of the four dimensions into a single analytical framework constitutes the *product evaluation matrix,* which is presented in Figure 2. Positioning all products within this matrix, based on hard data on sales, market share, and profitability, is an essential input to all marketing decisions.

A more advanced approach might be one in which each of the four dimensions is presented as a continuous variable and not as a categorical one that is based on some arbitrary decision rule. Yet, even the simple positioning of a product within this matrix provides clear understanding of the current position of the product on those dimensions that are most relevant for managerial control. Conducting such an analysis for all relevant segments of a product/market

Company Sales		Decline			Stable			Growth		
Industry Sales	Profitability / Market Share	Below Target	Target	Above Target	Below Target	Target	Above Target	Below Target	Target	Above Target
Growth	Leading									
	Average								A_{74}	A_{75}
	Marginal				A_{73}					
Stable	Leading									
	Average									
	Marginal									
Decline	Leading									
	Average	B_{74}				B_{73}				
	Marginal	B_{75}								

Figure 2. The product evaluation matrix: a hypothetical example.

strategic area provides management with a summary auditing form that high-lights the strengths and weaknesses of the firm's product line in all of its market segments.

This picture of the product performance (based on current hard data) can be supplemented by a historical trend analysis of the changes in the product's performance over time. Figure 2 also shows a hypothetical path for two products over a three-year period. Product A has been in a growth industry for these three years. In 1973, its company sales were at a stable level, but they did increase to the growth level in 1974 and 1975. Its market share position improved considerably from a marginal share in 1973 to an average share in 1974 and 1975. The major improvement, however, occurred with respect to its profit performance, moving from below target in 1973 to target in 1974 and above target in 1975.

Examination of the performance of hypothetical product B, however, reveals a bleak situation. The product is in a declining industry; its company sales decreased from 1973 to 1974; and while it maintained an "average market share" in 1973 and 1974, its share weakened to marginal in 1975. The only positive sign is that during these three years profits did not decline.

Phase C. Although the product evaluation matrix provides a useful tool for controlling the performance of the firm's product line and answering the question "where are we?" it alone cannot serve as a guide for future marketing actions. To provide such a guide, the analysis must incorporate an orientation to the future and the anticipated impact of alternative corporate marketing strategies. This is achieved by the following two steps.

1. Project the trend in sales, market share, and profitability assuming *no changes* in the firm's marketing strategies and no major changes in competitive actions and environmental conditions. This projection can be based on simple extrapolation of time series data or on any other forecasting procedure used by the firm. It should be done for each product in the strategic product/market area and should provide a range of possible results between the most pessimistic and most optimistic forecasts.

A simplified example of the current and projected positions of two hypothetical products is presented in the first eight columns in the upper panel of Figure 3. These data can then be transferred to the product evaluation matrix (the bottom part of Figure 3) to provide a clear picture of the anticipated trend in the position of each product. At this stage (even without engaging in conditional forecasting), the product evaluation matrix can start providing some useful guidance for the firm's product/marketing strategy for each of its products in the given strategic product/market area.

Product 1 is clearly a poor performer. It is in a declining industry, with declining sales, average market share, and below-target profitability, and if nothing is to change it is likely to stay in this situation (comparison of 1_c with 1_p). Product 2, on the other hand, is in a stable industry and is expected to increase its sales (moving from a "decline" to a "stable" level in this category), while its market share position and profitability do not change (a move from 2_c to 2_p).

2. Since the future performance of a product depends to a large extent on the firm's marketing efforts, a *conditional forecast* should be undertaken in which the sales, market share, and profit of each product are forecast under a variety of marketing strategies. Given a number of alternative marketing strategies, a separate forecasting analysis should be conducted for each and the results of the "best" strategy (according to the four dimensions) incorporated into the product evaluation matrix. If no dominant solution (i.e., "best" on all four dimensions) is revealed, all "best" strategies are to be incorporated into the matrix, as illustrated in Figure 3.

Product 1 has two alternative conditional forecasts. Forecast $1'_{cf}$ suggests no change in the sales position (it remains in a declining industry with decreasing company sales), worsening of market share (from average to marginal), but an improvement in profits from below target to target. A second marketing strategy, however, may result in position $1''_{cf}$, which enables the company to maintain an average market share, increase its sales (from "decline" to "stable" stage), but produces no improvement in its profit position, which remains below target. Assuming that only these two strategies are available, management should examine the trade-off between maintaining market share position but being below target on profits versus losing market share but achieving profit objectives.

Product	Current Position (C)				Unconditional Projection (P)				Conditional Forecast (CF)			
	Industry Sales	Company Sales	Market Share	Profita-bility	Industry Sales	Company Sales	Market Share	Profita-bility	Industry Sales	Company Sales	Market Share	Profita-bility
1	Decline	Decline	Av.	Below Target	Decline	Decline	Av.	Below Target	Decline	Decline	Marg.	Target
									Decline	Stable	Av.	Below Target
2	Stable	Decline	Av.	Target	Stable	Stable	Av.	Above Target	Stable	Stable	Dom.	Target

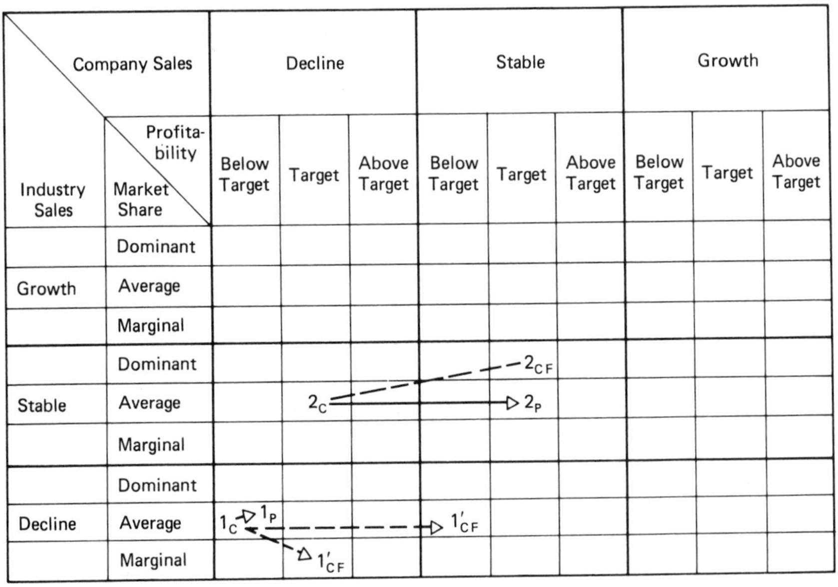

Industry Sales	Company Sales → / Market Share	Decline			Stable			Growth		
	Profita-bility →	Below Target	Target	Above Target	Below Target	Target	Above Target	Below Target	Target	Above Target
Growth	Dominant									
	Average									
	Marginal									
Stable	Dominant						2_{CF}			
	Average	2_c					2_p			
	Marginal									
Decline	Dominant									
	Average	1_c 1_p			$1'_{CF}$					
	Marginal		$1'_{CF}$							

Key: 1, 2 products   C = current   P = projected position
CF = expected position based on results of a conditional forecast analysis.

Figure 3. Incorporating sales, market share, and profit forecasts into the product evaluation matrix: a hypothetical example.

Product 2, on the other hand, has a single "best" conditional forecast that moves the product from 2_c to 2_{cf}. This suggests that the marketing strategy behind this forecast is likely to result in an improved market share position (from average for 2_p to dominant for 2_{cf}).

Phase D. To provide further guidelines for the firm's marketing strategies within the strategic product/market area, management may want to make additional diagnoses. Among the more useful diagnostic analyses are those that relate to the competitive structure and the effectiveness of the marketing efforts of the firm. Some of this information may be obtained as a by-product of the conditional forecast analyses, but some may require special studies.

Some of the more useful diagnostic tools are those that focus on the product's competitive position—product positioning[8] and brand-switching matrices—and on the effectiveness of the various marketing strategies, that is, promotion, distribution, and price. These diagnostic analyses can be undertaken using simple graphical analysis (e.g., plotting advertising expenditures or number of outlets against sales or market share or profitability), or they may take advantage of any one of a number of appropriate multivariate statistical techniques, such as multiple regression analysis. Such an analysis could establish the relative importance of each of the pertinent marketing variables for determining the firm's sales, market share, and profits. This, in turn, could result in three critical equations—one for sales, one for market share, and one for profits—that, in the simplified linear case, would be of the form:

$$Y = a + b_1 A - b_2 P + b_3 D$$

Where:

Y = Sales, market share, or profits
A = The appropriate measures of advertising and promotion (e.g., dollars spent on advertising)
P = The appropriate measure of price (e.g., actual price)
D = The appropriate measure of distribution (e.g., percent of effective distribution obtained)
b_1, b_2, b_3 = Parameter values, which are estimated separately for each equation

Phase E. The analysis so far has not included an explicit consideration of competitive actions and changes in environmental conditions. To incorporate these factors into the analysis, a market simulation model is called for. Such a simulation can be developed for a given strategic product/market area and be based on four major phases, all of which should result in simulated information on sales, market share, and profit for each of a set of marketing alternatives. These four phases include analysis under the following conditions:

1. No competitive retaliation and no changes in any major environmental factors

8. Yoram Wind and Patrick J. Robinson, "Product Positioning: An Application of Multidimensional Scaling," in *Attitude Research in Transition,* Russell I. Haley, ed. (Chicago: American Marketing Assn., 1972), pp. 155–175; and Yoram Wind, "A New Procedure for Concept Evaluation," *Journal of Marketing,* Vol. 37 (October 1973), pp. 2–11.

2. Competitive retaliation but no changes in environmental conditions
3. Changes in environmental conditions but no competitive retaliation
4. Competitive retaliation and changes in environmental conditions

Operationally, such a simulation may be based on a large-scale consumer study coupled with managers' subjective judgments. The consumer study should be aimed at establishing the following input base:

1. Consumers' utilities for various components of any marketing strategy (benefits sought). These utilities can be derived from a conjoint measurement analysis.[9]
2. Evaluation of the products of the firm and its competitors on the relevant benefits.
3. Assessment of the possible impact of different environmental conditions on consumers' utilities for the various benefits and their evaluations of the available product/brand offerings.

A market simulation based on this, a similar,[10] or even a different, structure[11] can serve both as a useful planning tool and as a way of generating inputs for the product evaluation matrix. In the latter context, the simulation can result in estimated sales and market share for any given product under a variety of alternative marketing strategies, anticipated competitive action, and alternative environmental conditions. To provide inputs on the anticipated profitability, it might be useful to couple the market simulation with an appropriate subjective risk analysis or simulation.[12] Thus, information on all four dimensions—industry sales, company sales, market share, and profits—can be incorporated into the product evaluation matrix in the same way that the information from the conditional forecast analysis was incorporated into the matrix, as illustrated in Figure 3.

9. Paul E. Green and Yoram Wind, *Multiattribute Decisions in Marketing: A Measurement Approach* (Hinsdale, Ill.: The Dryden Press, 1973); and Paul E. Green and Yoram Wind, "New Way To Measure Consumers' Judgment," *Harvard Business Review,* Vol. 53 (July-August 1975), pp. 107–117.

10. Yoram Wind, Steuart Joley, and Arthur O'Connor, "Concept Testing as Input to Strategic Marketing Simulations," in *Proceedings of the April 1975 AMA Conference,* Ed Mazze, ed. (Chicago: American Marketing Assn.).

11. Philip Kotler, "Competitive Strategies for New Product Marketing Over the Life Cycle," *Management Science,* Vol. 12 (December 1965), pp. 104–119.

12. David Hergz, "Risk Analysis in Capital Investment," *Harvard Business Review,* Vol. 42 (January-February 1964), pp. 91–106; and Edgar A. Pessemier and H. Paul Root, "The Dimensions of New Product Planning," *Journal of Marketing,* Vol. 37 (January 1973), pp. 10–18.

CONCLUSIONS

A firm's major strategic product/market decision alternatives for its existing product line and the component products of that line in a given strategic product/market area are:

1. Do not change the product or its marketing strategy.
2. Do not change the product but do change its marketing strategy. This may involve a change in the type and level of advertising, distribution, and pricing strategies associated with a given positioning and given product attributes.
3. Change the product. This can involve product modifications either within the boundaries of the product's current market positioning or within a new positioning. Alternatively, it may involve no product modifications but rather a pepositioning. In either case, a change in the associated marketing strategy is required.
4. Discontinue the product or the product line. This strategy may involve an interim product or product line "run out" (milking) strategy, pruning of the product line, or the immediate phasing-out of the product or the complete line.[13]
5. Introduce new product(s) into the line or add new product lines.

Traditional product life cycle analysis provides little guidance for making these decisions. It ignores the competitive setting of the product, the relevant profit considerations, and the fact that product sales are a function of the marketing effort of the firm and other environmental forces. The objective of this article was to propose a way of overcoming these shortcomings by taking these variables into account and hence providing management with the necessary product evaluation information for making the above decisions.

The results of experimentation with this approach in the International Harvester Company are encouraging, and the approach is now used on a regular basis in the preparation of all the firm's marketing plans. It is our belief that following the suggested approach (whether using the suggested criteria of sales, market share, and profitability, or others) may improve the strategic product/marketing decisions of industrial and consumer products companies.

The proposed approach requires five levels of analysis, each with an increasing specificity of guidance, for the firm's strategic marketing decisions. The first level is based on the evaluation of the product's current position with regard to industry and company sales, market share, and profitability, and it provides the

13. Walter J. Talley, Jr., "Profiting from the Declining Product," *Business Horizons,* Vol. 7 (Spring 1964), pp. 77–84; and Philip Kotler, "Phasing Out Weak Products," *Harvard Business Review,* Vol. 43 (March-April 1965), pp. 107–118.

Table 1. Levels of analysis and specificity of guidance provided by the product evaluation matrix.

SPECIFICITY OF GUIDANCE	NATURE OF OPERATION	STAGE IN THE ANALYSIS
Lowest	1. Current production position on industry sales, company sales, market share, and profitability	A and B
	2. Projected product position on sales, market share, and profitability, assuming no major changes in the firm's marketing activities, competitive action, and environmental conditions	C-1
	3. Projected product position on sales, market share, and profitability under alternative marketing strategies (conditional forecast), assuming no major changes in competitive action and environmental conditions.	C-2
	4. The above plus diagnostic insights into the competitive structure and the effectiveness of the firm's marketing activities	D
	5. Projected product position on sales, market share, and profitability under alternative marketing strategies, anticipated competitive action, and alternative environmental conditions (based on computer simulation)	E
Highest		

vaguest and most limited guidance. The fifth level, on the other hand, provides detailed and specific guidance based on projected product position with regard to sales, market share, and profitability under alternative marketing strategies, anticipated competitive actions, and alternative environmental conditions. Table 1 summarizes these five levels of analysis.

Not every product/market situation requires the complete analysis at all five levels. Even in its simplest form (level 1) the product evaluation matrix goes well beyond traditional product life cycle analysis and offers valuable guidelines for product line management. Product performance information based on *hard data* on sales, market share, and profitability by strategic product/market units puts into context the commonly collected consumer-based positioning/segmentation information. The approach can also be applied to competitive products, thus providing management with an ongoing performance audit of its own and competitors' products.

Integration of Financial and Marketing Plans

Charles L. Hawkins

A presentation to the 1978 International Conference of the Planning Executives Institute, May 15, 1978. Dallas, Texas.

Good afternoon ladies and gentlemen. I am pleased to be here today to share some thoughts with you. My discipline, obviously by my title, is in marketing. From what I know in scanning the roster of membership, most of your backgrounds are not from marketing and even fewer of you have a consumer package goods marketing background. I believe we have a lot in common, however, and can mutually benefit from a discussion of how we approach marketing planning in a consumer products company like Dr Pepper, and how that meshes and is integrated with the financial planning of the company.

I would like to start with a few general remarks about planning . . . some thoughts and theories I have collected through practical experience, through attending seminars like this over the years, and from reading. I would next like to discuss the key planning assumptions which start the planning process in our kind of business. Then, I would like to focus on marketing planning per se and take you through some of the steps in that process. Next, I will bring them together to show how marketing and financial plans are integrated both in concept and in the actual putting together of each plan. Finally, I will share with you some concepts on the long-term conceptual integration of marketing and financial plans.

First, some general remarks on planning. Planning is a word familiar to all of you here, and I suspect that in this room there are many different impressions and meanings as to exactly what planning is. You probably have your own favorite definition or set of words which describes for you best what planning is, so I won't try to impose one on you, but I believe all of us could agree that planning deals with the future.

By the future, I mean not only future decisions, but future implications of past and present decisions. When we think about what is going to happen in the future we have to project the future consequences of present thinking . . . something like a present value analysis . . . in order to convert possible future events to a decision that must be made now in the present.

Hawkins, Charles, L. "Integration of Financial and Marketing Plans," *Managerial Planning,* September/October 1978.

I think a definition that describes planning as primarily a means of eliminating or minimizing risks is accurate to a point, but I also believe it is limiting, because one of the main purposes of planning is to provide a context for understanding the long-term effects of present or short-term decisions.

Is there a need for planning? In a consumer package goods company, such as Dr Pepper, I don't believe that planning will insure success nor does lack of planning automatically mean failure. Good planning and the events associated with planning are more closely associated with predictability and probability. Let me explain . . . without planning, our results can be fantastic, out of sight, good, fair or a screaming disaster based on coincidence or chance versus design.

Lots of companies operate without a clearly defined plan, and many of them do quite well, but it is becoming more and more difficult to run a business without a plan because the cost of being wrong is becoming prohibitive. Planning, then, increases the probability of success. It will not insure success, but it will greatly improve the odds. In our business, planning helps improve the probability of long-term success by insuring that short-term tactics are consistent with activity that builds the strongest and most profitable consumer franchise long-term.

Planning, then, forces you to take a step back to look at the forest for awhile instead of the trees. Most line managers are so immersed in the day to day operations of fire fighting, the crisis of the moment and the urgency of making this month's sales and profit plan, that we don't conscientiously and systematically take a look at the bigger picture, . . . where we've been, where we are, where we are going. Planning is the process which enables managers to control the future by anticipating it and managing change.

Another benefit of planning is the involvement and commitment of the people involved. Planning must always start at the top management level of the company. The chief executive should state the mission and provide the broad direction. Depending on the organization, this is very specifically and definitively spelled out, or it can be broader in scope and subject to clearer definition at lower levels.

By being involved in the planning process, senior management really has the chance to manage, if you will, in the sense of guiding the future destiny of the business. At lower levels, a formal planning system is able to involve a large number of people and, in doing so, makes them aware of what the needs of the organization are. A formal plan involves them in where the company is going, some of the alternatives that could be pursued, and provides an understanding of how their departments function within the context of the overall company plan. A formal plan provides a reference point for managers at all levels to make sure that their departmental plans and operations are in synchronization with the rest of the company.

A formal marketing plan can be very useful in bringing objectivity to a very subjective discipline. As most of you are aware, marketing is not an exact

science . . . parts of marketing are still very much of an art even in the most sophisticated of consumer companies. Because of that, people involved in the marketing function exercise a high degree of subjectivity in managing the business.
The discipline of a formal marketing plan forces management at all levels to put
their thinking into writing, which can then be examined objectively. Often,
this simply serves to confirm the logic and wisdom of certain decisions, but often
a good plan will uncover different alternatives and open new avenues in order to
meet the needs of the business.

Finally, a written plan provides a measurement and control tool. A written
plan can and should be updated periodically so that it becomes a dynamic working document with flexibility built in to be responsive to change.

To summarize these general thoughts:

Planning is future-oriented, and good planning provides a context for
understanding the future.

Planning does not guarantee success, but increases the probability of
success and leaves less to chance.

Planning forces perspective—a look at the forest rather than the trees;
marketing planning brings objectivity to a subjective process.

The planning process enhances communications and involvement of management at all levels.

And a written plan should provide controls as well as flexibility.

Now, how do we go about developing a marketing plan and how is it integrated with other functions?

As I alluded earlier, marketing planning is generally quite different from most
other planning that takes place in an organization. On the assumption that
financial planning is a process and a discipline with which most of you are
familiar, marketing planning differs in that it is not absolute, there are generally
an infinite variety of alternatives from which to choose, and very often there are
very few proven techniques or courses of action to follow that will guarantee
results. Now, lest you think I am telling you that all we in marketing do is deal
in nuances and abstracts, I would like to assure you that there are some systematic approaches to marketing planning that are in common use, and nearly all
marketing activity is ultimately financially oriented. Every goal that we set is
ultimately translatable into the sales or profit line. Increases in market share, or
a substantial improvement in brand name awareness in a given marketplace, are
only relevant if they support and help achieve the company's sales and earnings
goals. So that is really our starting point. Taking the direction from the chief
executive level, the financial goals of the company are spelled out and become
the key planning assumptions from which the marketing plan is developed.

These goals are generally quantitative and are expressed in terms of growth rates, return on investment, return on gross assets, earnings per share goals, and the like.

When the key planning assumptions are developed (and by the way, these are generally developed in conjunction with top marketing management so there is no surprise), we essentially begin two parallel planning processes . . . development of the marketing plan and the development of the financial plan. Depending on the company, these two plans are independently developed and then integrated at the end.

Obviously, several check points are needed along the way to make sure the left hand knows what the right hand is doing, but it has been my experience that marketing planning takes place as a separate function and proceeds to a reasonably finished state before integration with the financial plan.

There are pieces of the marketing plan which are elements of the financial plan, and there are pieces of the financial plan which are key elements in the marketing plan. For example, it is very difficult to do much meaningful financial planning until you have a sales forecast, and marketing alternatives cannot really be fully developed until broad budget parameters are set that are consistent with the profit goals of the company. So this kind of integration happens at many points in the process. The financial plan is at its very root a marketing plan. They must complement each other and be totally consistent.

Over the years the marketing planning process has been refined and developed by consumer goods companies into a systematic and disciplined process. Much has been written on the subject so that most companies have access to the general structure of the marketing plan process. In addition, there is a fair amount of cross-fertilization which comes when people move from one company to another, and there is some mobility in marketing management. As a result of all of this, I would suspect that there is a lot of similarity in the way marketing plans from different companies look even though the industry in particular product line [s] might be quite different.

Marketing plans are generally written for a product or group of products and then these plans may or may not be brought together into an overall division or company plan. In the case of Dr Pepper, the brand marketing plan is in fact the company marketing plan because they are one and the same. However, in recent years, we have begun to develop different marketing strategies for our sugar free Dr Pepper product. At other companies with which I am familiar, there are separate product marketing plans written for each major brand. For example, at Proctor & Gamble, there are over 50 separate marketing plans generated each year.

What are the steps in developing a marketing plan and how do these come together into a cohesive document that provides direction for the future? To answer that question, I would like to take you through some of the steps we have just gone through to develop a long-term plan for Dr Pepper.

The starting point for our plan is the situation analysis. We attempted to provide an overview of external factors which affect the economy, which, in turn, affect our industry and, which in turn affect our brand and the Dr Pepper Company. For example, in analyzing the economy we projected what we thought the inflation rate would be and the reasons for it. We looked at GNP, unemployment, discretionary income, and then attempted to make conclusions on these projections as it affected and impacted the Dr Pepper business. Next, we made a forecast of population and consumption patterns by age groups. This very directly affects Dr Pepper business because our consumption is not evenly distributed across all age groups, and we need to have an understanding of which population segments are growing faster, which are growing slower, and what we can do about that as it affects marketing plans.

We made a projection of soft drink consumption that takes place in food stores where approximately half of the business is done today, compared to consumption of soft drinks outside foodstores or on-premise. We took a look at governmental influences; recent decisions that affect the franchise system; legislation that is pertinent to non-returnable containers; what the government is doing regarding saccharine; ingredients; disclosure; full ingredients; nutritional information; and government regulations in packaging proliferation and standardization. We looked at trends in packaging, ingredient costs, changes in the bottler distribution system which will affect our business.

Now to be sure, some of this was imprecise and difficult to quantify; however, it did provide us with a starting point and with a context out of which we could develop some broad conclusions about where we want to go and how we are going to get there. We summarized these key external trends and labelled them favorable or unfavorable as it impacts our business.

Then we turned inward and developed the summary of corporate strengths and weaknesses. We talked about the strengths of our product, our name, our franchise system, what momentum we have in the marketplace, potential we have with the brand. We took a long look at ourselves to identify weaknesses. Some of the things we haven't done. Where our share is weaker geographically, where we are vulnerable from a distribution standpoint, where our bottlers are not doing what we want them to, etc. The internal analysis took a look at the company's financial position, and several other financial aspects as they relate to marketing. The summary of external influences, and internal strengths and weaknesses comprise the situation analysis.

The next step was to confirm and specify the overall marketing objectives. We have our direction clearly stated by top management of the Company. Stated in only two ways—increase unit sales at a rate of at least 15% per year, and increase profits at a rate of at least 15% per year. This fulfills the broad objective of doubling our sales and profits every five years. It also is a very aggressive goal because this means that we will have to grow at more than double the industry growth rate and either take market share away from our competitors or expand the category. Those objectives are very precise and they are measurable.

In order to act upon those objectives, however, we had to develop specific marketing objectives that provide the focus for our program. These include objectives in trial levels, distribution, share of market and other specific measurable goals against which the success or failure of the plan may be measured. When we are developing these goals and objectives, we try to express them in reasonable, realistic terms instead of wishful thinking. We also try to incorporate into the plan the method to measure the progress toward accomplishments of the goal, and establish a period of time for their accomplishment.

Next, we formulated the strategies to accomplish the objectives. These marketing strategies are simply specific statements of how we expect to accomplish the objectives in the areas of advertising, distribution, sampling, promotion, point-of-sale and incentives. We also stated strategies in brand development and how we will use research in order to help measure progress against our objectives.

It is important to recognize that the strategies I am talking about are really decisions. They represent what we won't do as well as tell what we will do. As such, the strategies represent criteria against which we can evaluate any particular program. Does it meet the objectives and is it on strategy? For example, in our strategy, we have defined our prime target audience as soft drink users between the ages of 13-30. When programs are developed, they should be de signed to maximize the consumption of Dr Pepper among 13 to 30 year olds. There is no question that a program designed to generate brand trial among 55 to 65 year olds may sell Dr Pepper—but it is not on strategy and should not be a part of our plan.

Let me give you an example of this to show you how this process really channels the planning activity and dovetails the thinking of the managers into a consistent plan. Our point-of-sale advertising department is responsible for such things as menu boards in Burger King, the Dr Pepper clock you see in the local deli, the illuminated sign that is in front of the miniature golf course, and the push-pull signs that are on the restaurant door. One of the overview statements was that we have been and are in the process of upgrading the quality of the materials we offer in order to be more competitive and to be able to get our material placed more effectively. In reviewing the strengths of the department that are relevant to this, we took a look at such things as our relationship with external suppliers who give us expert consultation in this area. In the weaknesses we looked at such things as areas where our competition has an edge. In planning assumptions, we noted that some areas of the country passed legislation that either severely restricted or prohibited the use of signage of one type or another, and we looked at some specific trends like the trend towards more out-of-home meals being consumed each year. Out of all of this came a specific objective. The objective is to increase the penetration of our point-of-sale material in fast food outlets. We spelled out specific goals to reach in terms of numbers. The strategy to accomplish this objective talked about the number of items we want to introduce annually, lead time needed in order to insure that we meet the bottlers' needs as well as work within reasonable timetables with suppliers, and a specific definition of the particular type of point-of-sale material which should be developed for this type of outlet.

Now to this point, none of this spells out what we are going to do. That is, what precisely are the recommended new items for 1979 in the point-of-sale area. However, it does provide specific direction to the point-of-sale department in developing the program for the next few years. We believe that this systematic, thorough approach to planning insures a higher probability of success.

In the point-of-sale area, it would be an easy matter for us to give no more direction than "Go out and develop some new point-of-sale material for next year." Chances are that the material developed under such direction would be fantastic, or it might be a screaming disaster. Without direction, however, we would not have any standard against which to assess new submissions for point-of-sale items. What if we developed five new fantastic point-of-sale pieces for grocery stores, but neglected to generate any items for the important and growing fast food segment of that business? A systematic, thorough planning process can really help us increase the probability of success of each and every element of our marketing plan.

The annual planning cycle is very firmly grounded in long-term objectives and strategies, and is much more detailed. It really begins to spell things out in detail, and defines specific programs that are on strategy and which will help meet the objectives.

I might add here that one of the keys to a marketing plan is to allow flexibility within the plan for change. If we thought for a minute that we could sit down in early 1978 and develop the objective, strategies and broad plan that would take us through the next five years, then we would be sadly mistaken. Flexibility must also be built into each annual plan, allowing for adjustments that reflect changes in the marketplace, changes in the competitive environment, and changes within Dr Pepper.

The first major element of the annual plan is the sales forecast. Expressed in gallons of Dr Pepper syrup within the overall national sales targets, we develop area goals. The goals are based on answers to questions like:

How fast can we expect to grow in high development markets compared to lower development markets?

What is the competitive climate in the North that makes doing business there different from the South?

Will the cooperation or the lack of cooperation from our bottlers in the

West mean that we can grow faster than the national average or slower than the national average?

Etc.

These kinds of questions are really a part of the planning process because they bring into focus that real world in each market we do business in.

The end result of this explosion of the overall sales forecast into the pieces, results in an individual sales forecast for each of the 44 defined marketing areas across the country.

As planning is dominant to marketing, so marketing is dominant to the other major business functions. The marketing goals and objectives can be viewed as the guidelines for planning strategy. The basis for effective corporate planning is the marketing plan, with its emphasis on sound factual analysis of the present and projection of trends into the future.

Marketing is the catalyst that ignites the other major management functions of the corporation. Using the marketing plan as a basis, manufacturing can now concentrate on: (1) how best to meet the forecast commitments, (2) various production capabilities, (3) examining resources and facilities, including the availability and prices of raw material and other components. These items must be considered at the early stages of planning to indicate any modifications that might be needed in the marketing plan due to insufficient production capacity or shortages of raw material, and the like.

The human resources of the company are then planned. Can the existing organization structure support the market and manufacturing plans? Do we need more people, less people? Where and how should our production and management personnel be trained and further developed? These questions and others like them constitute the major components which must be examined to develop the manpower plan. After these plans are developed, the essential requirements are reduced to meaningful objectives and then the financial plan is drawn to support specific activities. All during the development of these plans, which are being developed separately and simultaneously by the different departments, they are being done in an integrated fashion so that a coordinated corporate plan is devised. So pulling it all together, the planning process begins with marketing translating its requirements into objectives based on the companys' capabilities. These objectives and forecasts serve as guidelines to manufacturing which then establishes production demands over the planning period. The manpower plan is worked up and finally all of these plans are underpinned and pulled together through the financial plan.

Along with the other departments, marketing projects its manpower needs and costs, our departmental operating expenses and capital requirements. These plan elements are common to every department, but marketing adds one more: the marketing spending plan. These are the dollars that are put against the consumer, against the trade, and against our bottlers in order to generate the pressure to accomplish the sales plan.

It is at this point that we turn to the development of the tactics and the specific programs that are to be launched in the coming year. This is where we finally get into tangible programs, the ads, the promotions, the incentive programs, and the point-of-sale pieces that we developed to impact our business. These are the things that really bring life to all the words that were developed to get us there. They are the end-results of the planning process, but we don't begin to develop the first one of them until we have a clear understanding of our objectives and strategies. What we are trying to accomplish and how we are going to accomplish it. Each of these programs that is generated has a price tag to it, and we go about allocating marketing dollars in two ways. One, we ask each sub-department in marketing to put together the programs which they believe will accomplish the objectives and are on the approved strategy, and then affix a price tag to each recommended element. At the same time, we have a top down system of developing marketing spending dollars. The starting point is a cents per gallon allocation which is based on historical trends and approved by the president. It is also a level with which the financial department is comfortable in terms of making the profit plan. This cents per gallon allocation is roughly allocated to type of marketing activity and then is further allocated to geographical areas.

If all of the recommended programs added up come below or on our total marketing allocation, then all is well. Any remaining money is put into a reserve for allocation later in the year. Quite often, it happens that recommended marketing programs cost more than the total dollars allocated to marketing. In this case, we attempt to set priorities for this spending and determine where we can expand our contract. If we get to the point where we believe we need more total marketing dollars, then it is time for renegotiation with top management. Obviously, our overall guideline has to be the protection of the profit plan.

The sequence which I have just described is how we go about marketing planning at the Dr Pepper Company and how this planning is integrated with financial planning. I recognize that some of the areas I covered were only highlights and grossly over-simplified, but my objective was to try to headline the whole process rather than cover any particular part of it in detail.

In summary, the marketing planning process is a formalized exercise in decision making . . . deciding what to do, how to do it, at what speed and at what cost. The planning process starts at the top and provides direction to management at all levels throughout the company. Objectives that are properly set provide a measurement tool and a built in monitoring system.

The planning process begins with the marketing plan, and I described to you a somewhat lengthy process that we go through in order to define objectives and strategies. The process includes a situation analysis and identification of strengths and weaknesses, both outside the company and inside, a meshing of the long-range direction of top management, and then the development of fundamental objectives—where do we want to be? These objectives and forecasts then serve as guidelines to manufacturing and all of the functional departments of the company, and they are held together by the financial plan.

At many points throughout the development of the marketing plan, we are communicating with the financial department, as they are ultimately responsible for delivering the financial plan to top management and the board of directors. As I indicated, much of the financial department's role is that of coordinator—to pull together the separate plans from all departments. So, in that sense, the plans are finely integrated from the beginning.

But that is far from being the only way in which the marketing plan and the financial plan are integrated. Let us go back to the basic goals of the corporation—in our case, to insure long-term viability by doubling sales and profits every five years—or on an annual basis, to grow by 15 percent each year in unit sales and profits. It is quite obvious that the marketing and sales department is chiefly responsible for the first of these. And unless we send the Controller and his people out into the grocery stores, the financial department has little effect in generating sales. Obviously, we seek the analytical support and advice of finance to tell us the profitability of the sales mix, and how we can improve profitability by emphasis on one size, flavor or distribution mode. This kind of integration reflects responsible planning and management of both the sales and the profit lines.

Except as it relates to bringing in the sales forecast, few people think of marketing as having a strong influence on the profit line—or at least as strong as the influence on the sales line. We will have an effect if we overspend the budget—or underspend—but is there really an integration of marketing and financial plans in the long term? In a consumer package goods company, I believe the answer is clearly yes.

And the reason is because of a few fundamental concepts which inextricably link the financial and marketing plans of a consumer products company. And I do not think it is much different for service oriented or industrial products companies. I would like to credit Mr. Robert Prentice for this list, because I think it is a good one. Here are the concepts:

1. To generate profit over an extended period, a brand must build a strong consumer franchise. It must establish a significant lasting value in the minds of an important segment of consumers.

2. Value, per se, is not enough. Consumers must also believe that the brand's value is worth the price. If they do not, the marketer will have to reduce the price—or increase the value—to the point where they are willing to buy it—to the point where consumers believe that value and price are in balance. If a high value is not established in the consumer's mind, a price reduction will affect profits.

3. A brand's share of market at any given time reflects how consumers perceive its price/value relationship in comparison with other brands.

4. The consumer arrives at his or her perception of a brand's value by experience with the product and its unique qualities and the satisfaction it provides. But a lot depends on the *ideas* the consumer gets about the brand which make it uniquely different—in some important respects—from competitive brands. These ideas come from the brand name, how it is positioned, the package and the various marketing activities that implant unique and meaningful ideas about the brand.

To the extent that the marketing plan reflects these principles, then it is truly integrated with the financial plan. A few examples will hopefully help to clarify what I am talking about and make the concepts more meaningful.

These are examples of marketing activities which build a consumer franchise and maximize long-term profitability by making the brand less vulnerable to short-term competitive tactics and less dependent on price, by enhancing the perceived value of the brand.

Advertising is the most visible and probably the best technique. What you say and how you say it is every bit as important as how much you spend. A lot of advertising does a poor job in this respect, I will admit, but for implanting the basic qualities and uniqueness about your product in consumers' minds, advertising is a very valuable tool. Under advertising, I include media advertising, point-of-sale advertising, and other paid means of getting your product name and message in front of the consumer.

Sampling is one of the most effective ways to gain consumer acceptance by trial. The proof of the pudding is in the eating, or in our case, the drinking.

Service Material that enhances the image of the product and establishes its uniqueness—such as recipes, educational material—are also important consumer franchise building activities.

They all have something in common: (1) they build long-term brand preference and (2) they help generate short-term sales.

All other activities in which marketing engages are generally meant for the latter. Their job is to accelerate the buying decision, to generate immediate sales. But they generally do not implant unique and important ideas about the brand in the consumer's mind. Instead, they simply reduce the price, or add temporary extraneous value (as in the case of premiums or contests), or help obtain retail distribution or cooperation.

These are important and necessary functions—but they do not register unique and important ideas about the brand in the mind.

When a marketing department is oriented toward the long-term—toward consumer franchise building activities which build brand preference and make a brand less vulnerable to price cutting and other short-term competitive activity, then it is integrated with the chief financial goal of maximizing long-term profitability.

To summarize, marketing and financial plans are integrated both conceptually and practically in the preparation of each. The controller's prime goal of maximizing long-term profits is precisely the goal of marketing.

To the extent that marketing plans for and manages its expenditures over time to insure that a higher and higher percentage of marketing dollars are spent in consumer franchise building activities, then the odds are considerably higher that long-term profitability will be maximized.

5
Operational Planning

Operational planners—the managers of a department or division—usually operate in time frames of up to 1 year. They are responsible for the efficient day-to-day use of the resources allocated to their area of operation, and they commonly carry out this responsibility within the framework of an operating budget. For example, a production manager may have to produce x units over the next 6 months. Furthermore, operational managers have a major advantage over strategic and administrative planners. Due to the short time span of the operating period, the degree of certainty of the information used by operational planners is far greater than with longer-range plans. As a result, many tools and techniques have been developed that are of great value to the operational planner, although they are generally not inappropriate for strategic and administrative plans.

As discussed in Chapter 4, functional planning is most applicable on the operational level. However, operational planning depends largely upon methodology; therefore, this chapter offers a comprehensive review of the tools and techniques available to the operational planner. Chapter 6, which deals with implementation and control, demonstrates their applicability to specific functions.

Certain types of operational plans have characteristics that are typical of strategic or administrative plans. For example, a short-range plan for product improvement or for market penetration by a division of a large firm may use the same planning elements as those used in strategic and administrative plans. Since such a planning approach has been covered in some detail in Chapters 3 and 4, the emphasis here will be on short-run planning techniques that are used for the most part by operational planners. However, because the use of planning techniques at the three planning levels overlaps, it is worthwhile to highlight the major differences between strategic and operational decisions. The following list is drawn from Steiner and Miner (1977) whose analysis was based on the work of Anthony (1964).

1. *Uncertainty*. Uncertainty is usually much greater in formulating strategy than when developing operating plans. Also, risks are more easily assessed for operational plans.

2. *Time horizons.* Operational planning covers a shorter time span than does most strategic planning.

3. *Nature of problems.* Operational problems are more structured and repetitive than strategic problems.

4. *Regularity.* Operational plans are generally developed over a periodic cycle with a fixed time schedule, such as the annual budget process. Strategic planning should be a continuous process, but its timing is determined by stimuli entering from the external environment at random, such as new opportunities and threats.

5. *Range of alternatives.* Strategic planners must choose from a far greater range of alternatives than operational planners.

6. *Detail.* Strategies are broad and have fewer details than operational plans.

7. *Reference.* Operational plans are formulated within and in pursuit of strategies.

8. *Information needs.* Formulating strategy requires large amounts of information derived from and relating to areas of knowledge outside the corporation. Operational information needs rely more heavily on internally generated data and involve greater use of historical information.

9. *Level of conduct.* Strategic plans are developed at the highest levels of management. Operational plans are employed at and relate to lower levels of management.

10. *Point of view.* Strategies are formulated from a corporate point of view, whereas operational plans are developed principally from a functional point of view.

OPERATING BUDGET

The budget is the major tool for implementing strategy. To be effective, it must function simultaneously as a planning tool, a coordinating tool, and a control tool. As a planning tool, it sets forth the anticipated results of the operations of a firm or of a subunit of the firm over a specific period of time. It thus provides both a target and a standard for those operating under the budget. The principal benefits of budgeting as a planning tool are:

- *Budgeting aids planning by charting the expected course of business operations.* Careful consideration is given to the general business climate, the future level of operations within the industry, and the firm's share of the industry's sales. Without budgeting, planning often takes the form of guesses made without considering all of the available information.
- *Budget plans are reliable because responsibility for their formulation is clearly defined.* The assignment of definite responsibility for a plan to each operating manager encourages precise thinking and careful evaluation.

- *Establishing a budget draws management's attention to alternative courses of action long before it has to decide which course to pursue.* This approach allows careful consideration to be given to all available possibilities. Furthermore, the mere awareness of long-term goals gives management a sounder basis for deciding short-term goals and making day-to-day decisions. These decisions are no longer made on a haphazard day-to-day basis. Budgeting coordinates each activity of the company with all others. A sales goal, for example, cannot be established without consideration of the productive capacity of the plant. On the other hand, budgeted production depends upon the goals established in the sales budget. Interdependence of all phases of the business is emphasized. Each department's operations are integrated within the overall plan of the business unit.
- *Budgetary planning fosters a spirit of cooperation.* All supervisory personnel participate in formulation of a budget and thus are personally involved in the outcome of the firm's operations. The budget therefore serves as a tool to enlist maximum cooperation of supervisory personnel.

The most useful budget is composed of individual budgets covering all phases of a business' operations: sales, production, purchases, production-department expense, service-department expense, etc. The larger the number of departmental budgets, the greater is the participation of supervisors in the establishment of the overall budget; furthermore, greater control is exercised if the unit of assigned responsibility is small. The development of a budget begins as far down the line of authority as possible. Supervisors prepare initial estimates for their departments. Such estimates are then converted into estimates for the larger units; these estimates are coordinated, in turn, into the overall plan for the firm.

TYPES OF BUDGETS

There are three types of budgets that can be used in developing a planning budget: the appropriation budget, the fixed budget, and the variable budget.

The *appropriation budget* shows the amount of money that can be spent on a particular activity during a given period of time. Usually planned at the beginning of the year, it consists of a fixed amount for that year. Appropriation budgets are used, for example, to control government expenditures. Advertising and R&D budgets are examples of appropriation budgets used in business.

The *fixed budget* is unchanging. Once a level of activity is determined (e.g., x units of sales, x units of production) the fixed budget is prepared for expenses at that one level only. If the volume of activity changes, the actual expense can be compared only with the figures established in the budget. Obviously, a fixed budget has limited value if the level of activity changes, since most expenses are affected by changes in volume. For example, assume a sales projection of $1 million and a sales commission rate of 5 percent. Under a fixed budget system, the sales commission expense would be budgeted at $50,000. If actual sales then turned out to be $1.2 million, the commission expense would be $60,000, and the budget report would show an unfavorable variance (unjustified additional expense) of $10,000 (i.e., $60,000—$50,000). However, $60,000 is still only 5 percent of actual sales and is perfectly justified.

The *variable expense budget* is a refinement of the fixed budget. It is constructed so that expenses can be adjusted as the level of activity changes. The variable expense budget recognizes that some expenses do not remain constant, but are affected by changes in production or sales. Variable expense budget construction involves (1) an analysis of the amount in each expense account; (2) its breakdown into fixed, variable, or semivariable components; and (3) the development of a formula by which each expense can be adjusted to the actual level of the activity.

CONCEPTS OF VARIABLE BUDGETING

Classes of Cost

All costs and expenses are dependent upon the passing of time or the level of activity, or both. They fall into three categories: fixed, variable, and semivariable.

Fixed costs are time costs, and they tend to remain constant within a certain range of activity. It is incorrect to assume that fixed costs will remain the same at all possible operating capacities. However, within relevant range, fixed costs generally will not vary. For example, it costs a firm x dollars per month to maintain an electric generator—where x is a fixed cost. The generator can furnish up to 1000 kilowatts of electricity. If the firm uses from 0 to 1000 kilowatts—i.e., the relevant range—x remains fixed. If 1500 kilowatts are needed one month, however, the firm must put another generator into operation, and generating costs would go to $2x$.

Although total fixed costs remain the same, fixed cost per unit of output declines with increased production. Fixed costs usually include supervisory salaries, rent, depreciation, insurance, and taxes.

Variable costs, on the other hand, change proportionately with changes in plant activity. Variable costs do not vary proportionately with activity from zero to full capacity, but their variability must be considered within the normal range of plant operations. A plant may have a capacity of 1000 units per day, but its normal range may be from 700 to 900 units per day. The planner is thus not interested in theoretical cost variations that may occur between 0 and 700 units per day, but focuses on the variability of costs in the range between 700 and 900 units per day.

In order to measure variable costs as they apply to some function or product, they must be related to a measure of plant activity that closely parallels the particular cost. This factor is called the *factor of variability*. Variable cost per unit of output is constant within the relevant range of plant activity. If a salesperson earns 5 percent of each sales dollar, then the commission expense is always directly proportional to sales. Thus, sales are a factor of variability for the commission expense. In most situations, raw materials and direct labor are treated as variable costs.

Semivariable costs are composed of both fixed and variable elements. They increase or decrease with the level of activity, but not proportionately. The most difficult problems that arise in constructing a variable budget are created by the semivariable costs. For example, invoices from an electric utility or the telephone company contain a fixed charge plus a variable amount depending on the volume of activity for the period.

Factor of Variability

As mentioned previously, the factor of variability refers to a measure of plant activity that is most closely related to a particular expense. In an ideal situation for preparing an accurate budget, the expense and measure of activity are directly proportionate to one another.

The most commonly suggested factors of variability are *direct labor hours, machine hours, raw materials used,* and *departmental production.* Before selecting an appropriate factor of variability, the operational planner should consider the following points:

1. The factor of variability that causes costs to vary. For example, past experience has shown that for every 1000 machine-hours it has used, a firm has spent $100 on maintenance parts. If the firm expects to use 8000 machine-hours next month, maintenance-parts expense would be budgeted at $800. If the following months call for machine use of 10,000 hours, $1000 would be budgeted for maintenance parts.
2. The factor of variability that is most sensitive to changes in volume of activity in the plant.
3. The factor of variability that is both easy to understand and measure.

Thus, machine hours used may be the most reasonable factor of variability for the expenditure of maintenance parts, while direct labor hours may be the appropriate measure of variability for indirect labor expense.

Once a factor has been selected for the variable budget, it should be used only as long as it remains the most applicable factor of variability. If the production process changes or newer machines are introduced, it may be necessary to select a different factor.

Determination of Cost Variability

After a factor of variability has been selected for a particular cost center or department, it is necessary to study each expense item to decide whether it is fixed, variable, or semivariable. The literature on budgeting describes some commonly found techniques for dealing with semivariable expenses. These methods are basically statistical in nature. (In "Variable Budgeting for Financial Planning and Control," which begins on p. 163, Mullis [1975] describes how variable budgeting is used for financial planning and control.)

BREAK-EVEN ANALYSIS

It would be frustrating to complete a planning budget and then find that a product selected for a special promotion during the year was uneconomical to produce or market. Break-even analysis is helpful in making decisions regarding changes in sales mix, sales price, sales quantities, and fixed or variable costs. (In the article beginning on p. 157, Harold Klipper illustrates how break-even analysis helps to explain a variation in gross profit caused by product-mix changes.)

The value of break-even analysis is based upon two assumptions. First, fixed and variable costs must be determined for use in the budget. Second. the factor of variable cost must have been selected and computed with accuracy. Break-even analysis is of limited value if the variable expense budgets are prepared haphazardly.

Procedure

Two procedures can be used in break-even analysis: *graphic* and *mathematical*. The 1980 planning budget for the Brown Tool Company illustrates these procedures.

Brown Tool Company
Condensed Budgeted Statement of Income
For the Year Ending December 31, 1980

Sales			$1,000,000
Budgeted costs	*Fixed*	*Variable*	
Materials	–	$100,000	
Labor	–	$325,000	
Manufacturing expense	$125,000	$ 75,000	
Selling expense	$100,000	$ 75,000	
Administrative expense	$ 75,000	$ 25,000	
Totals	$300,000	$600,000	$ 900,000
Budgeted income			$ 100,000

The break-even point is computed as follows:

$$\text{Break-even point} = \frac{\text{Fixed Costs}}{1 - \dfrac{\text{Variable Costs}}{\text{Sales}}}$$

Thus, for the Brown Tool Company:

$$\text{Break-even Point} = \frac{\$300,000}{1 - \dfrac{\$600,000}{\$1,000,000}}$$

$$= \frac{\$300,000}{1 - 0.60}$$

$$= \$750,000$$

This computation can be verified as follows:

Break-even sales	$750,000
Less fixed costs	- $300,000
Less variable costs (0.60 × $750,000)	- $450,000
Net profit	0

The break-even point is illustrated in Figure 5-1. The vertical scale represents revenue cost and the horizontal scale shows sales volume, both in thousands of dollars. The three lines that represent fixed, total, and variable costs were located as follows. First, three points are plotted on the cost and revenue scale at sales volume: the point for fixed costs at $300,000; for total costs at $900,000; and for sales at $1 million. The fixed-cost line is drawn horizontally through the fixed-cost point of $300,000. It is assumed that these costs would remain even if production were zero. The total-cost line is drawn through the total-cost point ($900,000) to the point at which the fixed-cost line intersects the vertical scale ($300,000). The sales line is drawn from the budget sales point ($1 million) to the zero point. The point at which the total-cost and sales lines intersect is the break-even point. As shown in Figure 5-1, the break-even point for the Brown Tool Company is approximately $750,000.

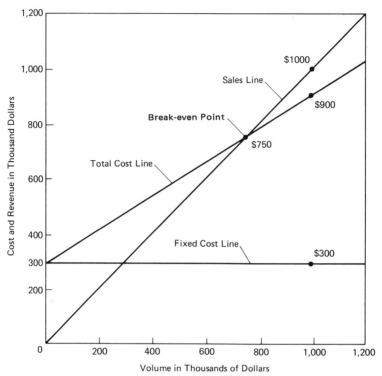

Figure 5–1. Break-even analysis, Brown Tool Company.

The Relevant Range

Break-even analysis serves as a useful guide to budget preparation within a certain range of plant activity called the *relevant range*. Break-even analysis indicates the level of fixed costs and the movement of variable costs within the relevant range. Different conditions may exist outside this range, which would change the relationship of the fixed and variable costs.

It should be apparent to the reader that the preparation of the planning budget is not based on one set of assumptions. Rather, the planning budget must be flexible to meet changed conditions—it cannot be based upon an unchanging plan.

SALES BUDGET

The operations of a company depend upon sound sales estimates. It is difficult to plan purchases or estimate direct labor requirements accurately if the sales budget has been constructed on a hit-or-miss basis. Thus, preparing an accurate sales budget is the first step in the preparation of a planning budget. The accuracy of the budget depends not only on careful preparation, but also on the effort expended by the sales force to attain its goals. The executive in charge of sales is usually responsible for developing the sales budget. (The importance attached to forecasting by the management of Alexander & Alexander is discussed on pp. 349–350 and 355–358.)

Long-Range vs. Short-Range Planning

In establishing a sales budget, planners must consider both the long- and short-range plans of the company. The purpose of long-range planning is to maximize profits over a number of years. Long-range objectives include introducing new products, exploring territories for new and existing products, and improving selling methods. Short-range planning, on the other hand, involves the preparation of a budget for the current year. One goal of short-range planning is to maximize annual profits. Often, however, a far-reaching program may reduce the current year's profits to accomplish long-range plans. For example, introducing a new product group may require extensive research-and-development expenditures in one year, thus reducing profits, yet the payoff may come in subsequent years.

In long-range planning, it is important to analyze external factors. For instance, in preparing sales forecasts, marketing planners must consider economic trends by making use of appropriate economic indicators (e.g., gross national product, inflation rate, etc.). Such an analysis leads to the formulation of a sales policy that guides operational planning in the areas of product line, pricing, promotion, and channels of distribution. The operational planner must supplement these policy guidelines with a comprehensive view of the effects of internal factors, such as managerial policy and procedures, upon past sales performance.

To analyze past sales performance, the operational planner requires a detailed breakdown of sales by product, territory, salesperson, or customer. Sales must be analyzed by either dollar amounts or units; however, it is preferable to use both. The purpose of this is to determine the causes of weaknesses in prior years' sales and to eliminate them in the future, as well as to determine the causes of success so that they may be reinforced. Analysis of past sales is a form of forced planning by which management can probe for "sore spots" and attempt to remedy them, as well as look for opportunities to exploit.

Examining the relationship of cost of sales and distribution costs to past sales is an invaluable aid in planning the future budget. It may indicate, for example, that a company has been promoting the wrong product in a certain territory. As a result, a *territorial analysis* may be conducted to locate areas where a company's products promise the most profitable sales. There are many factors to consider, such as climate, sectional prejudices and preferences, races and religions, occupations, and buying power. Territories may be subdivided by regions, states, counties, cities, trading centers, or prescribed market areas.

The number of potential customers in a selected territory may be estimated by means of a *demographic analysis.* Customers may be classified, for example, by industry, type of retailer (e.g., department stores, drugstores, variety stores), or by volume of annual purchases as determined by a buying power index.

Format of the Sales Budget

How a sales budget is presented depends upon the nature of the company and the detail with which the budget is prepared. The budget figures are usually analyzed by quarters, with monthly estimates detailed for the first quarter. If possible, both unit and dollar amounts are shown. However, if there is a large number of products, it may be necessary to indicate only dollar amounts. Another approach is to show the budget for the major products separately and to group the sales estimates for minor products. The sales budget should be detailed by sales districts if such districts have been established.

PRODUCTION AND INVENTORY BUDGETS

The sales budget furnishes the basis for planning production. Planners must then decide how much of a product must be produced to fulfill the projected goals embodied in the sales budget. They must also consider (1) maintaining satisfactory inventory levels and (2) stabilizing production. When these elements are properly balanced, a production budget can be developed.

In a typical manufacturing or trading company, investment in inventories is substantial. The dangers of obsolescence and possible decline in the value of inventories are always present. Even if prevailing market conditions do not jeopardize the value of the inventory, the cost of maintaining excess inventories could severely strain the financial resources of the company. On the other hand, the company must be able to deliver its goods within a reasonable period of time after accepting a sales order. The best inventory level, then, permits filling all sales orders quickly and yet keeps the dollar investment in inventories at a minimum.

When establishing inventory levels, the planners and production managers must consider stabilizing production. Stable production is desirable because it increases productivity by reducing idle plant capacity and minimizing labor turnover. Such stability can be achieved, despite sales fluctuations, by permitting the level of inventories to fluctuate within established minimum and maximum limits.

A sound management policy should achieve a balance between production and inventory levels after the sales forecast is prepared. A range of permissible inventory levels is set for each item of inventory. Stating inventory requirements in terms of a month's supply rather than in units or amounts eliminates the need for frequent changes in requirements. Inventory requirements are revised only if there are major changes in the production process or if general business conditions affect the availability of materials and credit.

The next step is to relate the inventory requirements to budgeted sales and production to determine the minimum and maximum inventory levels needed during the year. We can then estimate the annual production budget, which is based upon both the sales forecast for the year and established inventory requirements. It is preferable to record the production budget in units to be produced. If this is not practical due to the variety of items sold, aggregate dollar amounts must be used. For example, if the Brown Tool Company stated its budget in units and if inventory levels were established, the production budget would be stated as follows:

	Units
Sales Budget Requirements	95,000
Add: Desired Final Inventory of	
Finished Goods	15,000
Total	110,000
Less: Beginning Inventory of	
Finished Goods	−12,500
Required Production	97,500

If the sales budget is stated in dollars only, an inventory dollar value may be used.

The sales budget is usually prepared by months and quarters and shows seasonal variations. However, the ideal production budget does not vary from month to month. The amount of inventory may decrease to the minimum or increase to the maximum level in order to achieve stable production. The inventory budget is the buffer between fluctuating sales and stable production.

The production budget should not be viewed as an inflexible schedule but as a guide for planning production. It should serve as the foundation for planning material and labor needs, capital additions, and cash requirements, which are integral parts of the budget plan.

MATERIALS BUDGET

The production budget is the basis for the preparation of the budget of manufacturing costs. The daily activities of the manufacturing division, such as the purchase of raw material, hiring of personnel, and machinery maintenance, result in manufacturing costs. One of the most important phases of budgeting is to relate these costs to the planned rate of production. These costs are compiled in material, direct labor, and manufacturing expense budgets.

Raw materials consist of *direct materials,* which are specifically identified with the product, and *indirect materials* that are used in the production process. For example, in the apparel industry, cloth is a direct material; thread and buttons are indirect materials. The materials budget is concerned only with direct materials; indirect materials, such as labels and cartons, are considered in the preparation of the manufacturing expense budget.

Estimating Quantity of Materials for Production

If a standard quantity of material used in producing a unit of finished product is known, the quantity of materials required for production can be estimated by multiplying the budgeted production by the standard quantity. However, it is often difficult, if not impossible, to calculate such standards, and less definite bases for measurement must be used. For example:

1. Material-usage figures developed from prior years' experience.
2. Costs of materials developed directly without quantities. This is accomplished by developing a ratio of material cost to some predetermined factor such as direct labor cost, direct labor hours, or direct machine hours.

In developing a materials budget by using either of these methods, planners must rely heavily on the accounting information of prior periods. It is important that they evaluate the data on which such estimates are determined, since any change in the production process or costs might significantly affect material consumption and cost. In addition, allowance must be made for spoilage and waste.

Raw Material and Inventory Levels

As in planning the production budget, inventory levels must be considered in planning the raw material budget. Just as the finished-goods inventory furnishes a cushion between production and sales, so the raw materials inventory serves as the buffer between purchases and raw material requirements for production.

PURCHASE BUDGET

To determine the purchase budget, both the amount of each material to be purchased and the unit cost of each must be estimated. Establishing inventory levels for materials provides the basis for planning the amount of material to be purchased. If the inventories are maintained at fixed levels, the purchase budget would parallel and precede production requirements by a predetermined lead time. If the inventory were allowed to fluctuate with seasonal production requirements, purchases would not vary widely from month to month. Therefore, the timing of purchases depends greatly upon planned inventory levels.

The unit cost of material depends upon market conditions. Application of some of the economic analysis techniques used in forecasting sales also helps to estimate the market price of materials. Industry factors, the level of prices, and the condition of the economy as a whole affect material prices. Unit costs of materials will usually vary during the year. In preparing the purchase budget, the estimated average unit cost of materials may be used so that each price change does not have to be predicted for the purchase budget. Planners may study the pattern of past purchases along with the projection of future prices of materials in order to establish the average unit cost. They should also consider the handling of freight charges on materials purchased. Theoretically, freight is an added cost of materials, but for purposes of simplicity in budgeting, it can be handled as an overhead cost. Although the purchase budget may restrain impulsive behavior, it does not replace good judgment. As with all phases of budget preparation and operation, situations arise that require deviation from the purchase budget. If there is a temporary break in prices (such as a price war), it would be unrealistic to follow the purchase budget originally established. Thus, flexibility is required.

DIRECT LABOR BUDGET

The second element of manufacturing cost, *direct labor*, is labor time applied in the manufacturing of a product. All other labor time, such as that spent in maintenance and inventory control, is classified as indirect labor and is budgeted with manufacturing expense. When an employee works both on production and maintenance tasks, the direct labor budget is charged only with the production time.

The direct labor budget not only furnishes the estimate of direct labor cost, but it is used to plan personnel requirements throughout the year. The direct labor budget may be estimated from piece rates, labor hours, and cost, or labor costs only. If the labor time required in production can be readily determined, the direct labor hours can be multiplied by the average wage rate. If no operational times can be estimated, it may be necessary to develop a ratio of direct labor cost to a measure of productive activity.

How the direct labor budget is developed depends upon the method of wage payment, the type of production process, and the accounting records available. For example, a piece-rate wage system or a production process that allows a breakdown of operational times for each job permits a fairly accurate forecast of direct labor expenditures. Otherwise direct labor costs must be estimated by less precise approaches.

MANUFACTURING EXPENSE BUDGET

A manufacturing expense is a part of total manufacturing cost that is not included in direct material or labor because it cannot be specifically identified with a product. Manufacturing expenses include factory supplies, indirect (usually maintenance and service) labor, taxes, insurance, and depreciation. Budgeting these expenses is difficult for two reasons. First, these widely different costs must be accumulated in cost centers such as producing or service departments. Second, service-department expenses must eventually be allocated to producing departments and sometimes directly to a product.

Manufacturing expenses are incurred and accumulated in two cost centers in a departmentalized company: *producing departments* and *service departments*. Producing departments work directly on the product being manufactured. Service departments, such as engineering, maintenance, and warehouse, do not work on the product directly but furnish services to producing departments or other service departments.

Therefore, in preparing the manufacturing expense budget planners must first budget costs for the department that incurs them so that the costs can be controlled by type of expense. Then they should allocate costs to the product.

In summary, the construction of a manufacturing expense budget involves preparing a budget of each expense of a company, by time period, by department (if necessary), and according to accounting classifications.

SELLING EXPENSE BUDGET

After the three elements of manufacturing cost—materials, direct labor and manufacturing expense—have been budgeted, the budget for cost of goods manufactured can be completed. After completion of the manufacturing cost budget, the cost of getting the goods to market must be determined. This cost includes selling, delivery, and advertising expenses.

The chart of accounts classifies selling expense by assigned responsibility. The budget should be constructed on the same basis. For example, if a company has three regional offices, the selling expense budget should be prepared so that the regional supervisors know which expenses they are responsible for. Certain expenses included in the selling expense budget may be estimated when the sales budget is being formulated. These selling expenses are dependent upon sales plans and are estimated at a level in accordance with the overall sales program.

In sales and selling expense budgets, a definite amount is appropriated for advertising. This amount is dovetailed with the sales plan. The budgeted advertising expenses are broken down by type of advertising media and by month or quarter of expenditures. Advertising expense is commonly treated in the selling expense budget as a constant amount each month or quarter.

ADMINISTRATIVE EXPENSE BUDGET

The final category of expense to be included in the budget is administrative expense. Administrative expenses are incurred in the overall coordination and supervision of the entire operation of a business rather than in the operation of one particular function.

The chart of accounts should classify administrative expense by organizational responsibility. In a fairly large business, there may be divisions under the chief administrative executive, the controller, and the treasurer. A small business generally has one all-inclusive administrative category.

Administrative expenses have traditionally been thought of as relatively fixed. However, managerial decisions and policies influence many of these costs, so variable budget procedures are recommended in budgeting administrative expense. For instance, a frequently used measure of variability is *budgeted net sales volume*. Many administrative expenses vary with net sales and the level of production. Additional sales and production, for example, require larger expenditures on accounting, credit control, and general supervision.

Since administrative expenses are incurred so close to top management, it is common to overlook excessive spending. By intelligently planning such expenses and relating them to proposed sales volume, however, senior executives may realize that some of their expenditures can be reduced.

After the supporting schedules have been developed, the effect of changes in pricing policy, fixed expenses, and variable expenses on the profits of the company can be determined. The available budgeted statistics permit reconsideration of some of the policy decisions made in developing the budget estimates. Alternative courses of action can be evaluated by break-even analysis.

CASH BUDGET

A program for maintaining sufficient cash during the year to meet a company's requirements and for effectively using excess cash, if any, is vital in budgeting. The *cash budget* forecasts a company's expected cash receipts and disbursements within the budget period. It must be prepared after operations are planned because the timing of cash receipts and disbursements depends on planning budget schedules.

The cash budget serves several important functions:

1. It indicates how much cash will be available at any time as a result of planned operations.

2. It informs the company whether it will have to borrow additional funds or whether it will have excess cash available for investment.
3. It furnishes a sound basis for control of the cash position by allowing the responsible manager to manipulate available funds for the benefit of the firm and to compare actual disbursements to budget and take remedial action when the two are not in line.
4. It helps to support any bank-loan application a company might make and increases the chance of obtaining the loan.
5. It helps time specific capital acquisitions or unusually large purchases to coincide with periods of excess cash availability in order to avoid unnecessary interest charges.

OTHER TOOLS FOR OPERATIONAL PLANNERS

The almost universal adoption of the budget by organizations, especially on the operating management level, explains the extended treatment given to the subject herein. However, despite the value of the operating budget as a major tool for managerial planning, the complexity of organizational functioning required the development of techniques to supplement the budgetary approach. Historically, these techniques date back to the years following the Civil War, when the United States experienced a spurt of industrial growth. As companies expanded to accommodate increasing demand, managers discovered that their haphazard, hit-or-miss approach was inadequate.

During the nineteenth century, the ideas of the Enlightenment philosophers dominated the thinking of educated people in Western countries. They believed that all human problems could be solved by rational analysis and diagnosis. In addition, revolutionary advances in such fields as physics, astronomy, chemistry, and mathematics had paved the way for significant technological developments and greatly strengthened the belief in the value of rational problem-solving. Thus, as American industrial development accelerated after the Civil War, progressive management practitioners concluded that industrial problems could be solved, and thus productivity and efficiency could be increased. Frederick W. Taylor, the founder of the scientific management movement, applied scientific principles to the analysis of workers' tasks and as a result demonstrated dramatic increases in productivity. One of Taylor's disciples, Henry L. Gantt, invented a chart on which production was plotted continuously against time. The Gantt chart was the beginning of formal production scheduling in industry and is still in use in many companies today. Frank B. and Lillian M. Gilbreth used the scientific approach to advance the art of time-and-motion study, which, to this day, is one of the basic tools of industrial engineers. Harrington Emerson, an engineer by profession, persuaded higher management to introduce scientific management methods in its own planning and control activities.

During the early part of the twentieth century, various social sciences such as psychology, sociology, and anthropology began to develop. Behavioral scientists soon discovered that mathematics, "the handmaiden of the natural sciences," was not entirely appropriate for the symbolic expression of concepts in the social sciences. This led to the rediscovery and restudy of classical statistics as a potentially more valuable tool for the behavioral sciences. As a result, a new branch of knowledge developed, which came to be known as *decision theory*. The decision theorist uses probability theory to help managers use their own judgment in solving problems. Decision theory recognizes that classical mathematics can be used to solve problems where all factors pertaining to a problem are certain. However, managers face many problems in which some of the factors can only be expressed in probabilistic terms or even in which some factors are unknown. In such cases, the managers can derive probabilities from empirical, reasoned, or even totally subjective guesstimates.

By 1950, scientific management theory, classical mathematics, and statistical decision theory were well-known, but separate, disciplines. The next logical step was to put these three disciplines together to create a new planning and problem-solving tool. Two developments stimulated the necessary combination. During World War II, when Great Britain was suffering unacceptable shipping losses at the hands of the Germans, Prime Minister Winston Churchill called together an interdisciplinary team of scientists, mathematicians, and statisticians to help stem the losses caused by German submarine attacks on British vessels. Applying a combination of mathematical and statistical techniques, the team discovered that shipping losses could be minimized by increasing the size of convoys. They also recommended procedures for Royal Air Force pilots to significantly increase their "kill" ratio of German submarines. The team's great success during the war confirmed the validity of this approach, which had earlier become known as *operations research,* and stimulated its use in industry and other organizations during peacetime.

The emergence of the computer during the 1950s was the second factor that encouraged the development of these new operations research techniques. As specialists in the field developed quantitative models to apply to operational problems, it was found that the number of calculations required could mount to astronomical proportions. The advent of the computer made it feasible to use these techniques since the computer could process the calculations rapidly.

It is generally agreed that operations research is both a way of analyzing problems and a group of techniques. Whatever the nature of the problem, the operations researchers will adopt a *systems approach;* that is, they will try to identify and incorporate all elements that affect or are affected by the problem. They will use a scientific approach that considers all feasible alternatives and evaluates the consequences of each alternative. Due to the multidimensional nature of many problems, they will avail themselves of the interdisciplinary talents of colleagues in other specialities who can contribute to the solution. And finally, they will translate the problem into a quantitative model amenable to a mathematical resolution.

Problems tend to recur in formal organizations. Operations research specialists have classified these problems into six major categories and have devised mathematical models to deal with each one. A review of the most commonly found models in the field follows.

Allocation Models

Allocation models deal with the issue of allocating limited resources so that the overall efficiency of the activity or operation is maximized. The desired result may be achieved by applying a technique known as *mathematical programming,* which is designed either to minimize total costs or to maximize total profits. The choice of the specific type of programming model—linear, nonlinear, stochastic, parametric, or dynamic—depends upon the kind of data involved in the problem and upon the assumptions made by the decisionmakers. A common type of allocation problem is the decision on product mix. A given configuration of machinery and labor may be able to produce varying amounts of different products. Assuming different profit margins for each product, the programming technique will determine the optimal production quantity for each of the products for total profit to be maximized.

Allocation models may also be used to solve workflow problems in a job order shop. There are usually a number of ways in which an order may be produced. For example, during a given time period, if the most efficient production practice is selected for each order, some machines will probably be overloaded while others will remain idle. The production manager must select the method of manufacture in such a way that the total cost of production is minimized. Allocation models are also applicable in a situation where adequate resources are available, but it has not been determined how to assign or distribute them most effectively. Examples of such problems are the assignment of operators to machines, clerks to specific clerical tasks, or classes to rooms.

Inventory Models

The general problem of the storage of idle resources is handled by inventory models. The principal resources with which industrial managers are involved are personnel, goods, equipment, and money. As the level of inventory of a resource rises, so does the cost of carrying the inventory. Inventory carrying charges include such items as storage costs, obsolescence costs, taxes, insurance, and interest on the dollar value of the goods held. On the other hand, there are also costs associated with too low an inventory level. These include:

- cost of lost sales
- cost of customer dissatisfaction (due to delay or inability to meet delivery commitments)
- cost of many short production runs, which entail more inefficient purchasing practices (e.g., loss of quantity discounts), less efficient use of labor, and excessive setup costs

The appropriate inventory model provides a solution that minimizes the total cost.

The cash balance that a company should maintain may also be treated as an inventory problem. If a company holds too much cash, instead of investing it, it loses the potential earnings. On the other hand, if a company has too little cash available, it will have to borrow additional capital at premium rates, and there will be additional costs associated with obtaining frequent loans. Another problem can arise in planning future personnel requirements. If employees are trained in a specific skill and then the anticipated demand for that skill does not materialize, the result will be poor morale, turnover, and wasted training costs. Nevertheless, the training of an insufficient number of employees may result in a shortage of needed skills. Deciding which size of a piece of equipment to purchase is also an inventory-type problem. If the machine that is purchased is too large, idle capacity will result. If the equipment is too small, sales will be lost, and shortage costs will be incurred. In all of these cases, the inventory model will furnish a solution that minimizes the costs. The mathematical programming techniques referred to previously are used to resolve inventory problems. Where the inventory problem is so complex that the model can be constructed but not solved, using simulation techniques to obtain a solution may be appropriate. These techniques consist of imitating the operation of a system under varying conditions to find which set of conditions yields the least cost.

Queuing Models

Finding the best balance between the number of customers waiting for a service and the number of facilities available to provide it is the essence of what is known as the *waiting-line problem.* Examples of the waiting-line problem include the number of checkout counters needed in a supermarket, the number of tollbooths needed at a tunnel entrance, the number of receptionists needed in a hospital admitting room, the number of piers needed in a harbor, or the number of teller's windows needed in a bank. In an industrial setting, mechanics waiting at tool cribs or trucks lined up waiting for a vacant loading dock illustrate the same type of problem. The more excessive the waiting time is, the greater the cost of idle human and material resources. To minimize waiting time, a large investment in service facilities may be required. Queuing theory, which makes extensive use of probability theory, calculus, and simulation techniques, provides a least-cost solution to waiting-line problems.

Sequencing and Routing Models

Problems of sequencing and routing are subcategories of the more general scheduling problem. The essence of sequencing is to determine the best sequence of operation in order to minimize time or cost; with queuing problems, the sequence of customers is either irrelevant or is specified in advance. For example, if two products must be produced on the same machines, the sequence selected to produce the two products will largely determine the amount of each product produced as well as the amount of idle machine time. When the number of jobs required and the number of machines available are small, the Gantt chart is the most convenient tool to use. However, most real-life problems are far more complex and usually require simulation techniques.

Routing is also known as the "traveling salesman problem." Routing involves determining the best route for a seller to follow in order to visit a specified list of customers in various cities and return home in the shortest possible time and at least cost. A similar problem is faced by the dispatcher of a multiwarehouse company who must deliver a certain number of truckloads of material to various locations. The dispatcher must insure that the goods arrive at their destination in the shortest possible time or at the lowest possible cost, or both.

A technique has been developed for handling a variation of the sequencing problem that occurs in planning and monitoring a complex, dynamically changing program such as the construction of a new plant. The technique is based upon network theory; and the names given to the time-scaled network systems include PERT (Program Evaluation and Review Technique), CPM (Critical Path Method), or simply Network Planning and Scheduling. The problem is to establish starting times and due-date goals for each phase of the program, so that operation costs are minimized. To apply the technique, information is needed on the sequences required, the duration of each phase, and the costs for each part of the project. The technique makes it possible to determine labor needs, budget requirements, procurement and design limitations, and the effects of delays or speedups and communication difficulties. The networking approach provides the following advantages to the operational planner:

1. It provides an integrated picture of the project.
2. It forces a more logical approach to planning.
3. It guards against omitting important jobs.
4. It facilitates coordination among the subunits involved in the project.
5. It simplifies replanning and rescheduling.
6. It identifies who must be notified of schedule changes.
7. It provides a means for project cost control.

Replacement/Maintenance Models

Replacement/maintenance problems involve relatively costly equipment items such as machine tools, trucks, or generators that deteriorate with use or the passage of time. As these items degenerate, maintenance is required to restore their efficiency, and this involves a cost. However, if the equipment is replaced frequently, the investment cost increases. Thus, it must be determined when such items must be replaced so that the sum of the operating and investment costs are minimized.

There is a class of items that do not deteriorate but that cease to function after a certain amount of use of time—for example, light bulbs, tire tubes, batteries, and electronic components. In this case, it must be determined whether a group of these items should be replaced at one time prior to failure and, if so, how often. If the policy adopted is to replace an item only when it fails, the number of items required will be minimized. However, failures will be relatively frequent, and costs associated with downtime and replacement will be relatively high. If it is decided to replace the items as a group prior to failure, the costs of failure are minimized, but the number of replacement items required is maximized. The task is then to establish a group replacement policy that minimizes the sum of the costs of the items, failures, and replacement operations.

Operations researchers have devised several effective mathematical or statistical techniques for handling this type of problem. In many cases, relatively simple mathematical applications are sufficient. For more complex situations, simulation techniques are available.

Competition Models

Competition models deal with a class of problems in which the decision of one decisionmaker is affected by the decisions made by one or more other decisionmakers. Operational planners confront such problems when they are considering pricing policies, advertising strategies, the timing of new-product introductions, or the development of bidding tactics. Decisions made by military planners are affected by the anticipated reactions of potential adversaries. Foreign-policy decisionmakers must consider possible actions by allies as well as unfriendly powers.

The ability to cope with such problems depends entirely upon how much the decisionmaker knows about the competitor's action. Such action may be known in advance with certainty. For example, in many industries, if one firm reduces its prices, the others will all follow suit. In other situations, nothing may be known in advance about what competition is likely do do; this may be the case when a completely new product is introduced. Finally, in many instances, although the competitor's decision cannot be known with certainty, it may be estimated. For instance, in the case of closed competitive bids, it may be possible to determine the likelihood of various competitive bids based on past history. In such situations, there is a risk of being wrong, which can be expressed in probabilistic terms.

Under conditions of risk or uncertainty, competitive problems may be handled by a series of techniques developed under the conceptual framework of game theory. These techniques allow a company to determine the particular strategy that will result in maximum gain or minimum loss no matter what its opponents decide to do. Unfortunately, the theory provides the solution for only the simplest types of competitive situations. In more complicated competitive environments, statistical decision theory can be applied. A special type of simulation, known as *gaming,* has been developed in which the competitive situation is simulated but the decisionmakers are real. As managers play the game, possible counteractions are explored and evaluated, leading to successive modifications of the model until the best outcome is reached.

SUMMARY

Operational planners deal with the short-term, day-to-day transactions of a firm. Compared to strategic and administrative planners, they have access to much more information, the accuracy of which they may rely upon in formulating their short-range plans. Their accounting- and control-oriented colleagues have provided them with the indispensable tool of the budget. We have described in some detail the workings of the various operational and cash budgets, and we have seen how the budget functions as a planning tool. In the next chapter, we will explore how the same operating budgets can serve also as tools of coordination and control.

In many functional activities of a firm, specialists in operations research provide the operational planners with effective quantitative techniques to cope with operational problems that may be anticipated in the planning process. Many executives who are entrusted with operational planning responsibilities have not been trained to view these management-science techniques as legitimate planning tools. However, as more managers come to understand the wide range of operational problems that may be solved with these techniques, they will surely be as widely used by operational planners as the budget.

REFERENCES

Anthony, R. N. 1964. Framework for analysis in management planning. *Management Science* 10: 18–24.

Suggests as the main topics of a framework for planning the processes of strategic planning, management control, and operational control.

Klipper, Harold. 1978. Breakeven analysis with variable product mix. *Management Accounting* 59(10): 51–54.

Demonstrates how to analyze a variation in gross profit due to the effects of product-mix changes or cost variations. *Reprinted herein on pp. 157–163.*

Mullis, E. N., Jr. 1975. Variable budgeting for financial planning and control. *Management Accounting* 56(8): 43–45.

Describes how variable budgeting is used for financial planning and control. *Reprinted herein on pp. 163–168.*

Steiner, G. A. and J. B. Miner. 1977. *Management Policy and Strategy.* New York: Macmillan.

Text, readings, and cases covering the major areas of management policy and strategy.

Breakeven Analysis with Variable Product Mix

Harold Klipper

A firm that produces a single product, has a constant product mix, or prices all its products for the same profit margin can use the standard form of breakeven analysis even when it changes its product mix. However, most firms must assume some constraints on their product mix for planning purposes. Such factors as market projections, factory capacity, resource limitations, and profit projections must be taken into account. An optimum product mix, within the constraints determined by management, can then be formed using linear programming techniques. The optimum product mix can then be employed in a breakeven analysis for the planning period.

A profit-volume graph that would be useful in monitoring performance of a three-product mix during a planning period, as shown in Exhibit 1, was described by Lane K. Anderson.[1] This technique uses an optimistic cost path and a

1. Lane K. Anderson, "Expanded Breakeven Analysis for a Multi-Product Company," *Management Accounting, July 1975, p. 32.*

pessimistic cost path, both of which are projected on a linear breakeven chart. The major assumption in this case is that the final product mix will be achieved by the end of the planning period for which the chart applies even though the actual product mix may vary during the period. At any value of sales revenue, the cost may vary between the optimistic and the pessimistic cost paths as a function of product mix, provided there is convergence at the end of the planning period. If the ratio of product mix is constant and equal to the planned mix, then the cost will always coincide with the central cost path. When the cost falls outside the area bounded by the optimistic and pessimistic cost paths, it will no longer be possible to achieve the planned product mix. However, even when the costs do fall within these bounds, it is not certain that the final product mix will converge as planned.

Another technique employs a number of alternative product mixes in a single profit-volume graph.[2] If, at any sales revenue, the costs fall on any one of the product mix curves, then it may be assumed that the indicated product mix has been achieved. Both this technique and the Anderson technique assume no deviation from planned fixed costs or variable costs for each product. Any such deviations could not be separated for analysis.

THE EQUIVALENT SALES PRICE

By using an equivalent sales price and breakeven analysis, it is possible to determine when the product mix is favorable or unfavorable. It is also possible to

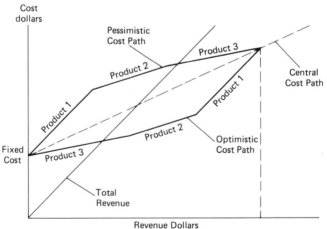

Exhibit 1. Area of possible product mix on linear breakeven chart.

2. See Morton Backer and Lyle E. Jacobsen, *Cost Accounting: A Managerial Approach.* McGraw-Hill Book Co., New York, 1964, p. 358.

determine if costs are at the planned level for the actual product mix achieved.

As with any other technique, it is necessary to start with an assumed product mix for the planning period. Then, an average contribution margin is established for all the products included in the assumed mix. The average contribution margin can be defined as:

$$M = \frac{R - V}{R} \tag{1}$$

where

M = Average contribution margin
R = Total revenue
V = Total variable costs

By using the standard variable cost for a product, it is possible to compute the equivalent sales price for that product:

$$ESP = \frac{ASP - SVC}{M} \tag{2}$$

where

ESP = Equivalent sales price
ASP = Actual sales price
SVC = Standard variable costs

Those products which have a contribution margin above the average will have an equivalent sales price higher than the actual selling price; those with a lower contribution margin than the average will have an equivalent sales price lower than the actual selling price. In any period, the total ESP revenues may be compared to total revenues. If the total ESP is higher, then a favorable product mix was achieved during the period; if the total ESP is lower, then an unfavorable product mix was achieved. A total ESP equal to total revenue does not signify that the planned product mix was achieved, but only that the mix obtained yielded the same gross profit as the planned mix. The total ESP figure can be used to determine the cause of any variation in gross profit due to product mix changes or to cost variations.

EXAMPLE

An example of a firm with three products is shown in Exhibit 2. The fixed costs for the period are assumed to be $20,000 and are spread uniformly over

Exhibit 2. Budgetary data for three-product mix and planning period of one year.

PRODUCT	UNIT SELLING PRICE	UNIT VARIABLE COST	PROJECTED QUANTITY	TOTAL SALES REVENUE	TOTAL COST	UNIT ESP	TOTAL ESP
A	$10	$ 8	5,000	$ 50,000	$40,000	$ 5	$ 25,000
B	15	5	2,000	30,000	10,000	25	50,000
C	20	10	1,000	20,000	10,000	25	25,000
Sub-total variable costs					$60,000		
Fixed cost					20,000		
Total				$100,000	$80,000		$100,000

the planning period. From the data provided and equation 1, the average contribution margin is determined to be 0.4. Using equation 2, the ESP for each of the products is: $ESP_A = 5$, $ESP_B = 25$, and $ESP_C = 25$.

Note that the equivalent sales price for products B and C are identical although the selling price and the cost for each is different. The reason is due to the fact that the contribution margin for both products is the same. Note also that total ESP is equal to the total sales revenue for the period, although the total ESP and total sales revenue are not the same for each product. This example illustrates that when the actual product mix is achieved, the total ESP and total sales revenue will be the same.

The results of actual sales and costs at the midpoint of the planning period (six months) are summarized in Exhibit 3 and on a linear profit-volume chart as

Exhibit 3. Summary of performance for three-product mix at mid-point of planning period—six months.

PRODUCT	UNIT SELLING PRICE	UNIT VARIABLE COST	QUANTITY SOLD	TOTAL SALES REVENUE	TOTAL COST	UNIT ESP	TOTAL ESP
A	$10	$ 8	2,200	$22,000	$17,600	$ 5	$11,000
A	9	8	1,000	9,000	8,000	2.50	2,500
B	15	5	1,000	15,000	5,000	25	25,000
C	20	12	200	4,000	2,400	25	5,000
Sub-total variable costs					$33,000		
Fixed cost					7,000		
Total				$50,000	$40,000		$43,500

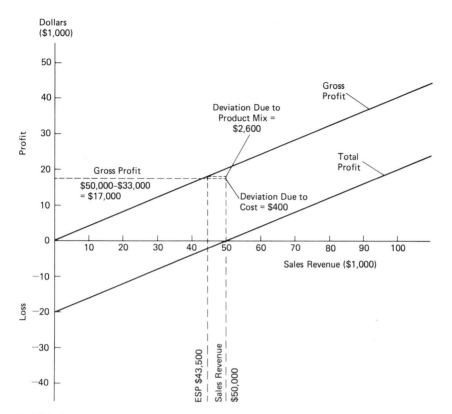

Exhibit 4. Linear profit-volume chart for three-product mix.

illustrated in Exhibit 4. If management only reviews the final results, it may be assumed that the firm is exactly on budget. Sales revenue is exactly one-half the yearly budget and total profit is exactly one-half the yearly budget. A closer examination will show that there are a number of factors that have actually deviated from the budget and these have cancelled each other to yield the same overall effect.

With reference to Exhibit 3, note that a quantity of 1,000 of product A was sold at a price of $9 instead of the normal price of $10. This is the only item for which a new ESP had to be determined. Also, product C showed a variable cost of $12 per unit instead of the budgeted cost of $10, and that the various quantities actually sold of the three products are not one-half of the yearly budgeted amounts.

In order to separate the effects of product mix and deviation in variable costs on gross profit by use of equivalent sales price data, two additional formulas will be required. (For this analysis, the special price on a quantity of product

A is considered to be for a fourth or different product and its effect is included in the product mix.) The percent deviation in gross profit, due to product mix, is given by equation 3, and is defined as the difference in gross profit resulting from the different total equivalent sales price and total sales revenue multiplied by the average contribution margin:

$$\Delta P_s = \left(\frac{MS - MR}{R} \right) 100 \qquad (3)$$

$$= M \left(\frac{S}{R} - 1 \right) 100$$

Where
ΔP_s = Percent deviation in gross profit due to deviations in sales mix
S = Total equivalent sales price

The percent deviation in gross profit due to a deviation in variable cost is given by equation 4. It is defined as the difference between the gross profit that was actually achieved and the gross profit that should have been realized if there was no deviation in unit variable costs.

$$\Delta P_c = \left[\frac{(R - V) - MS}{R} \right] 100 \qquad (4)$$

$$= \left[1 - \frac{V}{R} - \frac{MS}{R} \right] 100$$

Where
P_c = Percent deviation in gross profit due to deviation in cost

Applying Equations 3 and 4 to the example in Exhibit 2 will result in:

$$\Delta P_s = 0.4 \left(\frac{43,500}{50,000} - 1 \right) 100$$

$$= -5.2 \text{ percent}$$

and

$$\Delta P_c = \left[1 - \frac{33,000}{50,000} - \frac{0.4\,(43,500)}{50,000} \right] 100$$

$$= -0.8 \text{ percent}$$

The effect on gross profit of a product mix (including the special price on a quantity of product A) not in the same proportion as the original plan was un-favorable by $2,600 ($-0.052 \times \$50,000$). The effect on gross profit of a devia-tion in variable costs was unfavorable by $400 ($-0.008 \times \$50,000$). This can also be seen, from Exhibit 2, to be a result of a $2 increase in the variable costs of product C multiplied by the quantity sold of 200. These two factors account for the $3,000 deviation in gross profit (i.e., variable costs were $33,000 instead of the anticipated $30,000). The results of this analysis have been included on the linear-profit-volume chart, Exhibit 4, to show how the same results can be obtained graphically.

Although the effects of product mix and cost deviations could have been obtained directly from the data contained in Exhibit 2, the major advantage of using the equivalent sales price is that the only data required, which is not normally available from the profit and loss statement, is the equivalent sales price. Thus, detailed costs, selling price, and quantities need not be known to separate out the causes of gross profit deviations.

CONCLUSION

The ESP technique described in this article has been applied over a six month period to a medium sized manufacturing firm. It has not, to date, projected any large deviations in gross profit, but it has sorted out for management major deviations due to product mix and/or costs.

Variable Budgeting
for Financial
Planning and Control

Elbert N. Mullis, Jr.

There are many sophisticated methods for analyzing costs and their relationship to levels of output. One of the best ways is through the budget, and one of the most meaningful of these is the variable budget. The variable budget is tailored to any level of activity, so that the evaluation of efficiency is not contaminated by comparing a budget for one level of activity with results for another level of activity.[1] If you know what your volume will be, the variable budget will tell you what your cost should be. Thus, the heart of a variable budget is the cost/volume relationship of its components.

1. The prime objection to static or fixed budgets is that when sales volume and/or production levels fluctuate, the cost comparisons become meaningless.

In order to establish the budgeted performance at any particular level of activity, the related costs must first be determined. One basic method is to place all costs into the variable category if they are controlled only by the level of output, and into the discretionary category if they can be increased or decreased by a decision of management.

As an example, to the franchised bottler for a popular soft drink the one true variable is the cost of bottling syrup. Each change in volume automatically brings a change in syrup cost. Management has no control over this cost other than in controlling waste. So, this system basically categorizes direct materials as variable costs since the total costs are dictated by volume alone.

However, two other items of expense, not related to the manufacturing process, may also be based on volume with this system. These are salesmen's commissions and advertising. Salesmen's commissions are variable because management has formulated a pay scale which includes a flat commission rate of six cents per case sold. In the same way, advertising is a variable because it is allowed six cents for advertising media for each case sold. Should case sales for a particular month be 200,000 cases, then salesmen's commissions and the advertising budget would each be $12,000. Here a management decision has transformed advertising into a variable expense similar to commissions for profit planning purposes.

PROFIT PLANNING

The starting point in preparing a budget, or profit plan, is to determine the unit cost for each item produced. After the total variable cost has been developed, this amount is subtracted from the selling price to arrive at a marginal contribution per unit. So at any level of volume, it is easy to determine the contribution that should be generated to cover the fixed cost and provide profits.

Step 1

The first step then is to develop a unit cost for each element of variable cost by product. For instance, the elements of cost for a nine-bottle case of 48-ounce bottles, based on assumed prices and yield records, are as follows:

Syrup	$ .83
CO_2 gas	.01
Crown	.04
Bottle	1.19
Label	.05
Manufacturing cost	$2.12
Advertising	.06

Commission	.06
Unit variable cost	$2.24

With a selling price of $3.60 per case, a nine-bottle case generates a marginal contribution of $1.36 per case.

Step 2

The second step in preparing the profit plan is also very critical. It involves the yearly sales forecast. Since plans are built around the anticipated level of sales activity, much thought should be given to forecasting a realistic sales level and product mix. In this case study, the method of forecasting is based heavily on prior sales results and market surveys. The Company had determined that the major factors which influence the sales forecast are:

1. The number of Mondays and Fridays in a given month as well as the total number of working days (Mondays and Fridays are the two heaviest days in sales volumes.)
2. The general economic condition of the franchised area in terms of level of income, etc.
3. Weather (Cold damp weather has a negative sales effect.)
4. Planned advertising campaigns and sales promotions
5. Competition plans

Step 3

The third step involves setting the budget for the remaining expenses, which we shall call discretionary. It is in this area that good planning makes for profitable operations. Additionally, keeping the budgeting process as simple as possible allows for more, and better, management participation.

Discretionary expenses are those that are under the control of a department manager, who becomes involved in the budgeting process at this stage. His judgment as to the level of expenditures necessary for the budget period is based on past experience and knowledge of current and future conditions. Payrolls are an example of discretionary expense under this method. The manager responsible for a certain department can, without the benefit of cost study and engineering standards, determine the payroll dollars required to operate his department over the budget period. He factors in the overtime required to get over peak periods and allows for new people to keep up with normal growth. Also merit increases and general companywide pay increases are considered. All other expenses in the manager's department are determined in a like manner.

Step 4

The fourth and last step is the profit plan itself. Here we multiply the contribution per case by the sales forecast and subtract from that product the discretionary expenses to arrive at the operating profit for a period of time. At this point it may be necessary to re-examine some discretionary expenses if the profit margin does not meet the objectives of the company.

Exhibit 1 illustrates each of the planning steps. Note that the profit plan has forecast a net profit of $58,500 for the month of January based on the amount of sales according to the sales forecast. In this case, the planning was the com-

---

Exhibit 1. Forecasting the profit plan.

Step One: Determining variable cost

Ingredient	Per Case Cost		
	10-oz Ret	48-oz NR	12-oz Can
Syrup	$ .46	$ .83	$ .57
CO_2 gas	.01	.01	.01
Crown	.04	.04	
Bottle: returnable*	.20		
Bottle: non-returnable		1.19	
Can			1.34
Label		.05	
Mfg. cost	$ .71	$2.12	$1.92
Advertising	.06	.06	.06
Commission	.07	.06	.10
Unit variable cost	$ .84	$2.24	$2.08
Selling price	1.85	3.60	2.90
Contribution	$1.01	$1.36	$ .82

*Per trip amortization

By using the 10-oz (king-size) returnable bottle, the 48-oz non-returnable bottle, and the 12-oz can, we have examples of high and low marginal products.

Step Two: Sales forecast

Based on market studies and other factors, the sale for the month of January were forecasted to be 200,000 cases as follows:

10-oz ret	90,000
48-oz NR	60,000
12-oz can	50,000
	200,000

Exhibit 1. (Cont.)

Step Three: Setting discretionary cost

Through management analysis and past operating results, the following budgeted expenses had been approved for January:

Manufacturing	$ 40,000
Sales	65,000
Fleet	28,000
Administrative	22,000
Total discretionary	$155,000

Step Four: The profit plan

By combining the previous three steps we have a forecasted profit plan:

Product	Cases	Unit Contribution	Total Contribution
10 oz ret	90,000	$1.01	$ 90,900
48 oz NR	60,000	$1.36	81,600
12 oz can	50,000	$ .82	41,000
	200,000		$213,500
Discretionary cost			155,000
Forecasted profit			$ 58,500

mitment or strategy to achieve an economic result and the budget was the tool that translated this commitment into financial terms.

THE CONTROL FUNCTION

Control begins with the establishing of a standard. It is then possible to measure performance against the established standard, and to take corrective action when there is a deviation from standard. The control function depends upon an analysis of variances from forecasted and budgeted results. The analysis of profit variance highlights those areas needing management attention.

To illustrate the control function, let us assume that actual total sales for the month of January was 210,000 cases, 10,000 cases greater than the 200,000 forecast. However, because the marketing mix was not met as planned, our standard contribution is lower by $4,500. See Exhibit 2.

Since the budget is variable, it may be adjusted to the actual sales volume experienced for the month. In this way we can eliminate any variance due strictly to the difference between planned and actual volume. Thus, in addition to the $4,500 variance from forecasted profit due only to sales mix and volume, there

Exhibit 2. Budget and operational variance.

Marginal contribution for January

	Cases				
10 oz returnable	80,000	×	$1.01	=	$ 80,800
48 oz non-returnable	40,000	×	$1.36	=	54,500
12 oz can	90,000	×	$ .82	=	73,800
Total	210,000				$209,000
Forecast	200,000				213,500
Over (Under)	10,000				$ (4,500)

January Income Statement

	Actual	Budget	Difference
Sales	$553,000	$553,000	
Variable cost	345,000	344,000	$ (1,000)
Gross	$208,000	$209,000	$ (1,000)
Manufacturing	41,000	40,000	(1,000)
Sales	64,500	65,000	(500)
Fleet	28,100	28,000	(100)
Administrative	22,500	22,000	500
Before tax profit	$ 51,900	$ 54,000	$ (2,100)

is a further $2,100 variance due to unfavorable operations for a total decrease of $6,600 from budget. (Budgeted contribution margin of $58,500 minus the actual before tax profit of $51,900 = $6,600.)

Further analysis would show what caused the operational variance. For example, the $1,000 unfavorable variance in variable cost could be due to direct material production losses and poor yields. The other variances could be due to labor overtime not in budget or extraordinary fleet repairs. Each manager responsible for that particular area is issued an operating statement so that he may see where his attention should be directed.

CONCLUSION

The planning process centers around the variable budget's cost/volume relationship for variable expenses, and upon discretionary management judgment for fixed expenses. The control process, on the other hand, highlights areas which need the attention of management to meet the financial target.

6
Implementation
and Control

According to Herbert Simon (1965), there is a means-end chain in hierarchical organizations—that which is a means for a superior becomes an end (goal) for a subordinate. In other words, superiors achieve their objectives by means of their subordinates' performance, which, in turn, is a goal for the subordinates.

The various levels of planning are implemented in a similar manner. The efficient formulation of administrative plans is, in effect, the implementation of the strategic plan, whereas the development of efficient operational plans leads to the implementation of administrative plans. Thus, implementation and planning overlap at the two higher levels of planning. (This phenomenon is illustrated by Schendel [1976] in "Implementing Strategic Planning Systems," which begins on p. 195.)

At the operational level, there is also an overlapping of implementation and control. The marketing plan formulated by the administrative planner is expanded by the operational planner—through the device of the budget—into a sales plan. The sales plan sets quotas for sales of individual products by territory and by customer; sets targets for achievement of specific volume levels by customers and by salesperson; sets limits to returns and allowances; and provides budgetary figures for advertising, public relations, warehousing, transportation, sales aids, sales promotion, and other distribution expenses. The operational planner in the production department then develops the facilities and production plan given by the administrative superior into detailed budgets covering direct labor costs, expenses for raw materials and supplies, and various manufacturing overhead expenses including indirect labor, maintenance and replacement of machinery and equipment, production planning and scheduling, engineering, quality control, safety, and contracting costs. The line financial planner prepares a cash-flow budget to pinpoint daily cash needs so that all financial obligations can be met promptly, yet without a buildup of idle, excess funds.

BEHAVIORAL ASPECTS OF IMPLEMENTATION

Much of the literature on planning treats it as a mechanistic, almost completely rational activity. Formal plans are filled with statistics and analyses that purport to objectively evaluate the problems facing an organization and the optimal solutions to them. It must always be kept in mind, however, that plans are formulated by human beings, whose actions and behavior are significantly influenced by their personal views and assumptions. It can thus be misleading to rely principally upon charts, graphs, columns of figures, market-research reports, and other objective data to evaluate proposed plans. Such data are often arranged and even exploited by the planner to justify a plan that has been decided in advance.

If these subjective elements are significant on the planning level, they are pervasive on the level of implementation, which involves all members of the organization. We must recognize that the planning undertaken by managers is inextricably related to the values, needs, attitudes, and behaviors of all those concerned with the formulation and implementation of company plans. The difficulties associated with implementation are hinted at in the old saying, "The road to hell is paved with good intentions." It thus behooves the planning manager to give serious thought to the role of people in implementation.

At first, organizational research had focused on task analysis, organizational structure, and on the impersonal principles and functions of management. As the social and political climate in the United States changed during the second quarter of the twentieth century, however, various studies revealed that the classical theories of management could not elicit the kind of employee commitment to the organization that was needed to achieve its goals. In the 1930s, Mayo (1977) and his fellow researchers conducted a series of experiments at the Hawthorne plant of the Western Electric Company in Chicago. They found that the average worker was not primarily motivated by economic incentives, as had been asserted by the classical theorists. On the contrary, the studies revealed that the worker was a "social man" who responded best as a member of a group that accepted him fully and provided him with a sense of belonging. It was also shown that productivity improved when supervisors treated subordinates with dignity and showed an interest in them as individuals.

Barnard (1938), who had served as president of the New Jersey Bell Telephone Company, offered theoretical support to this behavioral view. In contrast to the authoritarian approach of classical theory, Barnard defined organization as a "system of cooperation" in which all members worked together for a common purpose. He introduced the concept of the inducement-contribution balance, whereby companies must offer inducements to get people to do what is necessary to have policies implemented. For example, the Alexander & Alexander case history recommends developing incentive systems to motivate personnel to perform as well as they can (p. 369). Barnard saw the relationship of the employee to the firm as a two-way negotiated process in which the organization obtained the employees' willingness to contribute time, effort, and ability in return for certain rewards. These rewards need not be purely economic, but they must be equitable and consistent with the contribution requested. Furthermore, the use of authority to implement policy must be viewed as legitimate by the subordinate. Thus, whereas classical theory implies that authority is delegated from the top down, Barnard thought of it as delegated upward. According to Barnard's acceptance theory of authority, managers possess authority only when their subordinates are willing to accept their orders.

During the past 30 years, additional studies of the individual in a work setting have increased our understanding of human behavior and of organizational practices that maximize the voluntary participation of employees. A number of psychologists have investigated the question of what motivates human beings to behave as they do. Some believe that individuals are born with or acquire a set of needs and that their behavior is primarily directed at satisfying these needs. Thus, in 1943, Maslow proposed a hierarchy of five universal needs. In ascending order, they are physiological, safety or security, social or the need for belonging, esteem needs, and the need for self-actualization. According to Maslow, all human beings strive to satisfy their needs in the sequence that he presented. Once they satisfy a lower-order need, it is no longer a motivator of behavior, and they seek to satisfy the next higher need. Thus, according to the theory, managers can motivate their employees to perform better if they (1) identify their specific needs and (2) help employees to understand that the rewards they will receive for proper performance will enable them to satisfy these needs.

McClelland (1962), on the other hand, believed that many of humanity's needs were acquired from the culture. He identified three primary needs: the need for achievement, the need for affiliation, and the need for power. Based on the results of his research, McClelland described the person with a high need for achievement as one who likes to take responsibility for solving problems, tends to set moderate achievement goals, in inclined to take calculated risks, and desires feedback on performance. A person with a need for affiliation desires to interact socially with people, and a person with a high need for power concentrates on obtaining and exercising power and authority. Managers who are guided by McClelland's theory would select a person with a high need for achievement to fill a challenging and problem-oriented job. They would choose an individual with a high need for affiliation for a job involving a great deal of personal contact. Finally, in considering candidates for a management-development program, they would give priority to those with a high need for power.

A third approach based on human needs was proposed by Herzberg et al. (1959). According to Herzberg, the satisfaction of a person's lower-order needs was necessary, but not sufficient, to provide job satisfaction. Thus, if an organization provided good working conditions, job security, fair company procedures, and competent technical supervision, the employees would have no grounds for dissatisfaction, but neither would they have any incentive to improve their performance beyond the minimum acceptable level. On the other hand, if an organization gave the employees the opportunity for satisfying their higher-level needs by structuring the task environment so that employees could feel a sense of achievement, receive recognition, be given greater responsibility, and be rewarded with career advancement and growth, the employees would be motivated to achieve the best job performance possible. Herzberg's two-factor theory has taught managers that the way to obtain greater employee commitment is to create more challenging and responsible tasks that will provide intrinsic and motivating satisfactions.

The motivation theories presented thus far focused mainly on the needs and incentives that cause behavior. Other theorists have been more concerned with explaining how individual behavior is energized, directed, and maintained. Adams (1963) studied motives that are developed through a reference person comparison. He found that employees compare their efforts and rewards with those of others in similar work situations in the organization. Equity exists when employees perceive that the ratio of their input (effort) to outcome (reward) is equal to that of other employees; inequity exists when these ratios are not equivalent. The existence of perceived inequity creates inner tension to restore equity. Equity may be achieved by trying to increase outcomes or, failing this, to decrease input. The tension will remain until the ratio balance is restored. Managers have learned from Adams' theory that inequitable situations can cause poor morale, quick turnover, and absenteeism. Because the theory emphasizes the importance of comparisons in the work situation, it may serve as a useful guide to managers who are concerned with equitable reward programs.

The most widely accepted process theory of motivation is known as *expectancy theory*. While several refined versions of the theory have been offered in recent years, Vroom (1964) proposed the original theory. Expectancy theory is based upon an assumption of rational human behavior and bypasses the needs that may stimulate this behavior. Individuals have certain personal goals in life that may be achieved by obtaining certain outcomes in their job situation such as promotion or salary increase. They will rationally deduce that a high level of performance (first-level outcome) will be instrumental in their attaining the desired second-level outcome, such as salary increase, social approval, or other goal. Furthermore, they will evaluate whether their efforts will lead to high performance. Finally, this thought process takes into account the valence (i.e., the value) that both the first- and second-level outcomes have for the individual.

The theory thus explains how rational people size up their jobs. They first ask themselves what is the probability (expectancy) that a given level of effort will result in a given outcome. If, due to lack of ability, experience, or a reasonable work environment, they perceive the probability as small, they will be discouraged from making the effort. They then evaluate whether good performance will lead to a valued outcome. Again, if they do not feel that the chances are good, they will be tempted not to make the effort.

House (1971) proposed the path-goal theory of leadership based on the expectancy-theory model. According to path-goal theory, the manager must clarify the path between effort and performance by training the employees to acquire the skills needed for proper performance and must give the employees the confidence that their efforts will indeed lead to the desired level of perfomance. The manager should then learn what second-level outcomes the subordinates are seeking and make it clear to them that achieving these outcomes is contingent upon high performance. The manager, of course, must be able to fulfill these implied promises.

The preceding theories of motivation have emphasized the individual. Other theorists have accepted the premises of these theories and concentrated on the structure and practices that organizations should adopt to effectively apply the findings of the behavioral scientists. One such theorist, Likert (1967), proposed "System 4 Organization," which summarizes the major aspects of an organization designed on the basis of behavioral-science recommendations. Likert's basic premise is that an organization can be successful only if its objectives are in harmony with the relevant needs and desires of its members. To achieve such harmony, the System 4 Organization proposes a structural design that encourages greater use of the human potential. Managers are urged to adopt participatory methods that stimulate the desired employee behavior; goal-setting, decision-making, and control processes should be decentralized and shared at all levels of the organization; and communications should flow freely throughout the organization—upward and horizontally as well as downward. To implement these processes, the organization design must support three concepts: (1) the principle of supportive relationships, (2) group decisionmaking and group methods of supervision, and (3) high performance goals.

The findings of behavioral scientists regarding human motivations and behavior and the subsequent proposals of organization theorists for structural and procedural modifications can serve as valuable guides for managers. Obviously, managers must recognize how important it is for employees to develop a strong sense of commitment to the goals of the organization. A person involved in making a decision will feel committed to it and want to see it implemented. For this reason, participation is the best answer to the implementation problem; however, various studies indicate that it is not an organizational panacea. Its major advantages have been shown to apply in small homogeneous groups at the lower levels of the hierarchy. At higher organizational levels, executives may be reluctant to resort to participation when the decisions are of great importance to the company. Furthermore, subordinates are likely to accept and implement top-level decisions by virtue of their source alone without the need for participation. Nevertheless, full implementation requires support at lower levels of the organization. At these levels, participation encourages employees to be committed to the organization and to its objectives so that they will accept policies, strategies, and plans that seem to be in the organization's interest.

The manager who is implementing a company's plans must be cognizant of two major dilemmas, which according to March and Simon (1958), are inherent in all structured organizations. To maintain adequate control of an organization, top management must insist upon a certain conformity of behavior as laid down in policies, rules, and procedures. Such practices are necessary to insure a commonness of objectives and a perception of shared goals. On the other hand, the desired conformity may develop into rigidity of behavior, which may strain the relationship among subunits of the organization and between members of the organization and various elements of the environment such as clients or customers. Rigid behavior may also inhibit the flexibility and adaptability often required when implementation occurs under dynamically changing conditions.

The second dilemma is the dysfunctional consequences of delegation, which is one of the basic activities of organizing. The role of strategy is to guide the organization as a whole. Yet, except for very small organizations, the organizing process dictates the establishment of subgroups composed of divisions, departments, sections, and other groupings that develop their own sets of goals and objectives, which often are not congruent with those of the overall organization. The maintenance needs of the subunits dictate a commitment to the subunit goals over and above their contribution to the total organizational program often resulting in increased conflict among organizational subunits.

These two dilemmas highlight the importance of effective leadership in the implementation of a company's plans. Aware that rigid behavior is likely to be caused by the bureaucratic aspects of the firm, the competent leader will work toward modifying the structure to encourage adaptive behavior with a minimum loss of reliability. Recognizing the almost inevitable clash between some subunit goals and the overall organizational goals, the successful chief executive will strive to achieve the internalization of the organizational goals by all of its members. Above all, the chief executive will serve as a linchpin, coordinating the efforts of all the disparate units toward the goal of implementation.

PLANNING AND CONTROL

A successful planning system must:

1. Communicate a well-defined plan of reasonably attainable goals.

2. Engage the participation and support of all levels of managerial personnel.
3. Provide feedback for evaluation of results as a basis for appropriate subsequent action.

The third element refers to the control portion of the planning cycle. The management literature lists planning and control as two universal functions of management—every manager must perform them. At the same time, they are treated as separate functions, which implies that they are the responsibility of different sets of managers. The controllership is the unique responsibility of the financial executive who exercises control over all the operations of the firm. However, the controller's task is to exercise an internal audit responsibility, that is, to provide an independent check on the performance of all the units of the organization. This in no way relieves the line managers from the responsibility of controlling the effective implementation of planned programs in their own area of operation. Also, the controller will generally develop, and provide the line manager with, the mechanisms needed to exercise effective control, such as budgets, reports, information, control devices, etc. Again, such staff assistance confirms the obligation of managers to control their own activities and those of their subordinates. Within this framework, we will explore the control element of the planning manager's job.

One of the most widely accepted approaches to managerial control is the closed-loop model shown in Figure 6-1. This model begins its cycle with the establishment of objectives for the organization and completes it with their attainment. From the time goals are set until they are reached, important managerial functions take place. The control function requires that standards of performance be developed in those strategic elements that affect the attainment of the objectives. Then performance must be measured to determine whether it meets the standards. If performance is outside the acceptable limits of variation from the standard, corrective action leading toward the attainment of objectives is necessary. The model can thus be seen as a closed cycle of control, beginning and ending with corporate objectives. (The role played by the control function in Alexander & Alexander is discussed in the case history on p. 372.)

Anthony (1965) distinguished two levels of control. He defined management control as

> ... the process by which managers assure that resources are obtained and used effectively and efficiently in the accomplishment of the organization's objectives.

This concept thus combines both planning and control. Anthony explained operational control as "the process of assuring that specific tasks are carried out effectively and efficiently." Such tasks require little judgment to know what is

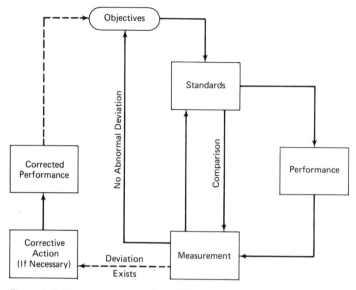

Figure 6-1. Management control model.

to be done. The planning manager is obviously concerned with management control as defined by Anthony.

Another way of viewing the control function was proposed by Greiner (1972); he described the evolution of different control techniques as organizations develop. The newly formed organization is generally small and entrepreneurially oriented. Control of activities comes from immediate feedback from the marketplace; the management acts as the customers react. The next phase of development is characterized by the introduction of professional management, which establishes standards of performance, cost centers, and a framework for budgetary control. As the firm grows, its structure tends to become centralized and is characterized by profit centers designed to stimulate motivation and the development of a reporting system based on the principle of management by exception. At this point, top management may sense that it is losing control over a highly diversified field operation. Some managements attempt to return to centralized management, which usually fails due to the scope of operations. The more successful organizations will adapt by developing special coordination techniques. During this fourth phase, formal planning procedures are established and headquarters personnel initiate companywide programs of control and review for line managers. Anthony's concept of management control is appropriate to the interweaving of planning and control at this stage. The structural characteristics of this phase of growth inevitably lead to a lack of confidence between line and staff, and to conflict between headquarters and the field. Therefore, Greiner described the development of a fifth and final stage that emphasizes interpersonal collaboration, greater spontaneity in management action through teams, and skillful confrontation of interpersonal differences. Social control and self-discipline take over from formal control, and organizational control is achieved by mutual goal-setting.

The control models proposed by Anthony and Greiner highlight the fact that control is a multidimensional concept inextricably intertwined with the planning function. The planner must recognize that it is not valid to monitor the performance of all planned activities, regardless of their present validity. No matter how good the company is at planning, events will differ from forecasts. The wise planner will accept this and will be primarily concerned that implementation changes are made responsibly and intelligently rather than mechanically. Managers should be expected to fulfill all plans that are still appropriate and to substitute modified plans when the original ones are inappropriate. Next, we will consider the major mechanisms available to implement control.

The Budget as a Coordinating and Control Tool

It has been shown in previous chapters how the budget serves as a planning tool. In addition, budgeting facilitates as well as forces the coordination of functional operations in both the development and carrying out of plans. Production must be coordinated with sales for efficient use of personnel, financial resources, facilities, and inventories. The planning budget helps to mesh all productive, promotional, financial, and administrative functions by indicating interrelationships and assigning specific responsibilities. The budget is the communication link between line and staff personnel; it forces the responsible individuals to perceive the relationships their unit holds to others, as well as to the total organization.

Probably the most widely accepted function of the budgeting process is control. Because of the nature and longer-term aspect of strategic goals and plans, it is difficult to use these as standards against which to compare results spanning yearly or even shorter operating periods. As discussed previously, specific plans and policies are established for these shorter time periods, usually in the form of various departmental budgets. As long as these more specific standards are consistent with the broader strategic elements, they can serve as milestones against which to measure the organization's progress toward attainment of its strategic plans. By comparing actual to budget performance, the decisionmaker can evaluate the effectiveness of performance and can take remedial action where the actual falls short of budgeted performance.

In practice, the operating manager encounters several difficulties in using the budget as a control tool. In a dynamic environment, unanticipated events may invalidate original budget figures. If the original figures are not modified, can the subordinate be held responsible for the resulting variance? If they are modified, should actual performance be compared to the revised figures or to the original figures? Another frequent problem is that the budget may include areas that are not controllable by the subordinate, or more likely are under the joint control of the subordinate and another individual. For example, if deliveries are not made to customers, did manufacturing fail to produce what the sales department sold, or did sales fail to sell what manufacturing produced? (The unreliability of budget standards is discussed in the case history, starting on p. 372.)

The attempt to motivate employees to meet budgeted targets raises yet another problem. If subordinates did not participate in preparing the budget, will they try to perform within the budget? On the other hand, are the subordinates privy to enough information to make a constructive contribution to budget preparation? These difficulties indicate that the budget will serve as an effective tool of control only to the extent that it is administered with managerial skill, wisdom, and judgment.

Other Control Mechanisms

Two techniques in reporting have evolved that have significantly improved the manager's ability to exercise effective control. The technique of *responsibility reporting* recognizes that the proper assignment of responsibility and accountability is essential to an effective management-control system. Thus, responsibility reporting incorporates a system that organizes performance data into information tailored to the authority-responsibility structure of the firm. The structure, in turn, should be developed with the organization's strategy as the basic criterion. If we consider the case of a division that is producing and marketing three product groups, a combined divisional statement may satisfy the needs of both investors and the Internal Revenue Service. Under the concept of responsibility reporting, however, the divisional performance would be broken down into the separate performance of each product group so that each product manager can be evaluated upon the quality of his or her efforts and contribution to the firm.

The principle of strategic levels or points of control underlies the technique of *exception reporting.* It takes only a minimum of work experience for a manager to discover that it is not feasible to personally control every aspect of an area of responsibility. Thus, organizations have evolved the concept of monitoring performance at critical stages of the workflow only. These points of control represented a significant advance in managerial efficiency. However, some innovative managers observed that, in controlling at strategic points, much of their follow-up activities served only to confirm that the operation was proceeding smoothly. As a result, given the availability of standards, guidelines, and benchmarks, there was no reason why control could not be exercised by the employee at the work station itself. Only when actual output varied drastically from the plan was it necessary to bring the situation to the attention of the manager. Such an approach is known as "management by exception."

The advent of the computer facilitated the wider use of exception reporting. Under manual systems, someone has to review all transactions in order to extract the exceptional cases. The computer can be programmed to compare the results of every transaction to a standard and to print out every deviation from the standard by more than a fixed quantity or percentage. For example, an inventory exception report will print out on a daily basis every raw material that went below a specified minimum inventory level. This permits the purchasing agent to reorder these items immediately without having to review the entire inventory line and in sufficient time to avoid running out of stock.

Motivation and Control

Obviously budgeting and the other control mechanisms we have described do not "control" the organization. Managers exercise control, and the mechanisms are tools to help them do so. Through this perspective, we can begin to understand why a management-control system will be effective in one organization and will fail in another. Why? As stated previously, organizations are made up of people, and it is people who will determine the success or failure of the organization.

If we were to examine a firm with a poorly functioning control system, we would probably find it characterized by:

1. Resistance and noncompliance by employees at all levels
2. Antagonism to controls and to those who administer them
3. Unreliable performance information because of this antagonism and resistance
4. The need for close surveillance of employees
5. High administrative costs

The employees did not join the organization imbued with these negative attitudes. However, if we consider conventional management-control systems from the viewpoint of those who are controlled rather than of those who do the controlling, we can see how these attitudes are formed.

The basic purpose of a control system is to obtain compliance with goals and standards. In theory, success in meeting the standards should result in rewards, whereas noncompliance should lead to punishment or to the withholding of rewards. In practice, the rewards are long-term, usually in the form of salary increases and promotion. Punishment for noncompliance, however, is an immediate and daily threat under a rigorous control system. Therefore, it makes sense that in daily behavior, an individual's chief motivation will be to escape punishment. Such behavior, moreover, is encouraged by the major concepts and characteristics of control systems, which were discussed previously.

The logic of accountability as a management principle is indisputable. In practical application, the principle is often used to discover and punish noncompliance with standards and controls. Accounting controls, budgets, and standards are elaborate systems of performance measurements; the potential result of each measurement may be punishment for the individual whose performance is being measured. Control through measures that stress variance from normal standards also emphasizes mistakes, failures, and substandard performance. Management by exception brings only one's errors to the attention of one's superior. Feedback of results is channeled through one's superior. Is it any wonder that the average employee may view the control system as a sword of Damocles constantly hovering overhead and react with defensive, protective, resistant, and aggressive behavior?

We seem to have exposed an irreconcilable contradiction in organizational life. On the one hand, we have maintained that an effective management-control system is absolutely essential for achieving the strategic goals of the organization. But we have also shown that the conventional control system may be perceived as a threat and lead to antagonism and resistance by employees, thus defeating its very purpose. Behavioral scientists have pointed to organizational characteristics that can motivate employees to identify with the goals of the firm. They have stressed that the primary managerial task is to help the organization achieve and maintain high commitment, and that identification and commitment rest on linking the individual's own goals with those of the organization. This is best achieved by open communication, mutual trust, mutual support, and effective management of conflict. In terms of the control function, the behavioral approach would propose the following practices:

1. Mutual goal-setting and congruence between subgoals and organizational goals
2. Participation in the setting of standards
3. Isolation of controllable from uncontrollable factors
4. Fostering of interdepartmental cooperation rather than intracompany competition
5. Use of the budget and accounting systems as motivational rather than policing devices

Since control systems are administered by managers, the style and leadership philosophy of the individual manager will, in large measure, dictate both the type and the effectiveness of a company's control system. In recognition of this close interrelationship, Camman and Nadler (1976), in the article starting on

p. 183, recommend that each firm should fit its control system to the style of its managers.

REFERENCES

Adams, J. S. 1963. Toward an understanding of inequity. *Journal of Abnormal and Social Psychology* 67: 422–436.

This article brought equity theory to the attention of behavioral researchers who were interested in understanding human motivation.

Anthony, R. N. 1965. *Planning and Control Systems: A Framework for Analysis.* Boston, Mass.: Division of Research, Harvard Business School.

A comprehensive presentation of the major elements of planning and control systems.

Barnard, C. I. 1938. *The Functions of the Executive.* Cambridge, Mass.: Harvard University Press.

This pioneering work by the former president of New Jersey Bell Telephone Company stresses the importance of cooperation by all participants in an organization. A forerunner of modern behavorial theories of management.

Camman, Cortlandt and D. A. Nadler. 1976. Fit control systems to your managerial style. *Harvard Business Review* 54(1): 65–77.

Points out that a control system can succeed only if it is compatible with the leadership style and philosophy of the managers who implement the system. *Reprinted herein on pp. 183–194.*

Greiner, L. E. 1972. Evolution and revolution as organizations grow. *Harvard Business Review* 50(4): 37–46.

A framework that proposes five identifiable stages of development in the growth of an organization.

Herzberg, F., B. Mausner, and B. Snyderman, 1959. *The Motivation to Work.* 2nd ed. New York: John Wiley & Sons.

A detailed presentation of the two-factor theory of job satisfaction.

House, R. J. 1971. A path-goal theory of leadership effectiveness. *Administrative Science Quarterly* 16: 321–339.

Presents a new theory of leadership derived from the expectancy theory of motivation.

Likert, R., 1967. *The Human Organization: Its Management and Value.* New York: McGraw-Hill.

A leading proponent of the human relations approach in work situations describes the System 4 Organization.

March, J. G. and H. A. Simon. 1958. *Organizations.* New York: John Wiley & Sons.

A proposed model of how organizations function based upon the limited rationality of human beings.

Maslow, A. H. 1943. A theory of human motivation. *Psychological Review* 50: 370–396.

Presents a theory of human motivation based upon an assumed "hierarchy of needs" present in all human beings.

Mayo, Elton. 1977. *The Human Problems of an Industrial Civilization.* New York: Viking Press.

An analysis of the effects of industrialization upon the worker drawing upon the author's experience with the Hawthorne studies.

McClelland, D. C. 1962. Business drive and rational achievement. *Harvard Business Review* 40(4): 99–112.

The economic success of the Western world is attributed to the cultural fostering of the needs for achievement, power, and affiliation in Western individuals. The author suggests that the best way the West can help the underdeveloped countries is by awakening these needs in their citizens.

Schendel, Dan. 1976. *Implementing Strategic Planning Systems.* Paper presented at the Academy of Management annual meeting, Kansas City, Missouri, August 1976. Reprinted herein on pp. 195–211.

A review of the implementation phase of strategic planning systems.

Simon, H. A. 1965. *Administrative Behavior.* New York: The Free Press.

Traces the behavior of people in organizations back to the limited rationality and biological limitations of human beings and enunciates a set of principles for organizations which recognizes these human limitations.

Vroom, V. H. 1964. *Work and Motivation* New York: John Wiley & Sons.

Presents the expectancy-valence theory of motivation to work.

Fit Control Systems
to Your
Managerial Style

Cortland Cammann
and
David A. Nadler

Not long ago, the Boy Scouts of America revealed that membership figures coming in from the field had been falsified. In response to the pressures of a national membership drive, people within the organization had vastly overstated the number of new Boy Scouts. To their chagrin, the leaders found something that other managers have also discovered: organizational control systems often produce unintended consequences. The drive to increase membership had motivated people to increase the number of new members reported, but it had not motivated them to increase the number of Boy Scouts actually enrolled.

The case of the Boy Scouts is a clear example of a widespread problem. Organizations spend large amounts of money, time, and effort in designing and maintaining control systems. These systems are intended to enhance an organization's ability to coordinate the actions of its members and to identify problems as they arise. Often, however, instead of increasing organizational control these systems reduce the amount of effective control that the organization exercises.

Why does this happen? Our research and the research of others indicate that the problem often lies with the ways that managers use control systems.[1] Most control systems, including budgetary, management information, and financial accounting systems, are essentially measurements. They regularly collect information about specific aspects of organizational performance.

The systems themselves are not capable of directly controlling organizational performance. Rather, they provide information to the managers who are in a position to exercise control. If managers use the information well, the control system works. If they use it poorly, the system may produce unintended effects.

Significantly, organizations seldom invest much effort in training managers to

1. Studies such as Chris Argyris's *The Impact of Budgets on People* (Ithaca, New York: Cornell University, 1952) and Frank J. Jasinsky's "Use and Misuse of Efficiency Controls," Harvard Business Review July-August 1956, p. 105, provide concrete examples of the problems that can arise from poor use of feedback systems.

use control systems. Instead, most spend a lot of time designing, constructing, refining, and improving the technical aspects of their systems. The result is that while organizational control systems continually become more precise, accurate, and technologically sophisticated, two questions are often overlooked:

1. How effective is the system (and the way it is used) in doing what it is supposed to do?
2. How could the system be better used?

Recent research in a number of organizations has provided some answers to these questions.[2] First, control systems influence the way organization members direct their energies on the job; the members are more likely to put time and effort into those areas covered by the systems. Second, how members respond to control systems depends largely on the way managers use the systems. Third, different managers develop different strategies for using control systems. Finally, each strategy has certain drawbacks and benefits.

Only when managers understand (a) how these systems influence the behavior of their subordinates and (b) what trade-offs occur in each control strategy, can they learn to use organizational control systems effectively.

In the balance of this article we shall discuss what managers should consider when they choose a control style. We shall examine the various ways in which control systems influence managerial behavior. Then, we shall discuss two major strategies for using control systems, the various issues that ought to be considered when choosing a particular control style, and the implications of the final decision.

INFLUENCE ON SUBORDINATES

When an area is covered by a control system, organization members concentrate on improving their performance in the measured area. There are three reasons for this direction of energy:

1. Measurement of an area of activity indicates that top management feels the area is important and bears watching.
2. Managers generally use control system measures when they evaluate subordinate performance. Since the subordinate usually feels that the manager's evaluation influences his or her rewards, the subordinate tends to put energy into the measured areas.
3. It is easy for an organization member to see changes in performance mea-

2. Anthony G. Hopwood's *An Accounting System and Managerial Behavior* (London: Haymarket Publishing, Ltd., 1974) and Geert H. Hofstede's *The Game of Budget Control* (Assen, Netherlands: Van Gorcum, 1967) look systematically at the ways in which accounting information is used and the impact these uses can have.

sures that are part of the control system. If his performance is improving, this can be a source of personal satisfaction.

Exhibit I provides an example of how performance measurement directs subordinate energy. In two different organizations—one a northeastern public utility, the other a midwestern bank—employees were asked to indicate to what degree different areas of activity were measured. At another point, they were asked how much time and effort they put into each area. As shown in the exhibit, the general pattern is that the more people perceive that an area is measured, the more time and effort they put into it.

Effects of Control Systems

It appears that control systems direct how much energy subordinates put into an area, but how is this energy used? On one hand, subordinates may be motivated to increase their levels of performance, producing larger quantities or higher quality work.

On the other hand, measurement may produce the results we saw in the Boy Scouts' example. Subordinates direct their efforts into "game playing" to "beat the system." Rather than performing well, employees often set low goals that can be easily met, manipulate measures to come out with the desired results, and actually sabotage the system's information base.

For example, a large government organization required each person to fill out a form accounting for the way he spent his time in 20-minute blocks. The intent was to motivate the employees to manage their time and to generate valid information about how much time they were allocating to different tasks. The result, however, was vastly different. The employees saw the system as an attempt to regiment their lives and activities.

Thus, instead of being a useful tool, the time sheets became a recreational activity. On Friday afternoons at the work break, employees got together to fill out their time sheets, each competing to see who could come up with the most preposterous record of activities. Needless to say, these records had no relation to actual work done. The system did not motivate people to increase performance; it motivated them to play games with the system.

Exhibit II summarizes the effects of control systems. The existence of measures in an area has an effect on subordinate behavior, but measurement is not the only factor. The measures have to be perceived by the employees as being reasonably accurate, and they have to be used skillfully by the managers.

STRATEGIES OF CONTROL

A manager must give serious thought to his use of control system measures in any one area. He must consider the consequences of his actions in terms of the

Exhibit I. Area measurement and effort in two organizations

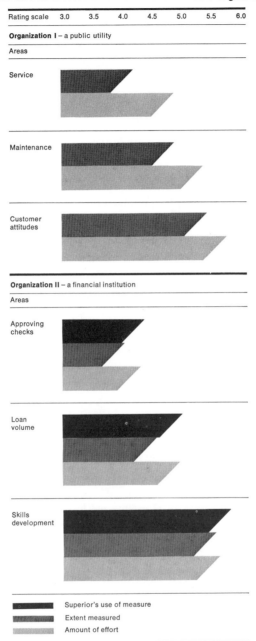

| Rating scale | 3.0 | 3.5 | 4.0 | 4.5 | 5.0 | 5.5 | 6.0 |

Organization I – a public utility

Areas

Service

Maintenance

Customer
attitudes

Organization II – a financial institution

Areas

Approving
checks

Loan
volume

Skills
development

Superior's use of measure
Extent measured
Amount of effort

Exhibit II. How control systems and their use affect behavior

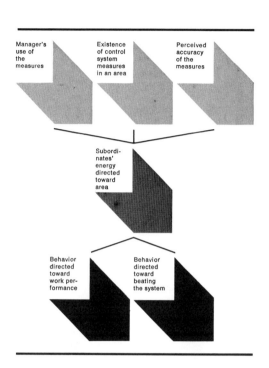

kinds of behavior that he motivates in his subordinates. Although there is a range of strategies for control, two major approaches—external control and internal motivation—seem to prove most useful for many managers. *Exhibit III* shows that each of these strategies requires different behavior on the part of the manager; each can have either desirable or undesirable effects on subordinate behavior.

External Control

This strategy is based on the assumption that subordinates in the particular situation are motivated primarily by external rewards and need to be controlled by their supervisors. To use the control system effectively in this way requires three steps.

First, the goals and standards associated with the system need to be made relatively difficult in order to "stretch" subordinates and leave little room for slack.

Exhibit III. Two different strategies of control

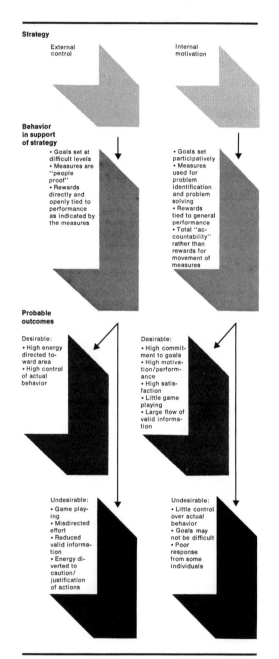

Strategy

External control

Internal motivation

Behavior in support of strategy

- Goals set at difficult levels
- Measures are "people proof"
- Rewards directly and openly tied to performance as indicated by the measures

- Goals set participatively
- Measures used for problem identification and problem solving
- Rewards tied to general performance
- Total "accountability" rather than rewards for movement of measures

Probable outcomes

Desirable:
- High energy directed toward area
- High control of actual behavior

Desirable:
- High commitment to goals
- High motivation/performance
- High satisfaction
- Little game playing
- Large flow of valid information

Undesirable:
- Game playing
- Misdirected effort
- Reduced valid information
- Energy diverted to caution/ justification of actions

Undesirable:
- Little control over actual behavior
- Goals may not be difficult
- Poor response from some individuals

Second, the area measures need to be constructed so that they are "people proof," to prevent individuals from being able to manipulate the measures.

Third, rewards need to be directly and openly tied to performance, as indicated by the measures in the control system, to ensure that the subordinates have an incentive to work hard.

An example of the external control approach would be to evaluate a manager solely on the performance of his profit center, with relatively high levels of profit being budgeted and with his compensation tied primarily and directly to the number of dollars of profit.

This external control strategy can have different effects. Ono one hand, subordinates may channel a great deal of energy into measured areas and may try hard to make their measures move, since they can gain rewards by doing so. Where the system is very tightly structured, the result will be a high degree of control of subordinate behavior. On the other hand, several undesirable results may occur.

First, such a strategy may motivate organization members to improve their performance measures but not create any commitment to their doing a better job. The subordinates will begin to develop an attitude toward performance in which "doing well" means doing well on the performance measures, not necessarily performing their jobs more effectively. As a result, if they can increase their "performance" by manipulating the measures, providing false information, intentionally setting low goals and standards, or sabotaging the system, the organization members can be expected to do so.

Second, such a strategy may result in misdirected effort. Subordinates may put all of their energies into the particular behavior that is measured, while forgetting other behavior that, although not measured, is also vital. For example, if all efforts are directed toward increasing sales volume, the amount of effort devoted to ongoing customer service may be decreased. In this case, the result is short-term maximization in the measured area with possible negative long-term effects on unmeasured areas.

Third, such a strategy may tend to reduce the flow of valid information, particularly negative information. If people are directly rewarded for positive movement of measures, they may become motivated to withhold information that would negate the meaning of those measures and to withhold negative information from higher-level managers who need it for decision making.

Finally, such a strategy may bring about excessive caution, directing energy toward justification of all actions. Subordinates may be motivated to ensure that the measures either continue to look good (by not taking any risks), or to assemble "just in case" files filled with information justifying a decrease in measured performance. In either case, energy is directed toward coping with the system, rather than toward the larger goal of making the organization more effective.

Internal Motivation

In this strategy, management assumes that subordinates can be motivated by building their commitments to organizational goals and by their being involved in the necessary tasks. They assume that employees will be motivated by the feelings of accomplishment, achievement, recognition, and self-esteem that come from having performed a job well. The strategy of internal motivation is implemented by using the control system in a very different manner than in the external control strategy.

First, although goals are set, the most important feature of this approach is not the difficulty in achieving the goals but the fact that they are set participatively. Those people who are responsible for achieving goals are given some influence over the nature of those goals.

Second, the measures are used for joint problem identification and solution rather than for punishment or blame. When a performance begins to move in an undesired direction, it is not the time for heads to roll. It is the time for managers and subordinates to meet together (a) to determine the reasons for the change, and (b) to develop solutions to the problems that have come up. Thus the system takes on an "early warning" function of surfacing problems, beginning the resolution process before those problems reach the crisis state.

Finally, although rewards are tied to performance, they are not tied to one or two specific measures. Rather, the reward structure emphasizes accountability for the entire job performance, only part of which may be represented by the measures. In general, the control system becomes problem-based and future-oriented. The system helps the manager exercise control of subordinate behavior by directing future efforts, rather than by punishing each person's past actions.

This internal motivation strategy may have different effects. It may generate high commitment to goals because the organization member participates in setting them and feels responsible for seeing that they are achieved. This may lead to greater energy directed toward task performance. As performance increases and as the individual monitors his progress through the measures of the control system, the strategy may also enhance the employee's satisfaction in performing his job well.

Thus the open nature of the control system and its general, rather than specific, accountability mean that there is little incentive for subordinates to play games or to behave dysfunctionally. More important, it encourages and rewards the flow of valid information, particularly negative information.

At the same time, such a strategy may have some undesirable effects. The comparatively loose nature of this approach means that the manager will have less control over the behavior of his subordinates. Because the manager gives up total control over the specific goals, subordinates may establish less ambitious goals.

In addition, since the information provided by the control system is for problem solving and not for evaluation, it becomes difficult to use it as a basis for giving rewards. Thus the manager has to sacrifice some of the value that is inherent in the external control approach in order to build internal motivation on the part of subordinates.

Finally, some individuals may not respond to the participative process because of differences in working style or personality. These people, therefore, will not be motivated to perform well within this strategy framework.

CHOICE STRATEGIES

Neither of the two strategies just discussed is necessarily the "right" strategy to use in all cases. Since each has certain drawbacks and benefits, a manager must consciously and carefully choose the approach that suits his particular situation. In making that choice, he needs to consider the following four issues:

1. *Consistency between strategy choice and managerial style.* In choosing a control strategy, a manager may have to modify either his style or the strategy so that his total approach to managing is consistent. For instance, if a manager generally makes all important decisions without involving subordinates, it would be a mistake for him to use an internal motivation approach. The subordinates would be accustomed to following the manager's lead. They may not be capable of setting realistic goals on their own; or worse, they may use their influence to set easy objectives that they know they can achieve. It is only in the context of a generally participative manager-subordinate relationship that an internal motivation approach to organizational control is likely to be effective.

2. *Organizational climate, structure, and reward system.* A control strategy, to be most effective, should be consistent with other factors in the organization that determine employee behavior. For example, a tight control system in an organization that normally provides a great deal of discretion and freedom for employees would soon run into problems.

3. *Reliability of job performance measures.* In some cases, control system measures accurately reflect job performance. In others, the measures do not adequately indicate how well the job is being done. When the control system is an unreliable indicator of performance, it is hard to implement a tight external control strategy since the use of inaccurate or unreliable measures as a basis for evaluation and reward could have disastrous consequences. Under such conditions, a looser and more internally oriented organizational control strategy is required.

4. *Individual differences among subordinates.* Because people are motivated by different needs, they may respond differently to the same organizational structure. The choice of control strategy assumes that the manager

knows something about the nature of the people who work for him. Individuals who are committed to the work itself (e.g., in many professional occupations) are likely to be less responsive to an external control strategy than those individuals whose primary motivation is financial reward or promotion.

A manager must also consider how much employees desire to participate in decision making. Some people may respond well to the opportunity for participation, while others may not want to become more involved or assume the responsibility. Thus the types of people who work for the manager should be a factor influencing his choice of a control strategy.

An Informed Choice

At first glance, it may appear that a manager has too many factors to juggle to enable him to make an effective choice. One way around this problem is for the manager to lay out the key decisions and choice points sequentially.

First, the manager needs to ask himself a number of questions (see *Exhibit IV*). What kind of managerial style does he generally use? What kind of organization is he in? How accurate and reliable are his important performance measures? Finally, how much do his subordinates desire to participate in decision making?

Second, the manager must systematically evaluate his answers to determine which strategy is most appropriate. One way of doing this is by using a decision-tree approach (see *Exhibit V*). As indicated by the exhibit, different combinations of answers to the key questions lead the manager to different recommended strategies with different issues concerning their implementation.

In addition to the decision steps outlined in *Exhibit V,* the manager also needs to consider the trade-offs between the different strategies that may apply to his particular situation. Obviously, he must weigh the desirable or undesirable effects (as listed in *Exhibit III*) that a control system may have on his particular group of subordinates.

For example, if the opportunities for game playing are few and the costs to the company of game playing are low, the external control strategy may be more feasible. In most organzations, however, the potential costs of game playing are high. Therefore, managers should give serious consideration to the internal motivation strategy, especially if the basic decision-making process indicates that subordinate participation is feasible.

A control system and the way that it is used constitutes a potentially powerful tool for influencing the behavior of individuals in organizations. Just as the manager needs to make a careful and informed choice among control strategies, the organization needs to be conscious of the alternative approaches to designing

Exhibit IV. Questions a manager should ask himself when choosing a control strategy

1. In general, what kind of managerial style do I have?	
Participative	*Directive*
I frequently consult my subordinates on decisions, encourage them to disagree with my opinion, share information with them, and let them make decisions whenever possible.	I usually take most of the responsibility for and make most of the major decisions, pass on only the most relevant job information, and provide detailed and close direction for my subordinates.

2. In general, what kind of climate, structure, and reward system does my organization have?	
Participative	*Nonparticipative*
Employees at all levels of the organization are urged to participate in decisions and influence the course of events. Managers are clearly rewarded for developing employee skills and decision-making capacities.	Most important decisions are made by a few people at the top of the organization. Managers are not rewarded for developing employee competence or for encouraging employees to participate in decision making.

3. How accurate and reliable are the measures of key areas of subordinate performance?	
Accurate	*Inaccurate*
All major aspects of performance can be adequately measured; changes in measures accurately reflect changes in performance; and measures cannot be easily sabotaged or faked by subordinates.	Not all critical aspects of performance can be measured; measures often do not pick up on important changes in performance; good performance cannot be adequately defined in measurement terms; and measures can be easily sabotaged.

4. Do my subordinates desire to participate and respond well to opportunities to take responsibility for decision making and performance?	
High desire to participate	*Low desire to participate*
Employees are eager to participate in decisions, are involved in the work itself, can make a contribution to decision making, and want to take more responsibility.	Employees do not want to be involved in many decisions, do not want additional responsibility, have little to contribute to decisions being made, and are not very involved in the work itself.

and using control systems. Becoming aware of the potential effects of control systems and of the great importance of the process of control—as opposed to the technology of control—is central to making an organization and its people more productive and effective.

Exhibit V. A decision tree for choosing a control strategy

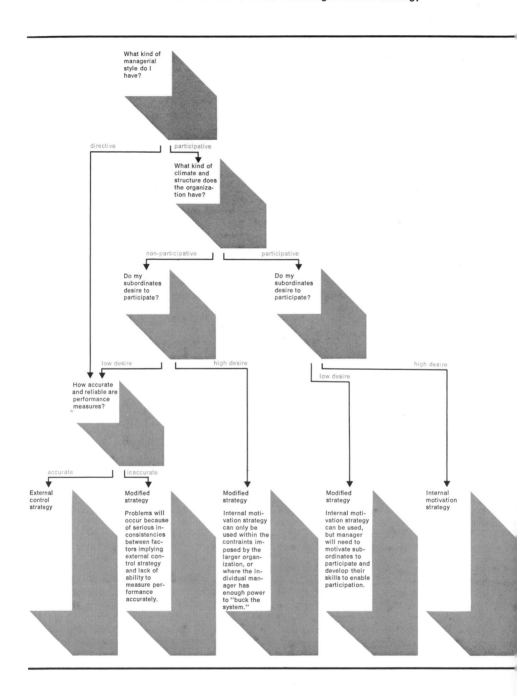

Implementing Strategic Planning Systems

Dan Schendel

Over the past 20 years, business firms have paid increasing attention to long-range planning—which is now often termed *strategic planning*. As the pace of our economic, social, political, and technical life quickens, top managers also have found themselves increasingly concerned with what Barnard (1956) once called *effectiveness* and what Drucker (1974) has variously called the *entrepreneurial decision* or "doing the right things."

A useful distinction can be made between *operations management,* those essentially day-to-day activities necessary to running a firm efficiently in whatever directions it is headed, and *strategic management.* Schendel and Hatten (1972), Ansoff (1972), and others have suggested that strategic management deals with entrepreneurial choice and the basic directions of the firm that help insure the future of the firm. For example, General Electric makes a distinction between strategic and operations management in its organization structure and in the ways in which it is managed (Springer 1973).

Although there is more to operations and strategic management than planning, to the practicing senior manager the distinction between the two modes of management is perhaps most evident in the different planning work that needs to be done for each managerial mode. More and more, planning systems are being sought and adopted that can insure that both the effectiveness and efficiency questions are answered, that the strategy will be explicitly managed, that its basic components will be kept in balance, and that it is being efficiently implemented.

Planning systems are developed to produce plans. In other words, a system produces a product, and this distinction is an important one to consider. Managers deal with results or are charged with producing them, and very often they are not concerned with *how* they produce them. Nevertheless, a good technique or system is as vital to producing good planning products as a correct stroke is to producing a winning score in golf or tennis. Our concern will be not so much with results or products, but with the planning system, specifically, the strategic planning system.

The purpose of this paper, then, is to present several basic issues that arise in

Reprinted with permission of Dan Schendel, Purdue University. Adapted from a paper presented at the National Meeting of the Academy of Management, Kansas City, Missouri, 1976.

implementing strategic planning systems in business organizations, and to develop possible ways of resolving these issues so that a workable strategic planning system results. We are not concerned with formulating or implementing strategy so much as we are with developing a system for accomplishing both of these important strategic management tasks in practice. A basic premise here is that strategic planning systems designed for a specific business organization and its circumstances can produce sound strategy.

There are three basic questions to be addressed in installation of strategic planning systems.

1. Do differing strategic planning systems exist?
2. If so, how can the proper system be selected?
3. Once chosen, what can be done to install the system to make it work?

THREE CASE STUDIES

During the past two years, three intensive cases involving three separate firms have been under study. In two of them, the author has served as a consultant charged with designing and installing a formal strategic planning system. In the third, the author was allowed close observation of a system, but provided only occasional input. The ideas and data underlying this work are taken from three intensive cases, either studied, or directly participated in, by the author.

Case 1: Multinational, Multidivisional Firm

The first firm is a conglomerate in the 100 largest manufacturing firms in the United States. It operates around the world, has profit-decentralized divisions managed in terms of groups of divisions, and operates with as complex an organization as exists in today's business world.

The development of its strategic planning system was viewed from an operating division with the oldest, and one of the largest, of the groups. The firm was developing a group-level strategic planning system, although it had already started work on a strategic planning system at the corporate level.

Case 2: Large Regulated Utility

The author assisted one of the largest natural gas utilities in the United States in designing and installing a strategic planning system. This company had an operations planning activity, but no separate planning staff. It had undertaken a 10-year long-range plan that was little more than an extrapolation of existing business trends. The company is organized along functional lines, and what planning work was done was superimposed upon the existing line management without staff assistance.

The assignment to develop a strategic planning system was made by the president, who also accepted a recommendation to establish a corporate planning staff reporting directly to his executive office. The planning office was separated into operations and strategic planning specialists, with initial emphasis given to the latter.

The natural gas industry is under threat of decreasing supplies, and as a result faces a finite future. Under such conditions, diversification becomes a strategic alternative of considerable interest. Although the interest in strategic planning arose from the threat of a substantially altered environment surrounding the energy field, a change in senior management and in managerial styles seemed to be the specific triggering device.

Case 3: Small Plastics Firm

The third company is a fabricator of plastic components for various industries such as electrical, plumbing, and business machines. Its products are custom-designed, high-margin, and low-volume with high value added, primarily in the form of technical content. Its current sales are under $25 million, which makes it very small in comparison to the multidivisional firm and the natural gas utility.

The company, which has strong growth opportunities, was led by a new young president into a number of newer managerial methods, including strategic planning. The company is organized functionally, and, given its small size, it is unable to afford the planning staff specialists or other staff specialists that are possible in a larger firm.

The company, while wholly owned by a large, privately held company, operates independently. It retains its own cash and to date has not incurred debt or had capital requirements that exceeded its ability to generate its own needs. This freedom permits it to do its own strategic planning as if it were a smaller firm entirely free of outside control.

Basic Strategic Planning Components

Schendel (1974) has suggested that there are three basic components to strategy:

1. goals or ends
2. resources and means used to achieve these ends
3. constraints arising out of the environment that limit what ends and means can be chosen.

If a specific, preferably good, strategy is to be produced as a product of the strategic planning system, then the system needs to address three strategy components.

Based on the case studies, as well as the concept of strategy and strategic management developing in the literature, and a review of other planning studies (for example, Henry 1967, and Steiner 1969), we suggest that a strategic planning system should exhibit these basic components:

1. A mechanism for developing the goal structure of the organization
2. A means of identifying and evaluating noncontrollable, environmental variables relevant to the organization
3. An analytical phase that evaluates the resources of the organization in terms of its goals and its environment
4. Creation and evaluation of specific sets of policies, action programs, and incremental resources designed to achieve the goals of the organization.

Goal structure. In a business organization, the primary goal over the long term is profitability. There are other important goals, however, which, in the short run, are sometimes more important, such as growth.

Where profits are satisfactory, other goals, including personal goals of managers, take on importance. Multiple, conflicting goals are possible. Moreover, there is a hierarchy of goals necessary for managing an organization, and any planning system must recognize the need for such a hierarchy. Indeed, goal structures have been suggested as one primary means by which any organization can be managed (Odiorne 1965, Humble 1970).

Any strategic planning system must take into account the multiple, conflicting goal problem, as well as the hierarchy problem. Moreover, the goal structure can be the basis for developing standards and measures of performance valuable to the control system. Hence, it is extremely important for strategic planning to deal with the goal structure of the organization.

Environmental assumptions. Any organization operates in a larger environment that it may influence in part, but which is largely noncontrollable. The organization must adapt to its environment. Because it cannot manage or control environmental variables, it must make assumptions about such outside influences. Explicit assumptions rather than implicit ones are to be preferred, and assumptions based on forecasts and analysis are preferable to those with less objective foundation.

Analytical phase. What the organization can do in light of its resources—that is, its strengths and weaknesses—must be analyzed across the planning horizon. This aspect of the planning system varies in sophistication, but must deal explicitly with whether the goals established are realistic and achievable in light of what can be done by the organization and what the environment will permit it to do. The barriers to goal achievement need to be defined and evaluated. In addition, whether goals need to be changed must be assessed in this phase.

Strategy development. The strategic planning system must develop the specific policies to be used by the firm in day-to-day operation and the directional action programs to be undertaken. It must also determine the incremental resources required to undertake such programs. This creative phase leads to the decisions that guide the firm. As such, evaluation of the impact of the goals, environmental assumptions, and the overall strategy must be consistent.

Types of Systems

Strategic planning systems differ in how they approach these various components. The different approaches might be categorized in terms of the following dichotomies:

1. Complete vs. incomplete
2. Reactive vs. proactive
3. Portfolio vs. business level
4. Top-down vs. bottom-up
5. Adversary vs. friendly
6. Open vs. closed communication
7. Staff vs. line involvement
8. Matrix vs. operating unit (elements)
9. Resource consumption vs. planned results
10. Short vs. long planning horizon

These dichotomies are really continuous. To gain some sense of the dimensions upon which strategic planning systems are based, let us examine each of the 10 factors.

Complete vs. incomplete. The degree to which the system covers the four major components outlined herein, not to mention the quality of the coverage, can vary. In an organization that is small, or at least in which managerial or analytical capacity is in short supply, it may not be possible or necessary to completely cover all of the components of the system. In installing a system, it is important to determine how rapidly the organization can assimilate a new management system. Hence, the rate of assimilation, as well as the capacity to manage the system, will determine the initially desirable degree of completeness. Clearly, the goal should be completeness, but that will not always be possible, and so it must be decided just which components require attention. For example, in a small firm it may not be very important to worry about the goal structure because the company's size and the proximity of managers should lead to a fairly clear definition of goals. In a stable environment, it may not be necessary to develop a complete environmental monitoring and forecasting capability.

Reactive vs. proactive. Management styles differ, including the risk level that will be assumed by the firm. Some systems can be triggered by threats, crisis, or perceived needs to change, whereas others cycle automatically or are prompted by search for opportunity. Reactive systems can work where there is stability and where change is slow. Proactive systems are preferable in principle because they emphasize anticipating change, avoiding impending threats, and capturing opportunity.

The natural gas firm was able to operate without an explicit strategic planning system for many years because environmental and internal changes were few and existing strategy was working. It is now switching to a more proactive system simply because it perceives greater threat and recognizes that its strategy will have to change more frequently. The small plastics firm operated successfully without a strategic planning system; however, it might have been more successful as a more proactive system. Nevertheless, it is possible to be successful with a reactive planning system and even with an incomplete system, where stable conditions and a viable strategy now exist.

Portfolio vs. business level. In a business organization, strategy is a concept with application at two organization levels. The first level is encountered in a multidivisional organization and is especially visible in a conglomerate organization, where capital resources must be allocated among competing demands. This allocation decision is essentially a portfolio decision involving the product/market scope of the firm; the analysis and overall planning system, and the strategy itself, differ from that required at the business level. At the business level, strategy is concerned with how to compete within a particular product/market. This question involves different issues than those involved in the portfolio question. These questions are obviously related, yet a planning system that has to deal with extensive portfolio questions operates differently than one that has fewer such questions, or none. At the very least, it is less complex in a coordination and communication sense; it does not require as long a cycle time, it involves less extensive environmental analysis, and its goal structure development is not as complex. Portfolio questions examine whether the products/markets undertaken remain the best ones for the firm.

The multinational firm needs a more extensive planning system than does the small plastics firm, which is dealing only with the how-to-compete question. Capital budgeting issues are far less complex for the plastics firm, as it is not inclined to reexamine plastics as a major basis for its existence.

Top-down vs. bottom-up systems. In the matter of goal-setting, especially where goals become the basis for performance measurement of individuals or organizational subdivisions, and also with respect to assumption generation and alternative proposals, it must be decided whether the planning system should begin from the top of the organization or from the bottom. By establishing goals and assumptions at the top of the organization, each further stage of the planning process is constrained by conditions that will be acceptable to its superiors. On the other hand, a bottom-up approach can proceed more freely and perhaps more creatively because it avoids the constraints from above. Both approaches appear workable, but which choice to make depends upon several variables, including:

1. the degree of participation, involvement, and commitment sought as a matter of managerial style
2. the technical nature of the business
3. the stability of the environment
4. the financial health of the organization.

As increased participation is sought, the more technical the product/markets, the more unstable the environment including competitive uncertainties, and the stronger the financial health, the more likely a bottom-up approach can be made to work.

Overall, no system can operate unidirectionally. Rather, a looping of information and decisions is required; i.e., a bottom-up approach will have top-down aspects, and vice versa. The general thrust, however, will be in one direction.

Adversary vs. friendly process. Should the system proceed in a confrontation, adversary manner, with each level challenging the next? Perhaps the most important area where the confrontation issue arises is in goal-setting, especially where goal-setting is used in the individual performance measurement and reward system. Under these circumstances, an adversary or confrontation system can result in goals that have "reach" in them. Such an adversary proceeding requires that a conflict resolution mechanism be built into the strategic planning process. A more friendly mechanism would generally proceed incrementally, i.e., last year's performance with some acceptable improvement would be set by the originating individual or group and would not be challenged. A friendly process would not require the cycling that an adversary proceeding would require. A confrontation process was chosen at the natural gas system, partly because it suited managerial style, whereas a more friendly system was used at the small plastics firm.

Open vs. closed communication. A plan must record and communicate information if it is to have any value in managing complex organizations. There are circumstances, especially in strategic planning, where it would be disastrous for strategic decisions to be made known. For example, premature release of a new product development, a closure or sale of an existing operation, and an intended acquisition, are major strategic actions that are better not widely communicated throughout an organization. The degree to which the system should proceed with a written record and widespread communication of the plan is a function of a complex of issues and variables. The military-secrecy concept of a "need-to-know" perhaps can give the greatest guidance here. If certain aspects of the plan must be guarded, then the planning process must recognize these sensitive areas and proceed in a way that can protect the integrity of the decisions. For example, an analysis to divest an operating division may have to proceed independently of the operating division personnel, with both the expertise and biases that they might provide.

Staff vs. line involvement. The amount of planning that can be done by staff personnel can vary, although no effective plan seems to be possible without the participation of line managers. If the product of the system is to be used, the plan must secure the commitment of those who must use it, the line managers. Such commitment can be obtained by involving the line managers in the system itself. Moreover, the technical input that can only be gained from line managers at all levels is necessary for the system to work.

In smaller organizations, it is impossible for a staff to be used to develop plans because they cannot afford the high overhead cost. Hence, this issue is of real concern only in larger organizations that can afford the labor specialization implied.

Matrix vs. operating organization. Organization structures are typically designed with the operations problems in mind; i.e., efficiency questions are of central interest. Although strategy guides the day-to-day operations of the firm, the planning system does not necessarily proceed along the same organizational lines selected for operations. For example, there may be important aspects of strategy that are not reflected in the operating organization. The natural gas firm is organized in functional terms, yet gas storage is not reflected per se in the operating organization. However, it requires strategy development that cuts across several functions. Marketing strategy, on the other hand, is reflected in an existing marketing function. Even when the operating organization reflects the strategic elements of a business, it may be desirable to use a "matrix approach" that cuts across the organization in terms of who has responsibility for developing strategy in particular areas.

The notion of dividing a business into its strategic elements and using a matrix approach is more relevant for the how-to-compete strategy level than the portfolio level. For example, some 11 basic strategic elements were chosen for the natural gas firm, and 10 were used with the plastics firm. The multidivision firm did its strategic planning in parallel with its operating organization, although at the group level a switch to a matrix approach may have been advisable.

Perhaps the foremost example of a matrix approach to strategic planning is General Electric's. Management has divided the firm into a series of strategic business units that cut across its operating organization. For each strategic business unit, strategic planning develops through a team selected for that purpose. The head of a strategic business unit may not have any responsibility for the operating results of an organization unit for which he or she has strategic management responsibility.

Resource consumption vs. planned results. We have already suggested that there may be a connection between goals established and the measurement of performance, i.e., results are emphasized rather than resources consumed. The basic distinction to be made is between the emphasis given input (resource consumption) and output (achievement of planned results). This distinction is relevant both to operations and strategic planning. Budgets or expenses are emphasized in a resource-consumption approach to control, while goal achievement, a management-by-objectives approach, is emphasized in a planned-results scheme. This latter approach requires that considerable attention be paid to establishing a goal hierarchy throughout the organization.

Short vs. long planning horizon. How far into the future must the strategic planning process look? The answer is ordinarily 5 or 10 years. Even though a length of time must finally be selected, the following two questions must be answered in order for a planning horizon to be chosen. (1) How fast are events occurring that can alter the balance of the basic strategy components, and in particular how rapidly is the environment changing? and (2) What lead times are required to react to changes? The longer the reaction time, the longer the planning horizon must be. Reaction times in the natural gas industry are quite long, at least insofar as exploration for new supplies and construction of distribution pipelines are concerned. Yet events are changing so rapidly in the industry that the effective planning horizon may be shorter today than it was in more environmentally stable times. The key consideration must be the degree of certainty that surrounds environmental forecasts, which is a function of how far into the future the forecast is made. It is fairly easy to assess reaction times.

Summary. The issues we have just covered, which help define the type of strategic planning system needed, have to be decided in terms of the organization, its characteristics, and its environment. To make these decisions requires specific knowledge of the firm and its environment, and we turn now to how this knowledge can be acquired.

SELECTING THE STRATEGIC PLANNING SYSTEM

For strategic planning to occur, the basic elements of the system must be covered, either explicitly or implicitly. For example, even if no attention is paid to environmental assessment, assumptions about the environment will still be made, even though they are likely to be hidden or implicit. Goals will still be used even if no formal attention is given to developing a goal structure. Of course, the goals may be those of individuals rather than those of the organization. In all, every organization has a strategy in the sense of goals-means-constraints.

In selecting a system, the circumstances of the firm, both internally and externally, must be assessed to identify just where on each of the 10 continuums the system should lie. This assessment, or *audit,* of the firm and its environment is not easy. Here we examine the elements that must be considered and an approach that can be taken to making the audit.

An audit should consider at least two areas: an internal examination of the firm and a look at the firm's external environment. The following elements need to be examined at a minimum:

Internal Audit

1. Goal structure
2. Planning readiness
3. Organizational complexity
4. Managerial style
5. Resources available
6. Relationship to operations planning

External Audit

1. Technological change
2. Social change
3. Political change
4. Economic conditions—Market demand
5. Economic conditions—Competitive structure
6. Economic conditions—General conditions

Internal Audit

Goal structure. Several questions that must be answered about the goal structure of the firm:

1. Does a goal hierarchy exist? If so, is it consistent from one organizational level to the next?
2. Does the organization use any kind of management by objectives system? At all levels of the organization?
3. Are both open-ended (goals) and closed-ended (objectives) statements used? Can the organization distinguish between them?
4. Are goals and objectives imposed from the top level of the organization downward, built upward from the bottom levels of the organization, or formulated through participation of both superior and subordinate?
5. Does the organization understand how to "factor" goals, i.e., take the derivative of goals for various operating units in the organization? Can strategic goals be reflected in operating goals?
6. What is the relative importance of personal goals and organizational goals in the organization?

The answers to these questions are relevant to understanding the level of professional management, how readily the organization could adapt to a matrix approach to organization and planning, what degree of training might be required to develop a goal structure, how closely knit the organization is in terms of its aims, and, generally, what approach it takes toward control.

Planning readiness. Planning readiness can be measured in these terms:

1. Are the attitudes held toward planning positive or negative? Do differing attitudes exist at different levels of the organization? Do they differ by age, experience, function of management responsibilities, or other relevant dimensions?
2. What knowledge of planning concepts and planning methods exists in the organization? Are some organizational levels more knowledgeable than others? Where is there a base upon which to build by using skills in the organization?
3. What level of analytical skills is available in the organization? Does the organization, or some part of it, know how to build models that will be of assistance to planning? What approaches are used to problem-solving?
4. Is there prior experience with either operations or strategic planning, either within or outside the company? Has this experience been positive or negative?
5. What is the perceived time horizon that managers possess? Do they typically take a short-range view, or do they look farther into the future?
6. What is the breadth of organizational concern? Do managers take a systemic view, or are they more narrow in perspective?

These variables tell a great deal about how ready the organization is to undertake a planning process and how extensive and sophisticated that process can be.

Organizational complexity. Complex organizations require more complex planning systems if they are to remain coordinated and controlled. The nature of the complexity must be understood if the proper planning system is to be designed and installed. Among the questions an audit must answer are:

1. How large is the organization in terms of organizational levels? Is the organization geographically dispersed? What is the overall size of the organization?
2. How are organizational subdivisions linked? For example, is the organization vertically integrated? Do different manufacturing sites share a common marketing, R&D, or other unit?
3. What is the product/market scope? Is synergy possible in terms of manufacturing, marketing, or managerial variables?
4. How complex is the financial structure of the firm?

5. Is the organization required to respond innovatively to a rapidly changing technical or competitive environment? If so, how does it respond?
6. What mechanisms has the organization devised to generate change in itself?

Managerial style. Styles of managing vary considerably from firm to firm, and, indeed, firms develop cultures all their own. It is important to understand these stylistic considerations (Edwards 1976) and to make certain that the planning system is in tune with them. These following questions must be answered:

1. What does senior management prefer in terms of style of participation, centralization of decisionmaking authority, concern for management development, and risk preferences?
2. Does the organization operate with open processes, or is it more secretive?
3. Is there a preference for objective, analytical problem-solving, or is intuition favored?
4. Does line management work closely with staff, or does it prefer to do its own work?
5. Is control strongly emphasized? If so, is it in terms of input used or results produced?
6. Which objectives and goals receive emphasis: growth, profitability, social concerns, or others?

Resources available. The resources available for planning need to be fully understood. Among the considerations are:

1. What assets—financial, facilities, and personnel—does the company have available to devote to planning? What resources does it lack?
2. What is the degree of top management's commitment to planning? Is it willing to manage with plans, or does it work outside them?
3. Do skilled planning staffs exist to assist in the planning process? If not, can they be built?

As the resources available for planning increase, there is clearly more freedom of choice in the planning processes available to the firm.

Relationship to operations planning. Any strategic plan can be effective only to the extent that it influences decisions and commitments of resources. Such commitments are made in the short term through the capital or operating budgets, which are both major components of operations plans. Because of the necessary relationship the plans must have, and because a strategic plan should dominate operations, it is valuable to identify the potential relationship the planning systems can have by asking these questions:

1. Does an operations planning process exist? Does it produce a workable plan? What is its relationship to control?
2. What is the calendar for the operations planning process? What are the timing requirements for the strategic planning system to influence operations?
3. Who is responsible for operations planning? Can the same staff or the line managers be involved?
4. Can corporate objectives be used as the basis for operations planning objectives? Generally, how can the components of the strategic planning system be reflected in operations planning?

Overall, answers to the kinds of questions raised in the internal audit should provide sufficient information about the internal working of the firm. Even so, additional information about the environmental setting that surrounds the firm is also needed to help select an appropriate strategic planning system.

External Audit

The rate of change or dynamic nature of the environment has an important impact on the planning process. The more dynamic the environment, the greater the need for strategic planning because of the increasing likelihood of strategy imbalances occurring. There are four general areas that give rise to the constraints and restrictions the firm must observe: technological, political, social, and economic. Within each of these areas, there are specific events or variables that must be monitored, and about which the firm must make assumptions:

1. How is technological change affecting the product areas in which the firm competes? Are existing products affected in any way by technological change? Is change occurring very rapidly? Is there uncertainty about the nature of technological change?
2. Are social, governmental, or political events occurring that must be monitored? What mechanisms must be established to monitor the events?
3. What competitive structure characterizes the industry in which the firm operates? What is the nature of competitive interaction and response? What is the firm's capacity for identifying competitive response?
4. Is there a demand for the firm's products or services? Is it stable or volatile? What substitutes exist for the product or service? What growth rates characterize demand?
5. Does the firm depend upon the performance of the general economy? Can the economy be a useful predictor of the performance of the industry? How can the economy be monitored?

HOW CAN THE AUDIT BE DONE?

To pose the questions in the previous section is one thing, to gain answers to them is another. If a large or complex organization is under study, the auditing task is very difficult, especially if it is performed by an outsider. The three-stage approach to the audit done for the natural gas utility illustrates what can be done:

1. background preparation through study of written materials such as procedure manuals, organization charts, reports, and memos
2. interviews with key executives and attendance at relevant meetings
3. use of a questionnaire.

A fourth step might be added in the form of training seminars that were a part of the planning system installation phase that will be discussed in the next section.

Since the first two steps are straightforward, we pass over them to examine the use of a questionnaire. It proved to be difficult to objectively assess, through observation and interviews alone, the planning knowledge and attitudes of key management personnel. Moreover, since there was a considerable number of managers, it was desirable to have assessment measures of all management personnel across the organization. Thus, a questionnaire was designed to assist in assessing the internal attributes of the organization. Of special interest was an assessment of the "planning readiness" of the organization at various levels within the firm.

The questionnaire contained over 100 items covering attitudes toward planning, knowledge of planning concepts, opinions held about the major goals of the firm, and prior experience with planning. A series of questions on age, experience within the firm, education, perceived organization level, and similar measures were used to permit a multivariate analysis between organizational attributes and planning readiness. The questionnaire was also designed so that it could be applied on a before-after basis to permit measurement of progress in installing a planning system. The questionnaire results proved to be of considerable value in designing the training seminars that played a key role in the installation of the strategic planning system.

It is interesting to examine briefly some of the findings based on the questionnaire. Attitudes toward planning varied considerably. Increasingly negative attitudes toward planning seemed to be associated with increasing age and experience in the company (but not with experience with planning). Such attitudes, however, can be changed with increased knowledge, such as can be provided by a training seminar. Individuals with positive attitudes toward planning seemed much more willing to reserve any skepticism and to join in making planning proposals work.

Increased knowledge of planning concepts seemed to be correlated with positive attitudes toward planning, which again suggested a role for training seminars and also broad topics the seminars needed to cover to improve planning knowledge.

In the questionnaire used, analytical skills were difficult to measure, but these skills appeared to be more prevalent among technically or scientifically trained or experienced personnel. Such personnel seemed to assimilate more quickly a normative, rational planning system.

In the three case studies, especially in the natural gas firm in which the questionnaire was used, the degree of planning readiness is positively related to positive attitudes toward planning, greater knowledge of planning concepts and methods, higher degrees of analytical skills, and greater experience with some form of planning. In general, it seems that the higher the degree of planning readiness, the more sophisticated the planning systems that can be used and the faster they can be installed.

INSTALLING THE STRATEGIC PLANNING SYSTEM

The natural inclination of top management that believes that a strategic planning system is necessary is to simply mandate some process or assign someone to install one. Very little care seems to be given to using explicit plans to guide the company's future, as well as its daily operations. In fact, when organizations lack experience with planning systems, the typical manager's reaction to the system is to see it as a form of control that will lead to a loss of managerial freedom. In actuality, a well-designed system will increase such freedom. Thus, such a negative reaction must be overcome to increase the likelihood of organizational acceptance of a new planning system.

What is the best way to instill positive attitudes? In two cases, training seminars were recommended. It was believed that out of better knowledge would come attitude change and a commitment to planning.

In the natural gas firm, the audit phase was used to help select and design the rough outline of a strategic planning system and its relationship to an operations planning process that had evolved over several years. The strategic planning system was not fully designed at the outset; important dimensions were left unspecified, awaiting further reaction and input from line management. For example, it was not clear whether it would be better to work through the operating organization or use a matrix approach. A top-down process was chosen because it fitted the normal managerial style. On the other hand, the degree to which a switch could be made to managing by objectives and planned results was unclear.

It was decided to use a training seminar both to increase planning knowledge and to design the details of the system. The seminar was designed as a series of single, day-long sessions separated by 4 to 6 weeks during which management study teams were assigned to work on specific elements of the strategic planning system. These study teams reported on their assigned projects and made recommendations. These teams played a key role both in designing specific elements of the process and in developing the overall educational process. Approximately one-half of each formal seminar day was devoted to the introduction of concepts and methods by a combination of outside experts and internal staff personnel. The other half of the day was devoted to study-team reports. This sequence was conducted during the 6 months devoted to the generation of a strategic plan.

Such a seminar, operated in phase with the specific major components of the strategic planning system, played a very significant role and led to the following gains:

1. A system was laid in place at the same time the first strategic planning product was produced.
2. The system was significantly influenced by key management personnel and greater commitment to the system and product was gained.
3. Key management's knowledge of planning was significantly improved, and, as a result, attitudes toward planning were improved.
4. Management was able to identify organizational weaknesses that it had to correct, especially analytical weaknesses.
5. A connection between strategic and operations planning systems was made stronger by the participation of managers who had to deal with both developing strategy and implementing it.

The training seminar was conducted in two waves of participants. The first sequenced wave dealt with the top line and staff personnel. It included the president, executive vice president, and all of the operating vice presidents, as well as key planning staff—about 15 members overall. This seminar was designed by the author in conjunction with the planning staff and president. The role played by the president was a key one, because his endorsement gave it early credibility and helped launch it successfully.

A second wave, offered to a group of about 50 middle managers, emphasized the relationship of the strategic planning system to operations planning. This seminar was designed to aid in the implementation of the strategic planning product through operations planning. This seminar was held on three consecutive days and repeated twice thereafter to keep each group small in size.

The combination of formal training and involvement with the evolutionary development of the strategic planning system was highly useful. Perhaps more than any other factor, it was responsible for what the natural gas firm's top management regarded as a successful introduction of strategic planning to its overall management practice.

CONCLUSION

The implementation of a strategic planning system involves far more than the imposition of planning steps. Three basic installation steps are suggested here. First, the basic planning process components and key dimensions that define a specific process must be defined. Some 10 dimensions were developed here. Second, an organizational and environmental audit is required in order to allow the choice of a strategic planning system and to lay the basis for the third step. The third step is to install the process and use it to produce a specific product. A key aspect of this step is the use of a series of training seminars. Such seminars can be used to increase the planning readiness of the firm, as well as help design specific stages of the strategic planning system. This third step is critical to securing organizational commitment to the product, a strategic plan, that comes out of the system. In addition, it is critical to helping insure that the system and the product it plans are suited to the needs of the organization's key management.

The success of the training seminars based on the questionnaire phase of the audit in increasing planning readiness was a key factor in the successful introduction of a strategic planninc system in both the natural gas and plastics firms. Without similar care, the multidivisional firm suffered lack of commitment and the lack of wide participation in system design. As a result, the strategic planning system was not as well designed as it might have been.

REFERENCES

Ansoff, H. I. 1972. Strategy as a tool for coping with change. *Journal of Business Policy* 1(4): 3–8.

——. 1972. The Concept of Strategic Management. *Journal of Business Policy* 2(4): 2–7.

Barnard, C. I. 1956. *The Functions of the Executive.* Cambridge, Mass.: Harvard University Press.

Drucker, P. F. 1974. *Management: Tasks, Responsibilities, Practices* New York: Harper & Row.

Edwards, John. 1976. *Strategy Formulation as a Stylist Process.* Paper presented at College D'Echanges Contemporains, St. Maximin, France, May 1976.

Henry, H. W. 1967. *Long Range Planning Practices in 45 Industrial Companies.* Englewood Cliffs, N.J.: Prentice-Hall.

Humble, John. 1970. *Management by Objectives in Action.* London: McGraw-Hill.

Odiorne, G. S. 1965. *Management by Objectives.* New York: Pitman Publishing.

Schendel, Dan. 1974. "A Concept of Corporate Strategy." Purdue University, Teaching note.

Schendel, Dan and K. Hatten. 1972. Business policy or strategic management: A broader view for an emerging discipline. *Academy of Management Proceedings*.

Springer, C. H. 1973. Strategic management in General Electric. *Operations Research* (Nov.-Dec. 1973): 1177–1182.

Steiner, G. A. 1969. *Top Management Planning*. New York: Macmillan.

7
Integration

When strategic, administrative, and operational planning are well designed, they should mesh into a unified total organizational plan. The integrating force among the three levels of planning is the concept of goals and constraints. Whereas goals at the corporate level are constrained mostly by external factors, these goals become constraints at the administrative level; in turn, the goals developed at this level become constraints at the operational level.

CARAM MOTOR CORPORATION

Let us use the plans of a fictitious organization, the Caram Motor Corporation, as an example. Currently the third largest automobile manufacturer in North America, Caram is aiming to become the first. Its goal is to raise its share of the market from 8 to 11 percent in the next 5 years. Caram's strategy is to develop an electric-powered car that is safe, efficient, economical, and capable of traveling long distances before recharging. Caram plans to produce and sell 500,000 electric cars annually within 5 years. Obviously, the fact that its strategic goal is to produce a fixed number of units in a specified time is an administrative planning constraint. Caram's administrative planners must now plan to design, develop, build, and acquire an organization structure and facilities capable of meeting the strategic goals imposed upon them from above. Next, the plant design, the selection of fabricating machinery, the organization structure, the means of distribution, and many other variables become constraints on the operational planners, whose major goal is to efficiently produce and ship 2273 electric cars a day, 220 days a year, within 5 years. To achieve their goal, they must plan to receive the required equipment and materials from reliable sources on fixed schedules, distribute the materials, and acquire sufficient, qualified personnel to perform the required manufacturing and distributing tasks. Eventually, Caram's operational goals become constraints on its outside vendors, who in turn must operate through their own chain of goals and constraints.

MASTER PLAN

To achieve its strategic goal, Caram must design, develop, and implement a total organization plan, i.e., a "master plan." To be of value to the company, this master plan must indicate how the strategic, administrative, and operating functions are to be integrated. Otherwise, it would be extremely unlikely that the company could achieve its strategic goal and approach its growth objective.

How does a firm achieve this integration in its planning process? Haynes and Massie (1969) recommend a master plan. They start with a strategic approach, labeled "formulation of economic mission," in which they ask, What kind of business should the company be in, and what should the performance objectives be? They present a flowchart, which moves from considering alternative fields of endeavor to evaluating the potential of each field. The comparative profile of the firm and the evaluated fields, the possible combinations of fields of endeavor, the feasibility of entering a field, and the performance requirements are all studied during the evaluation process. This allows the firm to determine what its economic mission should be.

Following the formulation of the economic mission, it must be determined what the competitive strategy should be. This problem is approached by considering product-market opportunity; how the firm's resources match up to those required in the product market being considered; the competitive advantages, if any; and finally, the positive and negative synergies involved. At this point, a strategic plan is formalized, and the competitive strategy is determined.

The requirements presented by the strategic plan are then fed into the administrative planning cycle. Next, an administrative plan is developed in order to integrate the constraints imposed by the strategic plan. The major tasks required to fulfill the product-market plan for each field of endeavor must be determined and evaluated. These include the required research and development, production requirements, organization structure, marketing requirements, financial requirements, managerial needs, the relationship between existing programs in terms of sequence, and timing and determination of time-cost characteristics.

Finally, when all the pieces of the puzzle have been put together, a program of action is formalized. The operational plan, although not addressed by Haynes and Massie, is the final integrating part of the entire planning mechanism. The operational plan required to breathe life into the chosen programs of action must consider, among many other factors:

- the allocation of labor and materials
- assignment of machinery and tools
- inventory controls
- flow of product within the plant
- maintenance of plant and equipment
- recruitment, training, and maintenance of the labor force
- job authority
- job responsibility
- cost effectiveness

- job satisfaction and motivation
- compensation systems
- development of managers
- quality control
- conflict resolution
- union relationships
- reporting systems
- distribution of product and vendor control

The control mechanisms that are part of the strategic, administrative, and operating plans are used not only to help implement the integrating mechanism, but as an early warning system as well. The control system should be designed to trigger contingency plans at the required level(s) when the master plan begins to falter so that the organization can take alternative paths to reach its goals.

MATRIX PLANNING CONCEPT

Another interesting approach to integration of corporate plans was presented by Cleland and King (1974). They believe that successful planning cannot be carried out within the framework of the existing traditional bureaucratic organization. A more suitable tool proposed for modern companies is a matrix form of planning organization. Although Cleland and King only emphasized long-range strategic planning, their matrix planning concept can be extrapolated throughout the entire planning set. They propose the formation of project teams that would be responsible for the various aspects of strategic planning.

It is also logical that project teams could be set up to handle the various facets of administrative and operational planning. In fact, the goal-constraint concept presented previously could be used to position these various project teams into a time frame. The administrative project team could come into play after the goals formulated by the strategic project team become administrative constraints. The same type of goal-constraint time schedule could exist between the administrative project team and the operational project team.

The matrix form of planning organization would be flexible so that individual planners could be placed into more than one project team at a time. The very fact that one individual could be assigned to a combination of strategic, administrative, and operational tasks at one time would have to lead to a self-integration of the various planning modes. The teams by necessity would be interdisciplinary, containing not only staff personnel, but line personnel as well. This mixture of skills and talents would increase the firm's ability to develop new ideas.

The individual employees and teams would also benefit from this approach. The planners would become actively interested in all phases of corporate planning and, in turn, would become more personally involved with the aims and goals of the organization. This involvement normally leads to increased input by the individual employees since they now have a personal interest in the outcome of the plans they helped to develop.

The matrix type of planning organization would also create a flexibility not available in a traditional bureaucratic organization. The placement of personnel and the vertical and horizontal flow of information are enhanced in a matrix. The information on goals and, in turn, their constraints would not only flow downward in the planning hierarchy, but also horizontally and diagonally. There would be a cross-fertilization of information among people employed in all three phases of planning. Control information would also flow more freely since it would not be constrained to vertical channels only. All in all, the concept of a matrix planning organization using interdisciplinary project planning teams is well worth exploring.

INTEGRATIVE PLANNING CONCEPT

Lorange and Vancil (1975) on strategic planning do not deal directly with the concept of integration. Their approach, however, is an integrative one. They propose a system for strategic planning in diversified companies, using a framework that incorporates two main-linked planning dimensions. One dimension, which is hierarchical, is an organizational one that operates through the three organizational levels, i.e., headquarters, divisions, and their functional departments. These three organizational levels happen to interface well with the three planning levels discussed throughout the book, i.e., strategic, administrative, and operational.

The second dimension considered is a chronological one. As the planning process moves between organizational levels, it also moves through three time cycles. Movement is from headquarters, after corporate objectives are stated, to the divisional levels where calls are made for division inputs. The divisions, after analyzing their own needs and strategies, propose their goals and resource requirements. The corporate planning group, after incorporating the divisional inputs, reinterprets its own overall strategy and forms tentative corporate goals. All this occurs within the first time cycle. At this point, the second time cycle begins; the corporate group calls for division programs to be developed. To meet headquarters' request, the division moves down the organization level by calling on its functional departments to analyze and recommend alternative programs. The division now moves up the organization hierarchy by recommending programs and stating resource requirements to the corporate planning group. This group again resets the corporate and division goals and makes tentative resource allocations to division programs. The third time cycle begins with a call by the corporate group for division budgets. The division calls upon its functional groups to develop budgets, which are then submitted to the division for initial

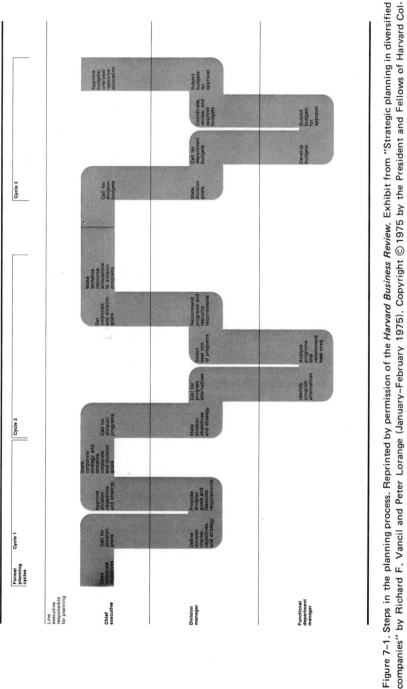

Figure 7–1. Steps in the planning process. Reprinted by permission of the *Harvard Business Review.* Exhibit from "Strategic planning in diversified companies" by Richard F. Vancil and Peter Lorange (January–February 1975). Copyright © 1975 by the President and Fellows of Harvard College; all rights reserved.

approval before being sent to corporate headquarters for final approval. This planning process uses a constant flow of information, both upward and downward between the three levels of organization, to achieve an integration of plans. It differs radically from the matrix approach—there is no horizontal flow of information because each planning level is distinct unto itself. However, it does blend well into corporate goal-setting.

The integrative mechanism between division and corporate levels permits the corporate planners to determine how closely the summation of division goals satisfies the corporate goal. The difference between the two is termed the *planning gap* by Lorange and Vancil. (This concept is also discussed in Chapter 3.) The attempt to close the gap is again an integrating device. Corporate management either (1) calls upon the divisions for more ambitious goals, (2) decides it cannot meet its goals in its present configuration and may acquire additional components or even divest itself of present components, or (3) decides that its corporate goals are not attainable and need modifying. Again, as in the matrix organization, the people in this two-dimensional planning process go through a learning experience and to a lesser degree become committed to the overall achievement of the corporate goals. The concept of a goal-constraint chain is applicable to this planning approach. Corporate goals beget division constraints and division goals beget functional-department constraints. This process is illustrated in Figure 7–1 and described in the next section.

CARAM'S PLANNING PROCESS

Using the example of the Caram Motor Corporation, let us attempt to trace its planning process through a two-dimensional program. Caram's corporate headquarters states its objective to become number one in the automotive industry and calls upon its automotive divisions for ideas and plans. The divisions propose investigating the feasibility of producing an electric car that is safe, efficient, competitively priced, and capable of traveling 500 miles before recharging is required. In addition, the divisions estimate the funds they would require for the study. The divisions' information, required to prepare the proposal, has been derived from their own departments such as research and development.

Assuming headquarters has approved the divisions' plans and decided to finance the study, the divisions now conduct the proposed feasibility study with the help of their individual functional groups. They find that an electric car meeting the criteria set forth in the initial proposal is practical, and they notify corporate headquarters of this finding.

Headquarters then decides that the new vehicle can help raise Caram's market share from 8 to 11 percent within 5 years. To accomplish this, the company will have to manufacture and sell 500,000 vehicles annually within 5 years.

Having formalized its goal, corporate headquarters then calls upon its divisions for alternative plans for accomplishing the stated corporate goal. The divisions, in conjunction with their functional departments, develop the administrative and operational strategies and determine the resources required to structure, staff, and produce 2273 electric vehicles a day, 220 days a year. The divisions analyze the recommended programs submitted by their functional groups and select the best mix of alternatives. Alternative strategies and plans may be submitted to headquarters. They may include recommendations to:

1. manufacture all the new electric cars in one plant to achieve manufacturing economy of scale
2. manufacture the cars in three geographically dispersed plants to achieve distribution economy of scale
3. have the cars manufactured in a foreign country where they can be produced at lower cost.

Corporate headquarters now resets its corporate and divison goals by obtaining as much internal and external input as possible and determining the parameters set by available resources. It may determine that its dealer organization does not believe it can sell and service so many of a new type of vehicle. The cost of financing such a major project may also be nonfeasible. If top management verifies the preceding objections, it may decide to change its corporate goal from 11 percent of the market to 10 percent.

Of course such a change in corporate goal changes the divisions' plan of producing 500,000 cars a year within 5 years to producing perhaps 350,000 cars. After a definitive goal is set, resources are allocated to the various divisions, and a request is made for division budgets. The divisions then restate their goals, which have been imposed by corporate goals that have become constraints, and call for department budgets. Budgets then move up the hierarchy until final corporate approval is given for a resource allocation of one or more years. As discussed in Chapter 6, budgets play a vital role in the control mechanism of a corporation and, in turn, act as integrating forces because of the goal-constraint nature of monetary allotments at each level of the corporation.

The Caram scenario pictures the company increasing its market share in the automobile industry from 8 to 11 percent within 5 years. It also anticipates the company becoming the leader in the electric-car business with a potent technological capability in the field of noncombustion power sources. If these things happen, the company will approach its objective of becoming the top manufacturer of automobiles in North America.

What happens if Caram's best-laid and integrated electric-car plans and strategies fail? Can the company survive? If so, how? Have contingency plans been drawn up in case the original plan fails. A "yes" answer to these key questions often means the difference between a company succeeding or going bankrupt. If a company is large enough, with sufficient resources, failure can be somewhat ameliorated. However, even giant companies suffer when their carefully made plans do not materialize. Let us consider the case of Ford Motor Company's Edsel.

THE EDSEL

The 1958 model Edsel, which was introduced to the American public in September 1957, was supposed to capture 3.5 percent of the entire American automobile market. This percentage, which translated into 210,000 cars in a 6-million car year, was considered to be an extremely conservative estimate. After all, the Ford Motor Company had put 10 years of planning into the Edsel. In addition, a great deal of effort and approximately $50 million were expended for advertising and promotion before the car was introduced to the marketplace. The company was sure it would have a tremendous success and would recover all of its $250 million investment by 1960. It even expected the Edsel division to operate profitably in 1958.

The results speak for themselves. In 1958, the 1200 new Edsel dealers that had been set up sold a total of only 34,481 Edsels. Moreover, between 1957 and 1960, only 109,466 Edsels were sold. On November 19, 1959, the Edsel was declared dead; production was discontinued. Ford lost over $100 million and experienced a tremendous loss of prestige within the automotive industry and among the buying public. Fortunately, the company was large enough and financially sound enough to absorb this gigantic loss. It was also able to recover $150 million of its basic investment by recycling Edsel tools and plants among its Ford, Mercury, and Lincoln divisions.

Why was the Edsel a flop? Among other reasons was the inability of the planners to project into the future. The Edsel was introduced into a recession environment. Few new cars, if any, could weather the economic storm of 1958. In fact, sales of new cars in 1958 were 4,257,812, down from 6,113,344 cars in 1957 and the lowest since 1948. The planners also misread the market, or they would surely have recognized the trend toward smaller cars evidenced the by tremendous surge in Americans buying smaller, less expensive, and more economical foreign cars. The foreign-car market responded in a more appropriate direction than did the domestic market in 1958. The sale of foreign cars, which was 259,343 in 1957, rose dramatically to 430,808 in 1958.

The Edsel itself was a letdown. After the public had been bombarded by $50 million worth of advertising and promotion, it expected a dramatically different and innovative product. Instead, they found it to be just another Ford with a different face and a few unnecessary gadgets. On top of everything else, the organization design called for a separate Edsel division with separate dealerships for Edsels. This required additional plants, machinery, and personnel, which became very expensive. In addition, Ford management was spread so thin that there was insufficient management personnel to adequately staff all of its divisions.

The separate-dealership concept was based upon the premise that the Edsel would bring in sufficient sales to carry the dealership, which would then motivate the dealers to an even greater effort. Ford, from previous experience, knew it would require 1200 new separate dealerships to obtain national distribution for the Edsel. Some of the new dealers were not automobile people; some were undercapitalized; and many ran their dealerships as satellites of their existing automobile agencies. The maintenance-and-repair shops of the new Edsel agencies had little work except that which had to be done on previously sold Edsels— of which there were very few. Thus, shortly after Edsel's introduction, the entire dealer organization began to suffer financial problems. Within a comparatively short time, many dealers were forced to close their doors, further compounding the problems faced at Ford corporate headquarters. What happened?

Obviously, no one reason can explain this costly failure except perhaps the lack of a properly integrated plan with a contingency feature. The upward and downward flow of information, which is the lifeblood of the integrating mechanism of a planning organization, was either ignored, sidetracked, or misinterpreted. Many warning signals were either ignored or not communicated. For instance, the name Edsel conjured up negative associations when tested in various parts of the United States, yet it was still the name chosen for the car.

Consider the goal of Ford headquarters; the sale of 210,000 Edsels in 1958. As in any goal-constraint chain, this goal became a constraint on the existing Ford divisions. The recommendation of the divisions, which flowed back to top management, was to create a separate new division. Management's acceptance of this decision was an error. The error was further compounded when it was decided that separate dealerships, divorced completely from the sale of Fords, Mercurys, and Lincolns, should be created. These new dealers would be responsible for the sale of 200,000 cars from the new division.

The problems associated with a new division, especially those with a new dealership organization, should have been well known to the responsible top officials. If these problems were known, understood, and communicated, then adoptive changes could have been made in the company's master plan. In turn, when danger signals began to appear on the horizon, such as extremely poor sales, a contingency plan could have been initiated immediately to help avert the collapse of the division.

It is very easy for those on the outside to pick apart the efforts of a group of knowledgeable, dedicated managers. In this case, however, mistake was piled upon mistake until the decision to discontinue the Edsel was inevitable.

A good strategic plan must lead to a learning experience for the company and especially for the planners involved in the three organizational levels—i.e., corporate, division, and functional departments. The learning process is more important than the plan itself if it generates questions—and also answers—about proposed alternatives and future projects. The planning organization must be receptive to criticism and advice from all levels. It must also be able to keep its channels of information open in order to profit from the concept of integrative corporate planning. It appears that Ford learned its lesson well, as proven by the success of the cars it has produced since the Edsel era.

An article by Hobbs and Heany (1977), "Coupling Strategy to Operating Plans," begins on p. 224. It delves into short-term plans and programs developed by functional managers in order to carry out the plans and decisions of upper-level management. Hobbs and Heany stress the idea that a gap exists between corporate planners and those at the operational or functional level.* This gap is caused by the inability of corporate plans to integrate operating functional procedures, practices, and measurements. The authors recommend five steps to help overcome the gap problem. These steps, which include communicating between levels within the organization, keeping the strategic team intact throughout the entire planning process, and activation of the plan, roughly follow the main-linked hierarchical and chronological planning dimensions proposed by Lorange and Vancil (1975).

"Planning the Process of Improving the Planning Process: A Case Study in Meta-Planning" by Emshoff (1978) is presented starting on p. 234. Emshoff addresses the problem faced by most planners at some time "of moving from a relatively ineffective planning process to one that meets the prescriptive characteristics it theoretically ought to contain." Emshoff's premise is that "the conversion of a planning system needs as much planning as the process being planned." The author presents two hypotheses for discussion. The first deals with the relationship between the effectiveness of the proposed planning changes and how these changes will help a manager solve a specific, important problem. The second proposes that to be worthwhile, meta-planning strategies must include the overall organization's culture and the management style of key individuals.

REFERENCES

Cleland, D. I. and W. R. King. 1974. Organization for long-range planning. *Business Horizons* **27** (4): 25–32.

Future organization strategies are vital to organizational survival, yet the classic approach does not provide the needed focus. The authors claim a matrix form of organization shows promise.

Emshoff, J. R. 1978. Planning the process of improving the planning process: a case study in meta-planning. *Management Science* **24**: 1095–1108

Addresses the problem of moving from a relatively ineffective planning process to one that meets the prescriptive characteristics it theoretically ought to con-

*This should not be confused with the concept of "gap closing" wherein the planners of a company attempt to develop long-term strategies to close the gap between where top management would like the firm to be in x years and where they perceive it will be if nothing is done.

tain. The author's basic premise is that the conversion of a planning system needs as much planning as the process being planned. *Reprinted herein on p. 234–252.*

Haynes, W. W. and J. Massie. 1969. *Management: Analysis, Concepts, and Cases.* Englewood Cliffs, N.J.: Prentice-Hall.

An introductory text to management that stresses theory without neglecting the skills required to relate theory to practice. Especially worth noting are the authors' chapter on planning, and the article by F. F. Gilmore and R. G. Brandenburg.

Hobbs, J. M. and D. F. Heany. 1977. Coupling strategy to operating plans. *Harvard Business Review* **55** (3): 119–126.

The authors give a five-step program to help close the gap between the outputs of the strategic and functional planners. The profit-center manager, by using power and control of resources, can couple strategic and operating plans in a realistic way. *Reprinted herein on pp. 224–233.*

Vancil, R. F. and Peter Lorange. 1975. Strategic planning in diversified companies. *Harvard Business Review* **53** (1): 81–90.

Presents a three-cycle planning process for consideration by executives in both large and small companies. However, the article is directed to the decisionmakers of large, complex, multidivisional companies that require formal planning processes.

Coupling Strategy to Operating Plans

John M. Hobbs
and
Donald F. Heany

In recent years a growing number of companies have expended considerable amounts of time and money to develop strategic planning skills in their profit centers and at higher organizational levels. We applaud this effort, but as we stand   back and observe large and small companies alike apply this new talent and expertise, we are struck by the widespread disappointment with the pace at which new strategies are often implemented. To say the least, it appears to be much easier to conceive a new strategy than to carry it out.

Corporate executives especially are aware that changes in strategic direction do not always occur at the promised tempo. Therefore, they discount the claims advanced by advocates of each new strategy. One executive offered this pithy description of his strategy review procedure: "Halve each earnings projection indicated in the strategic plan. Then double the amount of additional investment sought to implement that strategy." Behind this cynical discounting one can sense a keen appreciation of the problems of maintaining the coupling among the functions as a mature business attempts to change direction.

One barrier to successful implementation is the residue left by strategies formulated by past managers of the business. These strategies have left their imprint on shop procedures, work methods, job descriptions, work measurements, and business lore.

Advocates of bold new strategies have not recognized that they must first "uncouple" the functions from the viselike grip of past strategies *before* they can expect an appropriate response at lower organizational levels. The more that marketing, engineering, and manufacturing perfect their low-cost, efficient systems, the greater the likelihood that their operating plans will fail to discriminate among signals originating above them. They will instinctively resist changes in the way they get things done.

Take, for instance, the time-honored custom in certain segments of the capital goods industry to produce to requisition. Each product is unique. No finished inventory is carried. Each new order calls for individual handling, first by engineering, then by manufacturing, and so many months can elapse between date of order and date of delivery.

The manager in charge of a business that competed in one such segment embarked on a new aggressive strategy. He believed he could increase the business's market share by selling the value of product availability rather than technology alone. The key to his strategy was to release certain models to manufacturing before firm orders were in hand, thereby significantly shortening the delivery cycle.

Months later, this manager began to have second thoughts about this idea. For one thing, the models built in anticipation of demand required costly rework in order to match them to the orders ultimately received. Furthermore, customer complaints made it crystal clear that the publicized reduction in the delivery cycle had not been met. Missed schedules were also creating costly penalties.

An investigation proved the root of these problems to be the measurements used in district sales offices. For years, the bonuses of the sales engineers had been based on the dollar size of orders. Such a system prompted the engineers to give full rein to their customers' normal inclinations to demand tailored products rather than to worry about which model the customers ordered. Allusions to "king customer" were taken quite literally by field personnel. They did not recognize that their general manager's new strategy required a particular response from them.

Why did this happen? To some the answer is simple. The general manager was at fault. Had he communicated his strategy to the district offices, his sales managers would have perceived the need to amend their time-honored bonus system for sales engineers.

We think that a more basic reason can be found in the relentless quest for efficiency that characterized each functional area. Marketing procedures and practices had evolved over the years to control costs and to take full advantage of decentralization and specialization. Unfortunately, this pursuit of efficiency had one unintended result: marketing's operating plans were often independent of higher management's strategic shifts. The authors of these operating plans did not couple functional procedures, practices, or measurements to a given business strategy. In other words, functional momentum dulled marketing's responsiveness to the general manager's imaginative strategic move.

A second factor at work in this case was that the general manager underestimated the impact his new strategy would have on the marketing function. It is no trivial matter to inject a line of standardized products into a business that has been marketing customized products for more than a decade. To make this strategy work, marketing would have to take these steps:

- Develop a new measurement system for sales engineers.

- Hire salesmen or retrain sales engineers already on the payroll.
- Design a promotional campaign that would attract new customers but not divert old customers to the standardized products.

In fact, it is far from obvious that the same district offices can handle both customized and standardized products. As companies that have pioneered in the use of strategic planning can testify, this case is not an isolated instance of a functional failure to support a decision made at a higher level. Their functional managers are not always able to prevent foremen, purchasing agents, stock clerks, warehouse managers, district managers, engineers, and a host of other employees from following a competing strategy.

WHAT GOES WRONG

In short, corporate reviews often fail to detect such weak links, and profit center managers do not always foresee uncoupling problems. We would like to suggest some steps that a profit center manager might take to minimize the risks in uncoupling. But first we shall cite two more actual (though disguised) cases to illustrate how operating plans can become uncoupled from the very strategy they are supposed to support.

Faulty Perspectives

The manager of a consumer durable goods business concluded that, in a climate characterized by recession and rapid inflation, the fastest way to improve profitability was to fill out his product line. Accordingly, he authorized engineering to design a new appliance and asked manufacturing to tool up for an initial production run of 2,000 units. For his part, this manager included in his strategic plan profit targets that reflected the market's (hypothesized) favorable response to this new offering.

Signs that something was amiss soon reached his desk. Performance data revealed that the field failure rate for the new product was significantly higher than that for older models.

An investigation pinpointed what had gone wrong. Engineering had prepared an operating plan that recognized the broad intent of the new strategic plan. Unfortunately, the design engineers had not specified a quantitative quality standard for the initial prototypes. It seemed safer for engineering, if not for the business, to await field results on the initial 2,000 appliances. This low-level decision took little heed of the following facts:

- Manufacturing had invested millions of dollars in a new production line for this prototype. If engineering were to renege on the original product specifications that manufacturing had followed in laying out that line, much of this investment would have to be written off.

- The financial goals that the profit center manager had set depended on the timely and profitable introduction of the new appliance. If engineering took six months to finalize product specifications, these goals would not be met and the corporate office would be asking why.

When this instance of uncoupling was eventually brought to the attention of the profit center manager, he could not believe his ears. How could such an obvious deficiency in functional planning skills go undetected for so long? He intervened. The linchpin between the strategic plan and engineering's operating plan was reinserted, by edict!

This case illustrates how mismatched perspectives can cause uncoupling. On the one hand, modern businesses strive to achieve low costs via high volume, specialization, and automation. Each step down this road fosters a narrow, inward perspective. The specialists who draw up operating plans focus on the dimensions of their internal world: parts lists, drawings work standards, shop rules, production schedules, plant layout, and so on. On the other hand, the authors of business plans look outward. Their focus is on the external environment in which the business operates. Thus the profit center manager must match these two perspectives. There is no one to whom he can delegate this responsibility.

A related cause of frayed linkages is the existence of a sizable bloc of people at the lower organizational levels who are convinced that strategic planning is just not practical. In their eyes, strategic planning is a synonym for blue-sky thinking, something undertaken to satisfy the corporate office. They feel little loyalty to a document that reflects few, if any, of their inputs. They are not involved in, nor committed to, the strategic plan.

Incompatible Demands

The announced strategy of a manager running a business that offered a full line of mature, market-tested products was to hold market share in the face of persistent sniping by smaller competitors. His customary response to their pricing moves was to pressure his engineers to squeeze still more efficiency out of their mature technology. For years engineers had obliged, largely by increasing the physical size of their product. The first signal of uncoupling appeared at the final test station of the production line. Costly rework became necessary in order to repair deficiencies discovered so late in the cycle. Naturally, profit margins suffered and delivery schedules slipped.

A corporate study team discovered the problem: Manufacturing could no longer maintain the quality levels specified by engineering. Particles in the air became trapped in the products as they were being assembled. While these particles had always been present, they represented no threat to quality as long as the traditional performance levels were sufficient. Once engineering had escalated these standards to attract new orders, substantial changes in manufacturing processes were mandated. These had never been made because the manpower needed to modify the in-place operating systems was not available.

Operating plans were prepared by people with pressing line responsibilities. These people are not always in a position to monitor the linkages between their operating plan and plans prepared by other functions or by the profit center manager.

For example, the manager of manufacturing was responsible for 2,000 employees, 900 work stations, 75 miles of overhead conveyors, and dealt with more than 300 vendors. He had to contend daily with changes in product specifications, alterations in the production process, unexpected variations in the quality of raw materials, pleas from customers to expedite given orders, and a host of other short-term crises. These realities claimed his allegiance, all day, every day. He was not disposed to search deeply for frayed linkages between his concrete world and a future environment described in the profit center's plan. Invariably, programmed tasks had prior claim on his limited resources over unprogrammed tasks such as the coupling between his operating plan and engineering's new product specifications.

Penalties of Uncoupling

Coupling errors of the type indicated in the three cases we have cited can be quite costly, both in terms of resources as well as people's attitudes.

Wasted resources: For instance, it is accepted that the role of raw material inventories and work-in-process inventories is to guard against possible delays at earlier points in the procurement or production process. But what about excessive inventory levels? What about the idle capacity and surplus labor built into operating plans to make doubly sure that operating systems do not halt or falter because of strikes, vendor error, weather, acts of God, or jittery customers? Lower-level supervisors decide what is excessive. Their decisions are not always visible at a distance, nor are they always documented in a form that invites a periodic review by higher management. Once made, these decisions become sanctified by the passage of time. "We always did it that way. . . ."

Bias toward the status quo: In some companies, the tenure of managers of profit centers average less than three years. One factor contributing to this rapid turnover is the difficulty of eliciting prompt, integrated, functional responses to a new strategy. New managers commit themselves and their profit center to performance goals far beyond the capability of existing operating systems. The corporate office holds them to these goals. When the announced goals are not attained, a fresh managerial team is brought in and the cycle repeats itself, with one exception: The old strategy is often discredited along with the deposed manager. His replacement feels compelled to differentiate his strategy from that of his predecessor. This launches the functions on still another cycle of operational planning. If the latest manager is in a great hurry to win his spurs, he will not allow his subordinates time to analyze his new strategy or to investigate alternate operating systems. He wants action, now!

When profit center managers observe the risks assumed by colleagues who embark on aggressive moves, they wonder if the rewards reaped by these innovators are adequate. Many conclude that the risk/reward dictates a "hold" strategy. They silently resolve to become efficient administrators of established profit centers rather than midwives of new businesses. In their eyes, the established functional systems are too complex, too deeply rooted to be changed by a manager on his own initiative. They judge the turning radius of their profit center to be incompatible with their time horizon and performance measurements. Hence, they disavow any responsibility for nominating strategies that might renew mature businesses or initiate new ones.

In such a company, the de facto strategy is: stand pat. In time, the chief executive is likely to discover that his portfolio of businesses is positioned in mature markets and offering commodity-type products. This, of course, is the perfect recipe for low profits. It is a direct consequence of a measurement system that is biased against major strategic moves.

MINIMIZING UNCOUPLING RISKS

Just how might a manager go about forging better linkages between his new strategy and the detailed operating plans, procedures, and measurements prevailing two, three, and even four levels below him? How does the man in the middle cope with this troublesome problem without becoming hopelessly entangled in day-to-day affairs?[1]

Some managers react to evidence of uncoupling just as the Queen of Hearts might have done. "Off with their heads!" An injunction follows in a few hours indicating that all functions are expected to get behind the new strategy.

Another favored reaction is to form a task force to ferret out unnecessary expenditures in each nook and cranny of the company. In other companies, the normal response to flaws in operating plans is to offer a short course in planning to as wide an audience as possible.

We have found the following five steps to be more effective:

Step 1: Before nominating ambitious strategies, make certain that a serious functional overload does not exist. Measures to avoid unnecessary strain on the linkages between a strategic plan and current operating systems are always

1. Hugo E. R. Uyterhoeven, "General Managers in the Middle," Harvard Business Review. March-April, 1974, p. 75

preferable to after-the-fact remedies. We have no reliable meters for monitoring functional stress and strain. Yet the symptoms are easy to detect.

For example, Business X was in trouble. Its return on investment had sunk far below the company average. New competitors had penetrated its market and challenged its product leadership.

A new manager was dispatched to revive this business. His prescription for a return to a satisfactory level of profitabliity included the following:

- Upgrade the old product lines.
- Retaliate against foreign competitors by entering their traditional markets.
- Modernize the costing system.
- Build or acquire a new manufacturing facility.
- Switch the method of payment for factory workers from piecework to daywork.

He submitted a new strategic plan based on this program. Soon, Operation Rejuvenation was under way. Unfortunately, the profit center did not adhere to the timetable specified in its strategic plan nor deliver on its profit goals. In retrospect, the rejuvenation program was recognized to be overly ambitious. The functional managers could not cope with all these changes simultaneously. Calling for change did not make it happen. Inertia bested the bold new strategy.

The lesson is that a new strategy always sends shock waves throughout a profit center. It is unrealistic to expect that a rebuilt strategy can be executed while some functions are being steered into new markets. Functional overload is unavoidable.

Step 2: Contain strategic shock waves. If a new strategic course is called for, managers can still avoid some uncoupling problems by insulating parts of the business from strategic shock waves. For example, many chemical companies isolate the coupling problems associated with new product introductions by constructing a new pilot plant for each major addition to a product line. Those who manage these pilot plants have no responsibility for existing products or their operating systems. They run their own experiments and finalize the new process apart from the old. When they judge their new pilot process to be safe and efficient, plans for a full-scale production are drawn up. The existing operating systems are not disturbed by work on the embryonic product/process. This same approach can be taken by most businesses when they make basic changes in their products or their manufacturing processes.

In addition, managers can insist that the advocates of a new strategy spell out the key issues raised by that strategy. For example, if your strategy is based on a new technology, the key strategic issue might be: Can this business successfully reduce to practice its R&D output and at the same time maintain competitive quality levels on its existing products?

Step 3: Give your personal attention to major coupling issues. A profit center manager can personally attend coupling problems on a selective basis. We suggest that he (a) establish a mechanism for coping with such problems before they arise, and (b) personally monitor the sources of major coupling problems. For example, it is prudent to scrutinize each capital appropriation to make sure that it faithfully supports the thinking in the manager's new strategic plan. It may not. The authors of capital appropriations often have little connection with planning.

We also suggest that a profit center manager lend a hand in linking his center to other organizational components within the company. This is very important in large, diversified companies.

For example, one manager of a profit center that sells complex, high-technology products, each costing over a million dollars, has aimed at building market share for the past five years. With the onslaught of the recession, the market for these products became even more competitive. Customers delayed the receipt of completed orders. Vendors began to increase the prices of components and subsystems. The combined effect brought the center's annual output dangerously close to its breakeven point, and the manager began to question whether he could continue to build market share.

Taking a fresh look at his operations, the manager found a way to salvage his strategy. By amending the specifications his profit center placed on its intracompany vendors, he was able to offset their recent price increases. Specifically, conventional value analysis demonstrated that his product's performance would not suffer if the variety of one type of component purchased from a sister business were reduced from sixteen to four. This single step produced cost savings equivalent to the earnings realized from a 20 percent increase in his volume.

Encouraged by this result, this manager called for a comprehensive review of the ancient specifications for all his major components. He dug for more profit improvement opportunities by challenging each specification, each work procedure, each method that former functional managers had written when another strategy was in force.

Uprooting these traditional practices required his leadership. Only he could handle the delicate negotiations with managers of other profit centers. Only he could negotiate the terms according to which cost savings were to be shared with vendors.

Step 4: Don't disband your strategic planning team until it has identified follow-through actions by the next organizational level. Left to itself, the strategic planning process can become an end in itself, so bureaucratic and so ponderous that all participants in that process yearn to return to more congenial work. They are exhausted before they translate their strategic concept into specific functional support programs. They will say, "It's all in the strategic plan." Often it is not. Only the initial steps are mentioned, only the costs incurred in the next year or so. What a profit center manager needs is a tool to help him monitor follow-through; he must hold his planning team in place until its members have produced:

- A list of the specific tasks each function must perform in its strategy support role.
- The specific milestones by which he can assure himself that his profit center is, in fact, changing to its new course.
- The names of the individuals who have accepted responsibility for each major functional program.

If he gets less than this, he has been shortchanged. His new strategy is at risk and will remain at risk until such controls on implementation are in effect.

Why are so many strategic plans lacking in such realism? Sidney Schoeffler, executive secretary of the Strategic Planning Institute, suggests that this lack occurs because planners undergo a subtle but deadly transformation as the strategic planning process unfolds. At the very beginning, business planners are objective and dispassionate analysts. They are ready to examine each and every possibility. At the end of the planning cycle, however, the same individuals have turned into fervent advocates of a single course of action—the one described in their plan. All their energies and political skills are then dedicated to selling that strategy. They are not disposed to seek out or listen to criticism from lower organizational levels.[2]

A general manager can restore a measure of objectivity to the terminal phase of the strategic planning cycle by personally inviting a few key functional specialists to his/her office and asking for their views of the proposed strategy and its impact on their area of work. This would do much to dull the criticism often heard at the functional level that strategic planning is an unimportant, blue sky activity undertaken merely to please the upper echelons.

Step 5: Communicate downward, not just upward. Many uncoupling penalties come about because the profit center manager is preoccupied with communicating his new strategy to higher organizational levels. As a result, he tends to slight the other, more difficult task, namely, how to reach managers and supervisors at lower echelons. The latter hold the key to his success. Furthermore, they need a deeper insight into proposed changes than managers at higher levels.

After all, the functions are expected to erect a structure of complex, interacting operating systems upon a new strategic foundation. They must dismantle or severely modify the systems in place. Hundreds of specialists have to be retrained and new work procedures documented.

2. 1976 PIMS Conference, Boston, Massachusetts, September 1, 1976.

If you think you have already developed an adequate downward communications program, we invite you to put it to the following acid test. Thirty days after you have announced a new strategy, ask a dozen subfunctional managers and specialists to write down what they believe to be the three most important factors that will determine the success or failure of the business and its new plan. If the answers received do not agree or if the functional people do not identify the same key issues you thought you spelled out in your plan, then your new strategy is already in big trouble. You may have given an eloquent speech to your subordinates on the merits of your strategy selection, but your message was not received.

This is your early warning signal that a gap exists between your intent and their understanding, and you may still have time to bridge it. At the outset of this article, we mentioned a business offering customized products. Had the general manager of the business made this test, he might have learned that people in his district sales office were not aligned to his innovative strategy.

CONCERTED ACTION

Do these suggestions place too much of a burden on the shoulders of a profit center manager? Will they tempt him to take on responsibilities better left with functional subordinates? Will he become hopelessly bogged down in operating work?

Not necessarily. Strategic decisions affect all functional areas of the business. If one area fails to move in concert with the others, the profit center will be swept along on its old strategic course. *All* functional areas must be coupled to the new strategic plan, not just a few. One laggard, one half-hearted functional commitment may endanger the goals established for the center as a whole.

Few planners have the political muscle to oversee the alignment of operating plans to the new strategy. Only the profit center manager has the power and the control of resources to make things happen cross-functionally. If he claims the right to chart a strategic course, he must also accept responsibility for monitoring and at times directing its implementation at lower organizational levels.

In conclusion, while companies adhering to a policy of decentralization may find this suggestion hard to swallow—indeed, slightly heretical—we would remind them that integration has always been one of the primary elements of managerial work. It is unrealistic for any company to promote strategic planning as a technique for coping with a fast-changing environment without taking into account how it affects the profit center manager's other duties of organizing, integrating, and measuring.

Planning the Process of Improving the Planning Process: A Case Study in Meta·Planning

James R. Emshoff

Most of the published literature on planning is either *prescriptive* (i.e., what ought to be the characteristics of a long range planning process) or *descriptive* (i.e., what is the status of long range planning as it is practiced in organizations today). Prescriptive writings such as those of Ackoff, Ayres, or Steiner examine methodologies, tools, and techniques that are believed to be effective for the development and implementation of long range strategies. Descriptive writings, such as those of Caldwell, Lucado, or Steiner and Schollhammer identify the strengths and weaknesses in current planning practices of organizations.

This paper addresses a subject that crosses the prescriptive and descriptive planning literature. It is concerned with the process by which an organization changes a relatively ineffective planning activity into something that meets the characteristics prescribed by planning theorists. The thesis of the paper is that the conversion process needs as much planning as the process being planned. The short-hand term for such a problem is *meta-planning.*

The intent of this paper is to sensitize both managers and researchers that meta-planning is a significant management problem. Many organizations have experienced huge costs and great trauma in their efforts to develop long range strategies. Often this situation is blamed on poor planning, when poor meta-planning is the real source of the problem. Thus, this is a call for increased ef-forts to develop meta-planning theories. Such theories will enable organizations to define on-going programs to improve the effectiveness of their planning systems, eliminating much of the unproductive, but expensive, crisis-oriented change processes characteristic of many corporate planning systems.

One must recognize that the development and validation of meta-planning theories is a huge challenge that will require years to complete. Meta-planning fundamentally deals with the process of change in managerial roles as it relates to the formulation of long range strategy. Thus, a meta-planning theory must not only treat all of the issues required to develop a theory of planning, but it must also incorporate crucial properties of the larger management system of which strategy formulation is only a part. Therefore, if validation of planning

Reprinted by permission from James R. Emshoff, Planning the Process of Improving the Planning Process: A Case Study in Meta-Planning, *Management Science,* Vol. 24, No. 11, July 1978, Copyright © 1978 The Institute of Management Science.

theories has been a difficult process, validation of meta-planning theories promises to be even more challenging.

TOWARD A META-PLANNING THEORY

Where will the inputs for meta-planning theories be obtained? Two major sources are likely to be used. One is the literature on process consultation, developed by Bennis, Schein, Beckhard and others. This material provides a solid foundation for developing strategies on the implementation of meta-planning; that is, *how* to execute the change process. But meta-planning theories must also specify *what* changes in the planning should be made and in what sequence for the organization. Until organized research on meta-planning is initiated, inputs for this part of meta-planning theories will come primarily from the experiences of individuals who have attempted to introduce changes in planning processes within organizations.

Clearly there is no lack of experiential information on planning, but it has not been well organized. Thus, the most immediate need to start the process of creating meta-planning theories is the synthesis and generalization of implementation experiences. As this information is distilled, generalized hypotheses should begin to emerge that provide explanations of the success or failure of alternative sequences of planning process changes based on properties of the organization, its management system, and its history of planning.

Once a significant body of experiential information has been developed, the first meta-planning theories can be formulated by integrating it with the process consultation literature to create an explanatory basis for the "what, how, and why" of planning process inprovement. Unfortunately, we currently don't have enough accepted generalizations of experience on the "what" elements to even speculate on integrated meta-planning theories. Therefore, the remainder of this paper has a more modest objective—to formulate specific hypotheses related to the content of meta-planning theories and to evaluate them in terms of an organization's actual experience with efforts to improve its planning process.

HYPOTHESES

Three hypotheses will be presented. Before discussing how they will be evaluated, each hypothesis will be stated and briefly explained.

Hypothesis 1. Meta-planning strategies will not be effective unless managers whose efforts are needed to facilitate the process change see the change as one which solves a specific important problem they face.

The issue here is the balance between product and process. Meta-planning emphasizes the improvement in managerial processes to provide better ongoing problem-solving capabilities. Most managers will support corporate efforts to achieve this. But few of them will invest their own time in such activities unless they believe the effort will have a clear and direct impact on a problem of concern to them. Hence, the sequence of steps in process change must have an associated sequence of managerial problems that can be used to justify the effort.

Hypothesis 2. Meta-planning strategies must be part of a larger organizational assessment and change process that incorporates (a) the overall organization's culture, and (b) the management style of key individuals.

In the context of this hypothesis, organization culture is defined as the personality of the system taken as a whole; that is, how it responds to and interacts with groups outside itself. For example, some organizations tend to initiate changes in the markets in which they compete while others are followers; some rely heavily on external information for their decisions and others rely on internal information, etc. Culture is a property of the system, and not specific individuals in it. Management style, on the other hand, is unique to an individual. It reflects preferences for ways of making decisions. For example, some managers tend to be authoritarian and others participative. The basic hypothesis is that effective meta-planning strategies cannot be developed independently of the particular cultural and management style characteristics of the organization.

Hypothesis 3. In the long run, meta-planning must produce strategic decision-making processes that are compatible with the organization's cultural and management style; in the short run, purposeful incompatibilities may be introduced through meta-planning to create necessary change in cultural and management styles to achieve future systemic effectiveness.

This hypothesis implies that perspectives must be developed as to the appropriate culture, management style, and strategic decision process the organization ought to have for overall effectiveness. Thus, there are two objectives of meta-planning: (1) to achieve the long run desired changes in the strategic decision-making processes, and (2) to use the decision-making process as a means to create desired changes in the organization's cultural and management style.

STRATEGY FOR EVALUATION

Because no research program has been explicitly established to test one or more of these hypotheses, there is no way to validate them at this time. All that is possible is an analysis of experience with the introduction of change in a planning system to evaluate the credibility of the statements. Such analysis can be conducted in two ways. The hypotheses can be considered one-by-one and, for each of them, relevant experiences from a wide variety of cases can be assembled to see if the statements seem plausible. The alternative is to examine one specific case situation in more detail over a more extended period of the planned change process and to determine whether issues relevant to the three hypotheses tend to re-occur in the ways hypothesized.

The second approach to assessing the hypotheses is chosen in this paper for several reasons. First, the practice of drawing selected facts or events from case studies can be very distorting when it is taken out of context of the overall process. Hence, the value of the evidence for or against the hypotheses using the first approach will be more questionable than for the extended study approach. Second, at this stage in the process of developing meta-planning theories, interest should be at least as great in the formulation of new and more general hypotheses as in the validity of those presently formulated. By describing the sequence of process changes for one organization over an extended period of time, the information can serve as a base for adding to or modifying existing hypotheses, a capability not possible using the first approach.

The major disadvantage of the second approach is that the particular case chosen may not be very representative. To minimize this problem the case study is based on planning for a company that fairly well typifies problems faced by organizations in the $100 million–$500 million sales class with some degree of product diversification, but having a well-defined core business. The material to be presented synthesizes experiences from an intensive three and a half year effort to improve the long range planning processes. The program involved nearly 100 man-years of effort by people inside the company and about 20 man-years of effort from a university-based research organization acting in a consulting capacity.

The material will be presented in the chronology in which it historically occurred to maintain the context of events. Where appropriate, short discussions relevant to the three hypotheses will be inserted. These will be placed in brackets—[ ]—so that the reader can separate issues relevant to the specific chronology of events in the case from those relevant to meta-planning generalizations as formulated in the hypotheses.

COMPANY BACKGROUND

The planning effort was undertaken in a private sector company, which we shall refer to as Company ABC. ABC is a producer of consumer goods, with one particular product dominating both sales and profits. The company is a subsidiary of a much larger holding company, which we shall refer to as XYZ. ABC was the original company in the group and most of the other businesses in XYZ were originally started as vertical integration efforts by ABC to protect the economics of its basic product profits. The other businesses in the holding company, which were primarily in industrial products areas, were very successful at expanding business opportunities in their particular product field, but none of them had generated additional new businesses for further diversification of the holding company. Therefore, XYZ looked primarily to ABC as the internal generator of new areas for corporate growth.

ABC was culturally well suited to being a catalyst for corporate development. It had a risk-taking spirit, and liked to see visible changes arise from major management decisions. So new ventures were constantly being explored as ways of expressing the action-oriented culture. If ABC had a cultural problem in fulfilling its development responsibilities, it was the company's tendency to act on relatively sketchy external information about action alternatives, and to concentrate actions only on business areas where the internal information already pointed efforts in certain directions. In other words, the motivations for change and the directions they took were largely internally driven.

The president of ABC recognized and accepted his development responsibilities for XYZ. However, he was concerned about the ability of his organization to carry them out. The president felt that strategies of vertical integration no longer provided significant new business opportunities for ABC. Therefore, he believed the company was going to have to start looking for diversification outside its basic business. But the president felt that his company's organizational structure and planning processes were not sufficiently developed to successfully undertake the diversification he sought.

ABC was organized with four vice-presidents reporting to the president. As shown in Figure 1, three of the vice-presidents had operating responsibilities for a functional area of the company's business, while the fourth coordinated staff development activities. The company had a decentralized management philosophy, and each of the four vice-presidents had a great deal of autonomy. Thus, the channels of communication were largely vertical with the vice-presidents individually discussing their own strategies with the president, but little direct interchange among the vice-presidents on overall corporate strategy. The president felt this pattern of interaction had to change before the company could diversify into new business areas. Therefore, he asked the V. P. for staff services to design a new long range planning system for ABC that would accomplish the desired results.

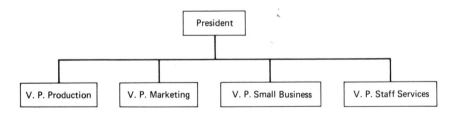

Figure 1. Top management organization struction at Company ABC.

INITIAL PLANNING EFFORTS

The planning system took about two years to design. The staff planners decided to concentrate their attention on resolving theoretical and methodological issues before addressing operational problems of the system's implementation. Hence, most of the resources were spent designing the planning system they ultimately hoped to implement in the company. When the project was completed, a system had been designed that integrated the latest thinking of many of the leading planning methodologists. It not only specified planning processes, but also linked planning with management information systems, organizational development, and control techniques. Processes were even designed for continually updating and improving the entire system. When the ideal system had been designed, the planning staff published several leatherbound volumes describing it and disseminated them to key managers throughout the company.

Unfortunately, the new planning system had virtually no impact on the decision-making processes in Company ABC. The vice-presidents and senior managers of the operating division were willing to discuss the new system on a conceptual level, but did not feel that it was feasible to convert ABC to the new philosophy. They felt there were too many differences between the proposed system and the way things were currently done to make the changes. Several off-site strategy sessions were held to try to work out an implementation plan, but nothing concrete came of them.

The president recognized that the staff effort had provided one important element for change, namely what the new planning systems should be. But they had ignored the issue of how the change to the new systems should occur. He felt the company needed an outside catalyst to get the change process started, and contacted a university-based research center to serve that role. He told this group he wanted them to develop and implement a program that would gradually shift the managerial processes of ABC toward the planning system that had been designed. In essence, he wanted to implement a meta-planning process.

The consultants began the study by interviewing each member of the company's executives, including key managers who reported to the vice-presidents. The purpose was to get a sense of the different perspectives of these managers on the company's overall strengths and weaknesses, as well as their opinions on the proper role for strategic planning in setting directions for future growth. Confidentiality was assured in each interview, and although words were carefully chosen by some of those interviewed, a number of issues were surfaced. Two concerns overrode all others, however, and those were (1) was a new planning system really needed, and (2) would a new system reduce individual power bases?

[Two issues relevant to the meta-planning hypotheses were raised by this diagnosis. The first relates to Hypothesis 1. The operating vice-presidents did not share the president's perception of the company's long range planning problem; hence, they did not see a need for a change in the process. Thus, from their point of view, process changes were proposed without a clear problem definition. Second, the situation provides evidence for Hypothesis 2. The changes were seen as having a potential negative impact on management style by reducing individual power bases. This was resisted and the resistance affects the planning process success.]

The consultants' first action was to arrange a meeting among the senior management to discuss the strengths and weaknesses of the company's planning efforts. On a qualitative basis, the managers tried to assess whether existing planning processes would be adequate to achieve growth objectives. Several of the managers had never before considered the fact that opportunities for growth were becoming more limited in traditional business areas. This issue had never been discussed by the senior managers as a group; hence, there had never been any explicit rationale for the efforts to redesign the planning system. Most operating managers thought it was happening as a matter of course because it "was part of staff responsibilities to propose such changes periodically." The meeting resulted in an agreement among the managers that the existing planning system was not adequate to insure continued expansion. Cross-functional strategic planning was needed and the vice-presidents agreed to become active participants in preparing and implementing appropriate changes.

The consultants felt the power base question had to be addressed very quickly in the meta-planning process or participation of senior management would not be productive. The consultants also felt the question could not be addressed directly because it might destroy the possibility of getting anything started. Therefore, a process was designed to answer the following question: "Could the senior management of ABC agree on a desired future for the company that: (a) would be feasible to achieve, (b) would provide acceptable overall performance, and (c) would insure each participant had at least as much managerial freedom and responsibility as at present?"

To answer this question (which was never formulated to the management group) the consultants proposed that the company begin a relatively informal planning process involving only senior management (i.e., the president, the four vice-presidents, and three senior managers who were regularly involved in key operating decisions). The process would be focussed on defining the desired directions for corporate development, an activity sometimes referred to as Ends Planning in the literature (see Ackoff [1]).

At the first working session of the new planning group, the consultants defined the Ends Planning process which would be followed. The process consisted of the creation of four separate scenarios of ABC as it might exist ten years from now. Each of the four vice-presidents was to take the responsibility for writing one of the scenarios. Each scenario was to be an integrated picture of ABC, including the businesses in which it operates, the products it markets, the methods of production and procurement, and the management structure of the company. The scenarios were to be written from a personal perspective; that is, each vice-president was to incorporate characteristics he wanted to see in the company of the future. Thus, the vice-presidents were encouraged to take a functionally-oriented perspective to the company's future. The only constraint was that the scenario also address issues of company-wide significance. The vice-presidents agreed to complete their scenarios in six weeks. The extent to which divisional staff would be involved in the process was left to the discretion of each V. P.

[The above process purposefully permitted a great deal of freedom in the means of preparing the scenarios in order that management styles would not be constrained. Consistent with Hypothesis 2, planning process acceptance by management was facilitated by maximizing the management style flexibility in individual participation during the process. Considerable differences in style emerged. One vice-president had maximum participation in the creation of his scenario, including secretarial staff. He constrained participation only by people's willingness to invest the time (including some week-ends) in the process. At the other extreme, one of the vice-presidents prepared the scenario almost completely by himself, with an occasional exposure to some of his key staff for comments. These stylistic differences became useful input for the design of subsequent parts of the planning process that required managers to assume different responsibilities.]

While the scenario writing was in progress, the consultants took the responsibility to expose senior management to selected environmental trends that could have significant impact on the corporate future. Papers were prepared by the consultants on topics such as ecology, worker participation in management, government regulation, and resource scarcities. These papers were intended to stimulate scenario development, but whether and how they were used were left to the individual vice-presidents. The material was largely ignored at the time it was prepared, but subsequently used by the consultants to challenge some of the underlying assumptions in the scenarios that were prepared. [This material was prepared to test the rigidity of the previously mentioned cultural tendency to ignore potentially important external information. The results illustrate Hypothesis 3 and the short-term need to create situations which change cultural characteristics to achieve planning effectiveness. This was the first effort to modify the company's culture to one more conducive to achieving the desired diversification.]

At the end of six weeks, all four scenarios were completed. The consultants took the responsibility to synthesize the issues generated and report back to senior management. None of the vice-presidents saw each other's scenario until all of them had been completed. The first step the consultants took was to identify every idea for change listed in one or more of the scenarios. This list was then analyzed and classified into topic categories. The categories used for the classification were: (1) products to be produced, (2) services to be offered, (3) new markets to be entered, (4) changes in the internal environment of the company, and (5) changes in relations with the external environment of the company.

When the classification had been completed, a two-day meeting was held with the president and the vice-presidents. At this meeting the consultants presented the composite list of ideas and proposed a procedure for consolidating the ideas. Each member of the senior management planning group would independently assign weights of importance to each of the proposed ideas. The weights would be tabulated and a composite weighting scheme would be developed to define the overall combined priority assessment. The weighting scheme would be done in a hierarchical fashion so assessment of importance of the five major categories (products, services, markets, internal environment, external environment) would precede weightings for sub-elements of each category, finally followed by weightings of specific individual activities within each category. The priority procedure was accepted by the group and carried out in the remainder of the two-day session.

At the end of the session, managers were amazed at how consistent their views of development directions actually were. Furthermore, the process of discussion during the two days had enabled this consistency to become even more unified. The obvious enthusiasm of the group over the consolidation seemed to dispel fears that no commonly-held future could be defined.

At the end of the session, the consultants proposed that the senior management group work together to prepare one integrated scenario based on the priority items identified in the two-day session. The group accepted the proposal and agreed to have the integrated scenario completed within a month.

The scenario was completed on time and another working session was held involving the consultants and senior management. The scenario was favorably reviewed by all members of the group. Time in the meeting was then directed toward identifying a set of development projects that should be initiated as soon as possible based on the scenario. Eleven such projects were identified, each addressing a major strategy that was implied by the scenario. The president and the four vice-presidents divided responsibilities for the leadership of the projects. Two or three middle managers were then chosen to participate as a planning task force for each project. Thus, a significant number of new managers became involved in the planning effort.

The definition of the projects ended the Ends Planning phase and initiated a Means Planning phase of work. It was agreed that there would be a major meeting to review the progress on each of the eleven projects in four month's time. The consultants' staff resources were to be used by any of the eleven project task forces in ways that they saw fit.

The last session of Ends Planning concluded with a great deal of enthusiasm on the part of ABC's senior management. Almost immediately after the meeting, however, the enthusiasm began to wane. As managers realized the extent of involvement required of them to spear-head the areas to which they had committed, while continuing their day-to-day managerial responsibilities, the overload looked impossible. Because each executive had committed to the effort, however, each tried to push forward in their area of responsibility. Within two months the strains became very visible. The priorities on the eleven projects began to be questioned. More important, the percent of time allocated to the planning projects steadily dwindled for most of the executives. An unforeseen problem with the process had arisen; the need for a reassessment was obvious. The consultants began to diagnose what was going wrong and started to reformulate the meta-planning strategy.

MANAGEMENT SYSTEM PLANNING

ABC faced a problem of scarce managerial resources at the top level of the organization. There simply wasn't enough time to manage day-to-day operations of the organization and at the same time lead new development efforts. The constraint had never been previously identified because ABC had never before defined its development priorities. Once having done so, and then having discovered the constraints on managerial resources, new challenges were faced in getting a more effective planning process implemented.

A meeting was held with the senior management group to discuss the problem and alternative solutions. The first question raised by the consultants was basic priorities: did senior management feel day-to-day operational activities so dominated development areas that long range planning should be substantially scaled-down or abandoned altogether? The group unanimously supported continuing the planning effort. In addition, everyone agreed that the Senior Management Planning Committee (as it began to be called) had to maintain leadership of the development areas.

[The decision to support a long range planning process in the face of severe time constraints created by day-to-day operating responsibilities was a significant test of managerial commitment. Justifications were almost entirely based on the importance of solving the problem created by limited areas for significant new development within existing businesses. Success in carrying out the process to date clearly played an important role, but this was seldom mentioned as a reason to continue. The product-orientation of management was very evident during this discussion, reconfirming Hypothesis 1.]

The planning committee decided to appoint a Management System Task Force to recommend ways of significantly increasing the efficiency of senior managment time utilization. [Although the task was process-oriented, it had a clear problem focus to the managers who initiated it, again adding credibility for Hypothesis 1.] The task force began what was to become a 15-month project on management system and organizational redesign. While this effort was going on, the eleven development projects were continued on a less intensive basis to insure they stayed alive.

The Management System Task Force began its work by analyzing how senior management spent time. That analysis showed that the bulk of it was spent monitoring and controlling the execution of operational activities. This suggested potential payoffs if current systems to support top management control functions could be improved. Since most of the formal sources of information for control were computer-generated reports, the study focused on the adequacy of the company's MIS. One problem with this system became readily apparent; although the MIS was used almost exclusively for control, the reports from the sytem did not meet a basic criterion of a good control system; namely exception reporting. In fact, when the computer reports were examined, one wondered whether they were designed to *minimize* the chance that management would be able to spot problems in the system. The task force found that the monthly computer output distributed to approximately 100 managers in the company exceeded 150 feet of computer paper in the normal folded form! When the density of output of these reports was taken into account, the task force calculated that if a manager read all the material he was given in the reports at a rate of 1,000 words per minute, he would have to spend more than 50% of his time doing nothing else.

As part of its analysis, the Management System Task Force conducted an extensive study of the computer department and its operating philosophy. The objective was to redefine the information support program so that its systems' output would be of greater benefit to managers. This study led to a complete restructuring of the computer department, converting it from a large centralized facility to one where both equipment and staff were decentralized to user departments. The decentralization led to intensive use of mini-computer technology with on-line information systems designed to serve the specific needs of managers. The change made the systems more responsive to managers and, hence, more useful to them.

The change also forced the computer systems staff to reassess their own long range planning activities. Decentralization made it more difficult for computer staff to work together on common developments. This issue forced the group to share explicitly their perceptions on the priorities of such developments. They discovered that there were not such common perceptions; i.e., an integrated planning perspective did not exist in the department. This situation caused a long range planning process to be initiated at the division level of the company for the first time.

[This is a good illustration of Hypothesis 1. There was a spontaneous initiation of a planning program at another level of the organization because the managers at that level recognized that they needed to plan in order to solve a problem that they faced. The problem-orientation drove the process-orientation.]

ORGANIZATION PLANNING

At about the time the changes in the computer department were introduced, a study was initiated on the informal processes for managerial control; that is, communication channels in the organization. This study was initiated to determine whether the organization structure facilitated relevant information interchange among managers. It quickly became evident from the study that there would soon be a serious overload on senior management because of their added business development responsibilities, regardless of how effective the new computer support systems could become. Thus, a reorganization of top management responsibilities in the company was clearly required.

Two alternatives to the present organization structure were considered. One option was to segment operating responsibilities, thus creating a new group of senior managers to take over some of these responsibilities. The second was to continue to have vice-presidential level managers maintain a dual responsibility for both operating areas and development concerns, but to significantly reduce the operating responsibilities of any particular vice-president.

The consultants discussed the advantages and disadvantages of the two options with the president. They pointed out that a reorganization had to be evaluated, not only from the perspective of the planning system, but also in terms of its impact on organization culture and on management style. [Senior management's recognition and acceptance of the interplay among planning, management style, and organization culture provide credibility for Hypothesis 2.] The advantages and disadvantages of each option were summarized to the president in a fashion similar to Table 1.

The difference between the options rested partly on whether there was a preference to reorient management styles into something more conducive to planning, or to change cultural aspects. A cross-functional planning orientation would have produced the most change in management style: a specialized product development activity would have accelerated an external orientation to the organization culture. The president decided management style considerations were of more immediate importance, hence he chose to keep development activities in the hands of the vice-presidents as a group. Therefore, five new vice-presidents were added to senior management, and the original four functions were divided into nine areas of day-to-day operating responsibilities. All nine vice-presidents were equally charged with corporate planning and development responsibilities.

When the functional responsibilities of the new vice-presidential positions

Table 1. Management system effects of reorganization options.

OPTION	PLANNING PROCESS IMPACTS	MANAGEMENT STYLE IMPACTS	ORG. CULTURE IMPACTS
Specialize the development function and keep broader responsibilities for operating managers	Potential implementation problems because operating managers may not accept development areas	Relatively consistent with existing management styles of clear management responsibility for one function or area	Organization more likely to obtain better environmental information because functional responsibility for development demands better information
Incorporate the development function with operating responsibilities and narrow the scope of operating responsibilities	Potential problems of balancing operating responsibilities with development responsibilities	Requires change in style to work as a decision committee on development decisions that cross functional areas	Culture relatively consistent with existing one because operating experience incorporated as primary information for development

were well enough established, attention turned to the development of procedures for integrating day-to-day operating concerns with strategic issues. One of the issues that remained unclear was the precise roles of the vice-presidents in strategic planning, since one of them had been officially designated V.P. of Corporate Planning. At the first meeting of the president and the vice-presidents after the reorganization, the consultants proposed a plan for future organizational processes. The key elements of the plan were:

1. That each vice-president be treated as the general manager of a profit center with cross charges for all goods and services provided by the profit center; the planning and development of each profit center would be a divisional responsibility with quarterly reviews of performance by the president and his immediate staff.
2. That an Executive Planning Committee, consisting of the president and the nine vice-presidents, be established and it be responsible for defining, implementing and controlling all company-wide strategic development for ABC (i.e., development in areas not considered to be the planning responsibility of one of the vice-presidents).
3. That the Corporate Planning division act as staff to the Executive Planning Committee; as such, it would be responsible for integrating information on major cross-divisional planning issues as well as monitoring the external environment for relevant corporate planning trends.

This plan made explicit the decentralized operating philosophy that ABC desired to maintain. It also made clear the dual responsibilities of each vice-president as both the head of an operating unit and a member of strategic management on corporate-wide development. Figure 2 shows the proposed process of interaction between divisional and corporate groups. The consultants proposed the corporate-divisional review sessions be held quarterly and that the Executive Planning Committee also meet quarterly following these divisional meetings. In this way updated analysis on divisional developments would be inputs to corporate strategy sessions.

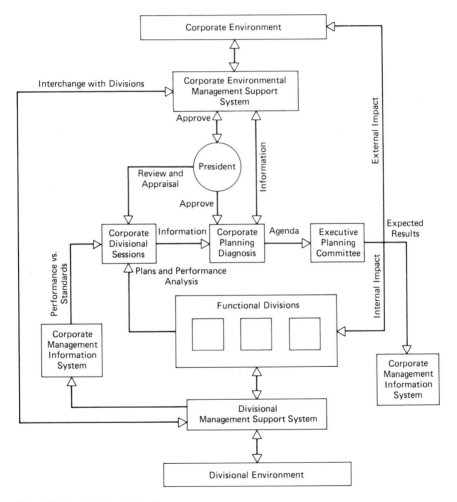

Figure 2. Organizational planning processes.

CHANGES IN CULTURE AND STYLE

The proposed organizational processes were accepted essentially as they had been presented by the consultants. However, the frequency of the Executive Planning Committee meetings was changed from quarterly to monthly to be sure a momentum would not be lost. The consultants expressed some reservations that the meetings might become unproductive because the appropriate staff work by the corporate planning division may not be completed with meetings so frequent. The senior management group was not overly concerned about this, however, and the change was made.

The agenda for the Executive Planning Committee meetings was prepared by the V.P. of Corporate Planning with input from the other committee members. It was agreed by the committee that its first activity would be an internal orientation program. Each committee member was asked to prepare a presentation on his divisional plans. The committee decided to begin with the Marketing Division because its efforts had the greatest impact on the activities of the other divisions.

The marketing review was expected to take about 3 hours. But questions during the course of the presentation resulted in only a fraction of the material being covered. The committee decided to continue to review and to meet more frequently to keep on schedule. At the second meeting there were even more questions and discussion than the first, so the progress of covering the material slowed even more. The committee continued to feel the interchange was useful, and so decided to increase its meeting schedule to a weekly basis and to extend the duration of the meetings to full-day sessions.

The increased time commitment did not achieve the objective of expediting the review process. Instead, it had the opposite effect. The more often the Executive Planning Committee met to review how marketing was planning its development, the quicker they seemed to bog down in the details of the strategies. In effect, the committee converted its function from planning corporate strategy to micromanagement of divisional operations.

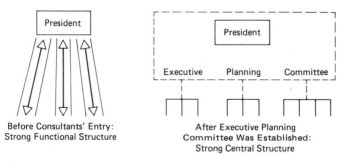

Figure 3. The evolution of managerial processes in Company ABC.

This evolution in orientation occurred over a several month period and was not clearly perceived by members of the committee. But, as illustrated in Figure 3, the managerial processes had effectively shifted 180 degrees from when the first planning efforts by the consultants had been initiated. Instead of clear delineation of responsibility areas for divisional V.P.'s and independent actions by them, all major decisions in every area of the company were coming under the control of the Executive Planning Committee.

This situation nearly destroyed all the progress that had been made to date. It became almost impossible for the company to get any decision approved because of the committee's review process. Further, almost all senior management time seemed to be spent in committee meetings. As a result, the lower level managers became isolated from their bosses. They drifted aimlessly with little idea what they should be doing, and even less feeling that what they did would mean anything anyway. It was a very dangerous situation.

While this was going on, the consultants had been playing a rather passive role in the Executive Planning Committee meetings to create a self-generated planning process in ABC. As the situation became more critical, the consultants decided they had to intervene. The consultants felt the problems arose because the committee was too anxious to succeed. Committee members knew cross-divisional cooperation was critical, hence enthusiastic participation in the divisional reviews was a natural tendency; it just seemed to have gotten carried away. More importantly divisional planning issues were tangible problems that could be tackled by the group. There were no issues already in existence that represented corporate concerns. Hence, faced with a choice between trying to help solve something already formulated at a divisional level or working on new problem formulations at a corporate level, the least risky starting point for the committee seemed to be to concentrate on divisional problems.

[This condition illustrates Hypothesis 2, and specifically how a planning process can fail for reasons unrelated to the quality of the process itself. Clearly, the Executive Planning Committee had been put into a role that was an unfamiliar management style for the participants. They dealt with the uncertainty in the best way they knew, which was to move away from vague roles as planners into more familiar roles as operating managers. An intervention was called for to reduce the uncertainty of dealing with planning problems, so that the new management style could be developed around productive, rather than destructive issues.]

The consultants felt it was critical to capitalize on the spirit the Executive Planning Committee had developed, but rechannel it to get the planning process back in balance. They did this by introducing a planning technique called Beliefs Assessment to the committee. (See Emshoff and Saaty for a detailed description of the technique.) The Beliefs Assessment process requires managerial participation in a series of sessions to define the key factors that will affect the organization's future and to formulate tentative planning policies to do something about the future. These sessions structure the interaction among participants, thereby reducing the anxieties about participative decision-making processes. However, the technique focuses exclusively on managerial beliefs to make the planning assessments: experiences, values, and prejudices are all incorporated, but staff analyses per se are not. Thus, the sessions facilitate active involvement by the managers who participate in them.

The Beliefs Assessment process worked well as an antidote to the micromanagement role the Executive Planning Committee had begun to assume. Major issues emerged from the process that were truly at a corporate level and clearly demanded long term attention by the committee. Hence, future meeting agendas could be focused on these problems with no fear of the process falling flat. This automatically reduced divisional oriented efforts of the committee.

There was another important change created by the Beliefs Assessment process. The process forced explicit assessment of environmental factors relevant to planned futures. Managers realized for the first time how little they knew about these factors. [The company thus began to recognize its cultural weakness; consistent with Hypothesis 3, planning problems induced changes in cultural attitudes.] As a result, the corporate planning staff began to act in the role originally intended for it, that is, as an analytic resource to gather, integrate and interpret factual information for the Executive Planning Committee relevant to the resolution of corporate issues. The staff immediately began to work on developing an Environmental Sensing System. Previously the staff, which contained many of the most capable middle managers in the company, had been occupied with busy-work projects that were self-initiated. As they became part of main-stream policy making decision, the staff's productivity increased enormously.

When the Executive Planning Committee reoriented itself toward corporate strategy, efforts were reinitiated to insure specific decentralized responsibilities for the operating units. The middle managers, who had previously gone through morale problems, became more visible and influential on operating decisions. They responded by taking the initiative to a far greater extent than they had in the past. Thus, for the first time, ABC was approximately balanced between an on-going strategic orientation and an effective operational orientation. This balancing occurred more than 5 years after the first initiatives were taken by the president and 3 years after the consultants entered the company. Once these capabilities were established, the outside consultants felt less and less need to actively define organizational directions. For a period of time they continued to operate in an advisory capacity to the Executive Planning Committee to insure development proceded in a healthy fashion. But they no longer controlled the planning activity. Thus, the company was in a position to determine its development by itself, which is the only way long run success was possible.

CONCLUSIONS

Obviously, the case study does not validate the hypotheses in a scientific sense. In fact, it raises many unanswered issues such as: Is there an appropriate sequence in which changes in planning processes, management style, and organization culture ought to proceed? How much change can be successfully incorporated in any phase of meta-planning? Who from the organization should be a party to overall meta-planning design? Are outside change-agents necessary?

This paper did not promise to provide answers to meta-planning issues. Hopefully, however, it will sensitize researchers and managers to the need to find the answers and integrate them into an overall meta-planning theory. Such theory development can potentially close the gap between the theory and practice of planning, a result that is desired by everyone.

REFERENCES

Ackoff, R. L., *A Concept of Corporate Planning,* Wiley, New York, 1970.

Ayres, R. U., *Technological Forecasting and Long Range Planning,* McGraw-Hill, New York, 1969.

Beckhard, Richard, *Organization Development: Strategies and Models,* Addison-Wesley, Reading, Mass., 1969.

Bennis, Warren G., et al., *The Planning of Change,* Holt, New York, 1969.

Caldwell, G. T., "Corporate Planning in Canada: An Overview," *Conference Board of Canada,* 1975.

Emshoff, J. R. and T. L. Saaty, "Prioritized Hierarchies as a Vehicle for Long Range Planning," working paper series, Wharton Applied Research Center, Univ. of Pennsylvania, Philadelphia, Penn., 1977.

Lucado, W. E., "Corporate Planning—A Current Status Report," *Managerial Planning* (November-December 1974).

Schein, Edgar H., *Process Consultation: Its Role in Organization Development,* Addison-Wesley, Reading, Mass., 1969.

Steiner, G. A., *Comprehensive Managerial Planning,* The Planning Executives Institute, Oxford, Ohio, 1972.

—— and H. Schollhammer, "Pitfalls in Multi-National Long Range Planning," *Long Range Planning* (April 1975).

8
Information, Planning, and the Computer

In previous chapters, strategic, administrative, and operational planning have been described through the managerial levels where planning is performed, the functions with which plans are concerned, and the techniques for the implementation and control of plans. Implicit in all these are the differences in the kind of information required for each type of plan, and planning effectiveness depends on the kind, amount, and accuracy of the information available.

THE DECISIONMAKING PROCESS

Decisionmaking is a process. Sequential steps are taken to arrive at a decision, and then more steps are taken to insure that the decision is carried out. The process continues and recycles as results are fed back, forcing reevaluation. And, in all instances—regardless, for example, of the managerial level or the magnitude of the decision—the decision process follows a general pattern.

This pattern has been described by many authors, and the steps have been given many different names. In his classic article, Eilon (1969) explains decisionmaking in eight steps:

1. *Information input.* First and foremost, the decisionmakers must recognize that a decision has to be made. They must be aware of a problem requiring resolution and of the details surrounding that problem. Perhaps profits are down, or inventories are up, or return goods are well ahead of last year's returns. What information do they have? What information do they need? Gathering as much information as they can, they are ready for the next step. (See pp. 254–256 on the nature of information and information-gathering.)

2. *Analysis.* In the analysis step, the decisionmakers attempt to reduce the information to manageable proportions. They try to determine that they are solving the problem and not a symptom. They establish the validity, appropriateness, and completeness of the information. If profits are down, it is probably a symptom of some other shortcoming in the organization, such as excessive scrap

in the production process or an inefficient distribution system. Depending on the cause of the problem, different kinds of information will be required and different kinds of analyses will be performed.

3. *Performance measures.* Based on the information and its analysis, as well as the objectives and policies of the organization, the decisionmakers now develop measures that indicate the performance required of the organization. (For example, what profit level is necessary? What criteria must be met in restructuring the distribution system?) Knowing the measures sets the objectives for the next step.

4. *Model.* The model is a representation of how the system will behave. It attempts to depict what happens—or will happen—in the process being evaluated. How does the product get to market? What could—or does—go wrong? What variables affect the system, causing different results at different times? The model might be elaborate or concise depending on the system being described or on the significance of the problem being solved.

5. *Strategies.* Strategies are the alternatives open to the decisionmakers. The word *strategy* does not necessarily imply that they are operating on the strategic level; rather, it is a term that is synonymous with alternative. Decisionmakers might have to choose between different delivery routes (operational alternatives) or different acquisition prospects (strategic alternatives). In Eilon's terms, both would be strategies.

6. *Prediction of outcomes.* Each alternative is analyzed and its outcome(s) calculated. This calculation may be quantitative or qualitative. For example, decisionmakers may be able to make an investment decision based on calculating a rate of return for each possible alternative, but in choosing a new advertising manager, they may have to rely mostly on emotion and intuition.

7. *Choice criteria.* A choice criterion is the actual standard for choosing one alternative over another. In the examples given in (6), such criteria would be a given level of return on investment in the first case and some "positive inclination" in the second.

8. *Resolution.* Resolution is the selection of an alternative. If the previous steps were accomplished with skill, then the last step should be almost automatic. The proper alternative should be obvious.

No one of these steps is sufficient by itself. All eight are important, and all eight must be performed properly—and successfully.

Just as in the planning process, a decision is only as good as management's ability to carry it out. After resolution, the implementation process begins. If new information is developed during this implementation phase, it may be necessary to return to an earlier step in the decision process and reevaluate the decision that has been made by redoing the process from that point. But, no matter how the process happens, Eilon's first step, information input, is the key.

INFORMATION

Information has certain attributes that reflect its quality and usefulness in a given situation. The degree to which these attributes must be present in a given information set is determined by the use to which the information is to be put. The attributes of information, according to Senn (1978), are:

1. *Accuracy.* Information should reflect a situation as it exists. The extent to which it does so is the responsibility of the person providing the information. Different situations require different degrees of accuracy. For example, information in a firm's accounts-receivable operation must be accurate to the penny. Otherwise, client complaints and delays in payment would result. On the other hand, information for analyzing sales by product type would not require such accuracy since whole dollars would still provide meaningful information. Whatever the situation, the user should be able to assume accuracy.

2. *Form.* Information should be presented in a useful manner. How this is done will depend to some extent on the degree of qualitative or quantitative content. The more quantitative the information, the more the users should be able to receive the information in a wide variety of forms and formats, such as numerical tables, written paragraphs, bar charts, tables, computer listings, summary reports, or cathode-ray-tube displays.

3. *Frequency.* There are two important aspects to the timing of information. The obvious one is how often information is needed. Moreover, how often should the information be collected? (That is, how often is it available?) For example, a sales-analysis report showing sales by item in gross dollar amounts is only needed by management on a quarterly basis. However, the detailed data about each item sold are available with each order processed on the computer. Thus, throughout each day as orders are processed, the sales-analysis information is accumulated and held for the quarterly processing into the management report. In this case, collection frequency is at the time an order is written, whereas report frequency is quarterly.

4. *Breadth.* Information may be broad or limited in scope. This is not reflective of the amount of detail or the quantity of information, but of the perspective. In the garment industry, top management might be interested only in style, administrative management in style and color, and operating management in style, color, and size.

5. *Origin.* Information may be gathered from within or outside a company. This topic will be covered in more detail later in this chapter.

6. *Time horizon.* Information is separated into three categories relative to time: (1) what has happened in the past, (2) what is happening now, and (3) what will happen in the future. The focus is on information use. All three categories are important to management. Historical information provides a record of

past performance. Its possession allows comparisons with the current situation. Information about the future determines which current actions are required to meet future goals. Such future information is essential to any planning effort.

When information is collected into sets, these sets have certain desirable characteristics (Senn 1978):

1. *Relevance.* If the information is not relevant to the situation, then it should be ignored. Extraneous and irrelevant information confuses issues, wastes time, and prevents clear-cut solutions.

2. *Timeliness.* Information should not be delayed in reaching the user. Late information can be just as useless as irrelevant information.

3. *Completeness.* Completeness is related to accuracy. The information a manager has may all be true, timely, and relevant; however, if the manager does not have all of the available information, then his or her decisionmaking will not be as efficient as it should be.

Paine and Naumes (1974) mention three additional considerations in evaluating the quality of information. The first is *cost/availability.* Much information is available if decisionmakers are willing to pay for it; however, if the price is too high, the information may not be worth the expense. The second consideration is *bias,* which is related to accuracy. However, there is a distinction. A person reporting information may be absolutely accurate, truthful, and even complete, but bias may be present in the form of undue emphasis in a given area, or in the order of the presentation, or simply in the tone of the presentation. For example, the information that your parents are coming to visit would probably have a different tone depending on whether you are telling it to your spouse or your spouse is telling you.

The third consideration is *competitive advantage.* An overriding question in the decisionmaking function is, what will your competitors do? By knowing what kind of information they have, you can gain insight into their possible actions. Also, the converse is true. If your competitors know the kind of information you have, then they will know some of your strategy. Thus, the value of information depends on whether the same information is available to competitors. If it is, it may be less valuable.

SOURCES OF INFORMATION AND DATA

Sources of information and data are generally categorized as primary and secondary. Primary data are collected by researchers themselves, through observation or some interviewing technique. Secondary data are collected by someone else. Both kinds of data can be available both within and outside an organization.

With observation, a whole event may be captured as it occurs. In addition, the observed subjects seem to prefer it to questioning, and observation may be the only way to get the information. However, it is a slow and expensive process, and it can only yield information that can be revealed by surface actions or indicators (Emory 1976).

There are many types of secondary information sources; the most common is published material. By far, in this country, the largest printer of such materials is the United States government. Its total publications number in the hundreds of thousands. A second major source is the various technical journals. There are 59,000 such journals in the world, and some 9000 are published in the United States. Another major source is the over 40,000 books published in the United States every year. Beyond this, much useful information can be found in reference books; university and company publications; reports of such research organizations as the Stanford Research Institute, the Rand Corporation, and the Brookings Institution; trade journals; and general business periodicals such as *Business Week,* the *Wall Street Journal,* and *Fortune.* The article by de Carbonnel and Dorrance (1973), which begins on p. 265, provides tables of source and content of both domestic and international economic and industrial information. The timeliness and completeness of the information sources are also indicated in the tables. Material from secondary sources can often be obtained cheaply and quickly, but it often does not meet specific research needs, or is not as accurate as desired, or both (Emory 1976).

In addition, there are numerous informal sources that managers use for acquiring information. These include the corporate "grapevine" and casual conversations with coworkers and industry associates. However, such information is less likely to be valuable to management decisionmaking.

COMMUNICATION/INFORMATION FLOW

Information is of little value to the organization unless those to whom it is transmitted receive it unaltered. This requires a well-run communication system that will overcome semantic problems and foster understanding. In some ways, this requirement is related to information accuracy. If accurate information is transmitted but the user receives inaccurate information, then nothing has been gained from the transmission. Should the recipient act on the inaccurate information, the result could be worse than if no transmission had been made.

The elements of a communication system are: an origin (*source information*), a transmitter (*data channel*), a receiver (*destination information*), and the message itself. The message may change form (*be encoded/decoded*) during transmission. Thus, errors in message transmission can be caused by improper encoding, bad transmission, improper decoding, or combinations of these.

Even the simplest message moves from its origin to its destination over some kind of data channel. For example, suppose Joe called Pat's office and left a message for her to pick up a loaf of bread on her way home. Such a message has all the elements of a communication system. The source information resulted from Joe's observation that bread was in short supply. A telephone line provided the data channel to Pat's secretary, who wrote the message on paper and placed it on Pat's desk. Pat received the note and interpreted it as requiring her to go to a food store on her way home. It is easy to see how errors can interfere with message transmission. Mistakes could have been made at any step in the preceding scenario. Joe could have said "bread" while meaning "milk"; the connection could have been so bad that "milk" sounded like "bread"; the secretary could have heard "bread" and written "milk"; and Pat could have read "milk" and bought bread.

We know of an executive whose hobby is tropical fish. One afternoon, his 10-year-old daughter telephoned his office, eager to announce, "The guppy had babies." However, the executive was in a meeting, so the daughter had to leave a message with a secretary. By the time the message found its way to the executive, it read, "The dog had puppies."

Communications *can* get garbled. When critical decisions are to be made based on the information communicated, management had better insure that a reliable communication system exists.

INFORMATION AND MANAGEMENT ACTION

In previous chapters, it has been made quite clear that the various planning perspectives—strategic, administrative, and operational—are linked to the management hierarchy. In other words, higher-level management is most concerned with the selection of objectives and policies, the broad allocation of resources, the broad structure of the organization, and long-term growth. Middle or administrative management is concerned with the acquisition and use of resources to create a maximum performance potential. Finally, operating management must assure that specific goals are achieved efficiently and effectively.

Steiner (1969) suggests that top-level managers should devote a small percentage of their time to issues that focus on the immediate future and the majority of time to decisions from 1 to 10 years ahead. Middle-level managers should concentrate on the period 3 to 6 months ahead, but some of their activities will require a longer perspective of perhaps 1 to 3 years. The operating manager is primarily concerned with today and the weeks ahead. Steiner admits that these allocations are arbitrary and perhaps form an ideal for the medium-size company. The larger the company, the more time top management will have to devote to activities beyond 5 years. For the smaller company, the top management focus would concentrate on the nearer term. And too, this time allocation would be modified by the nature of the industry that a firm operates in.

For example, innovation and change are slow-paced in the motor freight industry; an executive in that field would not have to look as far into the future as would a top-level manager in a high-technology firm in the dynamic, fast-changing computer industry.

The jobs to be done at each level of management differ extensively in subject as well as time perspective. The nature of the decisions to be made, therefore, is quite different. The kind of information required by each level of manager must fit his or her decisionmaking needs. Alexander & Alexander, recognizing the need to provide specific information for each level, built such a requirement into its implementation phase (see pp. 368–370).

As Zachman (1977) points out in "Control and Planning of Information Systems," which begins on p. 283, strategic decisions are highly judgmental, unstructured, and need tailor-made information. Middle managers make many subjective decisions, but they have prescribed procedures to follow and have structured information to work with. Low-level or operational managers rely on rules rather than judgment and need precisely defined information.

Providing information for strategic decisions is perhaps the most difficult of the three planning levels. Hayes and Radosevich (1974) list five characteristics of strategic information:

1. Information needs are rarely defined explicitly because of a lack of formal strategic planning and control systems.
2. Existing formal communications channels are ill-suited for strategic information.
3. The timing and phasing of strategic information gathering, transmission, storage, and retrieval are most critical.
4. Sources of strategic information are commonly external to the organization.
5. The strategic-information time horizon is often the distant future rather than the past.

Much of the information required at each level comes from similar sources, but is presented to the various management levels in different forms. Within an organization, each of the functional areas provides detailed information: payroll, personnel, production, marketing, sales, orders, inventory, purchasing, finance, etc. This information filters up the organization through operational and administrative levels to top (strategic) management. As it filters up, it becomes more general and less specific. Details are summarized, and information from various functional areas is integrated. Data reduction takes place; for example, inventory reporting includes the details of purchases, shipments, quantity on hand, returns, adjustments, and quantity on order. All of these are essential for the operational manager. For top management, however, this detail is reduced to a turnover ratio.

External information also affects all levels of management. Whether the information is provided by customers, stockholders, competitors, the public, unions, government, or any other groups or individuals outside the organization, it is useful in some way to management because it is one aspect of the external environment that management is constantly trying to accommodate. For example, at the operational level in an open-shop environment, it is important for the foreman to know whether an employee is in a union and what the procedures are for dealing with that union's members. Moreover, on the strategic level it is important to know the aggregate number of union employees, and whether this number is increasing or decreasing, to help determine the impact of organized labor on the future of the firm.

Because each level of management is faced with a different kind of decision-making problem and because each needs its own set of information to facilitate that function, it is critical that the right information get to the right level. Otherwise, one level of management may attempt to solve another level's problem. To direct information to the right level and to facilitate the reducing and forming of information appropriate for each use, an information system is required.

INFORMATION SYSTEMS

An information system is a systematic way of reducing raw data into meaningful information for the various levels of management. Theoretically, information systems can be either manual or mechanized, but in truth, only the simplest information system can be effective without some form of automation. Nonautomated systems become cumbersome to operate as data-file size and transaction volume increase. As a result, system-response time is reduced or there is a higher error rate, or both, as information-handlers strive to keep up with information demands. Therefore, the most realistic approach is to assume that the organization has a computer system that supports the information-processing effort.

A computer system in an organization, however, is not necessarily an information system. If a computer system does not provide meaningful information to all decisionmaking levels in an organization, it is not an information system, but just a collector of facts. Usually, the basic function of computers is the support of operational activities. Computers are programmed to handle the routine transactions of a business. As mentioned, this is a valuable function, for such detail is the source for much of the summary information that will filter up the organization hierarchy. However, a management information system (MIS) involves more than just hardware, software, and information itself. It must provide a means for storage and retrieval that facilitates integrating the information needs of the different operating areas of the organization. Today's computers have the ability to store, retrieve, manipulate, and transmit the data that are required for the integrating function. The key elements in such a computer-based MIS are data-file/data-base management, report generation/inquiry processing, and controls.

Data File/Data Base Management

The ability to store vast amounts of information at low cost is one of the key attributes of modern computers. Of course, the data stored within the system must be organized in a manner that facilitates retrieval and updating. A common approach is to place all information about a function into a file. Thus, all inventory information may be found in the inventory file. Often, however, the same information is common to more than one file. Under the unique file approach, the common data must be repeated, thus using extra file space and necessitating that the accuracy of both files be maintained. However, advanced hardware and data base management programs now allow the integration of the two files, thus creating a data base. In such a data base system, all files for an organization are structured so that any piece of information is recorded only once and is retrievable in combination with any other piece of information.

Report Generation/Inquiry Processing

The information must somehow be transmitted to the user. The most common way for this to happen is through a printed report. However, recent developments have made economical the use of cathode-ray–tube (CRT) computer terminals for displaying information in an executive's office or any other place where information is of value, such as factory, sales locations, etc. Inquiry programs allow a user to ask for specific information and have it displayed or printed in a meaningful format. For example, a manager may want to know the inventory status of an item and the number sold the previous week. The specific information can be requested and will be displayed on the CRT. If the manager wishes a detailed report of the previous week's sales he or she may request the detailed listing noting salesperson, customer, price, etc. This could be displayed on the CRT or printed as a report, or both.

Exception reporting is desirable in an MIS just as in any management system. The power of the computer is used to monitor activities; when the situation exceeds limits or violates the established norm, an exception report is flashed to management so that appropriate action may be taken.

Controls

An integral part of any MIS is controls and checkpoints. In addition to the accounting controls, there must be a provision to insure the integrity of files and to insure that information was not lost or falsely created. In addition, it must be insured that any changes that were made were made properly. There must also be a system to accommodate corrective action when things do go wrong. No system should be designed without a backup or bypass procedure. There must be some way to recover from either hardware, programming, or operator failure. With the management-decision system so dependent on the MIS, it would jeopardize the organization to do otherwise.

With the proliferation of minicomputers and microcomputers, a wide enough variety of computer capability and cost exists so that any organization should be able to install an effective system commensurate with its information needs. The key to the successful installation and operation of a computer information system is the same as for the planning system: top management involvement. In companies in which management has considered information processing as a resource to be managed much like other major resources (capital, labor, etc.), the computer installation has been a success. Where management has ignored this function, the information resource has become costly and ineffective.

In fact, as Zachman (1977) suggests, the information-management function should be established as a separate system, much as the cash-management system is held separate and assigned to a controller to manage. Information and its processing should then become the responsibility of an information-processing professional.

Even with a proper organizational structure and management involvement, developing an information system requires thorough planning. A number of approaches have been used, which can be classified according to two types: the *bottom-up* and the *top-down*. The bottom-up approach, which is more commonly used, is an evolutionary process. The system begins with transaction processing for one functional area. Subsequently, information and decision systems to support other than operational functions are added. It has the advantage of being an orderly step-by-step approach, using an existing data-processing operation. On the other hand, it could be expensive and inefficient since each iteration of the decision system will require a reworking or redesign of the existing system.

The top-down approach overcomes some of these design difficulties. Because an information system is designed to mirror the actual information flow in an organization, a single design satisfies the simplest as well as the most complex information system. However, to do this in practice is difficult. Objectives and policies have to be turned into realities, costs estimated, the value of each element in the system established, and a working system installed that crosses departmental and functional boundaries.

There is a hybrid approach that overcomes most of the problems and incorporates much of the good features of both approaches. It is detailed in Zachman's article beginning on p. 283.

COMPUTER-AIDED DECISIONMAKING

Having an MIS and having a computer assist in management decisionmaking may be two different things. It is possible to bring the power of the computer to bear on management-decision problems without an information system or even a computer on the premises. Even if the computer is only used for operational tasks, it does provide some information for management. Moreover, the many decision models, such as rate-of-return formulas and payback methods, as well as break-even analysis, allocation, inventory, queuing, sequencing, replacement, and competitive models, are made practical by the use of a computer. In addition, many companies are developing their own models suited to the circumstances of their industry and their firm.

The objective of this modeling is consistent with the objective of an MIS: to provide timely, accurate, and economical planning information. But models are not MIS's, they are adjuncts to an MIS, or, at best, a part of an MIS. The distinction here is based on completeness. The model will more than likely concentrate in only one area, such as financial. A typical financial model might compute the financial implications of various production and marketing policies under different environmental conditions and produce financial statements for each variation. Such a model, termed a *simulation*, is a representation of (potential) reality. It has the advantage of displaying outcomes without having to incur the expense of actually performing the required actions. It allows management to test various alternatives, weigh the outcomes, and then choose the one most desirable. But such a financial model will only relate to that one functional area, and other models will be required for testing options in other areas.

The kind of information needed for the model includes a certain amount of historical data as well as certain specific assumptions about the future. These assumptions might be contained in an outside data base available from the government or research organizations. Such a data base might contain demographic, economic, or other environmental information. The power of the computer rests in its being able to calculate the various outcomes rapidly in order to make it a simple matter to evaluate a number of alternatives. The managers play a "what if . . .?" game with the computer. For instance, they inquire, "What if labor rates increase by 7 percent? 6 percent? 8 percent?" or "What if sales increase by 6 percent? 12 percent?" They may also ask combinations of "ifs." In "Computers Games that Planners Play" (*Business Week*, December 18, 1978), a number of good examples of modeling success are reported. R. J. Reynolds Industries gathers information for its main strategic plan from its six operating divisions. Through the model, it can predict cash flow at any time. It can also predict shortfalls in any division, as well as the impact a shortfall would have on the corporate goals. Public Service Electric & Gas Co. runs its corporate plan once each day. It tests the impact that the level of fuel purchases has on costs, equipment use, and finances. At Ralston Purina Co., the model is used to determine the effect of soybean and corn price increases on the overall corporate plan long before the effect of those price increases is actually felt.

The success of the model is in direct proportion to the accuracy (quality) of the information used. And that seems to be the problem with many models in use. Although there is much corporate interest in modeling, the potential of this technique has been untapped by current practice (Hamilton and Moses 1974). In particular, the models have been unable to successfully predict economic conditions.

CONCLUSION

In this chapter, we have described the pieces that make up what might be termed a *decision support system for management*. We have emphasized the need for quality information and the necessity of presenting that information in a meaningful manner. The need for management involvement and support at all levels was emphasized. The point cannot be made too strongly that having a computer and having an MIS are not at all the same. According to Alter (1976), the computer data-processing system performs passive clerical activities aimed at mechanical efficiency and is focused on past events. It is a recordkeeping, business-reporting system that produces data in the form of standard reports. The management information system/decision support system does all this and much more. It is an active system oriented toward overall organizational effectiveness at all levels; it focuses on the present and future and has the flexibility to handle *ad hoc* situations. It can retrieve isolated data items, analyze data files, calculate the outcomes of proposed decisions, propose decisions, and make decisions. It is a decisionmaking and implementation system. Such a system is now essential to any planning function.

Just what does the future hold for planning besides the necessity for an information decision system? In the next chapter, we will attempt to forecast what future planning will be like.

REFERENCES

Alter, S. L. 1976. How effective managers use information systems. *Harvard Business Review*, **54** (6): 97–104.

Decision support systems are compared to basic data-processing systems. Examples of the various kinds of decisions and their information system support are given.

Computer games that planners play. *Business Week*, December 18, 1978, p. 66.

A brief synopsis of the current use of computer models in the planning function.

de Carbonnel, F. E. and R. G. Dorrance. 1973. Information sources for planning decisions. *California Management Review*, **15** (4): 42–53.

Describes the need for information in strategic decisionmaking. Presents tables of the sources for domestic and foreign economic information as well as industry information. Reprinted herein on pp. 265–282.

Eilon, S. 1969. What is a decision? *Management Science*, **16** (B): 172–189.

An analysis of the decisionmaking process and the impact of data processing on that process. Also includes a discussion of choice, rationality, and measuring utility.

Emory, C. W. 1976. *Business Research Methods*. Homewood, Illinois: Richard D. Irwin, Inc.

A compendium of techniques and tools explaining the scientific method and the planning and execution of a research project.

Hamilton, W. F. and M. A. Moses. 1974. A computer-based corporate planning system. *Management Science,* **21**: 148–159.

Describes a computer-based corporate planning system that combines the analytical power of optimization with simulation capabilities as elements of an interactive management system.

Hayes, R. L. and R. Radosevich. 1974. Designing information systems for strategic decisions. *Long Range Planning*, **7** (4): 45–49.

A discussion of the events that have given rise to a need for a new class of information related to strategic decisionmaking. Some characteristics of "ideal" systems to meet this need are described, and a program of less sophisticated systems is suggested which will develop toward that ideal.

Paine, F. T. and W. Naumes. 1970. *Strategy and policy formation an integrative approach*. Philadelphia: W. B. Saunders Company.

Provides a conceptual framework for information-gathering in the field of policy and for organizing and analyzing such information.

Senn, J. A. 1978. *Information Systems in Management*. Belmont, California: Wadsworth Publishing Co.

A text addressed to the user of information in government or business. The relation between data, information, and computer processing is explained.

Steiner, G. A. 1969. *Top Management Planning*. Toronto: Macmillan.

A formidable guide to the details of top management planning.

Zachman, J. A. 1977. Control and planning of information systems, *Journal of Systems Management,* **28** (7): 34–41.

Describes the steps necessary in planning business systems. The levels of planning and control are explained according to a number of characteristics. These are related to management and the computer. *Reprinted herein on pp. 283–295.*

Information Sources for Planning Decisions

Francois E. de Carbonnel
and
Roy G. Dorrance

Strategic decisions involve responses to changes or anticipated changes in economic and/or competitive conditions. Two types of strategic planning procedures are discussed herein: the first involves formulation of a competitive strategy developed from an internal appraisal of the company's product lines relative to the competitors faced (a recurring process which requires a continuous flow of relevant information); the second type of procedure is non-recurring and involves evaluation of new lines of business or products through an external appraisal of opportunities. This article will outline the informational requirements for strategic planning and indicate how the information can be obtained.

Generally, the firm needs two types of information for the purpose of strategic planning. It must first gather information on the characteristics of each of the industries in which it is involved or on industries into which entry is being considered. It must also be able to determine changes in behavior and plans of the major competitors of each of its product lines or to evaluate the competitive environment for a new line of business. In both cases the firm should develop a formal method for assimilating and updating relevant information. A "data base" for strategic planning should be designed. Figure 1 summarizes the structure of a planning data base and its relationship to the planning procedures.

Gathering information is often an extensive and costly task. Before undertaking it, the planner must know what kind of information he needs with respect to accuracy, specificity and frequency. The characteristics of the particular planning decision determine the informational requirements. For example, information will sometimes be desired for a narrowly defined, one-time analysis such as the study of future growth and competition in an industry in which the firm is considering an entry. Or, information may be required on a continuous basis as input to a system that monitors the competitive and economic environment of each of the firm's product lines. Since much of the information must be developed and therefore requires significant investment of time and effort,

© 1980 by the Regents of the University of California. Reprinted from *California Management Review*, volume XV, number 4, pp. 42 to 53 by permission of the Regents.

Figure 1.

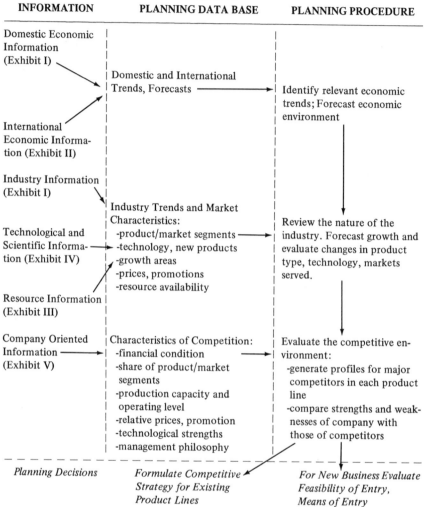

| INFORMATION | PLANNING DATA BASE | PLANNING PROCEDURE |

Domestic Economic Information (Exhibit I)

International Economic Information (Exhibit II)

Domestic and International Trends, Forecasts — Identify relevant economic trends; Forecast economic environment

Industry Information (Exhibit I)

Technological and Scientific Information (Exhibit IV)

Resource Information (Exhibit III)

Industry Trends and Market Characteristics:
  -product/market segments
  -technology, new products
  -growth areas
  -prices, promotions
  -resource availability

Review the nature of the industry. Forecast growth and evaluate changes in product type, technology, markets served.

Company Oriented Information (Exhibit V)

Characteristics of Competition:
  -financial condition
  -share of product/market segments
  -production capacity and operating level
  -relative prices, promotion
  -technological strengths
  -management philosophy

Evaluate the competitive environment:
  -generate profiles for major competitors in each product line
  -compare strengths and weaknesses of company with those of competitors

Planning Decisions

Formulate Competitive Strategy for Existing Product Lines

For New Business Evaluate Feasibility of Entry, Means of Entry

a careful definition of the purpose for which the information is to be used should precede any search effort, be it for a single project or for setting up and maintaining a data base for continuous monitoring purposes.

Sources of information vary in accuracy, accessibility and reliability. Much information is publicly available in the form of government or trade publications, and therefore is easily obtained and monitored. Other types of information are not directly available in a published source but must be developed from these sources or obtained from surveys or other types of research. Surveillance of competition, for example, typically requires some market research or survey activity. The firm may desire market share data which usually must be obtained in this manner. Such data collection techniques are particularly expensive and special care should be taken to explicitly define the end use for the information before gathering is initiated. And, finally, some of the most important information used in planning consists of forecasts to which most of the company's plans are very sensitive. A monitoring system for this data should be implemented to provide feedback on data reliability and forecasting accuracy.

Having defined the role of information in the strategic planning process, sources of information must be discussed, both for economic and industry analyses and for competitor analyses. (Sources of information are displayed in exhibits. There is an exhibit for each type of information discussed; since some sources contain several types of information, they appear in more than one exhibit.)

ECONOMIC AND INDUSTRY INFORMATION

Industry and general economic data provide information for generating yardsticks to which individual companies may be compared and are also useful for appraising trends and dynamic characteristics. Information relevant to an industry analysis includes general economic information, international economic information, resource and commodity information, and technological progress and production information. Many studies will not require such a wide spectrum of information, but we wish to give a general outline of sources.

Exhibit I contains a list of general statistical information available. Other data such as stock and money market quotations, available in financial newspapers such as the *Wall Street Journal,* are useful for monitoring interest rates (the cost of debt) and the cost of equity financing. Newsletters and periodic reports published by large Federal Reserve banks and the Dow Jones Company are also useful for following developments in the financial community. Trends in labor costs for major industries are available in the federal Department of Labor publications. A potentially useful source of industry information is maintained by state Departments of Commerce and the Federal Trade Commission. Although not easily accessible, reports on some industries maintained by these agencies are available to the public.

Trade association publications are particularly useful for industry analyses. They typically contain detailed information on shipments by product type, employment, capital investment, financial structure and foreign trade.

Exhibit II identifies sources of international economic information. More information can be obtained from documents published within each country. Most of the European countries also publish a national *Plan,* which outlines government economic intentions, and have established *Input-Output* tables

Exhibit I. Economic and industry information.

SOURCE	CONTENT	COMMENTS
I. U.S. Department of Commerce		
A. Bureau of Census		
Survey of Manufacturers	Annual statistics of industrial activity. 2-digit SIC classification.	Data 18 to 24 months old.
Census of Manufacturers	Summary of past data on industrial activity: production, employment, value of shipments, materials and energy sources, concentration measures. 4-digit SIC classification.	Published about every four years. Most recent-1967 data.
Statistical Abstract of the U.S.	Annual summary of population, prices, income, housing, foreign trade statistics.	Data 18 months old.
Census Tape: Industry Profiles	Following data for 4-digit SIC industry classification: number of employees, number of production workers, payroll, value added per worker, cost of materials, capital expenditures, inventory, various ratios.	Annual with 2 years lag. Good source of information for monitoring changes in productivity and other production characteristics for industry analyses.
Current Population Reports P-25 Report: Population Estimates and Projections	Population trends by age group, extended forecasts of population growth.	Concise and useful summary of population information.
Bureau of the Census Catalog	Catalog of new Bureau publications.	
Guide to Industrial Statistics	Catalog of industrial statistical programs, contents of reports, locator guide.	Annual publication.
B. Office of Business Economics		
Survey of Current Business	Monthly data on: general economic indicators – prices, income, employment. Industry summary at 4-digit SIC level although not specified as such. Banking, manufacturing, retail trade, raw materials industries. Data on shipments, prices, new orders, order backlog.	Published monthly. 2 month lag in data.

268

Source	Description	Notes
Supplements to *S of CB*: *Business Statistics*	Summary of monthly *Survey of Current Business* issues. Summary of business data.	Published every two years in August for two previous calendar years.
National Income Issue	Summary of monthly *Survey of Current Business* issues with detailed national income account data. Three year summary of industry statistics.	Published annually in July. Data through May of same year.
C. Bureau of Economic Analysis *Business Conditions Digest*	Monthly review of economic activity with statistical analyses of last ten years. National income and product information, cyclical indicators, anticipations and intentions, international comparisons.	One month lag in data. Data recent and well presented.
D. Business and Defense Services Administration *U.S. Industrial Outlook*	Statistics, comments, trends on major industrial activities for the coming year.	Forecast format not consistent – some in units, others in dollars. Data aggregated and not useful for detailed industry studies.
II. Council of Economic Advisors *Economic Indicators*	General economic statistics.	Published monthly.
Annual Report	Summary of economic activity and statement of general economic policy.	
III. Securities and Exchange Commission *Quarterly Financial Reports*	Financial statistics by industry, by asset size and by industry group. Profits, ratios, return on equity. 2 to 3 digit SIC industry classification.	Quarterly, 3 to 6 months lag in data.
Quarterly Report of Plant and Equipment Expenditures of U.S. Corporations		Same as above.
Quarterly Report of Working Capital of U.S. Corporations		Same as above.

269

Exhibit I. (Cont.)

SOURCE	CONTENT	COMMENTS
IV. St. Louis Federal Reserve Bank *Quarterly Report*	Monthly national economic statistics summary. Money supply, prices, employment, production, international trade. Data on U.S. and nine other countries.	A concise summary, convenient to use. Available gratis on request.
V. The Conference Board	23 publications, some statistical but mostly descriptive. Research reports, published irregularly on topics in finance, economic conditions, international business, antitrust.	Reference publications through *Conference Board Annual Index*; industry analyses done occasionally and provide useful background information.
VI. Trade Association Publications such as those of the: National Machine Tool Builders' Association; Glass Containers Mfrs.' Institute Iron and Steel Institute	Usually give history of sales in units and dollars by product type; industry financial and operating data.	Often the richest source of information for studies of competition and trends within the industry.

Exhibit II. International Economic Information.

SOURCE	CONTENT	COMMENTS
I. U.S. Department of Commerce		
A. Bureau of the Census		
Guide to Foreign Trade Statistics	Description of programs, published foreign trade reports, and availability of special services.	Published annually.
B. Bureau of International Commerce		
Overseas Business Reports	Data on foreign economies and economic policy. Economic indicators, data on sales, new businesses. Descriptions of trade regulations, market characteristics.	Published several times per month.
Foreign Economic Trends and their Implications for the U.S.	Reports from U.S. missions abroad on local economic conditions and trends. Summary of implications for U.S.	Several publications each month. Frequency varies with the foreign country reporting.
II. O.E.C.D.		
Economic Outlook and Main Economic Indicators	Statistical studies of O.E.C.D. member countries.	Monthly.
III. United Nations		
Statistical Yearbook	Statistics on world economic situation	Variable degree of accuracy. Not useful for detailed studies.
IV. O.I.T.		
International Labor Office		
Yearbook of Labour Statistics	Past and current data by country on: population, employment, productivity, wages, consumer prices. Some breakdown by industrial sector, roughly equivalent to 2-digit SIC level.	Annual publication. English, French and Spanish versions.

271

Exhibit II. (Cont.)

SOURCE	CONTENT	COMMENTS
V. *Business International*	Newsletter of current events relevant to international business. Some statistics, mostly descriptive. Government policy in foreign countries regularly reviewed with respect to tariffs, taxation, investment.	Quick and easy way to keep abreast of major international business developments. Published monthly.
VI. St. Louis Federal Reserve Bank	(See Exhibit I)	

of their economies. Another fruitful source of information is the local *American Chamber of Commerce* or the local *American Trade Center*. From international economic data the company can identify trends in foreign markets and forecast changes in the international trade conditions. In addition, the firm can monitor the economic environment faced by its major foreign competitors in their home countries.

Availabilities of raw materials and other resources can be a very sensitive factor for some businesses. The ability to forecast shortages and surpluses and price changes is crucial for these companies. Exhibit III indicates some relevant sources for this kind of information.

Information on technological innovations and estimates of future developments is frequently essential to the firm's planning effort. Unfortunately, this information is difficult to find and when available is often inaccurate because of the uncertainty involved. The firm's own research and development staff probably represents the most reliable source of information on technological developments. This information can be augmented by the government and academic and scientific publications shown in Exhibit IV. The subjectivity associated with this kind of information necessitates a careful definition of purpose before the search is begun. Because of the technical nature of the information, the research personnel who generate and collect the data should also interpret it.

The sources described herein provide information on general economic conditions and industry characteristics. A study using this information should produce clearer pictures of product-market structures, potential growth areas, profitability, technological trends, investment requirements, changes in capacity, and labor and capital requirements within the industry under study. Within this general framework, a study of competition in the industry can meaningfully be conducted.

INFORMATION ON COMPETITION

For each of its product lines, or for new products under consideration, the firm should gather as much information as is practically possible on major competitors. Important to planning are information on financial structure and condition, the relative size of major product lines, production capacities and capabilities, technological strengths, and management philosophy. Some of this information is readily available and some of it requires considerable effort. Our purpose is to indicate how most of the information can be obtained and, briefly, how it is used in strategic planning.

Financial Information

Financial data is relatively easy to find if the companies investigated are publicly held. Information on financial performance and structure is published by the

Exhibit III. Commodity and Resource Information.

SOURCE	CONTENT	COMMENTS
I. U.S. Department of the Interior		
Bureau of Mines		
Minerals Yearbook	Annual production data for metals, minerals, and fuels — refined and crude. Both domestic and international reports.	Published annually, 2-year lag in data.
Geological Survey	National and state data on water supply, non-metal mineral resources.	Annual.
II. U.S. Department of Agriculture		
Agricultural Abstract	Annual crop production data and forecasts.	Annual
III. Federal Power Commission		
Statistics of Electric Utilities/ Statistics of Gas Pipeline Companies	Annual financial and operating reports. Capacity and production data.	
IV. Publications of various institutions such as:		
American Petroleum Institute U.S. Atomic Energy Commission Coal Mining Institute of America American Steel Institute	Production capacities, inventories of resources, forecasts.	

Exhibit IV. Technological and Scientific Information.

SOURCE	CONTENT	COMMENTS
I. National Science Foundation *Annual Report*	Describes purpose and composition of year's research expenditures.	Gives general insight into research areas of current interest.
II. Government Data Publications *Research and Development Directory*	Describes nature of government contracts. Organized by company, agency and nature of research done.	Published annually. Compiled from *R&D Contracts Monthly*. Gives latest trends in various kinds of new technologies. Useful information on competitors if they do government research work.

companies themselves in annual reports and is summarized in several publications by information service organizations such as *Moody's* and *Dun and Bradstreet*. Sources of financial information for companies are listed in Exhibit V. Also listed are comments on each source based on the authors' experience during an actual study. Information obtained from informal sources such as personal contacts is often quite interesting but should be used with an awareness of questionable reliability and accuracy.

From financial information gathered for each competitor, the firm can estimate the competitors' sustainable growth capabilities by analyzing dividend payout policies, profitability and capital structure. By comparing this growth potential with industry growth estimates, the firm can assess the strength of each of its competitors. Estimates of labor and capital inputs enable the planners to judge the vulnerability of each competitor to changes in wage rates, interest rates and taxation laws.

Product Line Information

Financial and operating information segmented by product line is difficult or impossible to find. For analysis of a multi-product competitor, this situation can be quite frustrating since information on the relative contributions to sales and profits of each product line is strategically important. Some product line data may be gleaned from annual reports and other documents. Occasionally, annual reports will show contributions to total sales of each division and even less frequently contributions to profit by division. The "10K Report" to the SEC filed since 1971 by each publicly held company includes profit and sales information on product lines and/or divisions accounting for more than 10 percent of total sales and/or total profits. We have found, however, that companies reporting will often attempt to limit the information disclosed by integrating into the same division very different product lines. The motivation to do this is greatest if they wish to minimize information released about a strategically important product line. The planner should use the 10K Report with these considerations in mind.

Product line information is especially important since it can be used to develop a feel for a competitor's willingness to fight to protect his product if competition in the industry stiffens. Presumably, he will fight harder for a product that accounts for a large portion of his sales and profits than for a less important product. Product line sales information for competitors is also important for computing market shares and trends in market shares.

Salesmen and distributors represent a potentially rich source of information and should be used. Through frequent contact with customers, the people often accumulate considerable amounts of information about competitors, their product lines, and marketing strategies. (Sources of product line information are listed in Exhibit V.)

Production Capacities and Capabilities

The firm's planners can gain insight into competitors' plans for sales growth and pricing policies to achieve that growth by monitoring plant expansion developments and capital expenditures. From past production requirements such as sales per employee and square feet of plant per employee, it is possible to estimate the maximum sustainable market share for competitors if it is assumed that manufacturing technology and the production function remain fairly constant. Changes in gross plant and capital expenditures can be found in annual reports. Sometimes annual reports also give details of the purpose of such expansions. Another useful source of this kind of information is newspapers, either local or national. Local newspapers often announce with pride the plans for a new or expanded plant and the projected number of employees. Often corporate officials, when speaking before securities analysts' meetings, will disclose information on capital expansion projects; these speeches are frequently reported in the *Wall Street Transcript*.

Information on productive efficiency can usually be developed from publicly available information and is a useful input to a competitive analysis. By comparing statistics such as sales per employee and sales per dollar of assets, competitors can be ranked by relative production efficiency. Data for the industry as a whole is often published by trade associations and can be used as a reference for judging the competition.

Trade journals are a good source of information on trends in manufacturing technology. For example, the *American Machinist* reports news on plant expansions and new production processes for the metal-working industry. (Sources giving information on production characteristics are listed in Exhibit V.)

Technology and New Product Introduction

Indications of a competitor's technological skills and dynamism can be approximated by the rate of new product introductions in the recent past either in the product category under study or in product lines with related technology. Trade journals often have sections devoted to discussing new products marketed by various firms in the industry. By examining a few of the important journals in the industry for the past several years, a new product introduction profile can be developed on each major competitor and an estimate of technological strength can be obtained. The firm's salesmen and distributors are again a potential source for information in this area.

Management Philosophy

Although information on management philosophy is subjective, it can be useful in forecasting competitor behavior. By studying how competitors have reacted in

Exhibit V. Company-Oriented Information.

SOURCE	CONTENT	COMMENT
I. Annual Reports	Financial and operating data. Some policy considerations.	The reliability of all data is very questionable.
II. Securities and Exchange Commission		
Form 10-K (10-K Report)	Annual report filed by every publicly held company. Gives the lines of business accounting for more than 10 percent of profit, losses or sales: competitive conditions, backlog of orders, sources and availability of raw materials, R&D budgets, employees, principal markets, distribution methods, financial and operating data, properties and plants (suitability, adequacy, productive capacity).	
III. *Fortune's 500* Directory		
Plants and Products	Products manufactured (by 5-digit S.I.C.), plant locations, of largest U.S. industrials. Gives also sales and number of employees.	Publishing stopped since 1966. Very out-of-date, and data quite inaccurate originally.
IV. Dun and Bradstreet		
A. *Million Dollar Directory* *Middle Market Directory*	For corporations, gives 4-digit S.I.C. description of products manufactured, location, number of employees, sales, top management.	Recent, although not always exact. Lists businesses geographically, alphabetically, by product classification. Annual publication and updating.
B. *Metal Working Directory*	(Same as above, but more specifically for metalworking industries)	
V. Noyes Development Corporation		
Chemical Guide to the U.S.	For the 500 largest U.S. chemical firms: number of employees, plant locations, products, subsidiaries.	Not very useful. Same and better information can be found in Dun and Bradstreet more accurately.

Source	Description	Comments
VI. Standard and Poor's *Corporations Records*	News and cumulative news on publicly held companies, alphabetically. Capital structure, acquisitions, background, stock data, income statements and balance sheets.	Updated every 2 months. Detailed information, financially oriented.
VII. *Value Line*	2-page summaries on publicly held companies. Background, activities, past data and financial ratios, forecasts and trends.	Convenient rapid span over a company. Some appreciations of situation, and fair forecasts.
VIII. Moody's A. *Industrial Manual* B. *Public Utility Manual* C. *Transportation Manual* D. *Bank and Finance Manual*	For publicly held companies, similar data to Standard and Poor's *Corporations Records*. Plus Bond ratings, and statistical data on nation's basic industries.	Annual publications. Also News Reports. Consist of compilations from Annual Reports, SEC documents, and corporation's disclosures. *One of the best* sources of information.
IX. *Wall Street Transcript*	Reports of analysts' meetings, executives' speeches, and other miscellaneous informations.	Companies' alphabetical index enables to retrieve data easily.
X. *Barron's*	(Similar to IX above)	Not easy to use for special purpose studies. Look under "Investment News and Views."
XI. Special Subscriptions to services such as *Starch Marketing*	Give market shares and information on competitors.	Costly. For continuous studies mostly.
XII. Trade Associations Publications such as: National Machine Tool Builders Assoc. Glass Container Manufacturers Inst. National Automatic Merchandising Assoc.	Give usually [product] breakdowns (units, sales), industry financial and operating figures, sometimes market shares	Often the richest sources of product [line] information for competition studies, and industry analyses.

the past to changes in environmental conditions, the firm may gain insight into competitor strategies and management style. The backgrounds of executives, management's statement of general policy as sometimes stated in the "letters to the stockholders" in the Annual Report, and statements by executives at securities analysts' meetings, all help define the management philosophy. Different managements have different hierarchies of goals and the planner should attempt to identify these for each competing company. By conducting this type of analysis the firm may be able to forecast how a particular firm will react to an aggressive competitor, for example. (Sources of information which identify executives and give some biographical information as well as sources that often contain statements indicating management philosophy are given in Exhibit V.)

Miscellaneous

A rather unorthodox source of information is records of anti-trust proceedings which are publicly available and which often contain a wealth of information on the companies involved. If possible this source should be checked during the information gathering processes.

AN EXAMPLE

In an actual study, we applied the framework discussed above to evaluate the feasibility of an entry into the machine tool industry. Having no prior knowledge of the industry, we gathered and analyzed information from publicly available sources. We first narrowed the scope of the study to the metal cutting machine tool industry (Standard Industrial Classification, SIC, 3541).

First, we defined the nature of the industry as a whole, obtaining much of this general information from a publication of the National Machine Tool Builders Association called the *Industrial Outlook.* This pamphlet contained recent data on industry unit and dollar sales by machine type, imports and exports, numerical control applications, capacity, productivity and overall financial conditions. We checked and consolidated this information with similar kinds of data found in *Census of Manufacturers* reports and in the *Census Tape* for SIC 3541. An article on the industry published by the Conference Board helped identify principal determinants of industry sales, the most important of which was plant and equipment expenditures. These relationships were used to assess the current state of the industry and the future potential for growth. For more detailed forecasting, we could have used the *Quarterly Report of Plant and Equipment Expenditures of U.S. Corporations* coupled with an Input-Output Table of the U.S. economy.

To determine the technological trends, we reviewed past issues of two major trade journals, the *American Machinist* and *Machinery.* By systematically screening for information on new products and processes, we developed an indication of the rate of technological change and of trends in new product development. Specifically, we noted the penetration of numerically controlled machine tools and the growth in controlled wear machines-grinders, Electrical Discharge Machines (EDM) and Electro Chemical Machines (ECM).

From our study of the industry we made the conclusions:

- industry is cyclical and currently depressed;
- industry is small ($1 billion in 1970);
- industry is characterized by three types of products:
  –turning machines,
  –drilling, boring, milling machines, machining centers, and
  –controlled wear machines;
- numerical control of machine tools is increasingly more important; and
- growth in controlled wear machining techniques.

The second step in our investigation was an analysis of the competitive environment. We identified major manufacturers of the three types of products, gathered information on each company, and constructed competitor profiles. We consulted Annual Reports, *Value-Line* publications and Dun and Bradstreet and Standard and Poor's references to derive market shares by machine type, relative importance of machine tool sales, and a financial summary including profitability and capital structure histories. Information in these documents and in the *American Machinist* "Field Report" section and the *Wall Street Transcript* enabled us to estimate production capacities for each firm and recent capacity expansions. In addition, we estimated the relative technological strengths by examining rates of new product or process introduction for each competitor.

As a result of this analysis we reached the following preliminary conclusions:

- one or two large firms dominate the market for each of the three major machine tool types;
- there exists an industry-wide under-utilization of capacity; and
- there seems to be a direct relationship between market share and profitability.

In evaluating the feasibility of entry, we concluded that the potential entrant would have to seize a large share of the market for a particular type of machine tool as a minimum requirement for reasonable profits. The entrant would face strong competition from existing firms in the industry. The industry is dominated by large, well diversified, technologically capable firms who are currently functioning under capacity. These firms would fight an entrant through price competition to protect sales (market share) and render entry very costly. We therefore advised against entry.

CONCLUSION

Strategic planning can be "irregular," as in searching for new business alternatives, but often requires some continuous process for monitoring current activities in their environment. As essential and basic support to the planning process, environmental information will, therefore, be needed sometimes for a special purpose study and most of the time for a continuous surveillance of the environment in which the firm operates. At times, when the business community is impregnated with the notion of "data bases" and "information systems," we feel the need to point out what the potentials and requirements of a data base for the kind of information described above would be and how automated it could be.

The main characteristics required from information to fit in an automated information system are commonly found to be: presence of interactive variables, need for accuracy of answers and of values, speed of responses to managements' questions, repetitiveness of the tasks performed from the data stored, and volume of information. In "irregular" planning, the simulation of different courses of actions asks for an interactive role of the informations collected and developed. None of the other qualities are usually required from an information system on planning. But for a continuous monitoring of the economic and competitive environment of each of the company's product lines, regular updating of computer stored information files for statistical studies and answers to simple questions could prove very valuable. Such an information system would contain past and updated data on industry and company sales for each product line, matched with past and updated series of the relevant macro-economic indicators, and an input-output matrix of each company's activities would be updated through periodic review of the technical coefficients. This information would facilitate structural analyses of the industry, help the forecasting process, and allow for the simulation of the impact of changes in technology and for economic indications on certain company lines.

Concerning competitors, the firm would monitor and store data such as sales (dollars and units), breadth of the product line, assets, wages, employees, advertising effort, financial structure, and dividend policies. With a few simple assumptions, this information could be used for several different types of analyses designed to answer questions such as: What growth can each competitor sustain? What productive capacity is being added or is available? What are the consequences on the market derived from the introduction of a new product? How would change in debt rates affect each company in the industry?

Such an information system should be central—the converging point for different sources of data collected at very different levels in the organization and in different divisions. This synergy in information gathering would fulfill the needs of both the planning staff and the divisional managers in quest of statistical data.

Control and Planning of Information Systems

John A. Zachman

The first concept for controlling and planning information systems has come to be called the Hierarchy of Management and it is usually depicted as in Figure 1.

Examination of the levels of management reveals that the responsibilities and activities differ substantially from level to level. General management is primarily involved in planning and control, with minimal involvement in the operational aspects of the organization. Planning and control are predominant at the functional management level, but there is an increasing involvement in operational considerations. Operational management is almost totally absorbed in operational considerations with minimal involvement in the areas of planning and control.

Because the responsibilities differ substantially from level to level of management, the problems also differ substantially from level to level. From an information systems standpoint, this implies that the person for whom the system is to be built must be clearly identified at the outset, or there is considerable risk that the "wrong system will be built for the wrong person."

PLANNING AND CONTROL

In "Planning and Control Systems: A Framework for Analysis," Mr. Anthony points out that, contrary to popular opinion, there is not a single level of planning and control functioning in an organization, but three levels of planning and control. He calls them: Strategic Planning, Management Control and Operational Control and they are usually pictorially represented in the form of a triangle as in Figure 2.

Figure 1

Reprinted from *Journal of Systems Management,* July 1977, vol. 28, no. 7. With permission of Association of Systems Management.

Figure 2

In broad terms, Anthony defines the three planning and control levels as follows:

- Strategic Planning—the activity of deciding on objectives, changes to objectives; policies that govern acquisition, use and disposition of resources.
- Management Control—the activity which managers assure resources are obtained and used effectively and efficiently in accomplishment of objectives.
- Operational Control—the activity of assuring that specific tasks are carried out effectively and efficiently.

Some more specific distinctions between Strategic Planning, Management Control and Operational Control are illustrated in Table 1.

In summary, Strategic Planning addresses long-range problems which have a single occurrence, are unstructured, require analysis of data which is specifically gathered for a specific problem. Management Control addresses problems of resource allocation, which are continuing, cyclical in nature, require summary data gathered on a systematic basis, and tend to be somewhat more structured than Strategic Planning problems. Operational control is transaction oriented, addressing problems which continuously recur, are repetitious, are well structured, predefined, and have "input-algorithm-output" characteristics.

The major conclusion that Anthony reached is that if it is not recognized that there are three different kinds of planning and control functioning in the organization, there is risk of:

- a. Stating generalizations as if they were applicable to all levels of planning and control when they were in fact only applicable to a single level.
- b. Stating a generalization that was intended to apply to one level when in fact it applies to a different level.
- c. Emphasizing one level over the other levels.

Table I. Comparison of the three levels of planning and control.

CHARACTERISTIC	STRATEGIC PLANNING	MANAGEMENT CONTROL	OPERATIONAL CONTROL
Focus of Plans	One aspect at a time.	Whole organization	Single task or transaction.
Judgment	Highly judgmental	Relatively much – subjective decisions.	Relatively little– reliance on rules.
Degree of Structure	Unstructured and irregular – each problem different.	Rhythmic – pre-scribed procedures	Repetitious.
Nature of Information	Tailormade for problem – more external and predictive, less accurate.	Integrated – more internal and historical – more accurate.	Tailormade to operation – precise – often in real time.
Mental Activity	Creative, analytical.	Administrative, persuasive.	Follow directions – (or none).
Source Discipline	Economics	Social Psychology.	Economics, Physical Sciences.
Planning & Control	Planning dominant but some control.	Emphasis on both Planning and Control.	Emphasis on Control.
Time Horizon	Tends to be long.	Weeks, months, years.	Day to day.

Considering the fact that the intent of planning and control is to protect profitability, the risks outlined in the above three alternatives could materialize in substantial impact on profit, particularly under resource short conditions.

In essence, planning and control is required to preclude the suboptimization (or dissipation) of resources when the responsibility for the management of those resources is delegated to a lower level in the organization. A plan is required to force resource decisions to be made consistent with the overall objectives of the organization as opposed to making those decisions to the benefit of a single segment of the organization. Then, measurement is required to evaluate the effectiveness of the plan and the effectiveness of the performance of the organization. Control action is taken either to change the plan or the performance as required. Since Anthony wrote his book, "control" has been broken down into measurement and control. It is useful to consider them separately for theoretical purposes.

Although planning, measurement and control appear to be three separate mental activities they are so closely intertwined that they do not exist independently. That is, if the capability to plan *and* to measure *and* to control are not all present, the entire system is ineffective. That is, once again, "you can plan all day long if you want, but if you can't measure performance as it relates to plan (or if you can't effect control action), you might as well not have a plan.

In summary, resources must be managed in order to protect profitability and the management of resources is effected through planning, measurement and control. In order to be effective, all three components of planning, measuring and controlling must be present and they must be present at all three levels of Planning and Control, that is, at the Strategic Planning, Management Control and Operational Control levels.

Since the characteristics of Planning and Control differ drastically from level to level, the information system approach to support any one level would differ drastically from the other levels. Another conclusion is that a weak point in the planning, measurement and control system is extremely detrimental to the system. Characteristically, the weak point in planning, measurement and control systems is the measurement component for two reasons. First, human beings tend to avoid defining measurements (because if you define measurements, you are likely to be measured). Second, in order to measure anything, consistent data is required, for example, miles *or* kilometers, but not both. Consistent data for management purposes is usually difficult to obtain.

MANAGEMENT LEVELS

In combining the ideas of the Hierarchy of Management and Planning and Control, it is evident that the different levels of management have different responsibilities relating to the levels of planning and control as shown in Figure 3.

General management, whether it is a single individual wearing two hats or a complex structure involving a number of people, is responsible for the Strategic Planning aspect of the organization. Additionally, general management allocates the resources across the overall business unit. Functional management, in turn, allocates the resources assigned to them across the function for which they are responsible. Additionally, functional management gets involved with the Operational Control aspect of their function. Operational management is almost entirely absorbed in the operational aspect of the organization.

Because the characteristics of the three levels of planning and control differ substantially, and the information system approach required to deal with each level also differs substantially, not only must the person for whom the problem is to be addressed be identified, but the kind of planning and control to be addressed must also be identified. Once again, failure to decide at the outset whose problem and what kind of problem results in risk of solving the "wrong problem for the wrong person."

COMPUTERS TO SOLVE BUSINESS PROBLEMS

Given the conceptual representation of an organization as depicted in Figure 3, it is apparent that business computers and their predecessors were employed

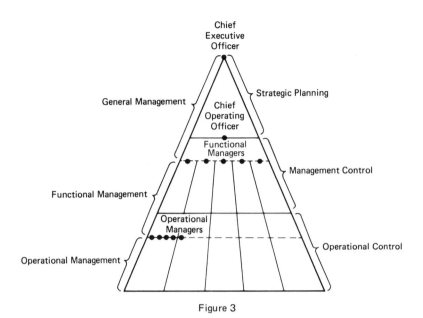

Figure 3

historically to solve problems at the Operational Control level of the organization. They focused upon the day to day, transaction oriented functions which were structured, definable, had specific input and output, were repetitious, and very precise in nature. Computers were capable of doing these functions better than people because they were faster, more accurate, and more flexible than people. Therefore, people displacement (or automation) was the primary justification for computer applications addressing Operational Control aspects of an organization.

Two factors have changed this early view of how computers could be utilized to best advantage. First, technology has increased rapidly and unceasingly since computers were conceived, and the substantially increased capabilities expanded the horizons of the problem solver in astronomical proportions. Specifically, he was enabled to address problems at the Management Control level of the organization and no longer was limited to addressing Operational Control problems. He could begin to focus on the resource allocation problems which had considerably greater impact on profitability than merely automating the transaction processing procedures.

At the same time, higher levels of management became acutely aware of the computers in their business because of the escalating costs of data processing coupled with the computer's notable failure to address management problems (a la "the myth of MIS"). The logical question to ask was, "Since I am spending so much money on these computers, why aren't they solving my problems?" The answer is: "Because management has a *different kind of problem*." If the computer systems have been designed to process transactions at the Operational Control level, they may be doing so very effectively; but in doing so, they may be complicating the Management Control problem.

What has happened is that operational management has been selected as the focal point for building computer systems. The systems have been designed from a very narrow perspective because the Operational Control manager is held responsible for processing his transactions, and has little concern for anything except those transactions. Therefore, the computer systems all grew up independent of each other with a focus on getting the transactions processed. The data utilized in the systems was defined as it related to the specific transaction being processed and was inconsistent with the data defined in all the other transactions being processed. Since the transaction data is inconsistent, it is of little value for measurement purposes in support of the planning and control system, which ultimately impacts profitability.

It is important to note that there are three dimensions to data inconsistency including definition, time and format. A simple example of each is:

Definition: Expense data is required in order to process transaction No. 1 and expense must be defined to include direct *and* indirect expense. Therefore, for computer system A, "expense" means direct and indirect expense. Expense data is also required in order to process transaction No. 2, but in this case, it must be defined only as *direct* expense. Therefore, for computer system B, "expense" means direct expense only.

Both computer system A and computer system B operate well and process transactions satisfactorily for operational management. No problem arises until someone at the Management Control level asks, "What are our expenses," in which case data from computer systems A and B is submitted, but is useless for measurement purposes because of the inconsistent definition of "expense," and therefore, expenses cannot be determined unless the data is developed by other means.

Time: Similar to the example of definition, if data is defined as monthly data, it cannot be added to daily data for any meaningful measurement.

More insidious from a time standpoint is the circumstance in which Organization Unit No. 1 collects data and processes it on a daily basis. At the end of the day it sends the data to Unit No. 2 where it is processed weekly. At the end of the week, Unit 2 sends the data to Unit 3 where it is processed monthly. Unit 3 then sends the data to Unit 4 at the end of the month for quarterly processing, etc. The problem is that the same data is being used in multiple organizations, but it is of a different age in each and can't be reconciled. Incidentally, each of the organization units tend to insist that their data is the correct version and it is very difficult to obtain any agreement on the "numbers."

Format: This means that one part number is 6 digits, alphabetic and the same part number for a different system is 10 digits, numeric which just superimposes another level of complexity on an already complicated problem.

The question becomes, "how do you solve the data inconsistency problems if you want to address Management Control issues at the functional management level of the organization." The answer is: "You must 'integrate' the data." (That's a friendly way to say you have to redesign the systems.) Designing systems around the transaction results in inconsistent data, therefore, a new design vehicle is required. Since implicitly or explicitly, the functional manager is now chosen as the focal point for solving a problem, it is logical to choose his organization unit as a design vehicle for information systems. In effect, the system designer gathers together all the transactions being processed within one functional area, designs the system to process those transactions, defines and accumulates the data in a consistent fashion, thereby resolving Management Control, data oriented problems as well as operational control, transaction oriented problems. This has become the era of the functional information system; e.g., the Marketing Information System, the Manufacturing Information System, the Material Requirements Information System, etc.

GENERAL MANAGEMENT STAGE

Computer technology, through increased capabilities, offers the opportunity to address even larger problem areas within the organization. This increased capability coupled with external economic problems, specifically resource short conditions, focuses attention at the general management level of the business. The continuing viability of the business unit may be dependent upon general management's ability to make most effective use of the resources across the overall business unit. This is the macro-productivity issue of the organization. This specifies effective planning, measurement and control at the general management level, which includes Management Control (resource allocation) and Strategic Planning (objective setting).

There is a requirement for consistent data in support of the planning, measurement and control systems; however, now it exists at the general management level of the organization. If this requirement was not foreseen while building functional information systems, once again there are inconsistencies in the data, including definition, time and format from functional information system to functional information system. Also, once again, the inconsistencies are resolved through data integration, that is, through system redesign. However, the decision to integrate the systems is more difficult to make, the higher the level at which integration takes place because of the magnitude of the investment in the currently installed systems.

However, the incentive to even consider addressing systems at the general management level is substantial, particularly if the business has grown to the point that one man cannot effectively manage the resources of the business singlehandedly. In this case, continued profitability most likely can only be maintained by formalizing the planning and control system and beginning to resolve the inconsistencies in the measurement data in support of that system.

A lesson learned during the stage of addressing functional management problems with information systems was that using organization units as design vehicles did not result in resolving data inconsistency at the general management level. A better design vehicle was required.

RESOURCES AS DESIGN VEHICLES

In "Industrial Dynamics," Forrester points out that by understanding the information flow throughout the life cycle of the resource, the resource can be effectively managed. Since managing the resources (profitability) is the objective at the general management level and since information flow is the factor required to determine the consistency requirements for the data, it follows that resources are good vehicles to use for information systems design. Information flow is merely the determination of how the information about the resource is used (that is, shared) by the various units of the organization throughout the four stages in the resource life cycle (Requirements Stage, Acquisition Stage, Stewardship Stage and Retirement Stage).

There is one special kind of resource that makes the most sense to use as an information systems design vehicle and that is the product or service produced by the organization. It is argued that this is a not "real" resource, but a "pseudo" resource. However, since the product or service has a life cycle identical to that of a "real" resource, for analytical purposes it looks like a resource. It is a particularly useful design vehicle because it is the one factor that integrates all the functions and levels of the organization, around which most of the information flows and in addition, it drives the requirement for all the other resources. (From a very practical standpoint, when doing information flow analysis, not only the product or service must be analyzed, but all the other critical resources must also be analyzed.)

DATA IS A RESOURCE

Data has value to the organization and must be managed as if it were valuable. It draws its value from its relationship to profitability through resource management and therefore, planning and control. Data is, in fact, a resource itself and like any other resource, must be managed if its value is to be preserved.

Resources are managed through breaking them out of the organization and establishing a management system (including planning, measurement and control) to preclude their dissipation, either intentional or unintentional. For example: cash is obviously valuable to the organization. Therefore, it is broken out of the organization (that is, the people in the organization don't carry the cash around in their pockets), specific responsibility is assigned to a Controller to manage the cash, and its use is controlled through a chart of accounts. All resources of value are treated in a similar manner.

Data, if it has value, must also be broken out of the organization, specific responsibility assigned for its management, and its use controlled through information systems. That is, if the value of the data is to be preserved, specific responsibilities and a management system must be established to plan, measure and control the data. This is usually referred to as the Information Systems Management System and its primary components are:

Plan Management—which includes the establishment of the objectives and the overall architecture within which short term data processing resources can be invested; the determination of the development priorities; and the measurement of performance against the plan.

Data Management—which includes the establishment of policies and standards regarding accessibility, security, definition, usage, etc.; ensures compliance; and physically manages the data.

The degree of formality of the Information Systems Management System as well as the degree of formality of the Management Planning and Control system both seem to be related to the size of the organization. As the organization grows in size, the management of resources is more broadly delegated which creates a Management Control problem requiring planning, measurement and control, along with the demand for consistency of data.

Before a long range information system plan can be prepared, some analysis must be performed in order to establish a framework within which information systems development can proceed and analytically, the following questions must be answered:

1. What data is driving the business?
2. How can that data best be managed in support of the business?
3. What are the priorities, or relative values of the various kinds of data, in order to determine where to invest the short term data processing resources? (Most likely it is not economically feasible or even desirable to attempt to manage all of the data.)

DEVELOPING INFORMATION SYSTEMS

There are a number of approaches that can be employed in developing information systems and they can be classified in two major categories, the evolutionary (or bottom-up) approach and the top down approach. A brief description of each follows:

The Bottom-Up Approach states that the way to develop an overall plan is to start with the operations modules for processing transactions and updating files and then to add planning, control, decision, and other modules as the demand develops.

The advantages of this approach are that it proceeds step by step, little by little in accordance with demand, building on transaction processing (which must be done anyway) and minimizing the risk of building a large-scale system which does not operate properly.

The disadvantages are that it is an extremely expensive approach in that every time an integration takes place, it is essentially a redesign of what has preceded. And, integration is required at practically every step as soon as the boundary between the Operational Control level and the Management Control level of the business is traversed. Additionally, the evolutionary process is easily halted if management in a particular area does not demand or refuses to be integrated.

This is the approach that was described in a preceding section (Evolution of Computers in Solving Business Problems) and it is easy to see why it was very useful in the early stages of computer application while the focus was at the Operational Control level of the business. However, it is also easy to see why it becomes dysfunctional as soon as the Management Control level of the business is addressed.

The Top-Down Approach seeks to develop a model of information flow in the organization and to design the information system to suit this information flow. Integration is planned as much as possible.

The advantage to the Top-Down Approach is that it is a very logical way to design anything. Essentially, this is the approach used to design airplanes, computers, buildings or whatever. It makes sense.

The disadvantages are that it is difficult to derive large scale information system plans from the objectives and activities of the organization, that it is difficult to assign cost and value to the modules, that the order of module development yielded is not necessarily related to organizational support or most potential use, and that there is the risk of building an enormous system that doesn't work properly.

It is clear that a hybrid approach is in order, employing the best attributes of each of the classical approaches where appropriate. The following is a description of such a hybrid approach.

Step 1. Using top-down analysis, establish a description of the business unit noting particularly the relationships between the business processes (activities), the data and the organizational entities.

Step 2. Develop an architecture, or network of information systems and modules that are required to manage the data, control its consistency and support the information flow through the business processes; that is, relate the network systems to the data, the processes and to themselves.

Step 3. Through direct management input, define, analyze, prioritize and relate the business problems to the network of systems in order to prepare a value analysis and the order of module development.

Step 4. Analyze the current status of the data and the data processing systems and relate them to the network of systems in order to determine the migration strategy from the present environment to this designed architecture.

Step 5. Given the analytical framework derived in Steps 1 through 4, prepare a long-range information systems plan which outlines the business environment, assumptions, information systems objectives, strategies, resources, short-range plans, etc., characteristically found in long-range plans.

Step 6. Execute the plan from the bottom up, that is, build the information systems modules, one by one, having preidentified their realtionships and data sharing characteristics.

Step 7. Put in place an information systems management system which will manage the plan both for performance and to ensure its continuing validity in relation to the business unit. Additionally, the system must provide for the management of the data from a policy and consistency standpoint as well as from a physical standpoint.

This hybrid approach in essence is the Business Systems Planning approach referred to earlier in this article. Experience has shown that it is useful to employ the approach in phases in order to enable graduated commitments of resources. Phase I should be very short with minimal resources but strong management perspective and credibility in order to obtain an early and inexpensive assessment of the value and direction for future phases. Phase II becomes a refinement of Phase I to a level of detail that allows preparation of the architecture and the long-range plan. Succeeding phases relate to implementations and can be overlapped with each other as well as with Phase II. The management system established controls the phases through the management of the planning process and protects the integrity and consistency of the data.

GENERAL MANAGER'S INFORMATION SYSTEM

The concepts presented in this article have been directed toward developing information systems that impact the general management level of the organization. The key to developing systems of this nature lies in addressing the issue of consistency of data, not merely processing the organization's transactions. This dictates the definition of the sharing of data both horizontally and vertically in the organization and implies central control of the data, although it allows for decentralized processing of the data if that is desirable. The resultant information systems environment is decidedly different than that which is currently prevalent. Table 2 summarizes some of the characteristics which differentiate the two environments.

Table 2. New information systems environment vs. old.

		NEW	OLD
a.	Level of management addressed	General Management	Operational Management
b.	Nature of responsibility	Plan, Measure, Control	Process Transactions
c.	Problem to be addressed	Management Control	Operational Control
d.	Value determinant of the systems	Business Process Performance Data	Transactions Processed
e.	Design approach	Top-Down	Bottom-Up
f.	Systems design vehicle	Resources, Business Processes	Organizational Functions
g.	Basis for modularization (Information System planning units)	Data Classes	Applications (Transactions)
h.	Objectives of information systems organization	Manage Data	Process Data

SUMMARY

World economic conditions in which resources are at a premium, coupled with a rapidly changing business environment create substantial incentives to focus on the issues at the general management level of the organization. Advancing computer technology facilitates this focus by enabling an organization to get control of its data.

Data derives its value from its requirement to support the management planning and control system which, in turn, is established to protect profitability thru precluding the suboptimization of resources. However, the value of the data is dissipated if it is not managed for consistency and integrity. Therefore, to protect profitability, some steps must be taken to define the data that is particularly valuable to the organization and begin to manage it.

Management of the data requires a "top-down" approach to information systems planning and architectural design with emphasis on planning and pre-integration of the data. It is improbable that the more traditional "bottom-up" approaches can be successful in this environment because of the exorbitant costs of data integration (systems redesign) which are inherent in these approaches. However, it is imperative to implement on an incremental basis from the "bottom-up" within the architecture as defined and planned from the top down.

Historically, it has been possible to hire programmers or analysts to define "automation" problems because systems were designed to operate in a structured (Operational Control) environment. In addressing the Management Control and Strategic Planning aspects of the organization, the structure deteriorates.

Therefore, if these aspects of the business are to be addressed, it demands the direct participation of management in the definition of the problems to be solved and the determination of the priorities.

It is evident that some structured approach is required to enter into this new environment. Depending upon chance or evolution is likely to cost dearly in terms of both money and time. An example of such a structured approach is Business Systems Planning. It is possible to use it in such a way that it will lead to the "data managed environment" as described in this article.

In relation to the current, traditional application of computers in business, these concepts represent a substantial departure into a decidedly different environment. Therefore, this decade is likely to be looked at in retrospect as a transitional era in which the focus of computers changed from data processing to the management of data. It is becoming very clear that computers can be a major management control tool having a significant impact on profitability in contrast to seeing them utilized merely as automation devices.

REFERENCES

"Planning and Control Systems, A Framework for Analysis," Robert N. Anthony, Harvard Press, 1965.

"Industrial Dynamics," Jay W. Forrester, MIT Press, 1961.

9
The Future

THE CHANGING NATURE OF
THE CORPORATION

The nature of the corporation is changing. Bagley (1975) warns of the effect of "supercorporations" on the worldwide economic scene. He defines these super-corporations as having four major characteristics:

1. at least $1 billion in size
2. an average annual growth rate of 10 percent
3. extensive diversification into at least three disparate industries
4. a rare degree of resourcefulness, flexibility, aggressiveness, and creativity

These corporations will probably be multinational as well.

Looking at the case history, there does not seem to be supercorporation status in Alexander & Alexander's future. Given a substantial annual growth rate and a chance to reach $1 billion in revenue, A&A contains its acquisition program to areas related to insurance. However, A&A does possess the fourth ingredient—aggressive management—so its future may see a shift in its acquisition policy if insurance opportunities continue their trend toward smaller size and marginal profitability.

To achieve the status of supercorporation, Bagley (1975) contends that different and better corporate planning techniques will have to be developed, and he sees these developments in the planning process as benefiting all organizations as they become better known and refined. Among the areas in which planning developments will occur are:

1. The systems approach to defining and solving intricate problems.
2. Computerized information systems and data processing. These will support the systems approach and other information needs and spawn a new breed of computer-dependent managers.
3. Marketing and the emergence of the entrepreneurship function.
4. Investment and commercial banking relationships with a potential shift in some functions to in-house.

5. New roles and compositions for boards of directors.
6. The quality of government employees as the supercorporations become more effective and therefore attract highly qualified civil servants to their employ.

What Bagley suggests for the supercorporation has implications for all enterprises. Bagley states that the supercorporations will develop techniques that will be made available to the managers of smaller corporations. In addition, the very presence of the supercorporations requires a renewed planning effort by every other firm in order to survive in the market. So, as the supercorporations change, all others will change as well, and planning will become even more important.

CORPORATE vs. BUSINESS STRATEGIES

In today's corporations, more and more distinction is being made between corporate strategies and business strategies. Corporate strategy covers all of the diverse aspects of a company, unifying them toward some overall goal. On the other hand, a business strategy is a plan for a single product or group of related products. According to *Business Week* (December 18, 1978), most of the activity today is at the business-strategy level. Sophisticated tools and techniques currently analyze the business and forecast market growth, pricing, and the impact of government regulation. Such plans meet threats from competitors, economic cycles, and social, political, and consumer changes. A business-strategy approach is reflected in Alexander & Alexander's strategy of concentric diversification of establishing new geographic markets (through acquisition) and of making an all-out effort to achieve a 15-percent return through effective marketing to new and old customers. (See pp. 364–367.)

The emphasis on business strategy indicates that corporate strategies are not well-developed. The *Business Week* article speculates that the reason for this lack of sophistication at the corporate level is based partly on a lack of clear, long-range goals set by the chief executive officer. Other chief executives fail to exercise their required entrepreneurship and merely play a caretaker role, settling for short-term profit growth or some other intermediate objective. They expect their line managers to act as entrepreneurs—to take risks, to be innovative, to be accountable—rather than accepting this responsibility for themselves. This supports Bagley's view that entrepreneurship is required for the new supercorporations.

But even when a chief executive has clearly defined goals that are imbedded in a rational strategic plan, certain organizational steps are required to insure the effective implementation of that plan. The article suggests these steps:

1. Shaping the company into logical business units that can identify markets, customers, competitors, and the external threats to its business. These units

are managed semiautonomously by executives who operate under corporate financial guidelines and with an understanding of the unit's assigned role in the organization.

2. Demonstrating a willingness at the corporate level to compensate line managers for long-term achievements, not just for financial results in the current fiscal year; to fund research programs that could give the unit a long-term competitive edge; and to offer the unit the type of planning support that provides data on key issues and encourages and teaches sophisticated planning techniques.

3. Developing at the corporate level the capacity to evaluate and balance competing requests from business units for corporate funds, based on the degree of risk and reward.

4. Matching shorter-term business-unit goals to a long-term concept of the company's evolution over the next 15 to 20 years. This is exclusively the chief executive's function—and his or her effectiveness in this capacity may be tested by the board of directors.

INCREASING ENVIRONMENTAL UNCERTAINTY

From another perspective, Welsch and Lee (1979), in the article beginning on p. 303, emphasize that due to increasing uncertainty in the external environment, planners can no longer consider a one-dimensional future. They must develop contingency plans to provide for a number of outcomes based on changing domestic and international economic conditions, technological change, social and demographic change, the political and regulatory environment, and ecological and environmental considerations.

Welsch and Lee suggest that these factors can be analyzed more easily if the planner understands future trends in the allocation of human and natural resources. They believe that the 1980s will see a shift:

- from manufactured goods to professional and personal services
- from growing monetary income to a desire to achieve a more gratifying quality of life
- from centralized management and control to local or regional influence over the decisions affecting our lives
- from the development of capital and physical capabilities to the improvement of human resources
- from the transformation of resources for production and economic growth to the conservation of these resources for future generations
- from the free-market economic-decision process to increasing accountability for the social and environmental impact of corporate decisions

Such massive uncertainty increases the desire for more certainty. However, even though more data than ever are available to management and even though computers are available to assist with the task, the problem of organizing and evaluating such vast amounts of data is formidable. And corporate planning models do not yet provide the answer either, at least not the whole answer.

The conclusions of Naylor (1976) are still true today. Naylor agrees that economic uncertainty is encouraging managers to turn more often to corporate planning models. He also attributes this trend to energy and raw material shortages, the leveling-off of productivity, international competition, tight money, inflation, political upheavals, environmental problems, and new business opportunities. However, he admits that although there have been marked increases in the use and usefulness of corporate models, the challenges now facing management require some dramatic improvements in this tool.

These improvements include making the model more user-oriented. Top management must be able to understand the model it is using. Production models must be linked to overall corporate models. Optimization techniques should be linked to corporate models to take advantage of mathematical programming routines. Finance, production, and marketing should be linked in a single model. Models of the external environment are required that reflect global economic, political, social, and environmental problems. And finally, the model must be integrated into the planning process. As these improvements are made, corporate planning models will become much more useful in reducing management uncertainty.

Alexander & Alexander is faced with a great deal of uncertainty too. For example, A&A faces such problems as the banking industry and its entrance into the insurance market, the threat of repeal of the insurance industry's antitrust exemption, and constantly changing state laws. Then too, uncertainty is one of the reasons why people buy insurance. Success in the insurance industry is directly related to evaluating risk and charging the insured proportionately. In this regard, the nature of the risk reflects various levels of uncertainty. For example, crop harvests (and weather) are much less certain than human life-span predictions. (For A&A's own forecasts, see p. 367.)

WHAT IS THE FUTURE?

So far, we have set a number of requirements for things that must take place for the benefit of the corporation, and we have speculated as to what the situation might be in certain areas. But how accurate can we be? How accurate were we in the past? Kahn and Wiener (1967) provide some insight in the article that starts on p. 318. They view change as taking place in 33-year intervals. Thus, they divided this century into three segments, recorded what took place in the first two, and predicted what would take place in the third. Since we are almost halfway through the third segment, it is interesting to observe what has and has not come to pass. In addition, we can speculate on what might still become reality and review any new factors that have entered the picture that were not part of the original prediction. Evaluating the Kahn and Wiener article should leave the reader feeling that the future is elusive indeed.

Some of the trends that Kahn and Wiener suggest are:

- Emergence of postindustrial society
- Worldwide capability for modern technology
- Need for worldwide zoning ordinances and other restraints
- High growth rates (1 to 10 percent) in gross national product per capita
- Increasing emphasis on "meaning and purpose"
- Much turmoil in the "new" and possibly in the industrializing nations
- Some possibility for sustained "nativist," messianic, or other mass movements
- Second rise of Japan
- Some further rise of Europe and China
- Emergence of new intermediate powers: Brazil, Mexico, Pakistan, Indonesia, East Germany, Egypt
- Some decline (relative) of the United States and Soviet Union
- A possible absence of stark "life and death" political and economic issues in the "old" nations

In addition, they list 100 technical innovations likely in the next 33 years. But even these trends and technical innovations are vague and open to interpretation. In short, they are flimsy guides for a corporate strategic plan.

THE PLANNER AND MANAGEMENT

Welsch and Lee (1979) remind us that both management and the planner have a place in the planning process. The planning specialist cannot do the planning and then turn it over to management anymore than management can do the planning without the specialist. What has to take place is an integrated team approach of line management and the specialists.

According to Taylor (1976), the job of the planner is not merely to design, install, and maintain a formal planning system, but to help the decisionmakers identify the key decisions to be made. The planner must realize that the solution generated must not only be rational; it must encompass an approach that is culturally acceptable and politically feasible.

For management, this implies the necessity for entrepreneurship. This term no longer applies only to those who found their own businesses; it also applies to those who run a business, recognize opportunity, have a sense of timing, and are willing to take charge and bear responsibility. Entrepreneurs are self-confident hard workers and innovators.

According to *Business Week* (December 18, 1978), ". . . at most companies, CEOs are content with the concept of the corporation as a holding company and they simply judge and assign resources to profit-making ventures." The article goes on, however, to argue for a corporate strategy that "exceeds the sum of its parts"—that is, a strategy that generates some synergy from the combined strategies of the various divisions of the corporation. And it is believed that some kind of audit should take place to evaluate the long-range planning of the chief executive.

That such a suggestion would be resisted by most chief executive officers goes without saying. CEOs are generally in their early fifties and want a few years of relative peace with the board of directors before retiring. Thus, their strategy often boils down to slow growth and no upheavals. The same article also speculates that today's CEOs come from a tradition where managers were forced to play a cautious game and so they are simply continuing that strategy. Today's line managers, however, are trained to be creative, flexible, and responsible. Thus, as they become the CEOs of the future, they may indeed meet the requirements of entrepreneurship.

CONCLUSION

Taylor (1976) takes a realistic view of where planning is and where it is going. He sums up what we have been saying in this chapter.

> As many practitioners and writers have pointed out, there is a gap between our theory which sees planning as a deliberate, rational, sequential process and our practice, where we find that many of the processes are *ad hoc*, informal, non-rational, and concerned with values or power.
>
> Every planner has to live with this incompatibility between his theory and his practice and it sometimes results in a kind of schizophrenia—a form of "Planner's Neurosis."
>
> We have an elegant theory of planning which argues very persuasively that planning should be:
>
> (1) comprehensive,
> (2) rational,
> (3) sequential, and
> (4) formalized.
>
> In practice, the planner finds that the process is not comprehensive but *partial*. Total integrated planning systems like total integrated information systems exist only in textbooks and in the dreams of management scientists. He finds that his planning process, to be kind, exhibits only "limited rationality." His ambitions for producing a sensible allocation of resources based on a

global strategy are frequently defeated through the machinations and the deviousness of operating managers who do not accept the logic that labels their division a "Cash Cow" to be "milked" for the benefit of other people's calves.

Often they find their financial and economic calculations, and their logical arguments are inexplicably discounted or altered because of some senior person's "intuition."

We do, of course, have a planning procedure—but that is not to say that this is where the decisions are made. The chief executive often seems quite happy that everyone else should use the system but one has the feeling that he is not always frank about his own strategies and future intentions. There are many planners who have first learned about company acquisitions and other important moves in the financial press. Added to all this is the problem known in the literature as "implementation." Planning theory is eloquent about formulating long-range plans but somewhat less forthcoming on the subject of how plans should be carried out. In practice it is sometimes difficult to know whether plans are being "formulated" or "implemented." Even when you think you have a plan agreed, it turns out simply to be a basis for further negotiation. It may be overturned by resistance from sections of management and groups of employees, the opposition of Trades Unions, protests from the community, legislation, moves by competitors or Acts of God. As one executive remarked, it seems that "No plan survives contact with reality."

With a plan, however, the confrontation with reality can be met with confidence—a confidence based on knowledge and forethought so that the proper changes can be made to accommodate a changing situation. Without a plan to guide managers in the directon of, or at least, the modification of environmental forces, the organization becomes a passive participant yielding to an uncontrolled situation and to so-called reality.

REFERENCES

Bagley, E. R. 1975. *Beyond the Conglomerates*. New York: American Management Association.

An analysis of what the author terms the *supercorporation*. What is it? What is its impact on the future of life and of business. Is it to be feared or welcomed?

Kahn, H. and A. J. Wiener. 1967. The next 33 years: A framework for speculation. *Daedalus* 96: 705–32.

An analysis of trends in change and innovation. The authors divide this century into three 33-year cycles and extrapolate from the first 67 years what the next 33 will be like. *Reprinted herein on pp. 318–341.*

Naylor, T. H. 1976. The future of corporate planning models. *Managerial Planning* 24 (5): 1–9, 13.

An analysis of the nature and acceptance of corporate planning models. The author is quite candid about the shortcomings of the models in use today and makes some significant recommendations for improvement.

The new planning. *Business Week* (December 18, 1978): 62–68.

A review of the current state-of-the-planning-art with particular emphasis on the role of top and middle management.

Taylor, Bernard. 1976. New dimensions in corporate planning. *Long-Range Planning* 9 (6): 80–106.

Five new dimensions of planning are discussed by the author: (1) central control system, (2) framework for innovaton, (3) social learning process, (4) political process, and (5) conflict of values.

Welsch, D. R. and R. W. Lee. 1979. Adapting systems to cope with multiple futures. *Management Focus* 26 (1): 6–17.

Proposes a new "wisdom" for today's corporate planners that requires a detailed knowledge of the external world. The systems should emphasize both variety and nimbleness, which are needed to mesh with a fast-changing and largely unknowable future. *Reprinted herein on pp. 303–317.*

Adapting Systems to Cope with Multiple Futures

Donald R. Welsch
and
Robert W. Lee

The corporate long-range planning approaches that were developed during the relative stability of the 1950s and 1960s are fast becoming inadequate to cope with today's turbulent climate. Planning was, for the most part, based on future assumptions that could be trusted to endure for five years or more. But the rapid-fire "major dislocations of the early 1970s made planning an anxiety-provoking exercise," says *Planning Under Uncertainty*, a report published last year by The Conference Board, a New York based research organization.

From *Management Focus,* Jan./Feb. 1979 issue, copyright © Peat Marwick, Mitchell & Co.

Exhibit I. Planning Systems

Exhibit I		
		Planning
Factors affecting systems	**Annual budget systems**	
	Marketing	**Production**
Domestic economic	• 1979 slowdowns likely • Consumer indebtedness at an alltime high • Pre-inflation buying patterns for consumer durables	• Availability and price of raw material continue to fluctuate with growing reliance on foreign resources
International economic	• Growing dollar incomes of foreigners due to strong foreign economies and weak U.S. dollar encourage foreign investment in United States	• More efficient plants abroad encourage foreign competition • Lower wage scales from LDC producers increase price competition • Restrictions on availability of materials purchased abroad
Technological	• Computer systems reducing normal inventory cushions in regional warehouses	• Use of energy saving equipment vs increasing labor productivity • Expanding the work force vs more overtime work
Social and demographic	• Greater diversity of taste and demand within similar demographic market segments requires better marketing policy • Two breadwinner family changes demand for traditional products • Growing senior citizen population creates new marketing opportunities • Awareness of new balance between work/education/leisure alters consumption patterns	• More women in work force • Demand for more flexible work schedule • Labor union attitudes toward productivity and technology • Alternative life styles for white collar workers mixing work and education
Political and regulatory		• FTC and FDA require more restrictive product safety standards • More rigid safety standards in the work place (OSHA)
Professional		
Ecological and environmental	• Product design/marketing affected by ecological perceptions of the dangers of technology	• Urban vs suburban plant location decision • Introduction of new production methods requires lengthy study of environmental impact
Corporate objectives	• Deeper penetration of existing markets vs expanding into new markets	• Vertical vs horizontal integration of production
Corporate organization	• Marketing organization designed to serve domestic, regional or international customer base	• Worker participation in management decisions • Competitive position of technology used in production

systems

Financial	Capital budget systems	Strategic planning systems
• Credit crunch occurs in capital markets causing higher interest rates and limited funds for investment	• Period of slow economic growth with 3% annual growth in GNP • Innovations in financial instruments which are tied to current interest rates • Service and knowledge oriented industries dominate • Stable productivity and rising wage rates	• Changing consumer attitudes towards inflation and durable goods purchases • Capital markets and government may provide capital for small innovative companies
• Government policies such as commodity policies and foreign trade restrictions that prohibit orderly planning • Inflow of capital from OPEC and Third World Sources	• Increasing protection of local markets by government policy • Development of resources for local consumption by government policy • Attractive nature of U.S. economy for foreign investors as a source of stable investment opportunities	• More efficient international exchange of production, capital, and information • Entry of Third World and OPEC wealth into transnational business community
• Efficient transfer of funds will alter fund utilization patterns — EFTS	• Availability of computer-driven capital equipment for production • Service industry technology not meeting social demands in government sector and non-profit groups	• Availability of alternative energy sources • Reduced availability of petroleum energy • Increasing analysis and control of climate and weather
• Social welfare contributions for employees continue to grow	• Demands for community development activities where plants are located • Slowing rate of population growth	• Need for constant retraining of knowledge for industry workers • Rapid obsolescence of work force under changing production technology • Workers with higher education skills than required • Increased speed of communication and information exchange
• Demands for disclosure of information other than historical financial performance	• Tax policy to encourage capital investment by business • Equal employment and fringe benefit policies raise cost of labor	• No recognized economic theory underlying policy decisions • Awareness of corporate and professional responsibility to consumers through increasing malpractice suits and product liability actions
• SEC encouraging soft information disclosure • Data base accounting systems which provide no historical detail	• AICPA procedures to review non-financial and soft information	• Decentralized record-keeping and control require new control and review procedures
• Demands for disclosure of non-financial information by companies — human resources, social responsibility and environmental impact	• Requirements for non-polluting production facilities • Use and preparation of recycled raw materials	
• Centralized vs decentralized management structure • Financial structure and capitalization • Working capital requirements	• Growth through merger/acquisition activity vs plant and equipment expansion	
• Greater demands on corporate officials for ethical conduct • Finance at the division or parent level • Local or international financial markets used to raise capital	• Relationship between planning/operations/executive functions in decision making • Limits of corporate information system to provide planning information • Nature of production cycle and accounting periods • Position of major products in product life cycle	• Top Down theory of management or Bottom-up theory • Attitude of management toward risk taking • Adaptive planning for expansion vs integrative for consolidation

After an in-depth study of planning, its methodologies, its shortcomings, and efforts to improve it, the report concludes that many corporate planning systems must be redesigned to adapt to a broad spectrum of present and future uncertainties.

A majority of other experts attempting to diagnose the future is in general agreement with The Conference Board's outlook. They recognize that seldom, if ever, have U.S. businessmen confronted such a bewildering variety of rapid changes, few of which are predictable over a span of more than several months. The only certainty seems to be that the future may take a number of paths, each with a separate probability of occurrence.

GOOD PLANS DEMAND BROAD VIEWS

Nevertheless, fresh approaches promise to enable planners to seize advantages from an uncertain future, provided that their planning systems are sensitive and flexible enough to adapt to abrupt changes. *Planners can no longer safely consider only a single future.* Instead, they must allow for many possible outcomes—some more likely than others but all deserving examination and evaluation.

No longer can planners assume that they work in a world that is friendly or, at worst, neutral. They must take into account the numerous changing dimensions of society: the external factors that may greatly affect their planning process. Some of the many crucial factors and their manifold influences are shown in the lefthand column of Exhibit I. . . .

Readers will be able to add to the chart many more details relevant to their own experiences and also to judge how vulnerable their own plans and operations may be to the multiple alternative estimates of the future that lies ahead.

In addition to responding to these uncertain external influences, corporate planners must also be prepared to react effectively to new requirements of their own management. In most corporations, these goals and objectives are changing in reaction to the changing business and social environment. These corporate changes are creating new organizational forms which must be accounted for in planning systems.

The key factors affecting corporate organization and goals are listed in the Exhibit. The speed with which change occurs requires closer attention to the relationship between short term budgets and longer term capital evaluations and strategic plans. *Good planning must be disciplined by strict attention to the relationship between time horizons,* which are suggested by the three groups of columns shown: Annual budgets, which encompass no more than one year or, alternatively, a single production cycle; capital budgets, which extend as far out as three years for evaluating proposed business expansion; and strategic plans which reach out from three to five years (sometimes longer) and focus on determining future directions for the company, must all be coordinated and adapted to changing external conditions with the logical interactions examined. The second and third categories overlap somewhat, since capital budgets have strategic elements.

Whatever the nature and lifespan of the plan, it must be compared frequently against actual performance, then changed if it has become unrealistic. Otherwise, a company may find itself wandering through a future that no longer exists.

A WISTFUL GLANCE AT A SIMPLER WORLD

It is difficult for many planners and corporate managers to realize how drastically their worlds have changed in only a few years. The relative economic and social stability of the early 1960s has given way to the uncertainty of the 1970s. Controllable or predictable environments can no longer be relied upon. The firm and reassuring planning system of the 1960s has been transmuted into systems used for identifying uncertainty and minimizing risk. The targeted trend forecast is now blurred into a spectrum of alternative scenarios, and focus on prediction has shifted to awareness of a multiplicity of possible outcomes. The single strategic plan that served as a long-term guide has become a sometimes bewildering set of contingency plans.

Why have the rules of the planning game changed so swiftly and drastically? Box A . . . suggests the basic reasons. Throughout these trends the one common thread of concern to planners is that response times in business decision making have shrunk at an alarming rate. Communications are virtually instantaneous. Accounting and operating information pours out at a much faster rate from modern computer systems. Product life cycles are shorter. Economic and policy analyses are generated at astounding rates. Social and economic policies are changing faster and more frequently.

Similarly, the dimensions of society are undergoing changes that were scarcely contemplated as late as the mid-1960s. Life style preferences are different, not just for teenagers and young adults but also for many of their elders. Demographics have changed in many ways. The work force is now dominated by people born during the baby boom, who are now in their late twenties or early thirties. Many of these young adults are jobless or cannot find work commensurate with their education. Large numbers of women of all ages have entered the labor force, well educated, ambitious, seeking meaningful careers as well as fair compensation.

One provocative view of social change is expressed by Robert Theobald, an economist who is the editor of *Futures Conditional*. He writes: "The key issue of our time is our view of people. If people are incapable of understanding themselves and their society, then we are indeed caught in the dilemmas advanced by those who debate growth limiting policies. If, on the other hand, people are willing and able to make decisions about their own lives and help run society,

---

Box A

Understanding trends in the future

The complexity and rapidity of change in the environment affecting corporate planning systems requires detailed study and analysis. The corporate planning process should, however, seek to identify and interpret specific trends that are relevant to the company's performance. This task can be made easier with a defined framework within which to conduct analysis.

Since the allocation of limited human and natural resources among various needs is the goal of any society and the main concern of most economic systems, allocation goals can be used as a means of classifying the myriad trends requiring analysis.

The major trends to be faced in the 1980s represent a shift in the allocation of human and natural resources:

- from manufactured goods to professional and personal services
- from growing monetary income to the uses of affluence to achieve a more gratifying quality of life
- from centralized management and control to local or regional influence over the decisions affecting our lives
- from the development of capital and physical capabilities to the improvement of human resources
- from production of physical products to the creation and dissemination of information and knowledge
- from transformation of resources for production and economic growth to the conservation of those resources for future generations
- from the free market economic decision process to increasing accountability for the social and environmental impact of corporate decisions

---

then we need to provide them with more opportunity to be involved in effective decision making." This statement, in short, suggests a coming decentralization of knowledge and authority never before envisioned—still another challenge for tomorrow's planners.

Government intervention in many areas has changed its character. The shift, in part, results from our leaders' frustrations with the pace of change and their inability to grasp the entire scope of the problems. Protection of the natural environment, consumer interests, and preservation of resourcess are now almost universal concerns. They are causing federal and local government to undertake new initiatives in these areas. Industries facing maturing and less profitable life cycles, such as transportation and utilities, are beginning to shift responsibility to government. Meanwhile, federal regulators are beginning to assume more passive roles in areas such as commercial aviation where they believe the market mechanism may be more effective.

The increase in the number and speed of factors affecting business indicates why planning grows continually more elaborate, though less certain. Some of the major elements and their interrelationships are shown in Exhibit II. We can see from this simple diagram that the comprehensive planning system today must anticipate a multitude of external environmental influences, adjust to the changing historical information created by the company's accounting system, and react to new corporate objectives, goals, and forms of organization. The modern planning system must combine all these inputs into multiple scenarios for different time horizons. Strategic plans and capital spending evaluation must contribute to the company's ability to adapt to change. The annual budget must aid the company in integrating its response to the environment so as to improve corporate performance in the short term.

THE YEARNING FOR CERTAINTY IS UNABATED

The replacement of best-estimate forecasts by assortments of scenarios that describe possible futures in some detail has been forced upon planners. Yet in most corporate settings, decision makers still feel uncomfortable when presented with a stack of scenarios. They tend to tell the planner: "If you can't tell me what is going to happen, at least narrow your predictions down to the one that is most likely." As a result, many organizations fail to take full advantage of a range of contingency plans, especially those designed to cope with unlikely combinations of events. The importance of this advantage can be recognized when one considers the implication of emerging trends, such as California's Proposition 13 and the business tax reforms.

Many in the business world have, however, reconciled themselves to meeting uncertainty head-on. [They have indicated that they] are willing to accept risk and uncertainty. . . . Quite possibly the next generation of decision makers will think and talk in the numerical terms of probability. One participant in The Conference Board study (a bank executive) stated flatly: "Forecasts are meaningless unless they are accompanied by probabilities."

It is likely that a larger proportion of decision makers find comfort in the predictive reliability of business cycles. Many short term fluctuations represent changes that are no more than random occurrences and therefore barely more meaningful than radio static. Nevertheless, certain well-established cycles have been studied and may have an important role in long-range corporate planning.

One well-known analyst has formalized the study of various cycles into a computer simulation model that may or may not comfort today's corporate planners. Jay W. Forrester of MIT's Sloan School of Management has constructed a model that projects the responses of the U.S. economy to a variety of

Exhibit II. Overview of a Planning System in Context.

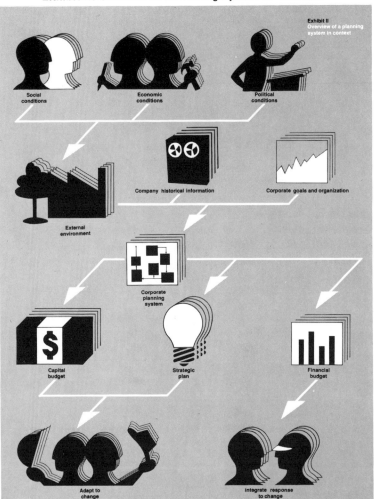

events. The reason for having and trusting such a cycle-driven model, he explains, is that "intuition and political debate are proving inadequate tools for managing economic change."

In a recent article in *Technology Review* he writes at length on three economic cycles that seem to have worldwide significance. They are the familiar three-to-seven-year business cycle first proposed by Arthur Burns and Wesley C. Mitchell; the 15–25 year investment (or Kuznets) cycle; and the 45–60 year Kondratieff cycle. The two longer cycles seem to be closely related to capital investment in such ways that they are potentially important considerations for corporate planners. Forrester states: "I am coming to believe that the long cycle is more important in explaining economic behavior than either the business or Kuznets cycles." He believes that the effects of this long wave may explain why simple extrapolation of economic trends no longer serves as a reliable guide to the future. Pointing out that the Kondratieff cycle seems to account for the depressions of the 1830s, 1890s, and 1930s, Forrester says that it may be of critical importance in explaining our current economic situation.

He concludes: "The challenge of the 1980s will be to cope with change. I believe we are at the top of a long-wave peak. If so, we are nearing the end of a technological era. . . . We are in a hiatus between the ending of our present technological wave and the vigorous development of the next. . . . A pause occurs while we shift gears."

Although Prof. Forrester represents perhaps the most conspicuous user of business cycles in futures planning, many noted economic consultants are influenced by the realities of business cycles in their forecasting work. Dr. Otto Eckstein and his Data Resources Inc. consulting firm prepare various ten-year economic projection alternatives based on the likelihood that cyclical factors will dominate the U.S. economy. In the near-future DRI projections, careful watch is kept on the underlying factors that may cause the economy to reach a cyclical peak or trough. The Wharton School forecasters, headed by Prof. Lawrence Klein, and the Chase Econometrics projections, prepared under the direction of Dr. Michael K. Evans, also reflect the underlying flows of economic and financial activity caused by cyclical influences.

PLANNERS ARE SWAMPED WITH INFORMATION

The current output of economists, psychologists, environmentalists, soothsayers, lawmakers, scholars, and spouses makes it easy for a planner to identify factors that may affect corporate performance. The difficult problem is to organize, rank, and evaluate the all-too abundant information. A basic framework for this organization is shown in Box B. . . . Then comes the still harder task of integrating this knowledge into planning systems that can lead to effective decision-making.

In the development of a planning system, two kinds of factors should be considered in broad terms. Those that do not affect the chances of achieving the plan's objectives can be ignored for the time being, although they should be reviewed periodically as conditions change. Factors that appear likely to alter the risk that the resulting plan will or will not succeed warrant painstaking analysis. A broadbrush view of important factors and their interrelationships is shown in Exhibit III. . . , which is essentially a rearrangement of the headings at the extreme left of the chart, Exhibit I.

This simplified diagram attempts to portray the complex linkages among the

**Planning for changing corporate
goals and organizations**

The sole purpose of planning is to assist management to make
"better" decisions. The test of a planning system is not its ability to
forecast the future accurately but rather its ability to perceive
enough of what is important about the risks and opportunities in
the future so that we can effectively chart our course for the present.

Depending on the businesses they are in, their relative size, the
nature of their competition and other unique factors, firms have
differing decision criteria, cycles, and styles. Capital intensive
companies or those that must invest heavily in new product development usually have extensive and elaborate planning systems in place.
This is not to say that these corporations do a better job of planning
than other firms but they generally will have the necessary structure. These firms have been forced to plan by their continuing need
to make rational decisions on investments to be repaid from operations over extended periods. Other firms, equally well managed,
without this pressing need for evaluating capital or new product
projects with long term paybacks sometimes never develop a sophisticated planning system.

With or without a defined system, however, planning occurs in
every firm. Every decision regarding resource allocation, new product introduction, current product retirement, acquisition, divesti-
ture, etc. is based on the results of that firm's planning. A formal
planning system makes this process visible. The planning system
must improve the quality of those decisions to justify its existence.
The system will vary significantly from firm to firm but should have
three basic qualities:

1. increase the scope, time horizon, and quality of manage-
    ment's awareness of the external and internal factors that
    affect the future of the company and provide a *realistic*
    appraisal of these factors;
2. provide an objective apolitical environmeent for the evalua-
    tion and resolution of competitive demands for critical
    resources and a method for review and enforcement of the
    decisions reached;
3. assure appropriate communication of company strategy,
    tactics and status to various levels of the firm.

In today's complex and volatile business climate, the attainment
of even these basic elements often requires the application of very
sophisticated techniques. Almost every firm has international
markets, divisions, or competitors so that a global knowledge of
markets, supply conditions, social/political stability and labor trends
is needed for many decisions. Further, rapidly changing financial
factors such as currency exchange rates, interest rates, and commodity prices force those making decisions regarding products to
utilize mathematical models for efficient and effective evaluation of

complex alternatives. Indeed, financing and monetary considerations may require the use of outside specialist skills. Finally, most of the members of any management team are "hard-nosed" realistic profit makers, not planners. The planning process may require the introduction of conceptual thinkers to broaden management's view of the horizons, both in terms of the timeframe involved and the range of issues considered.

The planning process cannot be taken from the firm's management and given to specialists to complete and return to management for implementation. Neither can the planning process be effective without the introduction of necessary specialist skills. The key therefore, is to meld the line management and the specialists into an effective team.

The formal planning system is intended to accomplish this melding. From a systems design standpoint there are several key questions. Foremost among these are:

- What are the appropriate planning horizons and cycles for the strategic, developmental, and operational plans?
- How can these planning cycles be integrated with the market and operations dictated by business cycles of the company?
- How can the company best accommodate the annual budget cycle within the planning cycle?
- What is the optimal makeup, reporting position, and review process of the planning function?
- How is it best to establish the information system that will support the planning process so that it minimizes reporting while maximizing the information provided to assure that current activities support the intent of the plan and that the planners are appraised of changes on the basis of the plan?

All these questions and others must be answered to provide a system that is an integral part of the company's decision making process, consumes the least management time consistent with an effective result, and enhances the company's performance.

This planning process is the one aspect of the management of the firm that is most dependent on the vision and style of the chief executive. The process is too critical to the future of the individuals involved and of the firm for the decisions to be taken lightly. Unless the people involved believe in the integrity, effectiveness, and reality of the process it can do more harm that good for the firm's morale and sense of direction.

The planning process will not point the way for the company but should help in the selection of alternative strategies. The criteria used in the selection of strategies to be evaluated are still entrepreneurial tasks even in the largest of companies and their quality depends on the chief executive. A superb or even a good executive can function more effectively with a planning process in place, but the planning process will do little to help a mediocre one.

Exhibit III. Dimensions of Society.

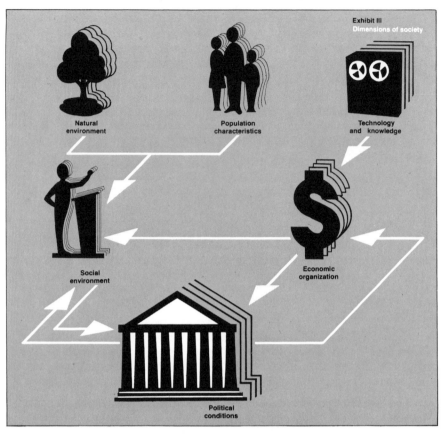

major dimension of our society. The dangers faced by our natural environment and the changing character of the U.S. and world populations contribute to the basic thrust of our social attitudes and institutions. As people become more educated, they react more quickly to the threats to our natural surroundings. The dangers perceived are translated into calls for political action and economic response.

Advanced technology has some sweeping negative effects that disturb environmentalists, government regulators, and other influential groups. Some of the best drugs have had side effects. Common chemicals, such as red dye #2, are suspected of causing cancer. Radiation and the disposal of nuclear wastes complicate plans for increasing energy output. The public has been sensitized to production methods that may endanger the health or lives of workers—e.g., black lung disease in the coal mines. Some management reorganizations result in severe personal dislocation that may lead to divorce or alienation from families.

The reactions to our environment and technology evoke our social moods and values. The state of technology and the depth of our knowledge profoundly affect our economic organization. Industrial technology determines the efficient scale of operation for various economic organizations. The accumulation of scientific and other human knowledge in our economic systems contributes to what and how we produce or provide.

A critical encounter for the business planner is the impact of the social environment on the economy. This dialogue reflects the difference between the values and needs of society and the current implementation of these goals. In the midst is a political system that reacts to and affects the outcome of our social system.

REDUCING THE RISKS OF MANAGEMENT

An article in *Harvard Business Review,* by George A. W. Boehm, editor of *Management Focus,* observed in the autumn of 1976: Managing is more of a gamble than ever, but systematically organized and analyzed information helps executives to hedge their bets. "The uncertainties of these times have forced a shotgun marriage between the executive decision maker and the systems analyst. . . . With enough ingenuity, it is possible to cope with an unsure future at least cleverly enough to minimize the chance of outright disaster."

To an even greater extent today, wrestling with uncertainty is the corporate planner's main task. The areas of uncertainty are difficult to identify and even more difficult to manage rationally. Here are a few specifics that most planners must contemplate and evaluate:

- What are likely impacts of the changing social environment?
- Will corporate and professional responsibilities to the consumer continue to grow as rapidly as they have in recent years?
- What will be the behavior of an aging population as the baby-boom bulge moves more people into their forties and fifties?
- How will steadily increasing participation by women affect the economy?
- Will the fear of technological advance grow?
- Can the nation sustain its historic optimistic view that somehow the future will work out well?

These kinds of domestic questions affect the planning process across many time horizons.

When the consumer markets and attitudes change, does the planner:

change his annual revenue budget, recompute his expected return on a capital project getting under way, or consider altering his company's competitive position in that market? Or perhaps, should he do all three?

When the price or availability of an essential production raw material changes significantly, does the planner:

> change his annual cost-of-goods-sold budget, reconsider the kind of technology built into a capital expenditure project, or review changing the mix of products sold by the company? Should he not do all three?

When the cost of borrowing in the capital markets rises sharply, does the planner:

> change his annual inventory and accounts receivable financing policy, recalculate the required rate of return on a pending project, or consider merging with or acquiring a similar competitor? Probably all three.

These kinds of questions and the need for complex, dynamic answers require that modern corporate planning systems be sensitive to external factors. The advantages of having externally sensitive systems are many in the uncertain environment that prevails today. Plans can be quickly adjusted to mesh with external change. The outcomes of various scenarios can be tested in advance with the aid of computers. The outcomes of management policies can be tested against different external scenarios. Internal performance can be measured against external conditions and modified if necessary. Finally, the implications of any mix of external changes can be coordinated from the annual budget through the five-year strategic plan.

PLANNING FOR THE INDIVIDUAL
IN A COMPLEX SOCIETY

E. H. Erikson, well-known student of human growth and behavior, describes the passage of a person's psychosocial life between the early and middle stages of adulthood. This period corresponds roughly to the present stage of the baby-boom generation, the dominant U.S. social force.

Although the characteristics of an entire society or era cannot be compared strictly to those of an individual, some interesting parallels include:

- the reexamination of life goals and objectives
- awareness of the complexity of life and the need to manage one's small piece of it
- evidence of one's vulnerability and helplessness to change or direct major social forces

- struggle between the desire to participate in society or to withdraw from it
- loss of optimism about the automatic success of events of the future
- movement toward more basic values of family, career, and community

If the parallel with Erikson is accurate, American society is approaching a middle stage of maturity. The realities of the natural environment have forced us to reexamine our priorities. The outlook for stable population growth has helped to bring expectations in line with the realities of our potential. These and many other reevaluations have become possible because our economic system has helped to create an affluence never before known in history.

THE PLANNER'S ROLE
AS TOMORROW'S PHILOSOPHER

Social analyses like that of Erikson may not be in the mainstream of day-to-day corporate planning. Nevertheless, factors and events triggered by the changing outlooks of people play a major role in most planning phases. Planners who hope to squeeze the most assurance from a basically uncertain future can profit by reflecting upon the observations of philosophically-minded psychologists and economists.

This is a worrisome—even frantic—era for those who must make plans and base decisions on them. But they can be heartened by the fact that even the economic and social turmoil of today was foreseen in broad terms as long as 20 years ago by humanistic thinkers such as Harvard economist Robert L. Heilbroner. In his book, *The Future as History,* he wrote: "Optimism as a philosophy of historic expectations can no longer be considered a national virtue. It has become a dangerous national delusion. . . . We limit our idea of what is possible by excluding from our control the forces of history themselves. . . .

"To rid oneself of this comforting notion is not to lessen one's ardor to resolve the difficulties of the present, but to arm oneself realistically for the continuation of the human struggle in the future."

And that, in capsule form, expounds the role of today's corporate planner.

The Next Thirty-Three Years:
A Framework for Speculation

H. Kahn
and
A. J. Wiener

The pace at which various technological, social, political, and economic changes are taking place has reduced the relevance of experience as a guide to public-policy judgments. Scientists, engineers, and managers who deal directly with modern technology and who are also interested in broad policy issues, often overestimate the likely social consequences of technological development and go to extremes of optimism or pessimism, while those more oriented to the cultural heritage often bank too heavily on historical continuity and social inertia. The problem, of course, is to sort out what changes from what continues and to discern what is continuous in the changes themselves.

At the Hudson Institute we have used three inter-related devices to facilitate making systematic conjectures about the future.[1] We first identify those long-term trends that seem likely to continue. These include, for example, the world-wide spread of a more or less secular humanism, the institutionalization of scientific and technological innovation, and continuous economic growth. We have, in this paper, identified a "multifold trend" consisting of thirteen inter-related elements.

We then cluster significant events by 33-year intervals, starting with 1900, in order to see which combinations give rise to new clusters, to define the qualitative changes in the combination of trends, and to identify emergent properties, such as the increasing self-consciousness of time and history.

Finally, we have attempted to construct significant baselines, statistical where possible, to project key variables in society—population, literacy, Gross National Product, energy sources, military strength, and the like. These variables and their growth rates tend both to furnish and to constrain the possibilities for any society. By selecting extrapolations of current or emerging tendencies that grow continuously out of today's world, and reflect the multifold trend and our current expectations, we create a "surprise-free" projection—one that seems less surprising than any other specific possibility. Consistent with this projection we

---

1. These and related issues are taken up in some detail in our volume for the Working Papers of the Commission, *The Next Thirty-Three Years: A Framework for Speculation,* published in October 1967 by the Macmillan Company as *Toward the Year 2000: A Framework for Speculation.*

describe a "standard world" and several "canonical variations" that form the likely worlds of the future.

In this paper we shall seek to illustrate these methods and to provide some brief examples of some of our conclusions.

I. THE BASIC MULTIFOLD TREND

The basic trends of Western society, most of which can be traced back hundreds of years, have a common set of sources in the rationalization and secularization of society. For analytic purposes, we shall separate these basic trends into thirteen rubrics, though obviously one might wish to group them into fewer and more abstract categories or to refine the analysis by identifying or distinguishing many more aspects. As basic trends, these elements seem very likely to continue at least for the next thirty-three years, though some may saturate or begin to recede beyond that point.

There is a basic, long-term, multifold trend toward:

1. Increasingly sensate (empirical, this-worldly, secular, humanistic, pragmatic, utilitarian, contractual, epicurean, or hedonistic) cultures
2. Bourgeois, bureaucratic, "meritocratic," democratic (and nationalistic?) elites
3. Accumulation of scientific and technological knowledge
4. Institutionalization of change, especially research, development, innovation, and diffusion
5. World-wide industrialization and modernization
6. Increasing affluence and (recently) leisure
7. Population growth
8. Decreasing importance of primary occupations
9. Urbanization and (soon) the growth of megalopolises
10. Literacy and education
11. Increased capability for mass destruction
12. Increasing tempo of change
13. Increasing universality of these trends.

Speculations about the future have ranged from the literary speculations of Jules Verne and Edward Bellamy to the humanistic and philosophical writing of Jacob Burckhardt, Arnold Toynbee, and Pitirim Sorokin. Although the observations and philosophical assumptions have differed greatly, some of the empirical observations or contentions have had much in common. Thus when Sorokin finds a circular pattern of idealistic, integrated, and sensate cultures, his categories bear comparison to what Edward Gibbon noted of Rome on a more descriptive level. If both the more theoretical and the more empirical observations are treated merely as *heuristic metaphors,* regardless of their author' diverse intentions, they may suggest possible patterns for the future without confining one to too narrow or too rigid a view. Metaphoric and heuristic use of these concepts broadens the range of speculations; one can then pick and choose from these speculations as the evidence is developed. Nevertheless, in using concepts this way, there is an obvious risk not only of superficiality and oversimplification but also of excessive or premature commitment to some idiosyncratic view. In this paper we shall illustrate only a few elements of the multifold trend.

The Increasingly Sensate Culture

The use of the term *sensate,* derived from Pitirim Sorokin, is best explained in contrast with Sorokin's other concepts: "integrated" (or idealistic), "ideational," and "late sensate."[2] One can characterize ideational art by such terms as transcendental, supersensory, religious, symbolic, allegoric, static, worshipful, anonymous, traditional, and imminent. Idealistic or integrated art can usually be associated with such adjectives as heroic, noble, uplifting, sublime, patriotic, moralistic, beautiful, flattering, and educational, while sensate art would be worldly, naturalistic, realistic, visual, illusionistic, everyday, amusing, interesting, erotic, satirical, novel, eclectic, syncretic, fashionable, technically superb, impressionistic, materialistic, commercial, and professional. Finally, there are tendencies toward what would be called late sensate, characterized as underworldly, expressing protest or revolt, over-ripe, extreme, sensation-seeking, titillating, depraved, faddish, violently novel, exhibitionistic, debased, vulgar, ugly, debunking, nihilistic, pornographic, sarcastic, or sadistic.

Sensate, of course, does not intend a connotation of sensual or sensational; a word such as *worldly, humanistic,* or *empirical* would have been equally useful for our purposes.

Within a culture there is a considerable congruence or convergence among the various parts. If, for example, a culture is sensate in art or in systems of truth, it tends to be sensate in systems of government and family as well. While a high culture may seem vividly defined to an outside observer and appear to be pervasive in a society, the situation may be much more complicated. For example, in Cromwellian England the majority of the people actually rejected puritan values, although this rejection might have been almost invisible to the visitor. Values are often enforced as well as exhibited by an elite. The degree of unity and pervasiveness of any particular culture is, in fact, a crucial issue, as is the question of the importance of the visible elites as opposed to the less visible, but perhaps more influential ones. In the United States today, for example, there is clearly a strong split between a large group of intellectuals and the government on many issues. Public-opinion polls seem to indicate that although these intellectuals hold a "progressive" consensus and dominate discussion in many serious

2. Pitirim A. Sorokin, *Social and Cultural Dynamics,* vol. 4, New York, 1962, pp. 737 ff.

journals, they are not representative of the country. In particular, the high culture can be thought of as secular humanist, and the public as more religious and less humanist.

Western culture as a whole is clearly sensate and possibly entering a late sensate stage. The sensate trend goes back seven or eight centuries, but its progress has not been uninterrupted. The Reformation, the Counter-Reformation, the puritan era in England, some aspects of the later Victorian era, and to some degree such phenomena as Stalinism, Hitlerism, and Fascism—all represented, at least at the time, currents counter to the basic trend of an increasingly sensate culture. Nevertheless, the long-term, all-embracing sensate trend expanded from the West and now covers virtually the entire world. Whether this will continue for the next 33 or 66 years is an open question. If the obvious implications of the description of late sensate culture are valid, the long-term tendencies toward late sensate must stabilize or even reverse if the system is not to be profoundly modified.

Bourgeois, Bureaucratic, "Meritocratic," Democratic (and Nationalistic?) Elites

By *bourgeois* we mean holding economic values and idealogies of the kind that characterized the new middle classes that emerged from the break-up of feudal society—values of personal and family achievement, financial prudence, economic calculation, commercial foresight, and "business" and professional success as a moral imperative. (The emergence of "bourgeois" elites in this sense is vividly described in such works as Max Weber's *The Protestant Ethic* and R. H. Tawney's *Religion and the Rise of Capitalism.*) Though Karl Marx and Friedrich Engels might have been surprised, it is now clear that these values can, and perhaps must, also be present in socialist or communist economies, especially if they are industrialized and "revisionist." By *democratic* we mean having a popular political base; this can also be totalitarian or tyrannical in the classical sense, provided it is not merely imposed from above and that there is some economic mobility and relative equality in access to opportunity. Bureaucratic and meritocratic administrations also characterize modern industrial societies, whether capitalist or communist.

Bourgeois democracy tends to rest on some form of "social contract" concept of the relationship between the people and their government. The people "hire" and "fire" their governments, and no group has theocratic (ideational) or aristocratic (integrated) claims on the government. Clearly, democratic government is also an expression of democratic ideology—it is sustained by the idea of the consent of the governed. The idea is contractual; and the factors of sacredness, occultness, or charisma are restricted.

Nationalistic values are also associated with the rise of the middle class. Kings used nationalism to gain allies among the middle class against the nobles, the church, the emperor, or enemy states. The nationalist idea later involved a recognition that the people (the nation) have the contractual right to government of (and by) their own kind and eventually to self-government—or that the right to govern has to be justified as representing the will of the people and serving the general welfare. Even the totalitarian nationalism of Mussolini, Hitler, Stalin, and the Japanese officer corps usually made its basic appeal to and found its greatest response in the middle class (or, in the case of the Japanese, the agrarian middle class).

One can argue that the long-term nationalist trend is on the decline today, at least in what might be thought of as the NATO area, though this remains in many ways an open issue. (The West European nations could conceivably become more nationalist in the future, and a European political community might emerge that would be nationalist in the sense that "Europe" becomes the "nation.") In any case, late sensate culture carries implications of cosmopolitanism and pacifism and lack of particularist ethics or loyalties, except on a shifting, contractual basis. Nevertheless, it is probably safe to argue that over the next 33 years nationalism will increase in most of the underdeveloped and developing worlds, at least in the minimal sense that modern systems of public education and mass communication will integrate even the most peripheral groups into the common language and culture.

Science and Technology

In order to provide a quick impression of science and technology (with an emphasis on technology) in the last third of the twentieth century, we list one hundred areas in which technological innovation will almost certainly occur.

Each item is important enough to make, by itself, a significant change. The difference might lie mainly in being spectacular (for example, trans-oceanic rocket transportation in twenty or thirty minutes, rather than supersonic in two or three hours); in being ubiquitous (widespread use of paper clothes); in enabling a large number of different things to be done (super materials); in effecting a general and significant increase in productivity (cybernation); or simply in being important to specific individuals (convenient artificial kidneys). It could be argued reasonably that each of these warrants the description technological innovation, revolution, or breakthrough. None is merely an obvious minor improvement on what currently exists.

We should note that the one hundred areas are not ordered randomly. Most people would consider the first twenty-five unambiguous examples of progress. A few would question even these, since lasers and masers, for example, might make possible a particularly effective ballistic missile defense and, thus, accelerate the Soviet-American arms race. Similarly, the expansion of tropical agriculture and forestry could mean a geographical shift in economic and military power, as well as a dislocation of competitive industries. Nevertheless, there probably would be a consensus among readers that the first twenty-five areas do represent progress—at least for those who are in favor of "progress."

The next twenty-five areas are clearly controversial; many would argue that government policy might better restrain or discourage innovation or diffusion here. These "controversial areas" raise issues of accelerated nuclear proliferation, loss of privacy, excessive governmental or private power over individuals, dangerously vulnerable, deceptive, and degradable overcentralization, inherently dangerous new capabilities, change too cataclysmic for smooth adjustment, or decisions that are inescapable, yet at the same time too complex and far-reaching to be safely trusted to anyone's individual or collective judgement.

The last fifty items are included because they are intrinsically interesting and to demonstrate that a list of one hundred items of "almost certain" and "very significant" innovation can be produced fairly easily.[3]

One Hundred Technical Innovations Likely in the Next 33 Years

1. Multiple applications of lasers and masers for sensing, measuring, communicating, cutting, heating, welding, power transmission, illumination, destructive (defensive), and other purposes
2. Extremely high-strength or high-temperature structural materials
3. New or improved super-performance fabrics (papers, fibers, and plastics)
4. New or improved materials for equipment and appliances (plastics, glasses, alloys, ceramics, intermetallics, and cermets)
5. New airborne vehicles (ground-effect machines, VTOL and STOL, super-helicopters, giant supersonic jets)
6. Extensive commercial application of shaped charges
7. More reliable and longer-range weather forecasting
8. Intensive or extensive expansion of tropical agriculture and forestry
9. New sources of power for fixed installations (for example, magneto-hydrodynamic, thermionic, and thermoelectric, radioactive)
10. New sources of power for ground transportation (storage-battery, fuel-cell propulsion or support by electromagnetic fields, jet engine, turbine)
11. Extensive and intensive world-wide use of high-altitude cameras for mapping, prospecting, census, land use, and geological investigations
12. New methods of water transportation (large submarines, flexible and special-purpose "container ships," more extensive use of large automated single-purpose bulk cargo ships)
13. Major reduction in hereditary and congenital defects

---

3. In compiling this list we have received useful suggestions from Jane Kahn, John Menke, Robert Prehoda, and G. Stine.

14. Extensive use of cyborg techniques (mechanical aids or substitutes for human organs, sense, limbs)
15. New techniques for preserving or improving the environment
16. Relatively effective appetite and weight control
17. New techniques in adult education
18. New improved plants and animals
19. Human "hibernation" for short periods (hours or days) for medical purposes
20. Inexpensive "one of a kind" design and procurement through use of computerized analysis and automated production
21. Controlled super-effective relaxation and sleep
22. More sophisticated architectural engineering (geodesic domes, thin shells, pressurized skins, esoteric materials)
23. New or improved uses of the oceans (mining, extraction of minerals, controlled "farming," source of energy)
24. Three-dimensional photography, illustrations, movies, and television
25. Automated or more mechanized housekeeping and home maintenance
26. Widespread use of nuclear reactors for power
27. Use of nuclear explosives for excavation and mining, generation of power, creation of high-temperature/high-pressure environments, or for a source of neutrons or other radiation
28. General use of automation and cybernation in management and production
29. Extensive and intensive centralization (or automatic interconnection) of current and past personal and business information in high-speed data processors
30. Other new and possibly pervasive techniques for surveillance, monitoring, and control of individuals and organizations
31. Some control of weather or climate
32. Other (permanent or temporary) changes or experiments with the overall environment (for example, the "permanent" increase in C-14 and temporary creation of other radioactivity by nuclear explosions, the increasing generation of CO_2 in the atmosphere, projects Starfire, West Ford, Storm Fury, and so forth)
33. New and more reliable "educational" and propaganda techniques for affecting human behavior—public and private
34. Practical use of direct electronic communication with and stimulation of the brain
35. Human hibernation for relatively extensive periods (months to years)
36. Cheap and widely available or excessively destructive central war weapons and weapons systems

37. New and relatively effective counterinsurgency techniques (and perhaps also insurgency techniques)
38. New kinds of very cheap, convenient, and reliable birth-control techniques
39. New, more varied, and more reliable drugs for control of fatigue, relaxation, alertness, mood, personality, perceptions, and fantasies
40. Capability to choose the sex of unborn children
41. Improved capability to "change" sex
42. Other genetic control or influence over the "basic constitution" of an individual
43. New techniques in the education of children
44. General and substantial increase in life expectancy, postponement of aging, and limited rejuvenation
45. Generally acceptable and competitive synthetic foods and beverages (carbohydrates, fats, proteins, enzymes, vitamins, coffee, tea, cocoa, liquor)
46. "High quality" medical care for underdeveloped areas (for example, use of referral hospitals, broad-spectrum antibiotics, artificial blood plasma)
47. Design and extensive use of responsive and super-controlled environments for private and public use (for pleasurable, educational, and vocational purposes)
48. "Nonharmful" methods of "over-indulging"
49. Simple techniques for extensive and "permanent" cosmetological changes (features, "figures," perhaps complexion, skin color, even physique)
50. More extensive use of transplantation of human organs
51. Permanent manned satellite and lunar installations—interplanetary travel
52. Application of space life systems or similar techniques to terrestrial installations
53. Permanent inhabited undersea installations and perhaps even colonies
54. Automated grocery and department stores
55. Extensive use of robots and machines "slaved" to humans
56. New uses of underground and tunnels for private and public transportation
57. Automated universal (real time) credit, audit, and banking systems
58. Chemical methods for improved memory and learning
59. Greater use of underground buildings
60. New and improved materials and equipment for buildings and interiors (variable transmission glass, heating and cooling by thermoelectric effect, electroluminescent and phosphorescent lighting)
61. Widespread use of cryogenics

62. Improved chemical control of some mental illness and some aspects of senility

63. Mechanical and chemical methods for improving human analytical ability more or less directly

64. Inexpensive and rapid techniques for making tunnels and underground cavities in earth or rock

65. Major improvements in earth moving and construction equipment generally

66. New techniques for keeping physically fit or acquiring physical skills

67. Commercial extraction of oil from shale

68. Recoverable boosters for economic space launching

69. Individual flying platforms

70. Simple inexpensive video recording and playing

71. Inexpensive high-capacity, world-wide, regional, and local (home and business) communication (using satellites, lasers, light pipes, and so forth)

72. Practical home and business use of "wired" video communication for both telephone and television (possibly including retrieval of taped material from libraries or other sources) and rapid transmission and reception of facsimiles (possibly including news, library material, commercial announcements, instantaneous mail delivery, other print-outs)

73. Practical large-scale desalinization

74. Pervasive business use of computers for the storage, processing and retrieval of information

75. Shared-time (public and interconnected) computers generally available to home and business on a metered basis

76. Other widespread use of computers for intellectual and professional assistance (translation, teaching, literary research, medical diagnosis, traffic control, crime detection, computation design, analysis, and, to some degree, as a general intellectual collaborator)

77. General availability of inexpensive transuranic and other esoteric elements

78. Space defense systems

79. Inexpensive and reasonably effective ground-based ballistic missile defense

80. Very low-cost buildings for home and business use

81. Personal "pagers" (perhaps even two-way pocket phone) and other personal electronic equipment for communication computing, and data-processing

82. Direct broadcasts from satellites to home receivers

83. Inexpensive (less than $20), long-lasting, very small battery-operated television receivers

84. Home computers to "run" the household and communicate with outside world

85. Maintenance-free, long-life electronic and other equipment
86. Home education via video and computerized and programmed learning
87. Programmed dreams
88. Inexpensive (less than 1 cent a page) rapid, high-quality black and white reproduction, followed by colored, highly detailed photography reproduction
89. Widespread use of improved fluid amplifiers
90. Conference television (both closed-circuit and public communication systems)
91. Flexible penology without necessarily using prisons (by use of modern methods of surveillance, monitoring, and control)
92. Common use of individual power source for lights, appliances, and machines
93. Inexpensive world-wide transportation of humans and cargo
94. Inexpensive road-free (and facility-free) transportation
95. New methods for teaching languages rapidly
96. Extensive genetic control for plants and animals
97. New biological and chemical methods to identify, trace, incapacitate, or annoy people for police and military uses
98. New and possibly very simple methods for lethal biological and chemical warfare
99. Artificial moons and other methods of lighting large areas at night
100. Extensive use of "biological processes" in the extraction and processing of minerals

World-Wide Industrialization, Affluence, and Population Growth

Many people—Kenneth Boulding, Peter Drucker, and John Maynard Keynes, for example—have pointed out that until the last two or three centuries no large human society had ever produced more than the equivalent of $200 *per capita* annually. With industrialization, mankind broke out of this pattern. By the end of this century, we expect that the nations of the world might be divided into the following five classes:

1. Pre-industrial	$50 to $200 *per capita*
2. Partially industrialized or transitional	$200 to $600 *per capita*
3. Industrial	$600 to perhaps $1500 *per capita*
4. Mass-consumption or advanced industrial	Perhaps $1500 to something more than $4000 *per capita*
5. Post-industrial	Something over $4000 to $16,000 *per capita*

We shall consider partially industrialized societies as being in a transition stage, without assuming that they will necessarily continue to industrialize. Those countries we call industrialized are roughly in the condition of inter-war America or post-war Europe.

Many pre-industrial or partially industrialized societies may also, of course, have dual economies—for example, northern and southern Italy. This problem, now defined in terms of urban and rural differences, may, by the year 2000, be most critical in the six most populous, least developed countries: China, India, Pakistan, Indonesia, Brazil, and Nigeria. These now contain, and in the future will probably continue to contain, about half of the world's population; they are now pre-industrial, but presumably will be partially industrialized by the end of the century.

Problems caused by great development in major cities and less in lesser cities and rural areas are already evident in these countries. Despite important differences in average development, one can argue that most great cities today have achieved startlingly similar conditions of modernization, and are at least "twentieth century." Rio de Janeiro, Bangkok, and Athens have many of the virtues and problems of the major cities of the United States: twentieth-century slums, computers, labor displaced by automation, great universities, skilled craftsmen, a trend toward tertiary and quaternary occupations, startlingly similar price structures for many commodities and activities.

The post World War II period has seen the emergence of the mass-consumption society, first in the United States and then in Western Europe and Japan. Japan, although it has less than $1000 *per capita*, is by every superficial appearance a mass-consumption society today, while the Soviet Union, with a *per capita* income of around $1500, seems far short of that condition. Similarly $4000 *per capita* will probably be sufficient for transition to a post-industrial economy for the Scandinavian countries or Great Britain, while countries with more ambitious goals in terms of world power (the USSR), stronger traditions of economic striving (West Germany), or higher expectations of productive affluence (the US) will not become post-industrial until higher levels of affluence have been reached.

The chart (p. 329) indicates a rather impressionistic, but not wholly unreasonable economic ranking for the nations of the world in the year 2000. The figures express national populations in millions, and the total world population is estimated at 6.4 billion. On the whole, the descriptions are optimistic, but we would not care to defend in detail the specific rank order we have suggested. The numbers identifying each group correspond roughly to the levels of income of the previous table.

If this scenario is realized, the year 2000 will find a rather large island of wealth surrounded by "misery"—at least relative to the developed world and to "rising expectations." But even the poor countries will, for the most part, enjoy

Economic Groupings in the Standard World

5 Visibly post-industrial		*3 Mature industrial*	
US	320	¼ of Latin America	150
Japan	120	½ of Arab world	100
Canada	40	½ of East and S.E. Asia	200
Scandinavia and Switzerland	25	Miscellaneous	50
France, W. Germany, Benelux,			———
Great Britain	215		500
	———		
	720		

| *5 Early post-industrial* | | *2 Large and partially* | |
		* industrialized*	
Italy	60	Brazil	200
Soviet Union	350	Pakistan	230
E. Germany, Poland,		China	1300
Czechoslovakia	135	India	1000
Israel	5	Indonesia	220
Australia, New Zealand	25	Nigeria	150
	———		———
	575		3100

| *4 Mass-consumption* | | *1 and 2 Pre-industrial or* | |
| | | *   small and partially* | |
		* industrialized*	
Spain, Portugal, Austria,		Rest of Africa	350
Yugoslavia, Albania,		⅔ Arab world	200
Greece, Bulgaria,		Rest of Asia	160
Hungary, Ireland	125	Rest of Latin America	40
Turkey	75		———
Mexico, Argentina,			750
Colombia, Venezuela,			
Chile	300		
Taiwan, S. Korea, Hong			
Kong, Malaysia, etc.	120		
	———		
	620		

great improvements over their traditional standards of living. The post-industrial and industrial societies will contain about 40 percent of the world's population, and more than 90 per cent of the world's population will live in nations that have broken out of the historical $50–$200 *per capita* range. Yet at the same time the absolute gap in living standards between countries or sectors of countries with developed economies and those at pre-industrial levels will have widened abysmally.

Urbanization, Literacy, and Education

The United States in the year 2000 will probably see at least three gargantuan megalopolises. We have labeled these—only half-frivolously—"Boswash," "Chipitts," and "Sansan." Boswash identifies the megalopolis that will extend from Washington to Boston and contain almost one quarter of the American population (something under 80 million people). Chipitts, concentrated around the Great Lakes, may stretch from Chicago to Pittsburgh and north to Canada—thereby including Detroit, Toledo, Cleveland, Akron, Buffalo, and Rochester. This megalopolis seems likely to contain more than one eighth of the United States population (perhaps 40 million people or more). Sansan, a Pacific megalopolis that will presumably stretch from Santa Barbara (or even San Francisco) to San Diego, should contain more than one sixteenth of the population (perhaps 20 million people or more). These megalopolises will all be maritime. Boswash is on an extremely narrow strip of the North Atlantic coast; Chipitts, on Lake Erie and the southern and western shores of Lake Michigan and Lake Ontario; Sansan, on an even more narrow strip on the West Coast.

While all three will be recognizably American in culture, they will most likely be quite distinguishable sub-cultures. Sansan will presumably provide an informal "bar-b-q" culture, which has sometimes been called "wholesome degeneracy," and will include large and self-conscious, alienated, new left, "hip," and bohemian groups. Chipitts, recently the site of successful architectural and urban-renewal programs, will probably still have traces of both the "Bible-belt" and Carl Sandburg's "raw and lusty vitality." Boswash will, of course, be "cosmopolitan"—the home of New York liberals, Boston bankers, tired or creative intellectuals in publishing, entertainment, and the arts, and political Washington.

The three megalopolises should contain roughly one half of the total United States population, including the overwhelming majority of the most technologically and scientifically advanced, and prosperous intellectual and creative elements. Even Sansan will have a larger total income than all but five or six nations. Study of the United States in the year 2000 may largely be of Boswash, Chipitts, and Sansan.

Such structures will be typical of other countries as well. Thus, most of south-eastern England is likely to be one megalopolis, though in this case it may be called a conurbation. The Japanese will no doubt coin or borrow a word for the Tohyo-Osaka strip. Nevertheless, although between 80 and 90 percent of the developed world's population will be urbanized by the end of the century, most people will still live in more traditional urban areas. Suburbia, then as now, will be a special kind of low-density urban living, quite different from rural patterns.

Decreasing Importance of Primary Occupations

Closely related to current trends toward very large urban agglomerations are the declining importance of primary and secondary occupations, and the growing importance of what are normally called tertiary occupations, though we shall distinguish between tertiary and quaternary occupations. (The primary occupations are, of course, fishing, forestry, hunting, agriculture, and mining. Secondary occupations are concerned with processing the products of a primary occupation. A tertiary occupation is a service rendered mostly to primary and secondary occupations. Quaternary occupations render services mostly to tertiary occupations or to one another.) There will undoubtedly be a large shift to quaternary occupations. Since these occupations are heavily concentrated in the government, the professions, the non-profit private groups, and the like, this implies—in conjunction with other things—a shift from the private business enterprise as the major source of innovation, attention, and prominence in society. The lessening dependence on access to inexpensive or convenient raw materials (rather than a situation of desperate shortages of usable or available raw materials). This, in turn, will make many factors of geography and location less crucial for the nation as a whole.

II. SOME PERSPECTIVES ON CHANGE

A second way of looking at the future is to identify the relevant clusters of events that have marked off different time periods in man's history. One can thus seek to identify the constants of each time, the secular trend lines, and the "turning points" of an era. For our purpose we begin by considering what a "surprise-free" projection might have been like in 1900 or 1933.

The Year 1900

One world (Western-dominated), though with many unassimilated, traditional cultures

Industrial, colonial, or "protected" societies

Declining United Kingdom and France—rising Germany, United States, Russia, and Japan

Parliamentary government and Christianity

Basic feeling in almost all classes of the white race (and in many non-white) of optimism, security, progress, order; a belief in the physical and moral supremacy of Western culture, and in rational and moral domestic and foreign politics; and perhaps most important of all, a relative absence of guilt feelings.

Intellectual acceptance of the ideas of Adam Smith, Darwin, and the Enlightenment.

It is interesting to note that the only two non-Western countries that had successfully begun to industrialize by 1900, Japan and Russia, did so more to serve their national security than to increase their standard of living. Except possibly for Turkey, Iran, Thailand, Ethiopia, and some Latin American countries, every nation that had failed to industrialize by 1900 was either a colony, a protectorate, or a *de facto* dependency. Thus, successful industrialization was widely perceived as a matter of national independence, if not of national survival. Today these incentives are greatly reduced.

In 1900 it was clear that the two established powers of Western Europe—Great Britain and France—were losing in power relative to Germany, the United States, Japan, and Russia. One can think of Britain and France as "core" powers of the West, Germany (or at least Prussianized Germany) as "semi-peripheral," the United States as "fully peripheral," and Russia and Japan as either fully peripheral or new "mixtures."

The Parliamentary ideal was widely accepted, and Christianity was almost everywhere triumphant or on the rise in 1900. National self-satisfaction, optimism, and faith in the future of most Western or Westernized people are, to modern eyes, perhaps the most striking characteristics of the year 1900—and ones which were soon to disappear in the tragic futilities of World War I and its aftermath.

The Period 1900-1933

The first third of the twentieth century brought some surprises:

Russo-Japanese War
La belle époque (1901-13)
World War I—Europe devastated
Five major dynasties (Hohenzollern, Hapsburg, Manchu, Romanov, and Ottoman) dethroned
Emergence of the United States as leading world power
Loss of European (and democratic) morale and prestige
Rise of communism and the Soviet Union
Great Depression

Rise of fascist ideologies and various dictatorships

Impact of new intellectual concepts (those of Bohr, de Broglie, Einstein, Freud, and Schroedinger)

The Period 1933–1966

The next third of a century experienced still more unexpected changes and disturbing events:

Continued growth of fascism and communism

World War II–Europe again devastated

Mass murders and forced population movements on extraordinary scale before, during, and after World War II

Intense, nationalistic competition in the development and application of radically new technologies for peace and war

Decolonization

The Cold War and neutralism in the Third World

Emergence of two super-powers (U.S. and Soviet Union); five large powers (Japan, West Germany, France, China, United Kingdom); three intermediate powers (India, Italy, Canada)

Rise and decline of Italy, Canada, and India

Decline and re-emergence of Europe

Decline and re-emergence of Japan

Reunification and centralization of China

Post-Keynesian, post-Marxian, and perhaps post-communal and sophisticated "development" economics

Emergence of mass-consumption societies

"Second" industrial revolution

Chinese achieve nuclear status

In looking at this 66-year kaleidoscope, an Indian national is quoted as saying:

For us in Asia there have been two epochal events in this century. The first was Japan's defeat of Russia in 1905. The second was China's atom bomb. . . . Asia and India are learning the uses of power in the modern world. The first lesson was taught by Japan in 1905. It demonstrated that an Asian country could master the West's weapons and use them to defeat the West. The second lesson was taught by China. It demonstrated that Asia could equal the West even in advanced military technology.[4]

4. As quoted by Harrison E. Salisbury in *The New York Times,* 18 August 1966.

To Asia—or some Asians—the century began with a non-white nation's successfully beating a white nation on its own ground, thus proving that Europe's supremarcy was not necessarily permanent, and the second third of the century ended with the acquisition of nuclear weapons by a non-white nation. Both of these events were thought at the time to be of crucial and worldwide significance. It is said that during the first decade of the century there were Africans who did not know what Russia and Japan were, and yet knew that a non-white people had defeated a white nation.

Most of these items would probably not have been predicted by any individual or policy research group "speculating about the next 33 years" in either 1900 or 1933. Probably the great divide was World War I. Preceded by the thirteen years that are still known as *la belle époque*, these years were, for almost all the civilized world, an unprecedented era of sustained growth. While some of the period's glory has been dimmed by the passing of time and comparison with the post World War II era of growth, the years are still remembered nostalgically. Not only did World War I terminate *la belle époque*, but it shattered the moral and political structure of Europe. The effective triumph of democracy over despotism (or at least unenlightened monarchy) might have created a situation of high morale, but the cost of the war had been too high—particularly the seeming senselessness of many of the tactics, the moral effect of various revisionist and anti-war writers, and the disillusionment with the post-war settlement. The loss of European morale and prestige following 1918 was both grave and world-wide. The pessimism that seized the West was reflected in the popularity of such an author as Spengler. Although many Europeans expected the Russians or Asians to succeed to the West's power, an aberrant of Western culture, nazism, came perilously close to conquering all of Europe. While fasicsm and nazism are no doubt heretical to the Western tradition, they are products of Western culture and result from identifiable and historically continuous religious, ideological, cultural, and structural forces within Western societies—trends that were emphasized by the pessimism and frustration that resulted from World War I.

Despite the widespread belief that poverty creates instability and messianic totalitarian movements such as communism and fascism, the four nations closest to catching up with or passing the advanced industrial powers—Japan, Russia,[5] Germany, and Italy—provided the serious instability of the first half of this century. This may turn out to be the prototype of some possibilities in the next 66 years as well. While poverty and pre-industrial economies are not themselves indicia of stability, neither is industrialization or Westernization.

In the first third of the century, many new theories were, at least intellec-

5. From 1890 to 1914 (except for the years of the Russo-Japanese War—1904 and 1905), Russia grew in GNP at an average rate of 8 per cent and was thus, in some ways, undergoing a very successful industrialization.

tually, profoundly upsetting. The self-assured, rationalistic, moralistic, and mechanically-minded Victorians were told, in effect, that solid matter is mostly empty; that time is relative and that perfectly accurate clocks run at different speeds; that the world is governed by the probabilistic laws of wave mechanics, rather than by simple determinist "cause and effect" as suggested by Newtonian mechanics;[6] and, finally, that a good deal of what passes for rational behavior is actually motivated by unconscious impulses and feelings of a socially unacceptable or reprehensible character. What is most striking is that these radical shifts in *Weltanschauung* were managed with so little disruption.

Perhaps the most significant aspect of the middle third of the twentieth century has been the sustained economic growth achieved in the post World War II era. This has raised the real possibility of world-wide industrialization and of the emergence in more advanced industrial nations of what has been called a post-industrial culture. Some of this economic growth clearly derives from a growing sophistication in governmental economic policies. As even the "classical" economist Milton Friedman recently said, "We are all Keynesians today, and we are all post-Keynesians as well." If this were not true, and the post-war world had been marked by the same violent swings between prosperity and depression as the inter-war world, we would not now take such a sanguine view of future economic prospects. Today it is widely believed that, except possibly for China, almost all the communist and capitalist governments are coming to understand how to keep their economies reasonably stable and growing; both the capitalists and the Marxists are, in this sense, "revisionist."

While we reject the so-called convergence theory, in which it is argued that communism and capitalism will come to resemble each other so closely that they will be practically indistinguishable, it is clear that they are borrowing from each other—with the Marxists, however, doing more of the explicit borrowing. The current governmental success in economics and planning is a major cause of the emergence of mass-consumption societies in Western Europe, the United States, Japan, and Australia, and is one reason why such societies can be expected to emerge rapidly in the Soviet Union and Eastern Europe.

It is still an open question, however, whether the same thing can be achieved in communal societies (such as China is striving to be) and in the less developed nations generally. But at least two groups of less developed nations are now doing so well economically that it is reasonable to think of them as undergoing a kind of "second" industrial revolution. Thus, those parts of Europe that were

---

6. Of course, many physicists now believe that the world is deterministic, but that there are unknowable 'hidden variables'. In the early days of quantum mechanics and the uncertainty principle, however, many philosophers seized upon the latter as allowing for, or being identical with, free will and thus providing a belated and unexpected answer to the mechanists and determinists of the eighteenth and nineteenth centuries.

left behind by the industrial revolution, or which were "transplanted," are now beginning to catch up.

Even more impressive are the growth rates in the Sinic cultures of the world outside China (including Malaysia and perhaps the Philippines, but possibly not Thailand). These countries seem able to sustain growth rates of about 8 percent, except for the Philippines with 5 per cent. Wherever the Chinese and their culture have gone in the world, they have done well, except in China. Until about 1800, China was, except for periodic inter-regna, an eminent culture in the world. It may once again be coming out of an inter-regnum, but whether or not it will achieve its "normal" status must now be judged unlikely or at best an open question.

The second third of the twentieth century ended with two super-powers, five large powers, three intermediate powers, and about 120 small powers. This structure and hierarchy seems likely to characterize the next decade or two as well. In fact, listing Japan and West Germany as the two largest of the five "large" powers is even more appropriate for the mid-seventies than for today.

The Last Third of the Twentieth Century

Continuation of long-term multifold trend
Emergence of post-industrial society
World-wide capability for modern technology
Need for world-wide zoning ordinances and other restraints
High (1 to 10 per cent) growth rates in GNP *per capita*
Increasing emphasis on "meaning and purpose"
Much turmoil in the "new" and possibly in the industrializing nations
Some possibility for sustained "nativist," messianic, or other mass movements
Second rise of Japan
Some further rise of Europe and China
Emergence of new intermediate powers: Brazil, Mexico, Pakistan, Indonesia, East Germany, Egypt
Some decline (relative) of US and Soviet Union
A possible absence of stark "life and death" political and economic issues in the "old nations"

Except for the possible emergence of what we call, following Daniel Bell, the post-industrial society,[7] the listing is "surprise-free": It assumes the continuation of the multifold trend, but excludes precisely the kinds of dramatic or

---

7. For a discussion of some features of the post-industrial society as Daniel Bell has used the term, see his 'Notes on the post-industrial society,' *The Public Interest,* numbers 6 and 7 (Winter and Spring, 1967).

surprising events that dominated the first two thirds of the century. More specifically, the "surprise-free" projection rules out *major changes in the old nations* that might be caused by such possibilities as invasion and war; civil strife and revolution; famine and pestilence; despotism (persecution) and natural disaster; depression or economic stagnation; the development of "inexpensive" doomsday or near-doomsday machines and nuclear "six-gun" weapons technology; resurgence of communism or a revival of fascism along with a racial, North-South, rich-poor, East-West dichotomy; an economically dynamic China, with 10 per cent annual growth rate, and a politically dynamic US, Soviet Union, Japan, or Brazil; development of the UN or other world-wide organizations, and possible regional or other multinational organizations; new religious philosophies or other mass movements, and a psychologically upsetting impact of the new techniques, ideas, and philosophies.

If the basic long-term multifold trend continues or is accelerated during the next 33 years, and there are no surprising but not-impossible disruptions of the sort listed above, then a post-industrial society seems likely to develop in the affluent parts of the world.

In a post-industrial world, *per capita* income is about fifty times that in a pre-industrial society. Most "economic" activities are tertiary and quaternary rather than primary or secondary; business firms are, consequently, no longer the major source of innovation. There is an effective floor on income and welfare, and efficiency is not a primary consideration. There is widespread cybernation, a typical "doubling time" for social change of three to thirty years, and a common technological foundation for a world society. Work-oriented, achievement-oriented, advancement-oriented values and "national interest" values erode, and sensate, secular, humanistic, perhaps self-indulgent, criteria become central, as do the intellectual institutions. Continuing education is widespread, and there is rapid improvement in educational techniques.

III. THE STANDARD WORLD AND ITS CANONICAL VARIATIONS

So far, we have been dealing with trends or clusters of "traits." To make any significant assumptions, we would want to combine the most likely predictions into a more or less coherent whole and specify them in more detail. This we would call our least improbable "alternative future," or our "Standard World."

One problem of long-range speculation is that the curve of probabilities often seems very flat—that is, no particular course of events seems more likely than another. In order to avoid the dilemma of Buridan's ass, we must make almost arbitrary choices among equally interesting, important, and plausible possibilities. If we are to explore any predictions at all, we must to some extent "make them up." The most salient of the projections we can make is one that is "surprise-free"; nevertheless it would be very surprising if in any 33-year period the real world did not produce many political and technological surprises.

For the skeptical reader this "surprise-free" projection may be useful chiefly as a norm for comparison and disagreement. Although the "surprise-free" projection is similar in spirit to the "naïve projection" of the economist, which assumes a continuation of current tendencies, it is more complex because it includes the implications of whatever empirical and theoretical considerations affect current expectations. (For example, a "naïve projection of world population to 2000 would be about 7.2 billion, but our "surprise-free" projection would be 6.4 billion.)

Each of the major alternatives to the Standard World that we have constructed fits into one of three categories: more "integrated," more "inward-looking," or in greater "disarray." The models in these categories envisage, respectively:

1. A relatively peaceful, relatively prosperous world with a relatively high degree of consultation among nations, with arms control and political coordination or even integration among all, or almost all, the "major" or minor powers

2. Almost as peaceful and prosperous a world but with little arms control or general coordination

3. A relatively troubled and violent world, but one in which no large central wars have occurred

The following are eight cononical variations:

1. More integrated
   (a) Stability-oriented
   (b) Development-oriented

2. More inward-looking
   (a) With an eroded communist movement
   (b) With an eroded democratic morale and some communist dynamism
   (c) With a dynamic Europe or Japan

3. Greater disarray
   (a) With an eroded communist movement
   (b) With a dynamic communist movement and some erosion of democratic morale
   (c) With a dynamic Europe or Japan.

By focusing attention on each of the above possibilities in turn, we get a sense of comparative structures and of a range of possibilities, while remaining within or fairly close to the "surprise-free" projections. Yet it should be clear that only a Procrustean theory could attempt to define the next 10 to 15 years (much less the next 33) in terms of such single themes. The reality undoubtedly will be one in which one theme alternates with another, or in which there is a dialectical contention among political trends or open conflict. But for our standardized and canonical contexts (and for some but not all of the scenarios that illustrate them) we assume that there is little fluctuation from simple secular trends.

In these projections we assume that the ten major powers (which we have divided into the categories "super," "large," and "intermediate") develop more or less according to the figure below. One might have wanted to assume that the "Integrated World" develops more rapidly and with smaller disparities in income than the "Inward-Looking World," and that this in turn develops more rapidly than the "Disarray World." While this is reasonable, it is not by any means inevitable.

Figure 1 shows how the ten largest nations compared in GNP and population in 1965 (numerals in circles), and the points they seem most likely to reach by the year 2000 (numerals in ellipses). The numerals identifying each country are in the order of our "best estimate" for 2000 GNP, although the differences among Canada, Italy, and India are not significant. The ellipses indicate a range of reasonable uncertainty for each year-2000 projection. In 1965, for example, the US had a GNP of about $692 billion (by UN definition), a population of about 195 million, and a *per capita* GNP of about $3560. By the year 2000 its GNP could reach nearly $4000 billion (almost the top of the chart) with more than $15,000 *per capita* GNP; or, assuming a much lower growth rate, the GNP could be less than $1500 billion and GNP *per capita* under $5000. The range in population estimates is narrower. Our "best estimate" is for a GNP close to the top of the "reasonable range" and for a relatively moderate population growth. (Our report contains more detailed figures.) The ellipses for India and China slope backward because they are more likely to achieve relatively high GNP growth if they can limit population. We have labeled the GNP *per capita* groups in terms of the classes discussed above.

Finally, we separate the 135 nations of the world into two classes—"old" (about 55) and "new" (about 80). "Old" nations are those that have had a relatively continuous existence at least since World War I; "new" nations are for the most part post World War II creations of ancient countries recently emerged from colonial status. (Thus we consider West Germany to be an old nation; East Germany and China, newly integrated; Taiwan and India, newly independent; Egypt, new.) We assume—again in all worlds, and for the 1967–2000 period as a whole—the fulfillment of certain widespread current expectations of more or less sustained economic growth among all the major (and most minor) nations, and more or less sustained (but usually slackening) population growth.

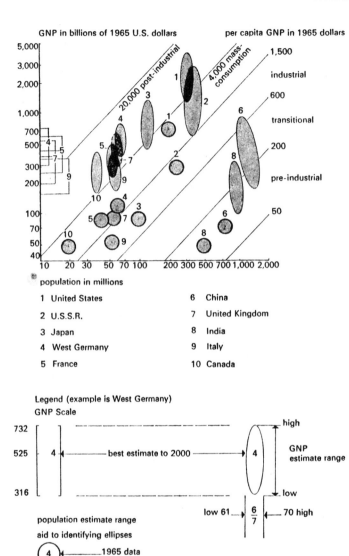

GNP in billions of 1965 U.S. dollars   per capita GNP in 1965 dollars

population in millions

1	United States	6	China
2	U.S.S.R.	7	United Kingdom
3	Japan	8	India
4	West Germany	9	Italy
5	France	10	Canada

Legend (example is West Germany)
GNP Scale

population estimate range

aid to identifying ellipses

Figure 1. "Surprise-free" projections for the ten major countries.

We also assume that except in periods of actual war or great crisis there will be freedom of the seas, with foreign commerce moving freely without explicit reliance on national naval or other military power. We assume that there will be few and minor frontier changes, if any, in the old nations, chiefly because of general conditions of political stability or inertia rather than because of the balance—or lack of balance—of local military situations. We assume that most of the old nations will not be called on to use military power to advance their national interests—at least in any simple or direct way. Obviously nations may none the less experience benefits (or disutilities) from military power—for example, from their ability implicitly or explicitly to protect (or threaten) various other nations. Some small nations may obtain security benefits (or disutilities) from having sizable national military forces—for example, from being a more valuable ally or feeling freer to accept or reject offers of protection by larger nations. But by and large, for *most* of the old nations and many of the new, national security is assumed to be "free"—derived from the general condition of stability rather than from a nation's own efforts.

Of course, this stability, if it exists or is to continue, will be maintained in part by the willingness of various nations, especially the US and the USSR, to intervene judiciously when situations arise that threaten the general equilibrium. Presumably the balance could be tipped by one of these nations trying either too hard or not hard enough—by intervening too readily in an attempt to control events or by failing to check forces tending to instability.

To go beyond the year 2000, we can speculate briefly on world society in the first third of the next century. We expect the rise of new powers—perhaps Japan, China, a European complex, Brazil, Mexico, or India. There will be new political, perhaps even "philosophical," issues, and a leveling-off or diminishing of some aspects of the basic long-term multifold trend, such as urbanization. The post-industrial and industrial worlds will have been largely realized, as will population control, arms control, and some kind of moderately stable international security arrangement, though probably not a "world government." In the industrializing world, disorder, ideology, and irrational movements will probably continue to play disruptive, though geographically confined roles. In the US and Western Europe, there will presumably be either a return to certain Hellenic or older European concepts of the good life, or an intensified alienation and search for identity, values, meaning, and purpose, a search made necessary and facilitated by the unprecedented affluence and permissiveness of the post-industrial economy.

Case History

In "Insurance Brokers' Stocks: A Defense Against Adversity" (*Fortune*, February 12, 1979), Alexander & Alexander Services Inc. (A&A) was shown to have had the highest average return on equity from 1975 to 1977 and the highest average annual growth in dividends from 1973 to 1978 among the five largest, publicly held insurance-brokerage firms in the United States. In its annual report for 1977, the firm's management stated, "There must be good, sound business reasons why Alexander & Alexander is now the second largest insurance brokerage, consulting, and actuarial firm in the world."

One of these sound business reasons is A&A's planning process. In April 1976, a study group under the leadership of A&A vice president Raymond Lynn Pfeister prepared a report, "The Strategic Planning Process for Alexander & Alexander Services Inc. and Subsidiaries." This report is reproduced here with editorial changes. Closely following the model presented in the preceding text, the report reviews A&A's present status and outlines its corporate objectives and goals. It considers various strategies that can be employed to achieve these objectives and evaluates the capabilities and the resources that are available. After the appropriate strategy is recommended, the steps needed to implement the decision are indicated. How the process should be monitored and coordinated is then described. Finally, the contingency mechanisms required for adaptive design alterations, adjustments, and revisions are presented.

Many case studies leave the reader wondering whether the plan worked. The A&A case study, however, is followed by an epilogue that evaluates the results of the proposed plan after several years. It reports which of the forecasts actually came to pass and which did not. In addition, it indicates how the plan is modified by changing conditions and presents the recurring and cyclical nature of the planning process.

The Authors

The Strategic Planning Process for Alexander & Alexander Services Inc. and Subsidiaries

Raymond Lynn Pfeister
Vice President
Alexander & Alexander Services Inc.

The study group has prepared and presents herewith a comprehensive strategy for Alexander & Alexander Services Inc. (A&A) and subsidiaries.

In order to draw conclusions relative to A&A's current corporate management and its philosophy, members of the study group interviewed various officers and executives of the firm. In addition, information needed for the study was obtained from internal records and from external sources such as *Standard & Poor's Industry Surveys, Moody's Bank and Financial Manual,* and *Value Line Investment Survey.* Further data were gleaned from such periodicals as the *Wall Street Journal, Wall Street Transcript, Insurance,* and *Business Week.*

The planning process is initiated by comparing present activities, objectives, goals, and decisionmaking policies to future expectations and constraints. This is done in light of available forecasts at both the detail and general level. The difference between the present activities and the desired future is the planning "gap." This gap is then viewed as the object of the plan.

The plan considers the synergy and capability profiles of various alternatives, including the possibility of diversification. Once all appraisals and considerations have been taken into account, a strategy is chosen.

A system to implement the plan is then delineated. To insure the optimal functioning of the strategy, concurrent monitoring and control techniques are discussed. Finally, since adaptability is the key to the superior functioning of a strategy, the possibility of periodic revisions during the life of the plan is considered.

Raymond Lynn Pfeister is an independent consultant, owner of the Pfeister Corporation (Arthur Treacher's Fish & Chips), and chairman and chief executive officer of Pfeister Barter Inc. (The New York Reciprocal Trade Exchange).

This process, as implemented by A&A through 1976, is outlined below.

STEP 1: A REVIEW OF ALEXANDER
& ALEXANDER SERVICES INC.

Status

A&A and its subsidiaries are engaged primarily in the following lines of business:

1. General insurance brokerage
2. Actuarial consulting
3. Employee-benefit communication

The firm negotiates and places casualty, property, and marine insurance with insurance companies for its clients. The types of casualty insurance handled are:

1. Legal liability
2. Workmen's compensation
3. Commercial and private-passenger automobile insurance and fidelity
4. Surety
5. Burglary

The types of property insurance handled are:

1. Physical damage
2. Interruption of business and extra expense due to perils such as fire and windstorm

The types of marine insurance handled are:

1. Inland marine and transportation
2. Ocean marine
3. Aircraft hull and liability

A&A provides additional services to clients in the process of placing property and liability insurance with insurance companies. A&A's high level of performance in this area differentiates it from its competitors. The services include:

1. Risk surveys and analyses
2. Loss control and cost studies
3. Claims and loss processing assistance
4. Marine average adjusting

5. Formulation of safety procedures and programs
6. Research and development in new insurance coverage and consultation on insurance programs

The other facet of A&A's general insurance brokerage business is life and various types of group insurance. The company designs, places, and services all forms of individual life and group life, accident and health, hospitalization and medical, and dental expense insurance programs. It also provides consulting services in connection with group insurance plans.

Actuarial consulting is a line of business in which A&A provides technical and consulting services primarily in connection with the design, establishment, and supervision of pension and similar employee-benefit plans. Services provided include:

1. Annual pension-cost calculations
2. Long-range projections of pension costs and pension-fund growth
3. Analyses of funding methods, investment performance, and related studies
4. The design of new employee-benefit programs and the establishment of funding arrangements
5. Assistance in labor negotiations with regard to benefit plans
6. Advice on coordination of existing employee-benefit plans following mergers and acquisitions
7. Assistance in international employee-benefit programs
8. Advice to clients with self-administered benefit plans

Benefacts Inc., a wholly owned subsidiary of A&A, is engaged in the organization's third major line of business—employee-benefit communication. Benefacts Inc. specializes in explaining to employees of clients the value of their respective employee-benefit plans. Other services provided include:

1. Analysis of client's employee-benefit program
2. Advice in the layout and design of individualized benefit reports to employees

A personal Benefacts report specifies dollar amounts of current and retirement benefits for the employee and his or her family. In addition, it enumerates social security and other statutory benefits.

General insurance brokerage revenue is largely generated via commissions. Actuarial consulting and employee benefit communication revenues are earned by service fees. In 1974, a cash-management program was inaugurated at A&A, which resulted in a significant generation of earnings. The program led to the improvement of investment income. Tables 1 through 3 summarize A&A's financial performance during 1970 through 1974.

Table 1. Revenues by source of revenues, Alexander & Alexander Services Inc.

	1974		1973		1972		1971		1970	
	($000)	%	($000)	%	($000)	%	($000)	%	($000)	%
General insurance brokerage										
Casualty, property, and marine	78,449	78.0	67,588	79.0	73,415	80.5	58,540	80.3	53,379	80.9
Life and group	8,157	8.1	7,634	8.9	7,014	8.9	6,593	9.1	5,192	7.9
Actuarial consulting	4,341	4.3	4,186	4.9	3,655	4.7	3,379	4.6	3,261	4.9
Employee benefit communication	4,736	4.7	3,581	4.1	2,996	3.8	2,463	3.4	2,342	3.5
Interest	3,392	3.4	1,634	1.9	633	0.8	719	1.0	1,112	1.7
Premium finance	864	0.9	527	0.6	321	0.4	194	0.3	34	–
Other	596	0.6	529	0.6	746	0.9	944	1.3	704	1.1
	100,535	100.0	85,679	100.0	88,780	100.0	72,832	100.0	66,024	100.0

Table 2. Financial Highlights, Alexander & Alexander Services Inc.

	1974	1973	1972	1971	1970
Sales ($000)	100,735	85,679	78,780	72,832	66,022
Annual growth (%)	17.6	8.8	8.0	10.3	
Pretax profits ($000)	19,136	16,251	13,707	12,133	10,478
Annual growth (%)	17.8	18.6	12.9	15.8	
Pretax profit (%)	19.0	19.0	17.4	16.6	15.9
Income taxes ($000)	9,799	8,293	6,791	6,260	5,476
Net income ($000)	9,337	7,958	6,916	5,873	5,002
Annual growth (%)	17.3	15.1	17.8	17.4	
Net income (%)	9.3	9.3	8.8	8.1	7.6
Earnings/share	$1.75	$1.50	$1.30	$1.11	$0.94
Annual growth (%)	16.7	15.4	17.1	18.1	
Cash dividend/share	$0.65	$0.45	$0.35	$0.345	$0.30
Annual growth (%)	44.4	28.6	1.4	15.0	
Cash flow <drain> ($000)	<9,736>	7,969	<1,799>	<2,017>	NA

NA = Not available.

Table 3. General Insurance Brokerage, Alexander & Alexander Services Inc.

	1974	1973	1972	1971	1970
Net income before taxes ($000)	14,831	12,886	11,373	10,135	8,029
Prorated income tax ($000)	7,564	6,572	5,775	4,885	4,175
Net income ($000)	7,267	6,314	5,598	5,250	3,854
Percent of total net income	77.8	79.3	80.9	89.4	77.1

Environment

A&A operates both in the United States and abroad. The economic environment cannot be separated from its social and political context. The United States is a country that encourages the entrepreneurial spirit. There is a pro-business bias in the United States that is stronger than that in all but a few other nations in the world.

There is a strong possibility that the United States Congress will pass a national health act. This would have an adverse effect upon A&A. Management, however, is sanguine about this possibility. It points out that in several Canadian provinces where A&A operates, such government-sponsored insurance exists and that actuarial consulting expanded there as a result. Moreover, management indicates that many salaried employees in Canada prefer to go to private hospitals, and thus, on balance, revenue has increased because of government health insurance. Top management believes that a similar scenario is likely in the United States.

Another political act in the United States that is potentially adverse to A&A is the passage of national workmen's compensation insurance. However, management does not foresee this occurring for at least 5 to 10 years. It believes that state governments will not yield their control of this field.

In order for A&A to act as an agent for an insurance company in a state, it is normally required to enter into an agency contract with the insurance company. In addition, certain A&A resident officers or employees must be formally designated as agents.

State laws also require insurance companies to be licensed before they are permitted to write insurance in that state. In certain situations, a company may wish to place insurance with an insurance company that is not admitted in a particular state. In such a case, the insurance may be placed, under certain circumstances, by one of the firm's offices in the particular state where the appropriate licenses are held.

In all states, insurance laws and regulations are subject to amendment or reinterpretation. Moreover, licensing authorities have broad discretionary authority over the granting, revocation, and renewal of licenses. Accordingly, the possibility exists that an organization may be precluded or temporarily suspended from continuing its business or otherwise penalized in a given state.

The strong consumerism of the 1960s has abated, and the insurance industry is no longer as threatened by its influence on regulatory bodies. Whether consumerism has waned temporarily is a serious question for the industry. However, rises in rates are being approved as insurance companies attempt to earn a profit on property/liability underwriting. A&A gains from such rate increases, since its revenues in this line of business are in the form of commissions.

A&A operates in all Western European countries except Norway, Sweden, Denmark, and Switzerland. However, except for Canada and Japan, it serves only American businesses internationally. Canada and Japan provide business environments that are closer to that found in the United States than in any other nations in the world. A&A is very wary of socialistic governments and egalitarian societies, for capitalism does not find friends in these locales.

The rising tide of a "new economic order" in Venezuela has made foreign insurance companies unwelcome there. In fact, within 3 years, all insurance companies in Venezuela will be nationalized.

Management Philosophy

The philosophy of A&A's management consists of five precepts dealing with both the conduct and the realm of the firm's business activities. These precepts are to be followed in the pursuit of A&A's stated financial performance objectives—namely, a steady annual earnings growth rate of 12% to 15% and a cash dividend equal to 45% to 55% of earnings. These precepts are:

1. Alexander & Alexander Services Inc. must grow.
2. This growth will be a result of mergers and acquisitions.
3. Alexander & Alexander Services Inc.'s growth will come from businesses closely allied to fields in which it currently operates.
4. Those lines of business that have demonstrated the highest growth rates during the past 5 years will be expanded.
5. The firm will actively pursue the marketing of innovative products. These products will complement those products currently being sold and will be marketed in the same marketplace.

Permeating these philosophical precepts is the spirit of fair play with customers. A&A's chief executive officer, Kenneth W. Soubrey, summed up this point of view succinctly when he stated, "We're careful not to be hoggish." Mr. Soubrey was alluding to the fact that while casualty insurance premiums increased 300% to 400% during 1969-1975. A&A cut back its commission rate "because we thought we weren't entitled to a 300% or 400% increase in income."

Review of Current Forecasts

A&A's current forecasts encompass both the external environment and the internal environment. Among the former, current forecasts exist for the international economy, the national economy, the insurance industry, the insurance brokerage and agency industries, government legislative and regulatory activity, and competition. Among the latter, forecasts exist for line-of-business volume, cost-reduction potential, acquisition activity, and personnel requirements.

A&A currently forecasts that inflation will continue to increase both in the United States and throughout the world. An international insurance broker such as A&A will benefit from an inflationary environment because commission income rises as rates rise and the increases in income will outpace the cost increases caused by inflation, according to Mr. Soubrey. In addition, A&A forecasts that large insurance firms will be raising rates to stop underwriting losses that are attributable to inflation. The firm also predicts that insurance companies will enact rate increases to overcome the ill effects of price wars and inflation that have occurred during the last few years.

A&A currently forecasts that the insurance brokerage industry will continue to witness the growth of the Big Five (Alexander & Alexander Services, Inc., Marsh & McLennan, Inc., Fred S. James & Co., Frank B. Hall & Co., Inc., and Johnson & Higgins) at the expense of smaller brokers. Because the large firms have national and international market coverage, they are better able to get coverage, make placements, and handle high-risk insurance at lower rates than regional brokers. A&A predicts that corporate business will continue to move to large national brokers because such brokers can afford to support the staff of experts that is necessary to service these clients.

Usually new business is taken away from small brokers; is is not taken away from direct writers or the other large brokers. Thus, A&A predicts that its growth rate and those of its major competitors will be comparable over the next 5 years. The market share of the Big Five is only 3% to 4%. However, it is growing gradually.

A&A believes that there will be no federal workmen's compensation plan in the next 5 years. However, the firm does predict that a national health act will be enacted. This will have a modest effect on A&A because currently the company does not derive a significant portion of its business from this kind of insurance. A&A believes that any adverse effects of such legislation will be offset by fees derived from consulting activities necessitated by this legislation. Mr. Soubrey cites A&A's experience with national health plans in various Canadian provinces. There, A&A has had a steady increase in its consulting work in group medical and hospital plans because companies still buy plans for employees who want to go to private hospitals.

A&A forecasts that the human resource management division will increase as a percentage total of A&A's business over the next 5 years. The year 1975 witnessed a spurt in the rate of growth in actuarial consulting and in group benefits due to pension reform legislation. More legislation in the pension area is predicted, and this will benefit Benefacts since small, trusteed pension plans are switching to thrift plans and insured plans to avoid the paperwork and reporting requirements under Employment Retirement Income Security Act (ERISA) of 1974. All other lines of business are expected to follow the revenue pattern of the last 5 years.

A&A forecasts that foreign corporations will be placing more insurance through brokers in Europe. Accordingly, the firm is building up its business in Europe.

Finally, the firm believes that it must attract good personnel in order to fully exploit the opportunities of the marketplace for the company's products. After all, the people are the product.

STEP 2: THE PRESENT

Present Activities

The key activities of A&A are:

1. national and international insurance brokerage
2. Benefacts, Inc.

The number of national offices has grown from 22 in 1969 to 55 in 1975. Joint venture operations are in effect in all Western European nations except Sweden, Norway, Denmark, and Switzerland. Joint ventures also exist in Brazil, Argentina, Uruguay, Mexico, Colombia, Australia, and South Africa. Currently, except in Canada and Japan, all customers in foreign countries are American corporations.

A&A has established the following corporate objectives:

1. International expansion
2. Domestic expansion
3. Increased market penetration
4. Productive employees

A&A has established the following corporate goals:

1. Increased profit margin. (Salaries and operating expenses will grow at a lower rate than revenues.)
2. Domestic expansion through acquisitions
3. Reduction of bad debts
4. Increased accounts receivable turnover rate
5. Increased investment income
6. Reduction of personnel costs from 60% to 54% over the next 5 years

A&A adheres to the following corporate policies:

1. Growth through acquisition.
2. All acquisitions are to be made via tax-free exchange of stock.
3. No diversification without synergy.
4. Earnings will never be diluted by merger.
5. Each account must be profitable.
6. Never promise earnings or any operational results to stockholders.

Domestic expansion is being pursued primarily via acquisition. This is true of all Big Five firms, and the competition is fierce. A&A maintains the following criteria for a successful acquisition candidate:

1. Professional competence.
2. Five-year growth record.
3. Geographical location is one where A&A is currently nonexistent or weak.
4. Acquisition must not dilute earnings.

All corporate objectives and goals are to be pursued within the policy constraints enumerated.

STEP 3: THE ALTERNATIVES

Current alternative areas of action will now be discussed. Expansion of the product-market scope through flood- and crop-loss coverage will be considered. Ways to increase A&A's competitive effectiveness against large banks and to gain competence in direct-marketing techniques will be reviewed.

Concentric diversification will be considered through the wholly owned subsidiary, Benefacts. This form of diversification expands the product-market scope while maintaining a connection between the current method of operation and the avenue of diversification chosen. It accommodates both internal expansion and acquisition. Specific areas for Benefacts would include automated payroll-processing services, employee stock-plan administration, and pension-plan administration.

Finally, adaptive planning possibilities will be considered in light of ERISA and the future national health-insurance proposals.

The underlying planning philosophy embodied in this presentation is that of adaptation, both active and passive. In developing alternative courses of action, A&A's objective is to generate planning that will create a desired future for the firm. In passive adaptation, the company changes its behavior to cope with a changing external environment. With active adaptation, the company changes its environment so that its present and future behavior are more effective.

In the following pages, several broad-based alternatives are presented, which reflect both types of adaptation.

Alternative 1

The first alternative action is to increase competition with the federal government in its actions to subsidize the cost of social problems that have not been soluble on a private-insurance basis. The federal government is a direct insurer of savings banks, commercial banks, credit unions, and crops. All of these are not in a totally federal province, however, because there is a competitive private market for crop and flood-loss coverage.

The insurance industry's participation in the national flood-insurance program will be increased as a result of the Flood Disaster Protection Act of 1973. However, the solution to the flood problem is not to insure against it but, to the largest extent possible, to prevent floods and flood damage by intelligent land use, laws, and flood-control projects. In lowering the risk of floods, the industry can profitably enter this market by offering affordable premiums while minimizing devastating payoffs on claims.

Insurance companies are seeking to share with the federal government a booming line of insurance—namely, insuring the nation's farm crops against all risks. At present, most of this insurance is written by the U.S. Department of Agriculture's Federal Crop Insurance Corporation (FCIC). In 1975, the government's volume grew to $73.6 million, up 36% from 1974 and double the volume of a decade ago.

That doesn't compare with private industry's crop-insurance premium volume of $315 million in 1975; however, private insurance is much more limited, mainly protecting farmers from crop losses caused by hail. Farmers are finding that complete crop insurance is becoming more and more important because of (1) inflation, and (2) an increasing number of lenders who are refusing to loan farmers money unless they can obtain more complete coverage.

Over the past 80 years, there have been several attempts by the industry to write all-risk crop insurance; the results have always been catastrophic. For example, in 1974 private insurers received $2.7 million in all-risk premiums, yet a drought caused them to pay out $13.3 million to farmers—a ratio of almost 500%. Another case in point is the "dust bowl" times of the 1930s. In contrast, the FCIC has operated for the past 35 years with a favorable ratio of payouts to premiums of 91%. Of course, the agency receives an annual government appropriation of $12 million and does not have to cover administrative costs from premiums paid by farmers.

Private insurers would like to share the crop-coverage market and are lobbying for legislation that would bring the government and industry together as partners, enabling the insurers to sell complete crop coverage and to pay the FCIC a premium to accept part of the liability (reinsurance). The Ford administration has proposed legislation that would permit the FCIC to accept large amounts of reinsurance. The administration believes that private insurers are in a better position than the government to assure widespread marketing of the coverage and to tailor insurance to an individual farmer's needs. Developing this alternative into an effective strategy can open a heretofore untapped market.

Alternative 2

The second alternative is to increase competitive effectiveness by (1) keeping big banks out of the insurance field, and (2) dealing with the threat of third-party marketing, a form of direct selling through prominent department stores and banking organizations.

Regarding (1), at issue is a Federal Reserve Board attitude that the insurance agency business is closely related to banking. If allowed to stand, this attitude would clear the way for bank-holding companies and other financial lending institutions to enter the insurance agency business. If making loans and writing insurance are combined under the direction of the lender, there will be an irrefutable pressure on the consumer. What is needed is continued support, via contributions, of the Producers Action Fund of the National Association of Insurance Agents. The fund will be used to continue financing legal and legislative actions necessary to protect independent agents and insurance brokers from unfair competition.

Regarding (2), in order to compete with direct marketing, agents and brokers will require training beyond a memorized pitch. They must provide a practical insurance service, know the product, and be able to convey its benefits and limitations in a highly professional manner. The cost of developing thoroughly trained, imaginative agents, which can run into tens of thousands of dollars, often exceeds their economic value to a small firm.

Therefore, in addition to continued training and development of a sales force that can compete with direct marketing, the acquisition and/or development of a subsidiary to engage in the business of direct marketing should be explored. In this manner, a second marketing method is available for breaking away from the one-way traditional form of marketing. There is a place for both the agency system and direct marketing (through third party) within the same organization. This gives the agency the best of both approaches.

Alternative 3

The third alternative is to expand human resources management (HRM) services to client firms via further development of Benefacts Inc. Clients' needs in personnel-related areas have skyrocketed in recent years, and it is becoming less possible to serve those needs properly on a piecemeal basis. HRM will enable A&A to offer those services on a systems-planning basis. The areas for expansion include the following alternatives:

1. Enter into competition with banks and data-processing service bureaus (e.g., ADP) for client firms' payroll processing, either through direct processing by Benefacts or the sale of packaged payroll-processing systems, depending upon the size of the client firms and the extent of their internal electronic data processing (EDP) capabilities.

2. Where consistent with the client firms' compensation management, assume the function of employee stock-plan administration, again depending on the client firms' internal data-processing capabilities.

3. Perform pension-plan administration functions for client firms in the capacity of a consultant rather than assume fiduciary responsibility for the plan's administration.

A data-base systems approach can be developed and adopted, in which the data required for A&A's current employee informations systems (EIS) can be expanded and organized for the services embodied in these three alternatives. The basic data organization and applications programs included in the system can be tailored to meet the client firms' needs.

Alternative 4

Within the existing framework of insurance brokerage service offered by A&A, the fourth alternative is to prepare for upcoming federal health and pension bills. These bills are expected to mean considerable refiguring and rewriting of insurance.

For instance, a national health-insurance plan would compel corporations to take a new look at their employee-benefit policies. Many authorities within the insurance industry believe that national health insurance would encourage those who can afford to purchase insurance through the private sector to do so. Pending legislation would meet this objective by providing for private insurance to assume coverage of "uninsurables" as a cost of operation, while the government would subsidize insurance for those unable to afford it. The industry should view a national plan as an opportunity to provide creative input and direction to any pending insurance legislation.

The Employee Retirement Income Security Act (1974) is so complex that businesses are having trouble adjusting to it. This situation offers A&S the opportunity to expand its consulting activities, possibly through Benefacts.

STEP 4: THE FUTURE

We now consider A&A's future growth objectives, expectations, and constraints. This will encompass predicting the further possibilities and movements of anti-trust exemptions, rate competition, crop-loss coverage, and the impact of social and demographic changes.

The insurance brokerage business entails considerably more than just the placing of insurance. Each major firm has specialists and consultants to provide specific services to clients. They conduct risk surveys to determine where and how much insurance is needed; recommend safety measures to cut hazards found in their clients' plants or in other facilities; and assist in processing claims for loss. For insurance companies, they may even arrange reinsurance where the risk exposure is great.

Although the insurance-related services are most important, the fast-growing brokers are nevertheless broadening their horizons. Marlennan Corp., kingpin of the insurance brokerage business, has through its Marsh & McClennan subsidiary, widened its range of services by acquiring real-estate consulting, computer management, money management, and investment advisory services. Its smaller rivals have been ambitiously acquiring stakes in actuarial consulting by establishing employee-benefit plans, engaging in estate planning, and offering mutual funds.

Clearly, an industry that can package so many different types of insurance for varying types of corporate risk is flexible enough to cash in on new trends of the types discussed under Step 3.

A major development that could have significant impact on the insurance brokerage industry is the recurrent movement to end its antitrust immunity. Thirty years ago, the 1945 McCarran-Ferguson Act gave the insurance business a broad exemption from the federal antitrust laws, leaving it up to the states to regulate the industry.

The antitrusters hope that ending the antitrust immunity of the insurance business will cause more competition in terms of rates and the kinds of policies offered. Seventeen states, including Illinois and California, allow companies to set any rates they want, and competition in those states is brisk. However, many other state commissioners generally fear that more rate competition might lead to premiums that are actuarially unsound.

The repeal bill also proposes prohibiting the setting of minimum prices for insurance by state law or regulation. This will have far-reaching effects on the mass merchandising of insurance. In addition, it will give the insurance companies the option of fully passing along to the insureds the associated underwriting cost savings.

Regarding rate competition, although brokers are engaged by buyers of insurance, they are nonetheless usually paid a percentage of the premium by the underwriter. The tremendous competition in the past 3 years among the underwriters who do the actual insuring has reduced premiums and yielded lower commissions for the brokers. Although prices remain low, there are signs that the bottom has been reached and could reverse in the future (during the next 5 years) because of insurance carriers' financially poor results.

In addition, should the pace of inflation continue to abate, the brokers' growth rate would be adversely affected. This is because inflation prompts greater coverage to match increasing replacement costs. On the other hand, the domestic population has a mounting inclination to sue. Thus, corporate insurance is a necessity, with new claims arising out of suits by environmental and consumer groups. Therefore, coverage will surely grow. In addition, brokers who specialize in hard-to-get insurance and in loss prevention (helping corporations to lower their premium bills) will be in a position to do well.

A rise in the interest rates, which is expected to be concomitant with national economic recovery, should cushion lower commissions if the McCarran-Ferguson Act is repealed or modified, which would lead to another bout of rate competition. Brokers usually place money received from insureds in certificates of deposit or Treasury bills before paying the underwriter; then they collect the interest. A&A, which had interest income of $1.6 million in 1973, expects this source of income to continue to increase during the next 5 years.

The high cost of energy threatens the food-producing efficiency of the United States. At the same time, the weather has taken a sharp turn for the worse, perhaps as part of a long-term cycle. Some weather experts believe that the American farm belt is in the early stages of a long drought. Some believe that temperatures in the northern temperate zones are cooling, which will produce frequent frosts and shorter growing seasons. Even if the current weather is normal, experts say that Mother Nature was unusually bountiful during the 1960s, when there were no major weather-caused crop failures. Weather historians quote the odds against such a decade at 10,000 to 1! However, statisticians generally believe that each good year just increases the probability of bad ones occurring in the future.

The independent agency and brokerage system can be a leader in the fast-developing market for commercial group insurance buyers if it guarantees that each group member will be professionally serviced. It is estimated that this market will reach $30 billion by the end of this decade. Because commercial-group marketing combines expense savings and the opportunity for more effective loss control, it is estimated that by 1980 more than 25% of the $30 billion in commercial lines business on the market will be written under group or mass-marketing plans.

Regarding a national health-insurance system, it is expected that such a system would include a specified marketing approach that fully utilizes the existing private-insurance-producer force, which would be compensated at historic commission rates for its services.

The probable impact of social and demographic changes on pensions was outlined by Charles Watson of the Wyatt Co. at a pension meeting held by the Society of Actuaries and the Conference of Actuaries in Public Practice. He predicted that the following factors will influence the development of pension plans in the future:

1. Corporate size will continue to spread.

2. A greater share of resources and work force will be applied to services rather than production.

3. More workers will be salaried rather than hourly.

4. More workers will become unionized, including supervisory employees.

5. Employees will wish to have more choice and control over their work environment.

6. Career patterns will have greater mobility and variety.

7. Individuals will show an increased fondness for risk aversion-avoidance of, and protection against, uncertainty.

8. The trend toward longer years of schooling will persist.

9. Women will become increasingly important in the work force, and there will be increased effort to eliminate sex discrimination.

10. Mortality rates will continue to decline, even at higher ages.

11. Fertility rates may continue at a low level, perhaps even decreasing population size.

As a result of these social and demographic changes, Mr. Watson plotted the characteristics of the "ultimate" pension situation:

1. With the spread of corporatism, there will be a concomitant spread of supplementary pension plans, provided that Social Security increases do not preempt this expansion.
2. Because of the increasing convergence of the contractual employment position of all workers, there will typically be one plan covering most types of workers, or perhaps separate but identical plans covering different classifications.
3. Benefits will be based on compensation and as close to final compensation as possible.
4. Benefits will be integrated with governmental benefits to the fullest extent possible.
5. The retirement age will become more flexible.
6. Death and disability benefits will be most important and will be provided as part of a unified package.
7. All pension benefits will be adjusted to reflect increases in the cost of living.
8. Increased mobility, combined with desires for benefit security, will lead to earlier participation and improved vesting. Pensions will be portable.
9. The decline of fertility rates, combined with increased longevity and late entry into the labor force, will mean that the work force will be composed of a decreasing proportion of the total population, despite some increases in female participation.
10. Per capita productivity, measured in the traditional way, cannot be expected to increase markedly or at historical rates.

The foregoing provides the insurance brokerage industry with greater administrative participation in pensions if the industry adapts to these changes.

STEP 5: CAPABILITIES

Synergy, which is a major ingredient of A&A's strategic decision process, is mainly concerned with the compatibility of a firm with its new entries or acquisitions. In business literature, synergy is often referred to as the "2 + 2 = 5 effect," which denotes that the combined performance of the various components of a system is greater than the sum of the individual performances of components.

In order to forecast a synergistic effect, a firm must take three steps:

1. Evaluate the strengths and weaknesses within the firm.
2. Derive synergy characteristics that the firm can use to seek new opportunities.

3. Measure the synergy potential between the firm and its prospective acquisitions.

The concept of synergy can be described in relatively simple mathematical terms. Assume that each component of a firm contributes to the overall profitability. The annual rate of return for each component can be expressed as

$$R = \frac{r - e}{i}$$

where R = annual rate of return
  r = annual operating revenue for each component
  e = annual operating expenses for each component
  i = average investment put into each component

That is, the annual return on investment from each component of a firm is equal to the difference between annual operating revenues and expenses divided by the average investment. This expression can be obtained for all the components of the firm, assuming that they are unrelated. Now, the total return on the investment for the firm as a whole is

$$R_t = \frac{r_t - e_t}{i_t}$$

where t stands for the sum of contributions made by all the components.

This formula holds as long as the revenues, the operating expenses, and the investments are unrelated. This is true in a firm like A&A in which there is no interaction between operating units. For instance, A&A is presently operating through eight geographical regions in the United States, each of which is headed by a director who operates independently and autonomously while subject to the administrative goals and procedures of A&A.

A company's total profitability can be obtained by summing up the various components. For instance, A&A's executive committee receives monthly financial statements from each regional office, from which it determines the company's overall progress and evaluates individual performances.

A large firm with the same total revenue as a number of small firms combined can operate at a cost lower than the sum of the operating costs for the small firms. Likewise, a large firm can make a lower investment than the sum of the investments made by individual firms and generate the same total revenue. As a result, the potential rate of return for a large firm is higher than the composite return obtained by a number of independent firms, the dollar volume being equal for both. If the level of investment remains the same, a larger firm can usually realize higher revenues and lower expenses than several individual firms taken together.

The synergistic effect is far-reaching. In selecting new projects and new acquisitions, A&A takes great care to optimize the synergistic effect and is highly successful in doing so. A&A has thus been able to gain a larger share of the insurance and industrial markets than its competitors. For example, take Benefacts. Today, A&A has many competitors in the preparation of employee reports, yet A&A has thus far prepared more employee reports than all of its competitors combined. This year, more than 2.5 million employees in 400 companies—about 3% of the entire American work force—will receive Benefacts reports.

Regarding the rate of return, several types of synergy can be categorized within A&A: sales, operating, investment, and management.

Sales Synergy

Sales synergy can occur when A&A uses common sales administration for its various departments (property, casualty, marine, life, and group) and divisions. Common sales promotion and advertising, combined with A&A's past reputation and its present stance as one of the largest insurance brokerage and consulting firms in the world, can certainly multiply the productivity of the sales force and increase profitability for the same dollar amount as would be spent serving servicing each component individually.

Operating Synergy

Operating synergy can result from the joint use of facilities and personnel. As a large national firm serving business and industry, A&A maintains a large staff of safety specialists and loss-control engineers who make suggestions and prevent losses where possible.

Investment Synergy

Investment synergy can be brought about by A&A's research-and-development program. Through more than 80 years of operation, A&A has acquired experience and knowledge of insurance and industry markets. Through its Anistics division which is equipped with computerized programs, A&A has been able to predict patterns of change in the field of risk and loss and to come up with a funding method. In addition, as A&A makes additional acquisitions, its premium volume increases.

Management Synergy

Management synergy is also an important contributor to synergistic effects; it can be strong or weak, positive or negative. Obviously, management in different fields will encounter different problems. If a newly acquired area is unfamiliar to a firm, not only will its synergy be weak, but there may be negative synergy at times. On the other hand, if management finds upon entering a new field, that the new problems are similar and related to what it has faced before, it will be able to provide subtle guidance forcefully and effectively. Consequently, synergy will be strong, and profitability will increase.

Whether the synergistic effects will materialize depends upon the degree and manner in which the newly acquired area is harmoniously integrated into the present organization. The ambitious acquisition program at A&A serves as a fine example. With its highly sophisticated electronic data-processing center in Baltimore, Maryland, A&A has been able to integrate new areas into its system easily and quickly, while remaining fully competitive in its own field.

There are relatively few firms that have pursued acquisitions as aggressively and successfully as A&A. According to recent financial reports, A&A has marked its 26th consecutive quarterly increase in revenues and earnings since going public in 1969. In fact, few firms have made progress with such speed and consistency.

The reasons for A&A's unusual success are not hard to find. Almost all of the acquisitions made by A&A fall into two categories:

1. Insurance agencies and brokerage firms
2. Firms very closely related to the insurance business

Because A&A knows the insurance field, strong synergy is likely to result from such acquisitions.

Since 1970, A&A has acquired some 80 insurance agencies and brokerage firms. In 1969, when A&A went public, it had offices in 18 American cities. Today, it has offices in 54 American cities.

Synergy Measurement

Synergy can be measured in two separate ways:

1. By measuring the expenses to the firm from a joint operation and by keeping the revenue fixed
2. By measuring the increase in revenue and by keeping the level of investment fixed

In general, the acquisition of a new area will go through two successive phases, start-up and operating. During the start-up phase, the effects of positive synergy are seen in dollar and time savings. Although the expenses associated with start-up are one-time expenses, they are not capitalized, but are charged to operating expenses during the start-up period. They are not easy to estimate, for many of the factors are not apparent prior to start-up. Therefore, capital investment theory cannot be used to calculate marginal cash flow.

If a firm has the knowledge, skills, and resources to meet the requirements of the new area, there would be positive synergy. On the other hand, negative synergy and diseconomy could result in the parent firm, if the acquired area differed significantly from that firm. Since the firms acquired by A&A are very similar to A&A in structure and function, the company no longer incurs extra operating expenses during the start-up stage and therefore is not put at a disadvantage; thus, A&A has positive synergy.

In the operating stage, two types of expenses are incurred:

1. Operating expenses
2. Investment required to support the operation

Here, two advantages are involved in producing synergy. One advantage is the interaction between total volume and expenses. As the total volume is increased, operating costs per unit are lowered. The other advantage is the scattering of overhead expenses over a number of areas.

It should be noted, however, that the effects of synergy are symmetric. Thus while the parent firm offers benefits to the newly acquired firm, it will also receive benefits in return.

The mutual contributions of existing capacities, skills, personnel, and resources can stimulate growth and bring about prosperity, which otherwise might not take place. Synergy is an excellent way to accelerate growth without additional major investments. Many examples can be given. In March 1975, A&A merged with Shand, Morahan & Co. of Evanston, Illinois, which specializes in insurance underwriting management. This firm will bring in additional revenue of $2 million annually. The anticipated merger with ECCO Insurance Agency in Houston, Texas, will add nearly $3 million of revenue annually and will greatly strengthen A&A's Houston office. It should be pointed out that, in these acquisitions, A&A did not dilute its earnings and both mergers were treated as poolings of interests.

STEP 6: THE STRATEGIES

Strategy is defined as a rule for decisionmaking in business, whereas objectives are what a firm sets out to achieve. The concept of a firm's business is described by strategy and objectives taken together. They specify amount, area, and direction of growth, and direction for opportunity. Strategy is necessary because, to seek new opportunities, a firm needs a well-defined direction. Moreover, it is advantageous to a firm to find new entries with strong competitive potential. There are four criteria of strategy: scope, growth vector, competitive advantage, and synergy.

As we shall see, these four criteria are mutually complementary rather than mutually exclusive.

Scope

The scope specifies the target that A&A is pursuing and for which common statistics and forecasts are available. Too broad or too numerous a scope can diminish the payoff from the strategy.

Growth Vector

The growth vector indicates the direction in which A&A is expanding. It indicates that direction both within and outside A&A. Four of the most common expansion areas are:

1. *Market penetration* denotes a growth direction through the increase of market volume for the present market. Generally, if volume can be added through a type of diversification, the result will be quite positive in both the new and old business.

2. *Market development* seeks new uses, users, or both for the firm's products. In market development, A&A aims to (1) expand its geographical base by entering cities where it has not had any office and (2) strengthen its existing offices.

3. *Product development* seeks new products to replace the current ones. A&A aims to acquire firms that possess particular expertise in certain specialized areas in order to round out services to its existing and prospective clients.

4. *Diversification* is distinctive because both the products and markets are new to the firm.

The Competitive Advantage

The competitive advantage seeks to identify particular quantities of an individual area that will give A&A a better comparative stance. Thus, A&A always seeks acquisitions that give it a commanding market position.

Synergy

Synergy is needed in a rapidly growing area that is subject to keen competition and constant change. It can be both aggressive and defensive. It can be aggressive in the sense that A&A's new entries can use its highly competitive stance in the field. For instance, A&A has the best talent and the best teamwork in the industry. Moreover, A&A's representatives are keenly aware of their responsibility to bring new ideas and methods to its clients and prospects. On the other hand, synergy can be defensive in the sense that a new entry supplies a key competence that A&A lacks.

Diversification Strategy

A&A has a diversification strategy that is supported by the following:

1. A&A is well equipped to search for new opportunities, both inside and outside the firm. A&A's research and development has established guidelines and procedures for judging diversification opportunities, which provide the acquisition department with direction. Thus, the firm does not passively await opportunities to surface, but rather actively pursues them.

2. With its direction set, the staff of A&A can analyze different situations with speed and accuracy, to identify profitable opportunities, and to decide whether the opportunity is a rare one and whether better opportunities are likely to surface in the future. As a result, A&A is able to avoid making bad decisions, to minimize irrational risks, and to avoid losses.

3. Most importantly, A&A has the ability to anticipate strategic change. No firm can consider itself immune to threats of product obsolescence and saturation of demand. Thus, whether to concentrate on strategy is not the issue, but rather how and to what extent. At A&A, close observation of both the threats and opportunities has become a continual process.

4. Whether to diversify is a major decision in the development of a firm. In most firms, strategy does not remain static, but rather is dynamic in response to changes in environment. A&A, being fully aware of upcoming competition, challenges, and drastic changes, is able to cope with them at any time.

By adopting a strategy of concentric diversification, A&A could accomplish the following:

1. Although more subtle than other types of diversification, concentric diversification implies a structural and functional connection between the current method of operation and the avenue of diversification chosen. *Structure* is the way the firm is organized. *Function* refers to the technology used. As a general rule, synergy is strong where technology is related, but is weak, even negative at times, where technology is unrelated. By definition concentric diversification has plenty of synergistic effect, and it can be more profitable and less risky because of this synergy. This occurs because the new entry, for the most part, is closely related to the parent and is integrated into the parent organization. In the past, A&A quickly and easily assimilated its new entries.

2. Concentric diversification can render stability and flexibility to the firm through acquisitions and thereby increase overall profitability.

3. As a consequence of concentric diversification, the combined performance can uplift A&A's competitiveness without diluting its earnings. This effect has been evidenced by the many acquisitions made by A&A since 1970. A&A prefers to make acquisitions through an exchange of stock. Only infrequently

does A&A use cash payment or deferred arrangements. In considering these arrangements, however, A&A follows the hard-and-fast rule of never diluting its earnings in the year of the merger.

4. In the presence of synergy, the joint operation of a concentric firm can in general be far better off than it might have been if the new entries operated as independent entities. The concentric firm can therefore achieve competitive advantage over independent entities.

5. A concentric firm like A&A can have better earnings and better access to capital markets. As A&A makes additional acquisitions, its premium volume increases. As a result of the many mergers it made in the past several years, A&A set up a sophisticated system that allows it to draw advance balances from various banks into a primary bank on a daily basis. The funds can be invested on a very short-term basis, even overnight or on weekends. Since going public in 1969, A&A has maintained a growth in earnings per share every year of approximately 15%.

6. During periods of inflation, a concentric firm can have stronger stamina than do other firms. While no business is inflation-proof, A&A does have some built-in protection. In times of inflation, as property values increase, payrolls will increase too, which leads to the increase of both casualty and property premiums.

7. The concentric firm can build on a record of successful operation and evidence of competent management in an acquisition. Prior to a merger, the first thing A&A looks for is whether an entry's personnel are true professionals and whether the new entry itself is compatible. A&A looks not only at the past growth pattern of an entry, but also at the projected growth pattern for the future. A report is prepared that includes the following data:

Employees: age, duties, recommendations, years of service
Personnel policies: employee benefits, travel and promotional, advertising
Largest account: when produced, commission volume, how secure
Collections of receivables: analysis of bad debts

The last 10 years have been marked by a great merger movement in the business sector. In fact, the number of mergers that took place during 1970 was about 10 times that which occurred in 1950. In the 5 years from 1965 through 1969, the number of mergers increased by almost 3 times. Since 1970, for instance, A&A has made some 80 acquisitions. Recently, however, there has been a general decrease in the size of the transaction. This is probably due to the increasing interest of the U. S. Department of Justice in the growth of mergers, which substantially reduced the number of mergers among large firms. Over the last 2 or 3 years, the size of the average agency acquired by A&A has been smaller than in previous years.

Acquisition Planning

In planning of acquisitions, the planner faces certain special problems, all of which require an evaluation of the total performance of the going concern. The evaluation is quite difficult because it has to rely upon estimates of profitability and upon forecasts of future income. Thus, it is primarily complicated and sophisticated guesswork. Not only are there many different methods of evaluation, but variations in the use of each method may lead to widely different results. In the evaluation of acquisitions, three main areas should be noted and distinguished:

1. Exchange of new for existing common stock within a single firm
2. Promotion of a new entry by purchase of an existing business
3. Acquisition of one company by another

In making an acquisition, a firm may either purchase the assets of an existing business, as is the usual practice of A&A, or acquire the necessary assets piecemeal to form an entirely new firm. Although the basic evaluation process is the same in either case, there are additional considerations related to the method of acquiring a new business. Acquisition by purchasing an existing business has both advantages and disadvantages. Among the advantages are:

1. It will enable the firm to get off to a fast start
2. It will provide the firm with customers and a mix of resources with which to work
3. With this existing organization, a firm can immediately begin to realize a return on its investment

On the other hand, many businesses are offered for sale that are doomed to fail. For example, many businesses that are under poor management or in poor locations are passed from one hand to another. In the long run, they all join the statistics of business failures.

There are several steps involved in the evaluation of acquisitions. The first step is to make an exhaustive survey of the company's financial history to be sure that the income is accurately and fairly reported. The second step is to determine whether these earnings can continue at the same rate in the future. In addition, there are many questions that require quick answers.

1. What resources are used in the business?
2. How is the internal organization set up?
3. What is the relationship between the key officers and labor within the business?
4. What is the relationship of the business with its customers?

5. What do bankers think of the business prospects? Will they be willing to extend credit?

STEP 7: THE APPRAISAL

At this point in the analysis, a strategy has been formulated for A&A: concentric diversification. The question now is whether this is its best strategy. To find the answer, the following model or formula is used:

$$\text{Objectives} - \text{Current Forecasts} = \text{Total Gap}$$

The objectives of A&A are the following:

1. Maintain present growth rate
2. Expand internally
3. Increase the management resource
4. Cut down potentially bad debts
5. Continue to search for and to make good acquisitions

Following are the current forecasts for A&A:

- If inflation continues, large insurance companies such as A&A will benefit because they will increase their rates and commissions.
- In 1973, A&A's interest income increased to $1.6 million. We expect this trend to continue for A&A for the next 5 years.
- A&A foresees greater usage of Benefacts. There is a good chance of concentric diversification here.
- A&A will experience a larger rate of growth in actuarial consulting and group benefits.
- A&A will have the same growth rate as its five major competitors for the next 5 years.

In comparing objectives and current forecasts, it can be seen that they are compatible in both internal expansion and concentric diversification. Therefore, no gap exists between them.

Gap-Closing Process

If a gap did exist between objectives and current forecasts, A&A would have to revise its objectives to align them with current forecasts. Then an evaluation of A&A's strengths and weaknesses would be required. For example, an obvious strength of A&A is its cash-management program.

Once the strengths and weaknesses are measured, the A&A competitive profile is generated. This will determine the areas in the industry in which A&A is either outstanding or deficient.

Then the industry is analyzed in terms of competition. Next, the industry's economic growth potential is estimated. To do so, it is necessary to examine trends in growth, profitability, and market shares.

At this point, the original forecast would be reexamined and adjusted to reflect these analyses. After reevaluating the revised forecasts, the general model is again applied. If a gap between objectives and forecasts still remains, the revised forecasts must be modified again.

Since A&A has both a growth rate and profit rate of over 15% annually, there is not much need for its involvement in outside industries. This is not to say, however, that A&A will always achieve such rates of return. Therefore, an alternate or backup strategy of horizontal diversification should be considered. A&A should look for new products to market with its present organization. In the future, when concentric diversification on current products levels off, these new products can pick up the slack. One of A&A's prime objectives should be to remain active in the acquisition of new products.

One approach to this objective might be through Benefacts. Benefacts currently sells a software package for communication purposes. This software package contains regional employee data, personnel data, and educational data. Since A&A already has the computer facility, and the systems, and application programmers, it could develop new marketable software systems. For example, A&A's account executives represent all products of A&A and its subsidiaries. When the account executives go to major corporations to sell insurance, they are frequently asked by top executives of these corporations if A&A has a software payroll system or a software accounting system.

A&A (including Benefacts) does not now have these software packages although such are marketed by competitors. For minimal cash outlay, A&A could develop a more sophisticated payroll package and accounting package, which would be more marketable than current packages. The only disadvantage is that A&A would be a latecomer to the field. However, if Benefacts' software experts create a more sophisticated payroll system and accounting system, marketability of both systems would, in the long run, surpass that of Benefacts' competitors.

This strategy would be considered concentric diversification for Benefacts and also would be considered horizontal diversification for A&A. In conclusion, the possibilities are there for A&A strategy of concentric diversification potentially supported by horizontal diversification. The model holds; the objectives and forecasts balance.

STEP 8: IMPLEMENTATION

Now that a particular strategy has been chosen, it must be implemented. Implementation can be facilitated by the following procedure:

1. Identify physical and mental tasks that have to be done.
2. Group tasks into jobs that can be done well, and assign responsibility for doing them to some individual or group.
3. Provide workers at all levels with
   a. information and other resources necessary for doing their jobs as effectively as possible, including evaluation of their actual performance
   b. measures of performance that are compatible with organizational objectives and goals.
   c. motivation for performing as well as they can by using techniques such as incentive systems.

For A&A, this procedure translates into five specific phases.

Identifying Managerial Decisions

The first phase identifies the managerial decisions that are required to operate A&A and other relationships between them by answering the following questions:

1. Whose needs or desires, external to A&A, does A&A try to satisfy?
2. How will these needs or desires be communicated to A&A?
3. How is the needed information recorded and transmitted to others in the organization?

Since A&A has gone public, the external needs A&A tries to satisfy are, obviously, those of its stockholders. These needs are communicated to the board by the stockholders at the annual meeting; it will be up to the executives of A&A to communicate with the rest of the organization.

Model Construction

The second phase is model construction. Three types of situations can occur during the planning of a model:

1. A model of the decision involved can be developed, and a solution can be found. The decisions that can be modeled and solved are usually solved by management or computer. Examples of areas where decisions can be implemented into a model and solved include purchasing, production, and distribution.
2. A model of the decision involved can be developed, but a solution cannot be found. In this situation, no optimal solution can be found. Therefore, solutions must come from managers or others.
3. A model of the decision involved cannot be developed because of lack of time, resources, or knowledge. This requires details of how a man-

ager goes about making the decision. In some situations, model building cannot be used at all, and therefore old methods to solve these situations must be used.

Information Requirements and Job Formulation

The third phase for development for implementation is information requirements. There are basically three areas of concern:

1. Uncontrolled variables in decision modes, which specify what information is required for the decisions that are modeled.
2. Where models are not available, A&A's management must decide which information is relevant.
3. Information through voice communication must be provided.

The fourth phase encompasses jobs and decisions. We now have identified decisions and their informational requirements. These decisions should be put together to formulate jobs.

Measures and Modifications

The fifth phase is measures and modifications. Measures and modifications must be developed for each decisionmaker. Then the decisionmaker must evaluate the situation for consistency with overall objectives. Substandard measurement demands modification.

Completion of the five phases allows A&A to proceed with implementing its strategy.

STEP 9: CONTROLS

This section deals with the methods A&A uses for developing operating and staff policies and procedures.

Corporate policies present guidelines for action in very general terms. However, more detailed guidelines or procedures will be needed within the various staff and operating areas. These specific operating and staff procedures are designed to achieve the subobjective of the individual area for which they are written. They are an extension of the general policies and thereby help to insure action that will be consistent with the overall company planning. The individual planning at each level of management within the company should then be reviewed by the next higher level of management until all the individual plans are coordinated and integrated within the overall comprehensive company plan. Effective planning depends on the process of integrating the individual operating and staff plans, and reviewing and revising them in the light of their effect on other company plans and on company profits.

Coordinating the Plan

Coordinating and integrating individual operating and staff plans begin with assigning the responsibility to an executive or an executive planning group. The executive or group must then communicate to all levels of management the essential strategic planning information, along with the instructions on what their individual plans require. Lower-level managers must be encouraged to participate so that the comprehensive plan developed will be both realistic and well integrated. Top management's support is required. Appropriate rewards should be given to those who plan well. Finally, a strong administrator is necessary if company managers are to take the planning effort seriously.

The job of coordination and integration does not end with issuing instructions and communicating strategic planning information. All operating managers do not have the same background, training, and perspective, and thus a considerable amount of additional formal and informal communication is necessary. There is no substitute for personal contact in explaining the planning framework and in following up on individual planning efforts.

In the situation of A&A, a systematic approach to developing and reviewing preliminary plans is necessary. The coordinator requires a draft plan from the operating and staff departments prior to actual implementation. This is necessary because current operating problems are usually uppermost in middle managers' minds, and they generally put off formal planning. For this reason, top management must assert itself in favor of the planning effort, exerting pressure to obtain the plans when necessary. They should insist on compliance to the systematic approach, or the entire effort could fail.

Plan Review

At this point, the coordinating committee reviews the preliminary plans in detail for consistency with the objectives and philosophy of the overall policy guidelines. Their relationship to each other is then studied and differences and problems are highlighted. Now the operating managers come into the picture. Where one section's plans affect another, the managers of both must be brought together to insure that each has taken the needs of the other into consideration. When refinements are needed, or plans seem unrealistic or incomplete, or inconsistencies with overall corporate directions are noted, conferences should be held with the line managers to iron out the difficulties.

Furthermore, if questions are raised regarding the ability of the plans to provide adequate growth for the company, then strategies, opportunities, and programs must be reviewed to obtain the desired results. This process of conflict resolution is by no means easy; considerable communication, diplomacy, compromise, and teamwork are required to come up with an effective plan.

Upon completion of this review and refinement process, the final operating and staff plans are prepared. These plans are final only in the sense that they are the operating line managers' final views; subsequent reviews of the plans will be made by corporate management. However, if the planning director or executive group has kept in close contact with the corporate managers, the latter's review should not lead to major revisions.

Concurrently with the corporate review, the company control group or control and budgeting manager is to review the plans for it is this group that tests the plans' profitability. Thus, the preliminary plans and their budgets are studied together by the planners and budgeters. This phase of the review process leads to many refinements and should be used as a major planning tool.

The final corporate plan is prepared, based on the preliminary operating and staff planning and on the budgetary and top-management reviews. Considerably less detail is required for the overall corporate plan than for the individual operating and staff plans. The planning managers' job, therefore, is to extract the highlights of the individual operating and staff plans and to prepare a summary presentation of them for top management as part of the overall corporate plan and its budget.

The management control function sets performance standards consistent with planning objectives. It includes the design of information feedback systems to compare actual performance with these predetermined standards. When there are deviations, it measures their significance and takes whatever actions are required to bring performance up to standard.

STEP 10: CHANGES

At first glance, measuring the effectiveness of the planning effort through the budgetary process seems to be an easy task. For example, where there is a systematically developed budget plan, the planning director or committee can tell very easily when sales goals are not being reached, costs are higher than expected, the desired return on investment is not achieved, a deadline is not met, or funds become unavailable.

Such a review is only a beginning, however, for these are only symptoms of problems. Isolating the causes of these problems is generally not easy. Two pitfalls to be avoided in using budgets to measure and insure progress toward planning goals are: (1) failure to develop comprehensive plans for solving these problems and settling for short-term solutions instead, and (2) the unreliability of many standards used by managers in measuring and controlling planning performance—that is, these standards are sometimes "fudged" or adjusted by management. This could be done due to internal pressure or because managers wish to apply pressure to the organization by setting standards beyond expectations in order to get maximum performance. This will not be conducive to the long-run success of the plans because goals cannot be effectively reached and evaluated if they are distorted to accommodate higher management.

Contingency Planning

Contingency planning is required for the new planning organization. Contingency planning involves anticipatory alternate courses of action when performance does not measure up to standard. This process will involve answering four basic points:

1. What are the jobs to be accomplished, and how can we group them effectively?
2. How must the authority and responsibility be assigned?
3. Can anything be accomplished in the way of streamlining the inner workings of the company?
4. How should these organizational changes be brought forth?

Answering the first question involves reexamining all that has gone before in this project; objectives, strategies, policies, and implementation plans to determine generally what activities or tasks must be altered to achieve our objectives. These should be divided into operating tasks and management tasks. Operating tasks involve the work required to sell and maintain the product and services, whereas management tasks involve supervising the work of others. As our earlier planning is strategic, not tactical, it does not contain complete task definitions. Therefore, the individual section or group managers have to go beyond the initial plans and look at the specific tasks that must be performed to carry them out.

Regarding the second question, the planning committee, top management, or both must determine to whom each organization position reports and that position's authority. This can be accomplished by formulating job descriptions that spell out the tasks assigned to every position and that also give the responsibilities and authority limits. This use of job definitions will also reveal the interrelationships of organization segments, shared responsibilities, and other relationships not easily seen in the organizational chart.

The third question requires a study of the human resources affecting A&A's development. This will naturally lead to adjustments in the organization structure and job definitions. In this way, reorganization could take place using informal grouping and the specialized talents of particular people.

Finally, to determine how to introduce organizational changes, the executive committee must first examine the existing structure to see where the major changes are needed and where resistance will occur. Upon isolation of these problems, the individual manager can then face and overcome them.

Another organizationl problem can arise as additional layers of management are created. Communication and coordination with line-staff relationships could become difficult. The individual organization segments could lose sight of their basic objectives and become isolated. Some of these problems could become elevated by reorganization along divisional lines, thereby giving each segment specific responsibility. This divisionalization could occur around geographic areas, products or services, types of clients, or a combination of these, depending upon the situation.

Finally, while managers must determine what activities are necessary in their area to achieve the objectives, it is not always possible to fill out these plans to the letter because of the scarcity of resources throughout the organization. For this reason, it is imperative that higher-level management or the planning committee not only spells out objectives, but also the restraints controlling organizational development, if a workable organization structure is to be developed.

CONCLUSION

The group assimilated the large body of resources and information applicable to strategic planning and adaptively applied it to A&A in a 10-step process. Our extensive investigation of all aspects of the organization revealed that not only is it most profitable within its own industry, but it is extremely profitable compared to other firms in other industries.

A&A is primarily an insurance and employee-benefit service organization. It provides some products and owns a variety of synergistically related subsidiaries. In addition, it operates in over 46 foreign countries. Its industry is relatively recession-proof and usually not subject to swings in economic conditions.

At present, the organization wants to increase its profit margin and continue its aggressive domestic acquisition program. Acquisitions are made via tax-free stock exchanges. Currently, the organization's objectives are international and domestic expansion, and increased market penetration through productive employees.

Some of the alternative areas considered were: flood- and crop-loss coverage; increased marketing effectiveness with different direct-marketing techniques; concentric diversification through the largest subsidiary—Benefacts; adaptive alternatives relative to ERISA; and the possibility of a national health-insurance program.

The planning process concurrently predicts and considers preparations for the future, including antitrust exemption, rate competition, and the impact of governmental, social, and demographic changes. For international planning, ramifications of political, social, and economic conditions are projected.

For most of the alternatives considered, including concentric diversification, A&A shows strong synergism in sales, operations, investment, and management. This supports decisions to acquire firms of similar type and grow concentrically via the propitious combination of current subsidiary resources.

The resulting strategic plan calls for an expected rate of return of not less than 15%. The primary strategy is to diversify concentrically while continuing to aggressively prosper through the acquisition of compatible organizations and new business (i.e., new accounts). To enhance the competitive edge, the organization should continue to use its knowledge, experience, skills, resources, capabilities, and, most importantly, its personnel to strongly promote research and development in providing for internal expansion.

In appraising the strategies at this point, it is essential to review the logic of the process thus far. Growth trends, profitability, and market share are examined. The tests and revaluations support the choices. Vertical integration, on the whole, is not considered at this time, because there is more than enough room for expansion without facing the risks of new products and their markets.

To implement the strategy, the mental and physical tasks of the individuals within the functioning groups must be structured. This step involves managerial decisions, model construction, information requirements, job design, and measures and modifications. A&A is currently very well prepared to accommodate the implementation step.

The control of the process deals with establishing policies and procedures by which the strategy will be coordinated and integrated. These are well established within A&A. Even with these controls, however, unforeseen circumstances may present themselves. Thus, the process recognizes the need for flexibility and makes preparations for adaptive alterations, adjustments, and revisions.

In conclusion, if A&A can continue to ward off the possibility of takeover by another organization (which to date it has done through a variety of sophisticated financial planning and policy techniques), then it should be free to implement the appraised strategies, capitalize on its capabilities, and control the changes in achieving a most promising future.

EPILOGUE

Now, more than 4 years after the A&A report was written, it is worthwhile to examine it in the light of current happenings.

Financial Performance Objectives

The plan was quite optimistic about A&A's future, and rightly so. The company's results have been truly exceptional since 1974, which, when the case was written, was the last year for which financial data were available. Among the financial performance objectives was the desire for an earnings growth of 12 to 15 percent per year. Through 1978, the rate was almost twice that. Estimated revenues for 1978 were approximately $280 million.

A second objective was a cash dividend of 45 to 55 percent of earnings. From 1973 to 1978, the average dividend was 40 percent. In other ways, 1978 was a year of record-breaking growth: revenue increased 21.4 percent, new business from new clients increased 27 percent, net earnings increased 24.8 percent, earnings per share increased 22.5 percent, quarterly earnings per share increased 22.5 percent, and quarterly earnings increased for the 39th consecutive quarter since going public in 1969. Finally, for the period from 1975 to 1977, A&A's average return on equity was 30 percent, which was the highest of the Big Five.

Legislation

Much of A&A's performance depends on legislation and other forms of government action. Thus, A&A opened a government and industry affairs office in Washington, D.C., to track emerging issues and monitor insurance-related legislative and regulatory issues.

Among the legislation considered in 1976 was a national health act. At the start of 1980, although there is still talk, no such law has been passed. In addition, no national workmen's compensation bill has been passed, and such matters are still under the control of the individual states.

Also dormant are the issues of crop-flood insurance, commercial banks as major sellers of insurance, and the antitrust immunity of the insurance industry. Nevertheless, any one of these could be activated in a short time and thus affect the industry. Likewise, the consumer movement, which has been less visible than in past years, could become more active, particularly if one of the other issues sparks controversy.

The mandatory retirement age was moved to 70. Current predictions are that the mandatory retirement age may soon be done away with altogether.

Forecasts

Among the forecasts made about the business environment for A&A was that inflation would continue to rise both in the United States and abroad. This forecast was all too accurate. Inflation was also expected to encourage a rise in premium rates, which was to lead to additional commissions. This situation did indeed occur. Product liability premiums grew to such uncontrolled proportions that traditional forms of coverage became unattainable. A&A responded by synergistically combining resources to form a risk analysis and management group to develop approaches to meeting this market need.

Rates for some types of product liability tripled and even quadrupled in 1976 and 1977; however, these high rates did not remain. Insurers that had dropped such coverage from their line because of high claims payments reentered the market, driving premiums downward by as much as 15 to 20 percent. Of course, this was mitigated by rising inflation, so that the net effect was still higher revenues.

Not only have insurance companies become more competitive among themselves, but new insuring mediums are emerging. One of these is the Insurance Exchange, which is the American equivalent of Lloyds of London. As such, it is a place where an individual can place large amounts of insurance. Another is the Free Zone, a concept under which a company can insure a risk in another state if that company meets certain size requirements.

Another forecast was that the Big Five would prosper, achieving their growth, not from each other, but from the smaller brokers. This has been exactly the case. Not one of the five public brokers has ever had a year-to-year earnings decline since going public. And in the 5 years preceding 1978 (the last year for which figures are available), their growth in earnings per share has been spectacular.

A&A's Other Objectives

Among A&A's other objectives was a thrust toward overseas expansion. Toward this end, A&A has announced that it is holding discussions with two London brokers who themselves are discussing merging with each other. A&A has entered into a major business relationship in Saudi Arabia, which enhances its growth potential in this important international area. In addition, foreign firms seem to be increasing their use of insurance brokers. This would be an entirely new market for A&A as it now deals only with American (multinational) firms abroad.

Domestic expansion was another of A&A's objectives. In 1976, it had made some 80 acquisitions since going public. That number is now 150. This is further evidence that A&A's growth is at the expense of smaller brokers rather than the major competitors. However, A&A did have an acquisition outside this pattern. A&A's merger with R. B. Jones, the ninth largest broker, was the largest merger in insurance history.

Concentric diversification was another objective. A&A has moved into the financial services area, potentially offering additional services comparable to Merrill Lynch and American Express. A&A now provides comprehensive property-tax consulting service and has become a leader in this area.

The plan also advocates strong management and leadership, and A&A has reconsidered its all-internal board of directors. The company is now on record as seeking outside directors, and two nonemployees will be proposed at A&A's next annual meeting. The forecasted need for more professionals and managers was met by hiring 2000 additional employees. In addition, the personnel department was enhanced by streamlining its recruitment procedures and developing a professional-level management-training program.

If one person were to be singled out to exemplify A&A's commitment to develop professional management, it would have to be the current president and chief executive officer, John A. Bogardus. Mr. Bogardus started with A&A as a producer over 20 years ago. In 1976, when the plan was originally written, he was executive vice president. Today, Mr. Bogardus continues to perpetuate his strong, charismatic management and leadership style throughout this worldwide company.

Author Index

Subject Index